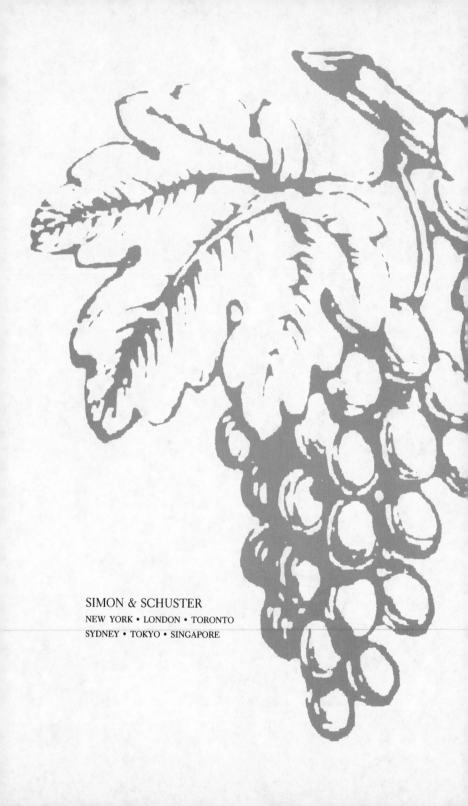

SIMON & SCHUSTER
NEW YORK • LONDON • TORONTO
SYDNEY • TOKYO • SINGAPORE

WINE
SNOBBERY

An Exposé

ANDREW BARR

SIMON & SCHUSTER

Simon & Schuster Building
Rockefeller Center
1230 Avenue of the Americas
New York, New York 10020

Copyright © 1988 by Andrew Barr
All rights reserved
including the right of reproduction
in whole or in part in any form.
Originally published in Great Britain
by Faber & Faber Limited
SIMON & SCHUSTER and colophon are
registered trademarks of Simon & Schuster Inc.
Designed by Edith Fowler
Manufactured in the United States of America

10   9   8   7   6   5   4   3   2   1

Library of Congress Cataloging in Publication Data

Barr, Andrew.
    Wine snobbery: an exposé/Andrew Barr.
        p.   cm.
1. Wine and wine making.   I. Title.
TP548.B335   1992
641.2'2—dc20

92-25261
CIP

ISBN 0-671-70804-X

Contents

Acknowledgments   7
Foreword: The British Edition   9

Part One

1 Prohibition and the Wine Boom   15
2 The American Sweet Tooth   27
3 Red Wine in Restaurants   37
4 Writers and Collectors   47
5 Wine Tastings Are Bunk   62

Part Two

Introduction: Art and Agriculture   77
6 A Kind of Makeup   80
7 The Sun in Sacks   96
8 The Champagne Game   112

9	The Law Is a Ass	131
10	Varietal Worship	159
11	Old Wine in New Bottles	184
12	Keeping Up With the Jayers	201
13	The Falernian Syndrome	232
14	What's Your Poison?	256

CONCLUSION

| 15 | A Plea for Flavor | 281 |

Conversion Tables: Alcohol Content and Yields	298
Wine Book and Magazine Snobbery	299
Notes	303
Index	319

Acknowledgments

Had I not been given a first opportunity to express myself by John Diamond, then the consumer editor of the London listings magazine *Time Out* (but now sensibly moved on to greater things), and offered a more prestigious stage by Georgina Boosey, Managing Editor of the British *Vogue*, this book would never have been written.

Many wine makers, importers, and retailers have shied away from any connection with a book such as this, and others who have been helpful have been unaware that they were being so or have preferred to assist me anonymously. On the principle that a journalist should not reveal his sources, I shall name none of them here. I would, however, like to thank Lance Foyster (now a Master of wine) for all his years of constructive criticism, and Mel Knox of Knox Industries, who was kind enough to read the manuscript of this edition and offer his comments. He has asked me to point out, however, that the opinions expressed are my responsibility alone.

This book is dedicated to my parents, because they do not drink.

Foreword:
The British Edition

THE BRITISH EDITION of *Wine Snobbery* was originally due to have been published on November 7, 1988, but this was prevented by Clive Coates, a wine writer to whom a review copy had mistakenly been sent. Coates objected to a comment made about him in the bibliography. In order to avoid the possibility of having publication delayed indefinitely by a long court case, it was postponed briefly while the passage of which Coates had complained was amended.

Coates's objection to *Wine Snobbery* was mirrored by the attitude of some of his colleagues. Edmund Penning-Rowsell, the 74-year-old wine correspondent of *The Financial Times*, described it as "an unnecessarily disagreeable book."[1] Margaret Rand, the editor of *Wine* magazine, described it as a "tiring and unenjoyable read" and pointed out that "Barr seems to have a remarkably low opinion of the trade to which he is (somewhat loosely) attached."[2]

Coates used to work as a wine merchant before he began publishing his own wine magazine, *The Vine*, in 1985. Penning-Rowsell was at the time, as he had been for many years, the chairman of the Wine Society, essentially a wine importing cooperative. *Wine* magazine, which Rand then edited, is economically dependent on advertising from wine producers, importers, and retailers. Her comments demonstrate the intimate involvement of British wine writers with a wine trade on whose products they are supposed to provide a

9

critical commentary. The belief of many wine merchants that it is the sole function of wine writers to support the wine trade—a support which they consider they pay for by providing free lunches, free booze ("samples"), and free holidays ("press trips")—is reflected by some wine writers, one of whom has defended his acceptance of "freebies" on the grounds that it is the purpose of wine writers to promote wine and the wine trade as a whole. That excuses him if he does not give the PR people their pound of flesh in terms of column inches every time he goes abroad.

This intimacy is most extreme in the case of those wine writers who are also members of the wine trade. One of these writers, Serena Sutcliffe, took out libel proceedings against *Wine Snobbery* at the end of 1988, objecting to my describing as "dishonest" her practice of recommending in her books and articles wines in which she had a financial interest without declaring that interest. Far from denying my allegation, Sutcliffe claimed that she had done nothing wrong; that writing about wines in which she had an interest, without declaring that interest, was something that many of her colleagues also did; and that her opinions were honest ones, without any deliberate bias toward her own wines. I had not suggested that she was deliberately biased. Nevertheless, she claimed that I had singled her out because I had a grudge against her: that I was motivated purely or principally by malice. We had (and still have) never met.

This case dragged on for two years. Then, suddenly, at the beginning of 1991, not long before it was due to come to court, Sutcliffe decided to settle—in return for a payment of £2,500 (about $4,000) and the opportunity to make a statement in front of a judge about her reasons for bringing, and settling, the action. The passage about her in the book remained unchanged. Sutcliffe announced her intention to settle the case just after she had been appointed the head of Sotheby's wine department in London. I have no means of knowing whether the two events were connected.

Although that was the reason why it attracted most attention, the principal reason for writing *Wine Snobbery* was not so much to criticize British wine writers and merchants as to question the fundaments on which their view of wine was based. I was originally impelled to write the book by the response of the British wine trade to the Austrian "antifreeze" story which broke in the summer of 1985. This scandal arose as a consequence of biochemist Otto Nadrasky Senior's discovery that he could make dry wines sweeter and thin wines fuller-bodied by adding diethylene glycol, a chemical

which is commonly used in antifreeze solutions for car radiators—
and which is potentially fatal to humans, as it can cause kidney and
liver failure. When I responded to the scandal by contributing an
article to the British edition of *Vogue* on additives and organic wines,
and wrote to the importer of one of these wines, asking how it was
made, he said in his reply that he hoped that, by the time the article
would have appeared, five months later, "the whole glycol saga will
be forgotten. This very mention of additives, whether natural or
artificial, always raises question marks in the consumer's mind and
it seems to me that any reference to additives seems to add another
black mark to the image of wine."

This importer shared the belief of many of his colleagues that,
if you ignore a scandal, it goes away quicker; indeed, it may never
become public at all. Certainly this approach has served politicians
well. Whereas John F. Kennedy kept his philanderings from the
public, Gary Hart was forced in 1987 to withdraw from the campaign
for the Democratic nomination for the presidency in 1988 because
he challenged journalists to prove allegations that he had been un-
faithful to his wife; and they did. In the same way, however, as sex
scandals expose the fundamental dishonesty and arrogance of many
politicians, wine scandals briefly expose what is rotten but generally
hidden in the wine business. It was found, for example, that a
number of German wines were contaminated with diethylene glycol,
but in much lower concentrations than Austrian ones. The authorities claimed: "The wines were not deliberately falsified, but . . .
unclean equipment in importing and bottling companies was at
fault."[3] Nonsense. German wines were found to be contaminated
because German wine makers were in the practice of adding illegally
10 to 15 percent of Austrian wine to their own produce.

This American edition of *Wine Snobbery* is necessarily different
from the British one. It has been substantially amended and updated
in order to take account of developments that have occurred since
the original text was completed at the end of 1987—and in order to
incorporate a large number of American examples. The last chapter,
and the whole of Part One, have been completely rewritten. Part
One of the British edition was concerned solely with the wine boom
in Britain and the various influences that affect the tastes of British
consumers. Part One of the American edition is concerned with the
same developments and forces in America.

Despite these changes, the core, and the essential purpose of the
book, remain the same. *Wine Snobbery* was written in order to

illuminate those dubious practices which are normally exposed only by occasional wine scandals. Only by appreciating why wine makers find it necessary to break the law is it possible to understand why wine tastes as it does, and why we buy the wines we do.

Certainly, it is in the interests of wine importers and retailers to encourage people to think that wine scandals are wholly unrepresentative. If the truth were to come out, would consumers be content with cheap wines and no longer be prepared to spend extra money to achieve the image that producers have so carefully created? It is the purpose of this book to explain why we pay for that image. We may think that wine snobbery has disappeared: we no longer shrink from admitting that we drink "naïve domestic burgundies" at home; we are no longer embarrassed by wine waiters in smart restaurants; we no longer try to get one over on "friends" at dinner parties. But to suggest that wine snobbery is dead is merely to fall victim to the skills of the marketing and advertising people. Wine snobbery today is more subtle and insidious than ever before.

PART ONE

1
Prohibition and
the Wine Boom

IT IS SOMETIMES suggested that the reason why the United States is not a wine-drinking country today is that Americans have shown a historical preference for hard liquor. It is pointed out that Americans were prevented from acquiring a taste for wine by the failures of the early efforts to grow European vine varieties in the eastern part of the country; and that no successful plantations of these varieties were made before the 1850s; and then only in California. Thomas Jefferson planted vines of every description at his vineyard at Monticello in Virginia over a period of at least half a century (from 1771 until 1822), but they suffered so badly from the diseases of phylloxera, mildew, and black rot that there is no evidence of any wine having been produced on this site before 1988.

Successful wines were made from the native grape varieties, however. In the first half of the nineteenth century wine made in North Carolina from the Scuppernong grape was not only served with the dessert at the White House on state occasions, but was consumed by poor farmers along the Cape Fear River "as freely as cider is used in New England."[1]

In the midnineteenth century the principal wine-producing state was Ohio. The sparkling Catawba made by Nicholas Longworth from his vineyard on Bald Hill in Cincinnati was sold throughout the East for one dollar a bottle, a vast sum at the time. It seems to have been worth the money, for Longworth once accused New York hotels of substituting French champagne for his. A gift of sparkling Catawba persuaded Longfellow to write an *Ode to Catawba Wine*:

> *Very good in its way*
> *Is the Verzenay,*
> *Or the Sillery soft and creamy;*
> *But Catawba wine*
> *Has a taste more divine,*
> *More dulcet, delicious and dreamy.*[2]

There was also a substantial connoisseur market for fine imported wine. Captain Thomas Hamilton, an Englishman who wrote an account of the eight months he spent in the United States at the beginning of the 1830s, expressed himself astounded by the succession of wines that was served at a dinner party he attended in New York, and by how they were all discussed in detail. He observed: "The gentlemen in America pique themselves on their discrimination in wine, in a degree which is not common in England."[3]

The spread of wine drinking was encouraged by immigrants arriving from wine-producing and wine-drinking countries in Europe in the second half of the nineteenth century. Between 1860 and 1890, 3 million people came to America from Germany; before long, the Union Square area of New York was famous for its *Weinstuben*. Between 1880 and 1920 a further 4 million people arrived from Italy, mostly from the south.

America would have remained a wine-drinking country had it not been for Prohibition. Ironically, the first attempts to control American drinking habits in the early nineteenth century had been directed only at spirits. Light, unfortified table wine was encouraged. In 1819 the federal government lowered taxes on imported wines in order to encourage temperance, which in those days meant drinking in moderation. One of the reasons why Longworth turned to vine growing in the 1820s was a desire to produce an attractive dry table wine in order to further the temperance cause. As Jefferson famously declared, "No nation is drunken where wine is cheap."

Prohibition may have originally been motivated by a desire to turn people from spirits to table wines, but its effect was precisely the opposite. The introduction of national Prohibition in 1920 did not cause people to stop drinking, but it did cause them to do their drinking illegally. The customers of speakeasies were not interested in table wines; they wanted hard liquor. The only types of wine available in speakeasies were sparkling and sweet fortified wine. These were therefore the types of wine that people wanted to drink after Repeal in 1933. Abdullah Simon, wine buyer for Château & Estate, the fine-wine section of the Seagram empire, remembers going to a dinner in a smart apartment on Park Avenue in New York in 1944 and finding Château d'Yquem served with the beef. The only people who drank dry table wine after the end of Prohibition were people who had drunk it before 1919 or had emigrated from Europe in the meantime.

Prohibition, moreover, affected grape growing for the worse. A section was added to the Volstead Act—which introduced Prohibition—in order to placate the Virginia apple farmers: it allowed a householder to make up to two hundred gallons a year of "non-intoxicating cider and fruit juices" for home use. In effect, people were allowed to make homemade wine. Not surprisingly, this loophole in the Prohibitionist legislation led to a boom in California grape sales. Many growers grafted over to coarse, thick-skinned varieties such as Alicante Bouschet, since these were the ones that shipped best. Prohibition left the nation with a vast acreage of vineyards growing the wrong grapes. As a result, the still wines that were made in California after the end of Prohibition were generally not very good.

In a seminal work on American wines published in 1941, Frank Schoonmaker and Tom Marvel suggested that Americans had been reluctant to turn to table wines since Prohibition because of the "mystery, ritual, and hocus-pocus which had accumulated around the subject of wine. Most Americans shrugged their shoulders at the whole business and stuck to highballs, cocktails, and beer. If wine entailed so much abracadabra, they just couldn't be bothered."[4]

It was principally Ernest & Julio Gallo who improved the quality of California wines by introducing better grape varieties and sensible viticultural and vinification techniques, and who took away the abracadabra by introducing inexpensive branded wines. The first of these, Paesano, made from late-harvested Zinfandel grapes, was launched in 1952. "Smooth" and low in tannin, it was sold as "the anytime wine." It was followed by Hearty Burgundy, which was introduced in 1954. This had the colors of the Italian flag on the label, and was sold in New York to old Italian home wine makers. It was a heavy, thick wine based on Petite Syrah, which the old Italians cut with water. A few years later these were followed by a white Chablis. Today Hearty Burgundy is the largest-selling red wine in the United States and Gallo's Chablis the largest-selling white. Overall, Gallo produces more wine than the whole of Australia.

The demystification of wine by the Gallos coincided with a renewed interest in European wines on the part of Americans. It is sometimes suggested that Americans took up wine drinking because of their experience in Europe during the Second World War; but there is little evidence of this. According to Simon, Americans who fought in Europe did not drink wine but brandy. Simon was in the army from 1944 to 1946 and never saw a bottle of wine during that period. Americans took up wine drinking in the 1960s, when the introduction of jet airplanes made it cheaper and quicker to fly to Europe. People who traveled to Europe and drank wine there took the labels off the bottles, brought them back, and looked for the wines. Not until 1968, however, did sales of table wine pass those of sweet fortified wine. The real wine boom occurred in the 1970s. The quantity of table wine sold in America increased from 53 million gallons in 1960 to 362 million in 1980. During the same period, dessert wines dropped from 87 million gallons (54 percent of the market) to 38.5 (7 percent).

A market-research survey carried out in 1955 had asked interviewees whether they thought wine was a drink for Americans. Ninety percent had said no. Then they were asked: if it was not a drink for Americans, then whom did they think it was for? They replied that it was for rich people, or for foreigners, or for drunken bums—but not for Americans.[5] The situation today appears, at first sight, to have been transformed completely. In 1990 *The Wine Spectator* had market research conducted into American wine-drinking habits. It found that 40 percent of the population drank wine— slightly more than drank spirits, slightly less than drank beer, and not significantly less than the proportion of the French population (49

percent) that drank wine. There is a major difference between France
and the United States, however. The people in France who drink
wine do so much more often than their counterparts across the
Atlantic. Of the 49 percent of the French population that drinks
wine, more than one-third drink wine every day. Of the 40 percent
of the American population that drinks wine, little more than one-
third drink wine once a week. Each American wine drinker consumes, on average, one glass of wine a week.[6]

America has not yet become a wine-drinking nation because
Prohibitionist laws have not yet disappeared. Although national Prohibition was repealed in 1933, state prohibition remained in Oklahoma until 1959 and in Mississippi until 1966. Not until 1984 in
Oklahoma, 1987 in Kansas, and 1990 in Utah was it made legal to
purchase a drink in a saloon. In these states, and in five others, the
law that now obtains is local option: that is to say, each county has
the right to decide whether it wants to be wet or dry. This produces
some ridiculous situations. Moore County in Kentucky is dry, which
means that the saloon in the town of Lynchburg cannot sell Jack
Daniels whiskey to its customers, even though that is where it is
made.

One of the main causes for the repeal of Prohibition in 1933
was the federal government's desire to make money out of taxing the
sale of alcohol. It was partly for a similar reason that a number of
states retained control of retails sales of liquor. Retaining control also
enabled them to control the drinking habits of the population. Iowa
established its state-owned stores in out-of-the-way places where they
were hard to find. According to Rolland Gallagher—until recently
the head of the state department of commerce—this was done in-
tentionally in order to stop people from drinking. Customers were
not allowed to browse, but had to line up at the counter and order
what they wanted. Until the early 1950s, Iowa had liquor cards that
were punched by the clerks after each purchase; this way, it was
possible to keep track of someone's drinking habits. If a man asked a
woman to marry him, it was customary for her parents to demand to
see his liquor license cards.[7] Iowa ended its state liquor monopoly
only in 1986—at which time fifteen states still retained control of
retail sales of liquor, including Pennsylvania. The Pennsylvania system was meant to have been dissolved the next year, but in fact

compromise legislation was introduced; this ensured that the state would be kept in the liquor business at least until 1992. The benefit, for wine sales, of ending state monopolies, cannot be exaggerated. The year after Iowa abandoned its monopoly, the volume of wine going into the state increased by nearly 60 percent.

A number of other states, instead of retaining a monopoly of retail sales of liquor, sell licenses to a limited number of liquor stores. Wine can be purchased only from them and not from grocery stores. To a substantial extent, the wine boom in Britain has been achieved by grocery stores, which have demystified and sanitized wine; they have made it an easy buy, and often an impulse purchase. The wine sections are placed at the far end of the store so that people can "reward" themselves after buying necessities. Roughly half of the wine drunk at home in Britain has been purchased in a grocery store. Buying a wine from a liquor store is quite different. It requires a special trip. Going into a liquor store is not part of everyday living; it is therefore capable of being regarded as a manifestation of wickedness. One of the reasons why consumption of table wines in the United States started to take off in the late 1960s was that a few of the monopoly states started amending their laws to allow table wine to be sold in grocery stores. It is believed by some people in the wine business that if New York and Pennsylvania allowed wine to be sold in grocery stores, wine consumption in the United States would double.[8]

The New York State government has on many occasions attempted to introduce legislation to allow grocery stores to sell wine, but each time it has been defeated by a well-financed lobby for liquor-store owners. The tide started to turn in the mid-1970s because a number of the big local wineries (notably Taylor in Hammondsport in the Finger Lakes), finding that their customers preferred wine with less of the foxy flavor of the native vine species labrusca than they had in the past, increased their purchases of bulk California wines for use in their blends—with a corresponding decrease in their purchase of New York grapes. Local grape growers therefore turned to establishing their own wineries. They were supported by Governor Hugh Carey, who in 1976 announced a state-sponsored program to promote the sale of New York State wines in stores and restaurants. Evidently, this only worked in part because in

1984 Governor Mario Cuomo proposed legislation to permit the sale of New York State wines in grocery stores in order to try and forestall bankruptcy among grape growers. Once again, this was defeated. Instead, a law was passed allowing grocery stores to sell wine coolers—low-alcohol mixtures of wine, fruit juices, and carbonated water—made from New York State grapes. The Federal Appeals Court overturned this law, however, declaring it to be unconstitutional. New York responded by allowing the sale of all coolers (under 6 percent alcohol) in grocery stores—which is a start. In his history of American wines, Leon D. Adams has suggested that, when a food-store wine bill eventually passes in New York, it will be followed by the other eastern states which have restricted wine sales to liquor stores: Pennsylvania, Rhode Island, Connecticut, New Jersey, and Massachusetts.[9]

Adams himself has played a major role in encouraging the growth of wine consumption in the United States. He lived through Prohibition in San Francisco and set up the Wine Institute afterward to encourage the consumption of wine. In recent years he has been instrumental in persuading many states to introduce laws allowing local wineries to start up and sell wines direct to the public. The first state to pass an Adams-inspired farm winery law was Pennsylvania in 1968. Since then twenty-four more states have passed such laws. Adams points out that there are now forty-three wine-producing states—exactly the same number that existed before Prohibition. The development of farm wineries has encouraged the abandonment of the idea that wine drinking is a vice—and thus the dissolution of a liquor-store system.

It should not be thought, however, that the gradual liberalization of state laws controlling liquor consumption—the residue of Prohibition—will lead to a continuing increase in wine drinking. Having risen rapidly between 1970 and 1980, wine consumption has been in decline since 1985; it seems likely that this will continue for a few years yet. According to *The Wine Spectator* survey, 21 percent of wine drinkers are consuming less wine than they used to and only 8 percent are drinking more. The cause of the decline is the growth of a national temperance movement, similar to the one which led to Prohibition in the first case.

The power of the temperance movement manifested itself most

strikingly at the beginning of 1989, when John Tower, who had been a United States Senator from Texas from 1961 until 1984, was nominated by George Bush to be Secretary of Defense. He was rejected by the Senate, at least in part, on the grounds that his drinking made him "morally unfit." Tower had admitted that he used to drink too much in the 1970s but had said that he would swear off drink if his appointment was confirmed. He was killed in an air crash in 1991.

The temperance movement won another major victory in 1990, when warning labels were introduced on bottles of wine. These warn that women should not drink alcoholic beverages during pregnancy because of the risk of birth defects, and that consumption of alcoholic beverages impairs your ability to drive a car or operate machinery and may cause health problems. Later that same year, *The Wine Spectator* survey found that 74 percent of the population favored having warning labels on bottles of wine.

What makes the warning labels so ridiculous is the substantial evidence of positive links between consumption of alcohol and *good* health. A number of studies have shown that moderate drinkers are less likely to die from heart attacks than teetotalers. Gerald Shaper, Professor of Clinical Epidemiology at the Royal Free Hospital in London, has sought to belittle the results of these surveys by arguing that teetotalers have performed badly because they include many former drinkers who have given up drinking for health reasons. In 1991 his argument was defeated by a survey of 51,529 male health professionals carried out by the Harvard School of Public Health. A third of the men in this survey were eliminated because they had had medical problems that might be related to heart disease. Of those remaining, men who drank the equivalent of two or more shots of spirits a day were significantly less likely to suffer from heart disease than teetotalers.[10] One possible explanation of why moderate drinkers should be less likely to suffer from heart attacks than teetotalers is that alcohol consumption is associated with higher levels of good cholesterol—HDL, high-density lipoprotein—which moves around the arteries eliminating bad cholesterol—LDL, low-density lipoprotein—which would otherwise clog them up.

Other surveys have suggested that wine drinking is beneficial in ways that other alcohol is not. In 1989 Terry Leighton, a microbi-

ologist at the University of California at Berkeley as well as the owner
of Kalin Winery in Marin County, announced that he had found the
anticancer agent quercetin in red wine. Quercetin is much more
powerful in reversing cancer growth than alcohol could be in causing
it. In 1990 researchers at Queen's University, Belfast, Northern Ire-
land, compared data from Belfast with that from three French towns
and found that the death rate from coronary heart disease in Belfast
was four times higher, even though the French consumed on average twice as much alcohol. They suggested that the difference might
lie in the fact that the French drank wine, whereas the Irish drank
beer and whiskey, and that perhaps the copper sulphate sprayed on
the vines remained in the wine and acted as an antioxidant, stabi-
lizing cholesterol and preventing its being taken into the heart wall.

The fact that French people suffer much less frequently from
heart disease than do Americans or British—despite their love of
saturated fat, their addiction to cigarettes, and their aversion to exercise—has come to be known as the "French Paradox." It was publicized in the United States by a report on the top-rated CBS weekly
news program "60 Minutes" on November 17, 1991. Serge Renaud,
director of research at the Institut National de la Santé et de la
Recherche Médicale (INSERM) in Lyons, was filmed saying that
the probable explanation of the "French Paradox" was that a high-
cholesterol diet was mitigated by a regular, moderate intake of alcohol, in particular red wine. This program unleashed a red wine
mania. Wine retailers and restaurateurs reported that people were
buying red wine who had never tried it before in their lives. In
Pennsylvania, the state liquor control board recorded a 97 percent
increase in sales of red wine in the week following the broadcast. In
supermarkets across the country, sales of red wine in the run-up to
Christmas were 44 percent higher than during the same period the
previous year. Evidently people would have drunk a lot more red
wine in the past if they had not been so worried that it might do them
harm.

It is ironic in the light of this sudden burst of publicity that wine
producers and retailers have encountered great difficulty in their
attempts to promote the positive links between wine drinking and
health. When the Leeward Winery in Ventura, California, published a synopsis of the "60 Minutes" program in its spring 1992

newsletter, it was ordered by the Bureau of Alcohol, Tobacco and Firearms (BATF) to remove the newsletter from circulation on the grounds that advertisements for wine were only allowed to suggest possible beneficial health effects if they also presented its possible negative effects.[11] In 1988 the Robert Mondavi Winery had started to affix a label to its bottles stating: "Wine is the temperate, civilized, sacred, romantic mealtime beverage recommended in the Bible" and that "Wine in moderation is an integral part of culture, heritage, and the gracious way of life." In 1991 it was ordered to remove this label by the Bureau of Alcohol, Tobacco and Firearms on the grounds that it was one-sided—despite the fact that it appeared directly above the one-sided government health warning label. Mondavi fought back, and a compromise was reached in which Mondavi removed from its label the statement that wine was recommended in the Bible, and changed the phrase "Wine in moderation is part of our culture" to "Wine in moderation is part of our family's culture."[12] Other wine producers have been more timid, having been warned by their lawyers that if they try to say that wine has any positive benefits, they could be a part of a class-action suit against wine from someone who has suffered as a result of drinking too much of it.

What is particularly appalling is the attitude toward pregnant women. They are instructed not to drink, not just by warning labels on wine bottles, but also by signs which must by posted in every establishment in several states (including California and New York) where drinks are sold. Such signs declare that the consumption of alcoholic beverages during pregnancy can cause birth defects. These instructions are supported by the fact that it is generally believed in the medical world that women who drink heavily during pregnancy run the risk of producing children with Fetal Alcohol Syndrome. Affected children suffer from behavioral and developmental disorders, and their organs may not work properly. It should be pointed out, however, that Fetal Alcohol Syndrome has largely been evidenced among the children of mothers who drank more than a bottle of wine a day (or the equivalent) during pregnancy. Moreover, it is not clear how much of the blame should be placed on alcohol. Many women who drink heavily during pregnancy are also heavy smokers and take drugs or tranquilizers; they tend also to suffer from poor nutrition and bad living conditions. According to Dr. Moira

Plant of the Alcohol Research Group in Edinburgh, the condition might just as easily have been called Fetal Tobacco Syndrome, had different questions been asked twenty years earlier.[13]

In July 1991 the results of a study of nearly six hundred Scottish infants and their mothers carried out by Charles Florey, Professor of Community Medicine at Dundee University, and colleagues, was published in *The British Medical Journal*. They had found no adverse effects on infants born to mothers who drank ten glasses of wine a week. This was not much less than the generally recommended limit for women who are not pregnant (fourteen glasses of wine a week). "I honestly believe that at some point over the next ten or twenty years, most of the drinks industry and all women will come to realize that during the 1980s they were victims of an enormous confidence trick," wrote Jancis Robinson in *The Wine Spectator*. "We have accepted the official line on alcohol and pregnancy because pregnant women represent a minority over whom the rest of the world likes to assume dominion; expectant female humans are meant to keep out of society's and harm's way."[14]

If history is anything to go by, restrictions on wine drinking are likely to increase. This is the third temperance movement in American history. The first movement began around 1820 and peaked around 1850. All of New England and many other states prohibited the sale of alcoholic beverages. This was followed by an upsurge in drinking, which peaked in 1890. Then Americans turned against alcohol again, and national Prohibition was introduced in 1920 and lasted for thirteen years. A new era of tolerance followed, which peaked around 1979. Dr. David F. Musto, a professor of psychiatry and a historian of medicine at Yale University School of Medicine, points out that the concerns and tactics of modern temperance groups very closely parallel those of the early nineteenth and early twentieth centuries—both of which led to Prohibition: public concern with the safety and healthfulness of food; a shift from attacking alcohol abuse to attacking alcohol itself; a shift from discussing beer, wines, and spirits separately to discussing one form, alcohol. He predicts that more groups will shift from urging moderation to urging abstinence. He believes that, if the current temperance movement follows the pattern of the previous two movements, it will last another ten or twenty years—becoming increasingly severe and moralistic—before ending with a wild backlash in an era of excess. He points out that the change in attitude toward drinking in the 1980s has been so profound that many people have not noticed that they have changed their views. For the 1990s, he predicts that consumption of alcoholic beverages will be ostracized in the same way as smoking in the 1980s.[15]

2
The American
Sweet Tooth

Ⅰf the wine boom in the United States has indeed come to an abrupt halt, it is perhaps not the neo-temperance movement that is to blame. It can be argued that Americans are not really interested in drinking table wine.

In 1985, the year in which wine consumption started to decline, Frank Prial wrote an article in *The New York Times* in which he declared: "We have never been and are not now a wine-drinking nation, and the jury is still out on whether we will ever be." He explained that the switch from sweet "dessert" wine to dry "table" wine in the 1960s and 1970s was not really a conversion to table wine, since it never occurred to most Americans to combine wine with meals. Instead, they thought of wine as a refresher or a cocktail; and that, as a result, it was usually white. The so-called wine boom of the 1970s was actually a boom in white wines. During the 1970s, when total table wine consumption nearly trebled, red wine consumption remained basically stable. White wines passed red in 1977, and by 1985 white wine consumption was three times that of red.[1]

There is a good reason why producers should want their customers to drink white rather than red wine—they can sell it sooner. Indeed, it has been suggested that the boom in white wines was at least in part the achievement of the wine producers who launched advertising campaigns to claim that white wine is the traditional choice of Americans. This was not really true: those people who drank wine in the 1960s drank red wine. But their claims were self-fulfilling.[2]

There are also a number of reasons why consumers should prefer white wine to red. It is considered to be lighter and less alcoholic. There is in fact no reason why it should necessarily contain less alcohol, and some reason why it should contain more. A red wine loses alcohol during fermentation in ways that a white one does not—up to one-twentieth of its total if it is fermented in open vats, as is traditional in the Côte d'Or in Burgundy; and the same if the stems are included in the vat, as is the usual practice in Beaujolais; and up to one-sixth of its total alcohol content as a result of the regular recycling of the skins in the vat in order to extract color and flavor from them. But it is popularly believed that white wine is less alcoholic than red, and there are those who would not wish us to be disabused—such as the wicked old Frenchman whom the English wine writer Cyril Ray described as recalling that he had found it profitable in his time that "nice young English girls" were unaware of the truth in this matter.[3]

Many people prefer white wine because in their experience it is less likely to give them a hangover, although it is not clear precisely why this should be. It has been suggested that the reaction which a number of people suffer after drinking red wine is allergic. Possibly this is caused by histidine, which occurs in the skins and pips of black grapes. Red wines contain more histidine than white because they are fermented in contact with their skins; for white wine the juice is separated from the skins before fermentation. If headaches are caused by histidine in red wines, this would explain why cheap red wine produces a headache and expensive red wine does not. In the manufacture of fine wines, the grapes are pressed very gently, whereas grapes for cheap wines are often pressed very hard, in order to get as much as possible out of them. This pressure extracts many more chemicals from the grape skins and pips. Alternatively, people could be reacting to histamine (a derivative of histidine) and tyramine formed during the malolactic fermentation—a secondary fermentation that converts malic into lactic acids and which occurs much more commonly in red wines than in white ones. In 1983, however, two American scientists carried out allergic skin scratch tests and antihistamine treatments in order to determine whether the reaction to red wine really was an allergic one. They pointed out that histamine and tyramine levels in red wine are very low and concluded that the reaction to red wine is not allergic, and is probably psychologically induced.[4] In 1988 six English doctors resurrected the role of red wines in causing headaches by suggesting that migraines which occur after drinking red wine might well be caused by the tannins in the skins and pips of black grapes rather than by histidine. They suggested that the tannins inhibited the bodily enzyme PST, whose job it is to detoxify certain chemicals in the intestine.[5] This said, there are several other causes of headaches which arise equally from both red and white wines, such as the enlargement of the cranial blood vessels by alcohol.

A more significant explanation of the popular preference for white wine is that it is served cooler than red—or rather, red wine is generally served warmer than white. It is generally believed that red wine should be drunk *chambré*, and *chambré* is imagined to mean warm. In fact, it means "at room temperature"—and even that is too warm. It made sense to serve red wines at room temperature in the nineteenth century, when they were generally more tannic than they are today. It is only the presence of tannin which requires that red wine be not served so cool as white: we are far more sensitive to bitterness and astringency at low temperatures. Moreover, the concept of room temperature has changed since last century. Fuel is now (relatively) cheap, and people have central heating. Except in midsummer, room temperature meant at most 60–65°F last century, not the 70–75°F we enjoy today. Fine wine is best enjoyed at historic room temperature, which should *never* exceed 65°F; above that level, too much alcohol evaporates and the smell of alcohol overwhelms the bouquet of the wine.[6] Modern red wines which are high in fruit and low in tannin are best enjoyed at 55–60°F—much the same temperature as that at which white wines show their best. But, as things stand, and particularly in restaurants—where red wines tend to be kept close to the heat of the kitchen and white wines in the cool of the fridge—red wines are generally served at 70–75°F and white ones at 40–45°F.

If most Americans prefer white wines to red, it is principally

because it is a national characteristic to insist that every drink should
be cool and refreshing. From a European perspective, Americans
appear to be obsessed with refrigeration. It is a bizarre sensation for
a European visitor to order a shot of bourbon and to be presented
with a small amount of liquor spoiled by an enormous amount of ice;
to eat a salad that has been frozen; to be unable to spread butter on
a slice of bread, but to have to lay it on in slabs.

European commentators have struggled to explain the American obsession with refrigeration. It is clearly not a matter of the
weather. Although, in some parts of the United States, it becomes
very hot in summer, other parts of the country can be very cold in
winter. Many parts of Europe are very hot in summer, too, but this
does not prevent people from drinking red wine at room temperature.

The underlying explanation appears to be the reverence that is
accorded to the role of technology in the development of the United
States. Refrigeration was invented at the beginning of the nineteenth
century in order that food could be transported long distances. Domestic refrigerators had become commonplace by the middle of the
century, a hundred years before they became standard fixtures in
Europe. It is an American habit to make use of technology in order
to distance oneself as far as possible from the primitive and brutal life
of the frontier. Simon Hoggart, who spent 1985 to 1989 as Washington Correspondent of the British Sunday newspaper *The Observer*, suggests that Americans often invert the temperature of their
homes to an exaggerated extent—chilling them to 60°F in summer
and heating them to 75°F in winter—because they have never rid
themselves of their fear of poverty and hunger and therefore exag-
gerate their responses to these dangers.[7]

Another reason why Americans generally prefer white wines to
red is that whites are sweeter. There is nothing in American wine-
making regulations to dictate how much sugar a wine labeled "dry"
is allowed to contain. Many allegedly dry California Chardonnays
are actually quite sweet. It may seem odd that a winemaker should
want to produce a Chardonnay containing residual sugar, but the
point is that sugar makes a white wine taste richer and more rounded.
It is partly the presence of residual sugar that explains the success, in
tasting competitions in the 1970s, of Chardonnays from Château St.

Jean, and in the 1980s of Chardonnays from Kendall-Jackson. Jed Steele, who was the wine maker for Kendall-Jackson until 1991, justified making Chardonnays with up to 0.7 percent residual sugar on the grounds that "The first duty of wine is to taste good." Certainly, sweetish Chardonnays are what most American consumers prefer. Whereas it is taught at wine-making schools in Europe that sugar in wine can be detected once it reaches a level of 0.3 or 0.4 percent, at the University of California at Davis it is taught that the threshold for perception is 0.5 percent. The explanation for the different figures is simple enough: Americans have a sweeter tooth than Europeans.[8]

Both the American sweet tooth and the national obsession with refrigeration are demonstrated by the popularity of White Zinfandel, the most successful wine category of the 1980s. The origins of White Zinfandel are to be found in the efforts made, from 1968 on, by Bob Trinchero (the owner of Sutter Home winery in the Napa Valley) to produce traditional red Zinfandel from grapes growing in Amador County. In order to make this as rich and concentrated as possible, he tried, in 1972, drawing off some of the juice before fermentation. He sold the wine made from this juice as a curiosity. He made it along the lines of a Chardonnay—dry, oak-aged, fairly complex. It sold well, but not amazingly so. In 1975 the fermentation stuck, leaving it with 2 percent residual sugar. The White Zinfandel boom was born. Sales of the Sutter Home White Zinfandel took off at the beginning of the 1980s, and by 1990 had reached 35 million bottles a year.

The success of White Zinfandel gives the lie to the suggestion made by some wine commentators that the fall in wine consumption since the mid-1980s actually conceals a maturing of American tastes in wine—a movement from drinking a larger amount of cheap wine to drinking a smaller amount of better wine. The commentators point out that three-quarters of the wine consumed in the United States comes from California; that in 1985 jug wines—cheap wines sold in big bottles with screw tops—accounted for 80 percent of California table wine sales and varietal wines for 20 percent; that by 1990 jug wines accounted for only 60 percent and varietal wines for 40 percent. The increase in the consumption of varietal wines has been attributed to the development of "fighting varietals," which are not plants related to triffids but are wines made from a single grape variety which sell for between $5 and $7. Fighting varietals, however, were not developed as a means of satisfying a growing interest in wine but in order to soak up the excess production of the wineries who had planted vineyards in the 1970s—not because they wanted to make wine, but because of favorable tax laws. Most of the growth in varietal wine sales must be attributed to White Zinfandel, which is the largest varietal category in America. Outselling Chardonnay by two to one, it accounts for 10 percent of all American wine consumption. Trinchero believes: "White Zinfandel is popular because it is easy to like. You don't have to have a degree in enology to enjoy it."[9] This is true enough. A chilled bottle of Sutter Home White Zinfandel tastes like strawberry mousse, or strawberries and cream. Trinchero does not believe that consumers of White Zinfandel will "trade up" to drink dry white wines. "For Middle America, White Zinfandel is as premium as it gets. They won't move on. It's their wine, and they'll die with it in their hands. Often they did not drink at all before they tried White Zinfandel—or else they drank beer. The United States will not become a wine-drinking country."

People prefer the taste of sweet wine—while at the same time pretending that they prefer dry wine, which is more sophisticated. So they like to drink White Zinfandel, which is never actually described as "sweet"; sweetish Chardonnays, which everyone thinks of as being dry; and sherries such as Dry Sack, which is undoubtedly sweet. Dry Sack is probably the cleverest example of a wine company's pandering to our taste for sweet wine that is labeled "dry." In his book on sherry, Julian Jeffs says that sack—a very popular drink in sixteenth-century England, particularly among Falstaff and his friends in Shakespeare's *King Henry IV Part I*—was a sweet wine. Dry Sack is a medium sherry: therefore, it is a very dry sack, though not a dry sherry.[10]

The American preference for sweet wine goes back a long way. The success of the sparkling Catawba made by Nicholas Longworth in Cincinnati, Ohio, has been referred to in the previous chapter. This was first produced (by accident) in 1842. Before that Longworth had made dry white wines which were much appreciated by German immigrants in the *Weinstuben* of Cincinnati, but not by American tasters, who often mistook them for cider or even vinegar. What

American wine drinkers enjoyed most was North Carolina Scupper-nong. At the very least, this was a sweet, fortified wine with a pro-nounced muscadine flavor; at most, it was not actually wine but a *mistelle* or cordial. Longworth dismissed it as "a compound of grape juice, cider, honey, and apple brandy."[11]

Likewise, it was sweet fortified wine that Americans started drinking after the end of Prohibition. According to Charles M. Craw-ford, who has worked for Ernest & Julio Gallo since 1942, in the early days of wine drinking after Prohibition people did not like imported table wine, which they found too acidic and called "sour wine." People wanted sweet wine, which, to be stable, had in those days to be fortified. This is no longer necessary. People have there-fore converted from fortified sweet wines to unfortified sweet wines; they have not converted from fortified sweet wines to unfortified dry ones.

The American preference for sweetness in wine is intimately linked to the national preference for sweetness in food. In their brilliant attack on the philistinism of the American palate, John and Karen Hess pointed out that, whereas other societies have separated their sweetening from their main dishes at meals, and usually con-sume sugary foods in a dessert or between meals, Americans are "a nation of sugar addicts" who look for sweetness in everything they eat—bread, meat, soups, vegetables, and salads.[12]

Most Americans grow up on sweet, fizzy drinks such as soda pop and cola. On average, each American consumes half a can of just one brand of cola—Coca-Cola—every day. Sweet though it may be, Coca-Cola is probably not sweet enough to satisfy the majority of people who drink it. At least that is the conclusion to be drawn from the launch of a new formula of Coca-Cola in 1985. This was un-doubtedly influenced by the "Pepsi Challenge," in which represen-tatives of Pepsi-Cola offered consumers two glasses of cola and found that in very many cases they preferred the one which contained Pepsi, a sweeter drink than Coke. Coca-Cola tried to counter the challenge by themselves moving to a sweeter formula in 1985. They were supported by taste tests in which consumers had consistently preferred the new to the old Coke, but they had failed to take into account the personal attachment felt by consumers of the original Coke. Consumers regarded the product as something immutable, as important a symbol as the American flag. A public outcry persuaded Coca-Cola to release the old Coke as "Classic Coke" after a few months.[13] Nevertheless, the premise was a fair one: for most American consumers, Coke is not sweet enough.

Much of the so-called wine boom can in fact be accounted for by the consumption of the alcoholic equivalents of soda pop, the new Coke and Pepsi-Cola. In 1955 the federal government authorized "special natural wines" to contain natural pure flavors without paying extra excise tax. This led to the production of flavored fortified wines, of which the first was Thunderbird, a lemon-flavored white "port" launched in 1957 by Ernest & Julio Gallo. Thunderbird attracted a great deal of criticism in the 1980s on account of its popularity down on skid row, but in its early days it was promoted a the "new American aperitif." People drank it mixed with soda and ice as an alternative to a spirits-based cocktail. In 1958 Congress voted to allow wines to contain enough carbon dioxide to make a slight pop when opened without paying extra tax. Manufacturers of flavored wines such as Thunderbird started making fruit-flavored "pop" wines, with about 8–10 percent alcohol. These were a great success in the 1960s, and by 1971 accounted for almost 10 percent of all wine consumed in the United States.

Sales of "pop" wines declined during the 1970s—but this did not mean that people had moved over to drinking more traditional wines. They simply converted to other, similar styles of wine such as Riunite Lambrusco, which was launched in 1967 and by 1984 was selling 130 million bottles a year. When Lambrusco sales declined in their turn, it was not because consumers had moved over to drier wines. It was partly because of the discovery of minute traces of diethylene glycol in some of the Riunite wines,[14] partly because of the damage done to the whole Italian wine business by the methanol scandal, and principally because of the sudden and unexpected success of coolers.

Coolers are mixtures of alcohol—whether wine, beer, or spirits—fruit juice, and carbonated water; they contain anything between 1 and 6 percent alcohol. They were invented at a Malibu beach party in 1979 and test-marketed among beach-goers. By 1986 sales of coolers had reached 60 million case (120 million gallons), accounting for 20 percent of the total American wine market and a revenue of $1,200 million. Since then, they have fallen back to roughly 80 million gallons. They have not taken over the whole country, as many people in the industry had predicted, but have remained seasonal—and biased to the West Coast and the Sunbelt. In 1991, however, Riunite recognized the significance of coolers by changing the taste of their red and white Lambruscos to make them lighter and sweeter, fresher and fruitier: less like wine and more like coolers than they used to be.

The preference for fizzy drinks shown by consumers of soda pop, cola, Lambrusco, and coolers is shared by many of the people who have taken up drinking dry wines. As Longworth had realized in the 1840s, if American consumers cannot have a drink that is sweet, then at least they would like it to be sparkling. That is why he converted from still to sparkling wine production, a change which enabled him to sell his wine all over America rather than just in the *Weinstuben* of Cincinnati.[15] The popularity of sparkling wines among American consumers has not diminished since. In 1990, 150 million bottles of sparkling wine were consumed in the United States.

There are various reasons for the appeal of sparkling wine. From the point of view of the wine maker, carbon dioxide accentuates the acid taste in wines and therefore makes them seem fresher. This is very useful for white wines made in hot climates, which tend to suffer from a lack of acidity. It also protects wine from decay, because the pressure of gas trying to escape prevents air from entering the bottle. When the "champagne method" was developed last century, making it possible to produce sparkling wines at will, it was used to preserve wines while they were waiting for customers. When it became difficult to sell red burgundies at the end of last century, even the *grand cru* wines were made sparkling by the new "champagne method." This method is still used today as an alternative to chaptalizing (adding sugar before fermentation) the produce of bad vintages in cool vine-growing regions. It is used by a number of producers in the Mosel, even for the most famous wine of all, Bernkastel Doktor; in the Loire, at Vouvray and Montlouis; and in cooler regions of California, such as by Ted Bennett at Navarro in the Anderson Valley in Mendocino County.

From the point of view of the consumer, the carbon dioxide enhances a drink's appearance, diminishes the taste of alcohol (which many people dislike), and at the same time enables the alcohol to be absorbed much more rapidly by the gut, thereby producing a much more rapid effect. This has rendered sparkling drinks sexually useful. As the English essayist Denzil Batchelor once wrote, "In the old days before World War I, [sparkling red burgundy] was a particularly favorite of ladies of easy virtue and also of young girls who were inclined to wish that their virtue was not quite so difficult."[16]

3
Red Wine
in Restaurants

APART FROM a preference for cold, sweet drinks, there is another reason why Americans drink so much more white wine than red. This goes back to our days as hunter-gatherers thirty thousand years ago, when a liking for sweet things was programmed into our genes. The caveman knew that if a fruit was sweet, it was ripe and ready to eat. At the same time, we developed an innate dislike of bitterness, since a bitter taste in a plant indicates that it contains poisonous alkaloids, a necessary means of chemical warfare for a plant that cannot defend itself from predators by running away. A liking for sweetness and a dislike of bitterness are the only two innate tastes that we have; all other tastes are acquired. Whereas the liking for sweetness explains why most people like sweet white wines, the dislike of bitterness explains why many people dislike red wines—because these contain tannins. It is the purpose of tannins to interfere with an animal's digestive process. They taste astringent because they react with the mucoproteins contained in saliva, thereby preventing the saliva from performing its lubricating effect. The more we drink, the more astringent the wine appears, as we simply run out of mucoproteins.

In order that we should come to enjoy dry wines more than sweet ones and red wines more than white (and make the transition from novice to sophisticated wine drinkers), it is necessary literally to "sophisticate"—to pervert—our natural tastes. The ways in which we lose our preference for sweetness and overcome our hostility to bitterness are different. In the first case, it is satiety: until our taste for sweetness returns in old age, the older we become, and the more years of plenty we have enjoyed, the less sweet our tooth. That is why children have a sweeter tooth than adults.[1] We lose our dislike of bitterness by taking pleasure in the sensation of danger. Drinking tannic red wine or coffee is unnatural and dangerous, and therefore pleasurable, in much the same way as riding in a roller-coaster. In both cases, however, our reason for doing so is to show ourselves to be sophisticated (in the sense of worldly-wise) by adopting tastes that can only be acquired with practice.

The American preference for sweet wines and white wines conflicts with that of the wine-producing and wine-drinking countries of Europe, where more red wine has historically been drunk than white. One of the reasons for Americans' not generally sophisticating their tastes is their relatively late introduction to wine. Whereas, in Europe, parents often encourage their children to start acquiring a taste for wine when they are still very young, the prevailing American attitude toward wine consumption by children was demonstrated by the school board in Culver City, California, which in May 1990 withdrew an award-winning adaptation of *Little Red Riding Hood* from a children's recommended reading list because a bottle of wine was included in the basket of goodies that Little Red Riding Hood was taking to her ailing grandmother.

Teenagers are not allowed to drink wine, either. Between 1984 and 1987, twenty-three states raised the minimum drinking age from eighteen or nineteen to twenty-one—under pressure from a federal law that, under the pretense that a significant proportion of highway deaths involving drinking are caused by people under twenty-one, threatened to withhold highway grants from those states which failed to raise their minimum drinking age to twenty-one. In theory, twenty-one is the minimum age only as regards public purchase or public possession of wine. Although your child may not be allowed to have his own glass of wine in a restaurant, there is nothing to stop his drinking from your glass—other than public opprobrium.

There is a simple enough explanation for the desire of Europeans to undergo a process of sophistication at as early an age as possible. They consider that red wine generally combines better than white wine with food. In Italy and France, most of the wine that is drunk is red, because wine is usually drunk only with meals. Indeed, in the 1950s it was said of the Italians that they believed that wine *was* a food. Every meal had to include wine, but wine could only be drunk at a meal. If Italians drank little in the way of spirits, it was because spirits were not recognized as food.[2] Evidently this attitude was, and is, encouraged by their practice of introducing children to wine as a part of family meals at an early age. In Anglo-Saxon countries the position is quite different. In Britain, twice as much white wine is drunk as red, partly because a lot of people drink wine at parties. In America, the party drink is usually beer, and wine is most commonly taken with food. One might therefore expect more people to drink red wine in America than in Britain. But they do not. Three times as much white wine as red is consumed.

Part of the explanation for this state of affairs lies with restaurants, which are (or should be) the motor of change in taste in food and drink, and thus of the movement from sweet white to dry red wine. Certainly, the part that is to be played by restaurants in turning America into a wine-drinking country is recognized by those California wineries that have opened up restaurants on site, among them Domaine Chandon in the Napa Valley, Château Soverain in Sonoma County, and Wente Brothers in Livermore. These wineries are operating on the principle that Americans tend to be comfortable with food but uncomfortable with wine, and that it therefore makes sense to introduce them to sophisticated wine through the medium of sophisticated food. Eating in restaurants requires a certain amount of experimentation, since what is served is inevitably different from what is consumed at home; therefore, restaurant customers are more prepared to experiment with what they drink than are people at home. Moreover, people go out to restaurants for the occasion, rather than for the food. (It cannot be for the food, since a decent home cook can produce better food than 95 percent of restaurants.) Part of that occasion is the drinking of wine, even if this is not something these people normally do.

Furthermore, since eating out is an occasion, it might be expected that restaurants would encourage people to try better and more expensive wine. Apart from anything else, it offers an opportunity for conspicuous display. In 1990 *The Wine Spectator* ran a story about people who had spent very large sums of money on buying wine in restaurants. It asked Nelson Durante why he had spent $6,500 (then £4,000) on a bottle of 1925 Brunello di Montalcino (made by Biondi-Santi) in an Italian restaurant in New York. Durante said that he had been trying to sell a communications business—for tens of millions of dollars—and had promised himself that, if he succeeded, he would buy the most expensive bottle of wine he could find. "Every sip I took of the wine, I remembered the bottom line of the contract."[3]

Now, if people are likely to drink more fine wine in restaurants, then they are likely to drink more red wine. This is because ordinary wine is more likely to be white, and fine wine is more likely to be red. In the opinion of Rodney Strong, a former dancer who founded an eponymous winery in Sonoma County in California, "White wine is wine drinking on a superficial level. Americans have yet to develop the introspective approach needed to appreciate red wines—and, let's face it, most of the great wines are red."[4] There is some substance to support his belief in the superiority of red wines. Most of the flavor in wines comes not from the pulp in the middle of the grape but from the skin that surrounds it. Red wines are fermented in contact with their skins; white wines are not. Therefore red wines have more flavor. The white wines that have most flavor are those which are made by leaving the skins in contact with the juice before fermentation (a method which was popular in California in the late 1970s but was abandoned because the wines turned brown at an early age) and those which are made by fermenting a turbid juice containing a lot of solid matter from the skins. This latter method is traditional for white wines in Burgundy, and is increasingly practiced by producers of the best California Chardonnays, such as Kistler in Sonoma County and Au Bon Climat in Santa Barbara.

Against these theories it can be argued that Americans are eating less meat than they used to, and therefore eating out in restaurants is more likely to encourage them to drink white wine, because white wine goes better with fish and red wine with meat. The rules about combining food and wine, however, were developed for reasons of practicality as much as those of taste. It makes sense to

progress during a meal from lighter to heavier: from fish to meat, and
from white wine to red. Our senses of smell and taste are most acute
when we are hungry; as our hunger is satiated, our senses become
dulled, and more intense flavors are required in order to provoke the
same response. Since fish has consequently been consumed at the
same time as white wine, and meat at the same time as red, they
have come to be thought of together—especially since most fish is
white and much meat is red. These rules are supported by the fact
that tannin in red wines reacts with fish to produce an unpleasant
metallic taste, and thus tannic red wine and fish do not make a good
marriage. Tannic red wines, however, are no longer so common as
they used to be. Robert Mondavi has blamed the wine industry for
having turned Americans away from red wine by making red wines
in the past that were too "big" and "strong" to go with food.[5] Things
are different today. More subtle wine-making techniques have produced an enormous improvement in Pinot Noirs in both California
and Oregon. Because Pinot Noir grapes have relatively thin skins,
the wine made from them is much lower in tannin than in Cabernet
Sauvignon. Pinot Noirs can therefore combine perfectly well with
fish. Indeed, Oregon Pinot Noir producers are promoting their wine
as the ideal accompaniment for salmon.

The reason why restaurants have not served to encourage Americans to move on from white wine to red is simply that, by the way
in which they treat wine, restaurants generally do more to discourage
than to encourage wine consumption.

All wine in restaurants is absurdly expensive. Restaurants make
much more money on wine than they do on food. Although they
mark up the cost of raw ingredients by 250 percent, restaurants in
fact make little money on food. Their customers would simply not be
willing to pay the sort of prices for their food which would cover not
only food costs (and wastage), but also labor costs (both cooking and
serving), the expense of equipment, electricity, rent, taxes, etc., and
the restaurateur's profit margin. Therefore the profit margin is transferred to wine. A restaurant's food prices may be low, but its wine
prices are high. The standard markup on wines is 200 percent on the
wholesale price—slightly less than the margin on food. But the
service of wine involves restaurants in little expense beyond a few
breakages and some pilfering by the staff, and minimal staff time

actually in serving the stuff. On top of these, they make a huge profit.

Some restaurateurs have attempted to overcome their dependence on earning money from the sale of wine, but without success. When he opened his restaurant at Thornbury Castle in Gloucestershire in the west of England in 1966, the restaurateur Kenneth Bell tried charging less for the wine and more for the food. He soon had to give up on this idea. His customers did not understand what he was trying to do, and considered his prices for food excessive. Ernie Van Asperen, the owner of the Californian Round Hill winery, which today produces good-value varietal wines, used to own two waterfront restaurants on the north side of San Francisco Bay. In the mid-1960s he attempted to get his clients interested in wine by offering it at retail price, but he had to give up on his experiment after a couple of years because it was not sufficiently profitable. One possible solution might be to charge an entrance fee to cover the cost of the restaurateur's overheads and to allow him a profit margin— and then to charge for food and wine at cost. I suspect, however, that this would discourage people from ever entering restaurants at all, as it involves paying something for nothing. It would also mean that small eaters subsidize big eaters—though that is no more unfair than the present system in which wine drinkers subsidize non-drinkers.

When asked why their wines are so expensive, restaurateurs attempt to justify themselves by saying that their customers would not want it otherwise. On one occasion in the early 1980s, Frank Prial of *The New York Times* was lunching with a wine importer in a neighborhood restaurant where the house white—which the restaurateur bought from the importer—cost $13. The importer told Prial that he sold it to the restaurateur for $2. Prial asked the restaurateur why he marked up the price by so large a margin. "Listen," was the reply, "I get a high-class clientèle here. They'd be insulted if I charged them less."[6] Some of this restaurant's customers may well have preferred to have been insulted; but it is sadly true that many diners-out become uneasy when faced with a restaurant wine list, and are reassured by high prices.

There exists a difference, however, between high prices and ludicrous ones. It is difficult to avoid describing the cost of fine wines in restaurants as anything but the latter. This is because restaurants mark up wines by a fixed percentage, so they make far more profit on expensive than on cheap wines. The ludicrous sums that are asked for fine wines in restaurants encourages their customers to resort to various ruses, such as saying that it is their birthday and asking to be allowed to bring a very special bottle from their own cellar. André Soltner, the owner of Lutèce in New York, used to allow regular customers to bring in wine from their own cellars—until, one day, his wine waiter walked past a wineshop where he saw one of these regular customers buying the wine he would, later that evening, claim had come from his carefully accumulated private collection. Other restaurateurs are perfectly prepared to let their customers bring their own wines, providing their customers are prepared in return to pay extortionate corkage charges. Sirio Maccioni, the owner of Le Cirque in New York, says that it is his policy to charge between $15 and $50 a bottle corkage, depending on the value of the wine.[7]

If good wine in restaurants were not so obviously a rip-off, more people might be encouraged to drink it. But, given the extra expense and effort involved in holding stocks of fine wine, there is no economic reason for restaurants to encourage consumers to drink by charging a lower percentage markup than they do on ordinary wines. Many a restaurateur is quite happy when his customers stick to ordinary wines, because then he does not have to worry about the ignorance of his staff in wine service.

Few restaurants treat wines properly. They are served in the wrong way by staff who mostly know no better. Even the smartest restaurants nowadays have great trouble finding *sommeliers* who have the slightest knowledge of wine. Unlike the position in Europe, the status of a *sommelier* in the United States is a lowly one—so lowly that there is no word in English to describe his job. Someone with enthusiasm for wine is more likely to work in a wineshop. What is the point in spending a lot of money on a good bottle of red wine if it is going to be served too warm, and if the staff insists on filling the glass up to the brim every time you have drunk enough to get a chance of swirling it around to enjoy its bouquet? Not that this would be very effective, anyway, given the shape of glasses that most restaurants use, and the fact that many of them stink either of detergent or of varnish—the latter the result of mistakenly storing them upside down on a shelf.

The ignorance and stupidity of many restaurant staff discourage people from drinking wine. For example, staff often refuse to take back bottles that are corked. It is true that consumers have sometimes claimed that wines are "corked" for their own nefarious purposes. In Britain before the Second World War, a popular restaurant ploy was for a diner-out to order a bottle of white wine to go with his fish course, drink half of it, then complain that it was "corked." As he had by now finished his fish, it was by now too late to replace it with another bottle of the same wine, so he was given, to go with his meat course, another bottle of the same wine for free.[8] Moreover, it is unlikely that many consumers are able to identify corked wines, since most members of the wine trade are not. I have been to a number of professional wine tastings at which I have tasted nearly empty bottles of wine which are evidently corked but about which no one has complained. Diners-out, who read in wine books such as Alexis Bespaloff's revision of Frank Schoonmaker's *Encyclopaedia of Wine* that "Corked wines arrive much less frequently than many consumers imagine,"[9] are generally disinclined to send back defective bottles, not least because, if they do so, they are liable to be told by their waiter that the wine is meant to taste like that.

In fact, corked wines arrive much more frequently than wine waiters or wine writers imagine. California wineries have told me that 5 percent of their bottles are corked. These estimates were confirmed by *The Wine Spectator*, which in 1990 carried out an analysis of the ten thousand wines it had tasted over the preceding three years and found that 4.7 percent of them had been corked, including a $350 bottle of Romanée-Conti 1985.[10] It is not hard to identify a corked wine—it has an overpoweringly musty smell, similar to damp cardboard—but restaurateurs seem to have difficulty noticing it.

The British journalist Joanna Simon once sent back a musty bottle of champagne at one of London's most fashionable restaurants. The waiter disappeared with the bottle and after some time reappeared with the manager, who said that there was absolutely nothing wrong with the bottle. Simon stood her ground, which led the manager to insist that she retaste it "with a little more in the glass." She did. More made it seem worse. The manager, who had clearly expected her to capitulate under pressure, then announced, "If anyone would notice something wrong, *I* would." Simon then played her trump card. Saying that she thought she, too, could

recognize a bad bottle, she handed over her business card, which
read: Wine Correspondent, *The Sunday Times*. The manager looked
at it and at her, then walked away, followed by the waiter carrying
the offending bottle. After another long wait, the celebrated chef-
proprietor himself appeared. He conceded that there was something
wrong with the bottle, but said that he probably would not have
noticed unless she had pointed it out. He replaced the bottle. Had
Simon been an ordinary customer, she would have been stuck with
the bad bottle.[11] She certainly seems to have suffered less than the
diner at Le Pavillon in New York who sent back a bottle, which
Henri Soulé, the owner, accepted without demur; then, at the end
of the evening, Soulè tore up the check and suggested that hence-
forth the customer should dine elsewhere.[12]

In 1991 *The Wine Spectator* asked a random selection of one
thousand of its subscribers what they thought about wine service in
restaurants. Sixty-five percent of those who replied rated service as
less than satisfactory, and only 9 percent rated it as good or excellent.
A reader from St. Louis, Missouri, wrote to say: "We don't eat out
nearly as often as we'd like because wine lists are so bad here. None
of the staff ever knows anything. We often share wines we order with
the staff because they've never tasted them."[13]

Instead of restaurants being the motors of change from white to
red wine, people have stopped drinking wine in them altogether. I
remember dining with a friend at Le Montrachet in the Tribeca
district of New York in the autumn of 1990. As its name might
suggest, it specializes in burgundies—at very reasonable prices by
New York standards. It was Friday night, yet ours was the only table
with a bottle of wine. Some people had a glass of wine; most had
mineral water. A few years ago many more people would have had
bottles of wine on their tables. But sales of wine in restaurants are
falling sharply, forcing many restaurants—which are dependent on
the easy money they make from wine for their livelihood—into
bankruptcy. Asked in 1989 why wine sales in restaurants were falling, Abdullah Simon, the director of Seagram's fine-wine division,
Château & Estate, pointed to factors beyond poor service: to the
recession, to a change in the tax laws which mean that 20 percent of
the cost of a business-related meal is no longer tax deductible, and to
a lifestyle change. "Until a few years ago," he said, "it used to be the

fashionable thing to spend an evening going out with your friends to a restaurant: it was like going to the theatre. Now people are eating more at home."[14]

People may drink wine at the table in the United States, but that table is at home and not in a restaurant. It has been estimated by various surveys that between 75 and 80 percent of wine consumption takes place in someone's home. The neo-temperance movement may not have stopped people drinking in private, but many people have become wary about drinking in public. This is hardly surprising, if one considers the experience of a woman who ordered a pink daiquiri in a Seattle restaurant in 1991. Because she was (very obviously) pregnant, two waiters lectured her about her unborn fetus and how it would probably be born a lopsided moron if she drank a daiquiri. The customer then complained to the manager about being treated like a child abuser, and the story has a happy ending: the waiters were fired.

4
Writers and
Collectors

I F THE CONSUMPTION of better wines is not encouraged by restaurants, then perhaps it is encouraged by wine writers. Certainly, they have an important role to play. Unlike, say, automobiles, which travel at different speeds, handle in different ways, and offer different standards of comfort, there are no objective criteria for differentiating between different wines. All wines are a solution of ethanol in water. Some Germans have tried to "prove" that their frequently maligned dry wines are better than dry French white wines because chemical analysis shows them to contain more sugar-free extract—which in theory means more body and flavor—but the practice of judging a wine by its chemical analysis has not caught on in the United States. The status of a wine depends on a subjective analysis by tasting by an expert.

In this respect the wine market is quite different from that for other drinks. There are specialist beer retailers; there is a growing number of microbreweries, each of which produces several different beers. But beers are consistent, branded products: once a consumer has tasted them for the first time, he is not in need of advice to help him to decide whether to try them again. In wine there is a much wider range of products; moreover, even if a consumer has tasted a wine before, he will not necessarily have tried the latest vintage or know how it has matured or how it is likely to in the future. It is in our choice of wine, not of beer, that we rely on the opinions of experts.

The influence of these experts is much greater in the United States than in Britain. This is partly a result of American liquor laws. In many states you are prohibited from tasting a wine before you buy it—a common practice in Britain, where wine merchants hold regular tastings, not just as a means of selling wine but also in order to enhance their image as serious wine retailers. Because of such laws, Americans have to take the advice either of the retailer or of a wine writer.

Advice is something that few American wine retailers are equipped to give. Wine retailers in Britain generally have a much greater knowledge of French wines than their counterparts in the United States have of California wines. Whereas many British wine retailers import wine on their own account, both from Europe and from America, retailers in the United States are—except in Massachusetts, California, and Washington, D.C.—forbidden from importing wine. So there is little incentive for them to travel to wine-producing regions. Many of them would not be interested in doing so, anyway. In New York State, according to Michael Aaron of Sherry-Lehmann, "The majority of wine retailers don't even know that you need a corkscrew to open a bottle of wine. A lot of the people who sell wine don't drink it. They treat wine as a commodity."

The ignorance of the majority of retailers was made evident by a scandal involving the export to the United States (between November 1978 and July 1979) of 250,000 bottles of cheap French table wine relabeled as Pouilly-Fuissé and Puligny-Montrachet. This scandal was eventually exposed by the vigilance of British trading standards officers, and the two Englishmen who had relabeled the wines were sent to jail for eighteen months. The owners of the wine stores in the United States which had sold the wines would have been happy if supplies continued. None of them complained to their suppliers about the quality of their wine; the proprietor of one retail store in Manhattan, who was selling the "Pouilly-Fuissé" for $11.45, said: "It's very popular. We sell all we can get." Frenchman Alain Leonnet, who ran wine stores in Los Angeles and San Francisco, tried to argue that "White wines like these are always chilled so cold

that they're practically frozen when they're drunk. Even an expert
would have trouble telling what they are."[1] No one, however,
obliged the wine retailers to freeze these wines before tasting them—
assuming, that is, that they did taste them before putting them on
their shelves.

In Britain, the standard of wine retailers may be higher, but that
of many wine writers is not. In Britain, wine writers are, for the most
part, not truly journalists, but amateurs. This is a matter of econom-
ics. Many magazines are not particularly interested in the quality of
the copy presented for their wine column, providing it is innocuous
enough. What matters to them is that the right image be created for
their magazine; the up-market status of wine drinking has not yet
been tarnished by its growing popularity. They feel that wine writers
write for love of wine only, and in their heart of hearts believe that
the writers ought to pay the magazine, not the other way around.
This belief is reciprocated by the many amateur wine lovers who are
perfectly prepared to write, as a hobby, for nothing. As a result,
magazines pay, on the whole, very little for wine articles. If professional journalists are not prepared to work for these fees, amateur
ones will.

British wine writers would seem to enjoy quite enough in the
way of perks to compensate them for being badly paid: all that wining
and dining at other people's expense, not to mention the regular and
continuous supply of free samples, and the occasional press trip
abroad. Obviously, a wine producer (or the promotional body for a
wine region) is not going to spend a couple of hundred dollars on
taking someone out to lunch, or a couple of thousand dollars on
sending a journalist on a trip abroad, without expecting a come-back
in the form of a favorable article. In the vast majority of cases, the
bribe is successful. Not only does an article appear, but the journalist
omits to mention that the research was sponsored by a company
whose job it was to show the product in its best possible light. In the
summer of 1991, Lucy Bailey, the wine correspondent of *The Sunday Telegraph*, a national newspaper, wrote a very complimentary
article about Muscadet—at a time when it was generally being criticized by other wine writers and by wine retailers as offering poor
value for money. "There are good reasons to continue drinking
Muscadet," she said. Nowhere did Bailey mention that she had

written the article following an expenses-paid trip to Muscadet *with her boyfriend.*[2]

The outstanding example of British wine-writing ethics is offered by the wine magazine *Decanter*, which first appeared in 1975, nine years before its only rival, *Wine*, and which, despite relatively small sales, enjoys a very good reputation internationally. *Decanter* clearly considers itself to be a consumer magazine, offering consumer advice, and boasts on its letterhead that it is "the world's best wine magazine." It is hard to see how these claims can be justified when many of the articles in the magazine have been written by wine writers about regions to which they have recently enjoyed a press trip; when wine companies have been told that articles will be written about them provided they are prepared to take out advertisements; and when its contributors have been pressed by the magazine's advertising department to mention a particular company, who will then be prepared to buy space. *Decanter* has got itself into this ethical mess for economic reasons. Because it is economically dependent on wine advertising, it is hardly in its interest to encourage articles that criticize advertisers, actual or potential. On occasions, a tacit understanding is reached between editor and advertiser, and a product is mentioned in an article in expectation of an advertisement being paid for. This relationship is sometimes made explicit, in the form of what are called "advertisement features" or "advertorials." More often, it is not. As a result, many articles in magazines end up, in effect, as puffs, as advertorials posing as editorials.

Some contributors to *Decanter* have tried to defend their uncritical approach by saying that critics should mention what they like, and simply ignore what they do not. But how, by definition, can a critic be uncritical? As well as recommending good wines to buy, giving consumer advice entails, for example, examining the latest hype—Beaujolais Nouveau, Bordeaux futures, wine coolers, or whatever—and trying to determine whether it is a rip-off. The idea that one should write only about those wines that are worth drinking is a dereliction of the first duties of a journalist. It is also highly misleading. Is one to assume that a product that is not written up is condemned by omission? If so, this will only increase the pressure from advertisers for favorable editorial mentions as a condition of their paying for advertisements.

Decanter, furthermore, publishes articles by wine importers or retailers about regions in whose produce they have a financial interest, without that interest being declared: for example, Liz Berry, joint owner of La Vigneronne, a wine retailer in London, who has in a number of articles put forward her shop as a supplier of wines she has recommended; Ian Jamieson, at the time a director of the wine importers Deinhard, who has written articles about German estates for whom Deinhard is the British agent; Simon Taylor-Gill, the wine buyer for Domaine Direct, a specialist importer of burgundies, who has written several articles about Burgundy.[3] *Decanter*'s competitor, *Wine*, publishes articles by David Gleave, the wine buyer for Winecellars, specialist importers and retailers of Italian wine, about producers whom his company represents in Britain or at least sells on a retail basis. Moreover, many of the most prominent British authors of wine books are in fact wine merchants: Anthony Hanson, author of *Burgundy*, is the wine buyer for Haynes, Hanson & Clark, retail wine merchants specializing in fine Bordeaux and burgundies; David Peppercorn, author of *Bordeaux*, and Serena Sutcliffe, author of *The Pocket Guide to the Wines of Burgundy*, are directors of Peppercorn & Sutcliffe, a wine brokerage business; Nicolas Belfrage, author of *Life Beyond Lambrusco*, a book on Italian wine, as well as David Gleave, who has written *The Wines of Italy*, are directors of Winecellars. David Gleave's interests may not have been admitted by *Wine*, but he includes at the front of his book a list of the fourteen estates he mentions whose wine he imports.[4] Others omit to declare their interest. Serena Sutcliffe is remarkably complimentary in her book about the wines produced by Burgundy merchants Delaunay and André Delorme, by Robert and Michel Ampeau in Meursault, and by Domaine des Varoilles in Gevrey-Chambertin. Nowhere does she reveal her commerical involvement with these estates. The most famous British wine writer, Hugh Johnson, although not a wine merchant, is nevertheless a director of Château Latour, which he describes in his 1992 *Pocket Wine Book* as the "grandest statement of the Médoc: rich, intense and almost immortal in great years, almost always classical and pleasing in weak ones." He may be right, but do his readers not have the right to know of his interest in the *château*?

Up until 1987, American wine writers had little reason to feel superior to their British counterparts. Then, that summer, the *Los Angeles Times* led its front page on two successive days with an exposé of the working methods of wine writers. The writer who was exposed most thoroughly was the *Los Angeles Times*'s own wine columnist, Nathan Chroman. The paper said that Chroman was widely discussed by California wine producers because he was "perceived by many in the wine industry as having abused the power conferred on him by his column. He is thought to be abrasive and imperious, and he is criticized for having involved himself in several situations where there is at least the appearance of a potential conflict of interest—having a financial involvement with at least three California wineries; accepting free meals and free trips abroad for himself and his wife; writing a book, one edition of which was partially subsidized by a wine maker."[5]

It was announced in the article that Chroman, a Beverly Hills attorney, would no longer be writing his column, which he had contributed once a week since 1968. According to Jean Sharley Taylor, the paper's associate editor, the decision to end Chroman's column and the appearance of the exposé were purely coincidental; she claimed that the *Los Angeles Times* had for a long time wanted to hire a full-time professional journalist in Chroman's place, but had only just been given the budget to do it.[6] At the same time, *The Wine Spectator* introduced a ban on its staff's taking press trips, although its proprietor Marvin Shanken now says that the decision to introduce this ban was taken before the *Los Angeles Times* article appeared. He said that *The Wine Spectator* had never permitted its staff or free lancers to take a press trip sponsored by an individual producer or brand owner; but that until 1987, when he was in a position to fund travel, he allowed them to take trips sponsored by national or regional promotional organizations.

Not only does *The Wine Spectator* distinguish itself from its British counterparts by its rejection of press trips, but it is prepared to criticize the wines it dislikes as well as praise the wines it enjoys. Marvin Shanken, a trade magazine publisher who bought *The Wine Spectator* in 1978, says that at first he caused "a major controversy within the industry. They said that we had no business listing the wines which we did not recommend. But this encouraged consumers to trust us." It also apparently led wineries to cancel advertising.

Shanken claims that in 1990 one company which had advertised a dozen times a year decided to pull out on account of the bad reviews it had been receiving, thus losing *The Wine Spectator* $100,000 a year in revenue. Certainly, the attitude of *Decanter* is quite different. It does not give marks to the wines it tastes and does not list the wines in its tastings which have performed badly. For a while it used to publish a list of all the wines included in the tasting in question, although not beside the report of the tasting but hidden away in the back of the magazine. Now it no longer does even this much.

The Wine Spectator has not shrunk from controversy. For example, at the end of 1989 it published an account of the dispute between the co-owners of Château Ausone, alongside Château Cheval-Blanc the most prestigious estate in Saint-Emilion, which was affecting the quality of the wines. It told how, during the 1989 harvest, Pascal Delbeck, the wine maker employed by one of the co-owners, Heylett Dubois-Challon, instructed the pickers to start harvesting the Merlot grapes (half the total crop), only for the other co-owner, Alain Vauthier, to stop the harvest three hours later. Then Vauthier and Dubois-Challon, his great-aunt, started arguing in the middle of the vineyard. Vauthier had stopped the harvest because he wanted riper grapes. In the opinions of both Dubois-Challon and Delbeck, the grapes were already ripe enough. "What are we waiting for?" asked Delbeck. "To make Ausone vintage port?"[7] Not only has *Decanter* failed to discuss the disputes of Ausone, but its attitude to controversies of this kind is demonstrated by its never publishing anything about one of the major scandals of the 1980s, the conviction in 1983 of the Burgundy merchant Roland Remoissenet for mislabeling his wines. Since Remoissenet's wines were sold by some of Britain's most prestigious wine merchants, such as Averys of Bristol and The Wine Society, one might have thought that it was in the consumer's interest that it should have done so.

The Wine Spectator has its critics, however. Many members of the California wine trade believe that there exists a relationship between the advertisements in *The Wine Spectator* and its editorial content, as there is in *Decanter*. They point to such items as the extraordinarily sycophantic interview of Ernest Gallo by Marvin Shanken, published in the September 15, 1991, issue. Shanken wrote of Gallo that "there is no-one for whom I have greater respect," and failed to ask him about the darker side of his business, such as the Thunderbird and Night Train fortified wine brands which he had been recently persuaded to remove from liquor stores in skid row areas because of the part they played in the creation of a "$500 million misery market."[8] Thunderbird and Night Train had up until then accounted for sales of 60 million bottles a year, hardly an insignificant proportion of Gallo's business. Shanken, however, concentrated on Gallo's new vineyard venture in Sonoma County, where Gallo said that he intended to produce $60 Cabernets and $30 Chardonnays. Shanken did not ask him how he proposed to manage this when the winery was not even built yet. There is no evidence, however, that this interview was tied to a Gallo advertising campaign: no advertisements for Gallo appeared in any subsequent issue of *The Wine Spectator* that year. Nevertheless, the belief that the good offices of *The Wine Spectator* can be bought is sufficiently prevalent for Shanken to have written an editorial on the subject in 1990.[9] Shanken later explained why he had brought the subject out into the open. He said that it had been common in the past for wineries which had received a bad review to claim that they were being punished for their failure to advertise but that he had thought that this prejudice no longer existed. Then he met a furniture salesman at a cocktail party who said that his local retailers had told him that the marks *The Wine Spectator* gave to the wines it had tasted were "phony" and that it was possible to "buy" a cover story if one spent enough money.

Ironically, although the marks in *The Wine Spectator* are not phony, they are often wrong. *The Wine Spectator* may have higher ethical standards than its British counterparts, but its judgments are less reliable. For example, when its European correspondents Per-Henrik Mansson and James Suckling wrote about the 1989 red burgundies at the beginning of 1992, they described the vintage as "the best since 1985" and gave it a higher overall rating than either the 1988 or 1978 vintages, both of which are considered superior by the majority of red burgundy producers.[10] The 1989s may well be more flattering in their youth than the 1988s or 1978s were, but that does not mean they are *better*.

The influence of *The Wine Spectator* has less to do with the accuracy of its judgments than with the fact that, by its preference for ripe, up-front, relatively accessible wines, it speaks to the man in the street—not above his head, as British magazines do. In this demotic approach to wine writing it was preceded by the world's most famous wine writer, Robert Parker. Although his newsletter *The Wine Advocate* is much less interesting to read than *The Wine Spectator* and its circulation is only one-third as large, Parker exerts greater influence on wine purchases than anyone else. One wine producer even thought Parker was important enough to take the extreme step of directing threats against his person, which led him to cancel a book-signing tour of California and a trip to Europe he had planned for the autumn of 1990.

The threats were pointless, because much of Parker's influence is exerted indirectly, through the use of his ratings by retailers. "The trade reads Parker religiously," says the New York wine merchant Peter Morrell, "and reacts by taking the wines [he recommends]. His ratings are used extensively, including by me. It is a matter of expediency. I can't go everywhere. I can't taste systematically." Parker's influence affects retailers and importers alike. Some British wine merchants make sure that they make their annual buying trip to Bordeaux before Parker publishes his tasting notes on the previous year's vintage at the beginning of May, or else all the good wines will have been bought by American importers on Parker's recommendation. Moreover, not only do wine retailers buy wine that Parker has recommended, but they refuse to buy wine that he has marked down. "I can't sell anything that he hasn't scored well," says Michael Aaron of Sherry-Lehmann in New York. [11]

Whereas the British tend to disbelieve journalists, Americans are prepared to believe what they see in print—even when their own experience is to the contrary. In 1985 a customer came into Wally's Liquors in Westwood in Los Angeles and bought a case of Chalone Chardonnay. A few days later, he returned eleven of the twelve bottles, saying that he did not like the wine. Steven Wallace, the owner, gave him his money back. Two weeks later he returned and bought another case of the same wine. Wallace asked him why he had changed his mind. He said that he had just read a rave review of the wine by Parker in *The Wine Advocate*. [12]

Parker was the first person to turn the hundred-point system that is used in schools into a tool of wine appreciation. He has done so with such success that many other American wine publications (including *The Wine Spectator*) have copied him. Certainly, the hundred-point system has its critics. The wine writer Robert Finigan has compared it to walking through the Louvre in Paris and saying, "That's a seventy-seven . . . that's a ninety-six." The system is generally condemned in Britain, where it is regarded as "intellectual self-indulgence" to believe that one can detect sufficiently fine distinctions between wines to validate using so precise a scale.[13] Before it was condemned in Britain, the practice of marking wines was misunderstood. When Hugh Johnson read a proof copy of his book on Bordeaux—sent to elicit praise that could be quoted on the book jacket—he mistook the ratings for printer's marks.[14]

Instead of giving marks, most British wine writers concentrate on describing the taste of what they drink, often in the most exotic terms they can manage. Charles Metcalfe, Associate Editor of *Wine* magazine, in one of his articles in the wine trade magazine *Wine & Spirit*, reported on some tastings of German wines, associating the Hattenheimer Wisselbrunnen 1981 from Schloss Rheinhartshausen with strawberry ice cream, the Johannisberger Erntebringer Spätlese 1982 from Deinhard with browned rice pudding, and the Erbacher Rheinhell Spätlese 1983 from Schloss Rheinhartshausen with baked bananas . . . before going on to describe the Forster Jesuitengarten Eiswein from Reichsgraf von Bühl as having "the pungent fragrance of old-fashioned sweet peas, but a softness as well, as if they had been stewed in butter but retained their perfume."[15] Whereas British attempts to describe sensual pleasure merely serve to increase wine snobbery and to turn new consumers away from wine, the American approach of giving marks appeals directly to unsophisticated wine drinkers. It helps explain why American wine writers are so much more influential than their British counterparts.

In Parker's case, this influence is strengthened by high ethical standards. In *The Wine Advocate* in 1986 he published a notice saying that he had given his brother-in-law financial support for the purchase of vineyard land in Oregon, and that he had no intention of ever writing about the vineyard or its wines. He republished this notice when he wrote again about Oregon in 1991.[16]

Parker is not infallible, however. He knows a great deal about Bordeaux and the Rhône Valley, but is a much less reliable source of information about Burgundy, on which he published a book more than a thousand pages long in 1990. Opinion is opinion, certainly, but I would not like to think that any of Parker's readers had followed his recommendation of the wines of Doudet-Naudin, to which he gave marks of between 83 and 86 out of 100, describing them as "rich" and "concentrated."[17] In my experience, they are earthy, common wines that do not taste of Pinot Noir. Germany is not a country of which Parker claims to have intimate knowledge. Nevertheless, his *Wine Buyer's Guide* contains a list of recommended German producers which was presumably based on personal experience. The list includes Geltz-Zilliken among the "Outstanding" producers and Forstmeister-Geltz-Erben among the "Excellent" ones; Landgraf von Hessen as "Excellent" and von Hessisches as "Good"; von Kesselstatt as "Excellent" and Josephshöf as "Good." In each case this is simply the same estate under two different names.[18]

This said, Parker owes his reputation in part, at least, to the fallibility of others. He started to get interested in wine in 1967, when his contemporaries were turning on, tuning in, and dropping out. When the parents of his high school sweetheart sent her to Alsace in order that she should be as far away from him as possible, Parker took a semester off from school and went to visit her. He liked Coca-Cola, but it was to expensive in Alsace, so he started drinking wine. He soon became fascinated by it. He trained as a lawyer, but launched his newsletter in 1978 as a response to his disenchantment with the "self-serving" state of wine journalism in the United States. In 1983 his *Wine Advocate* took over from Robert Finigan's *Private Guide to Wine* as the leading wine newsletter and Parker was able to give up the law. Parker had risen to prominence because he praised the 1982 red Bordeaux, whereas Finigan had sat on the fence. The 1982 vintage was a landmark, because the dollar was strong and many Americans were just starting to get interested in fine wine. Parker not only told consumers what they wanted to hear, but he was right to do so.

The Wine Spectator had missed out on the 1982s, which it had said were too expensive. It was therefore particularly keen to be the first to publish its report on the Bordeaux produced in 1989, which had been lauded as the "vintage of the century" even before the grapes were picked. The top *châteaux* do not permit their wines to be tasted before April 1, arguing that they are not ready to be judged before then. By the morning of April 4, James Suckling and James Laube had tasted 141 wines, marked them all out of 100, and written their report on the vintage. This was then published and made available on newsstands by the morning of April 10. They rated the vintage overall 98/100, the same as 1961 and higher than other outstanding recent vintages such as 1982, 1985, and 1986. They wondered whether it was not in fact the vintage of the century. If it was, that makes six vintages of the century in one decade.

Other commentators were rather more cautious in their judgment of the 1989s. In his magazine *The Vine*, the British wine writer Clive Coates condemned the hype that was already surrounding the vintage as "complete tosh . . . red Bordeaux is supposed to be a wine of breed and distinction. This is what 1989s seem to lack."[19] It was to *The Wine Spectator's* praise of the vintage, however, that American consumers responded. Despite prices that were 20–30 percent higher than for the excellent 1988, demand was greater than it had ever been before. Obviously it is not possible to calculate the degree to which this demand was the result of *The Wine Spectator's* opinions. The proportion of American fine-wine buyers on which it exerts a direct influence, however, is surprisingly large. Sales are a little under 100,000 copies an issue, but Shanken claims that his magazine is read regularly by between 300,000 and 400,000 people. Estimates of the number of purchasers of fine wine in the United States vary from half a million to a million consumers.

Why was it that consumers bought the 1989 red Bordeaux? As will be suggested in Chapter 12, their potential for investment is dubious, to say the least. Many of the purchasers of 1989 Bordeaux bought it solely in order to put in their wine collection. *The Wine Spectator* certainly encourages a collecting, rather than drinking, mentality by its general approach to wine and wine makers. Whereas the two British wine magazines, *Decanter* and *Wine*, attempt to describe the tastes of wines and appeal largely to people who already know about wine and already have fine wines in their cellars, *The Wine Spectator* tries to encourage new people to drink wine. It seeks to popularize wine by focusing on personalities more than on winemaking techniques or how the stuff actually tastes (although these aspects are not ignored). On the one hand, highlighting personalities makes wine accessible; on the other, it creates a new type of snobbery by creating superstars whose wines are too grand to be purchased by ordinary consumers. It turns wine from a comestible into a collectible.

The phenomenon of buying wines for collecting was certainly encouraged by the issue of *The Wine Spectator* dated January 31, 1989, which carried the cover story "The Ultimate Collectibles," and which charted the appreciation in value of twenty-seven collectible wines over the ten years between 1978 and 1988. The top California wines outperformed the top Bordeaux over the period: for example, Heitz Martha's Vineyard Cabernet Sauvignon 1974 appreciated in value by 700 percent, compared with 300 percent for Château Pétrus 1961.[20] A year later *The Wine Spectator* published an article on Heitz Martha's Vineyard Cabernet Sauvignon, describing it as "California's most collectible wine." It suggested that the 1985 vintage, which it said would be released the following month, "may be the crowning achievement in Heitz's wine-making career."[21] In fact, the 1985 was released on January 27. Fifty thousand bottles had been produced. The release price was $50 a bottle, a $10 increase on the price of the 1984. Because of *The Wine Spectator* article, people started lining up at 3:00 A.M., a phenomenon for which Heitz had not been prepared. The winery newsletter had promised that each customer would be allowed to buy two cases of bottles and one case of magnums, but the throng was such that this was cut to a case of bottles and two magnums at the beginning of the day, and further as it wore on. Tempers flared as the supply ran out. This problem was solved the next year—when the 1986 was released—by increasing the price to $60 a bottle and restricting purchases to six bottles per person.[22]

Are the Heitz worth the prices paid for them? *The Wine Spectator* thinks very highly of Martha's Vineyard and marked the 1984 and 1985 97/100 and 98/100, respectively. It did, however, point out that some bottles of the 1984 Bella Oaks suffered from a musty, woody taste and said that Belle and Barney Rhodes, the owners of the vineyard, were concerned about breakdowns in quality control.[23] My own experience of the 1984 Bella Oaks and the 1982 Martha's Vineyard is that they are both spoiled by a corky aroma and taste. Other people have suggested that there are problems with the 1985

Martha's Vineyard and the 1986 Bella Oaks, but I have not tasted them. When Chalone had a similar problem in the early 1980s, they concluded, after much heart-searching and the rumored expenditure of half a million dollars, that the cause was probably the infection of their barrels by the same mold (2,4,6-trichloroanisol) that causes bottles of wine to be corked. They cleared out all their old barrels and tried again.

In Parker's case, his influence in turning wine into collectibles is most evident in the case of French wines, such as—from the Rhône Valley—the three single-vineyard Côte Rôties produced by Marcel Guigal: La Mouline, La Landonne, and La Turque. When Parker tasted the 1985 vintage of La Turque in 1986, he marked it 98–100/100, later settling on 100/100. He described it as "a multi-dimensional, celestial wine which breaks all parameters and wine-tasting reference points. If one were to kill for a wine, this might be the one to do it for."[24] Fred Ek, the wine buyer for Classic Wines in Boston, the American agent for Guigal's wines, says that Parker's influence was "an important factor" in the large increase in demand for the single-vineyard wines from the 1983 and 1985 vintages, not just because he liked the wines but also because he promoted the idea of collecting the best. In 1989, bottles of La Turque were sitting on shop shelves priced at $650 each, although the price has fallen since.

Collectors buy wines to which Parker or *The Wine Spectator* has given high marks—not because they like them, but because they have been told that they ought to have them. One New York retailer, who has asked not to be named, tells how a woman came to his shop, said that she knew nothing about wine, and asked for $5,000 worth of assorted wines, "all rated ninety-three or above by Parker."[25] In one edition of his newsletter Parker described being invited to dinner a few years earlier by one of his readers. The reader showed Parker around his huge, temperature-controlled cellar, which was filled with rare vintages of top Bordeaux and burgundies. At dinner the reader opened for Parker a bottle of Bordeaux from his collection— Château Croizet-Bages 1969, the produce of a mediocre *château* in a poor vintage. It tasted unpleasant. The reader explained that he did not actually drink wine himself. "But it sure smells good," he added. This story led Parker to launch a blistering attack on what he called the nondrinking collector. "To him, wine is like a collection of crystal, art, sculpture, or china—to be admired, to be shown off, but never, ever, to be used."[26]

No one knows how many people who buy fine wines do so not in order to drink them but to have them in their collection. In Boston, Fred Ek has bought a number of complete cellars for Classic Wines, still in their original state with the cases unopened, all of them from Bordeaux. These can only have been owned by non-drinking collectors. Ek also believes that the practice of collecting wines has spread among many classes of society. "It is surprising how many drug dealers have collected wine," he says. "In New England, even they are conservative."

In 1990 *The Wine Spectator* published an article on what made collectors tick. It pointed out that wine collectors had collected items such as stamps and comics when they were children. It asked Henry Clay Lindgren, a wine collector and a psychology professor at San Francisco State University, whether there was a collecting personality. "People collect because of their need to organize the environment in a systematic way," he explained. "Collectors have a need for power, mastery, and control. They may also have a desire to show off."[27]

5
Wine Tastings
Are Bunk

AN ALTERNATIVE to relying on the prejudiced and often ill-informed views of a wine writer is to believe the results of a comparative blind tasting. "Blind" means that the tasters do not know what the wines are until they have tasted them. This is essential to avoid prejudice, in precisely the same way as the criminal record of an accused person is not made known to the court until after judgment has been passed. Just as the more important crimes are judged by the consensus of a jury, so are panels of tasters convened in order to judge wines in a blind tasting. The results of a tasting appear more authoritative if they appear to be the consequence of the deliberations of a committee. The difference is that, for tastings, experts are used—yet, their judgment can be depended upon with even less confidence than the decision of an untrained jury.

Tasting is entirely a matter of personal preference. Most tasters would give a higher mark to a champagne with a "good yeasty nose" than to one without. But Möet's enologist Edmond Maudiére says that "If a champagne does have a yeasty nose, it's a defect. It results from having too many generations of yeast cells develop in the bottle."[1] Would he be wrong to mark a champagne down for having a yeasty nose? I wonder how a panel convened to compare California

Cabernet Sauvignons, and including in their number James Laube of *The Wine Spectator* and Dan Berger of the *Los Angeles Times*, would judge the 1985 vintage of Stag's Leap Wine Cellars Cask 23, which, when it was released at $75 a bottle, was California's most expensive wine? Laube described it as "absolutely stunning . . . a wine of great magnitude, depth, and ageing potential"; Berger thought it was "stinky, weedy . . . a strange wine."[2] Tasting by committee seeks to perform the impossible by aggregating personal preferences.

I would always prefer to read one man's views on a particular wine than those of a committee. One may be biased—but he says what he thinks. Moreover, just as consumers learn to judge a theater review according to the tastes of a reviewer—and may perfectly well go to a play because Frank Rich did not like it, or avoid a film to which Pauline Kael has given a good write-up—so in the world of wine writing, it is possible to come to understand the prejudices of one taster. For example, Robert Parker's taste in red burgundies is for big, rich wines such as those made by Philippe Leclerc in Gevrey-Chambertin; and among ports he likes the soft, fleshy style of Fonseca. He freely admits that he is obsessed with young wine—with fruit—and says that for this reason he does not generally go to tastings of old wines. Knowing his predilections, one can judge his comments accordingly. For all their foibles, Robert Parker, author of *The Wine Advocate*, and Clive Coates, the British author of *The Vine*, deserve far more attention for what they have to say than do the views of committees convened to hold comparative tastings.

Not only does judgment by consensus seek to sum up personal preferences, but it groups together decisions that are made on wholly different criteria. Does one judge a wine according to its typicalness or its individuality? Should one expect the character of the vintage to dominate the style of the house, or vice versa? In a tasting of 1984 Bordeaux, should one prefer those wines which taste more austere and more predominantly of Cabernet Sauvignon than usual because their Merlot crop failed, or those wines which have been produced to conform to a house style, either by rejecting a significant proportion of Cabernet Sauvignon from the final blend or by including some Merlot from the previous vintage? In a tasting of 1983 white burgundies, does one rate more highly those wines which have over-

come the unusually hot weather conditions of the vintage and produced characteristically lean and stylish wines, or those which have
sought to express the particular character of that year and ended up
resembling California Chardonnays rather more than the usual run
of white burgundies? What usually happens is that some experts
choose one criterion, and some another. But these are subjective
questions, and how they can be determined by a committee within
the context of comparative blind tasting beats me.

In general, the wines that perform best in comparative blind
tastings are the most obvious and least subtle ones. The pioneers who
began planting the red burgundy grape Pinot Noir in Oregon in the
late 1960s and 1970s suffered initially from the taunts of professional
wine makers in California, who told them that fine-wine grapes
would not ripen in their cool climate. This led them to try and prove
themselves by making wines that were as big and tannic as possible.
It was these big, tannic wines that put Oregon on the map. In a
tasting of seven red burgundies and ten Oregon Pinot Noirs from the
1983 vintage, carried out by twenty-six writers and merchants at the
International Wine Center in New York in 1985, the top three all
came from Oregon: Yamhill Valley Vineyards and Sokol Blosser
(both of them made by Bob McRitchie at Sokol Blosser), and
Adelsheim. The next year, *The Wine Spectator* was begging the
question, "Is this the promised land for Pinot Noir?"

Four years later it decided that it was not. Following a tasting of
1991 Oregon Pinot Noirs, mostly from the 1983, 1985, and 1987
vintages, many of which it described as "dry, earthy, and tannic," it
concluded that Oregon Pinot Noir had "failed the test of time."[3] Bill
Blosser of Sokol Blosser Winery wrote to *The Wine Spectator* to point
out that, although it expressed disappointment with the 1985s, it in
fact gave them higher marks than it had done two years earlier, when
it said that American Pinot Noirs were "better than ever." David
Lett, who had, at Eyrie Vineyards, been the first person to plant
Pinot Noir vines in Oregon in 1966, accused *The Wine Spectator* of
employing "some of the most irresponsible journalism short of grocery checkout tabloids" and of applying a "preestablished negative
bias."

All that had actually happened was that the big, tannic 1983s
and 1985s that had shown so well in their youth had fallen apart.

They may have performed impressively in blind tastings, but they were not successful versions of Pinot Noir, a grape which at its best produces the sort of delicate wines whose finesse is generally passed over in the conditions of a comparative blind tasting. The vintages of Oregon Pinot Noir that made its reputation, 1983 and 1985, were atypical. "We don't like our 1985," admitted David Rice, marketing manager of Yamhill Valley Vineyards, in 1990. "It is a wine for Cabernet drinkers. Ultimately, it will go out of balance."

The Wine Spectator, which tastes wines by committee, makes a point of stating in every issue that its ratings are based on the potential quality of a wine at its peak, however short or long a period it will take to reach that point. Because its panel tastes the wines blind, and therefore does not know what it is tasting, it does not always achieve its aim. In July 1989 it marked the 1987 Chardonnay from Au Bon Climat only 58 out of 100, describing it as "sulphury, sour, and bitter."[4] The Au Bon Climat Winery in Santa Barbara County is one of the very rare producers of Chardonnay in California whose wines are made, not in order to flatter in their youth, but to improve in bottle; in a tasting of mature California Chardonnays in 1991 the most impressive wines were Au Bon Climat's 1985 and 1982 vintages. Similarly, in December 1990, *The Wine Spectator* rated the Vosne-Romanée from Domaine Mugneret-Gibourg only 64 out of 100, saying that it lacked fruit and charm.[5] This fine estate is notorious, even within Burgundy, for making very lean, dry, austere wines which do not show flatteringly in their youth but which explode in the mouth after a number of years' aging in bottle. Judging a wine's potential is very difficult, particularly in a blind tasting where you must compare a wine that is attractive now with one that may not taste very pleasant at all. As the British wine merchant Robin Yapp, the country's leading specialist importer of fine wines from the Rhône Valley, has written in the context of a tasting of immature vintages of Gérard Chave's Hermitage, which he imports, "a good rule of thumb for aspirant wine merchants searching for good Rhône red wines is to remember that the nastier the stuff tastes when young, the better it is likely to be ten years later."[6] Certainly, wines that taste thoroughly unpleasant when young—at least to the palates of tasters who expect immediate gratification—can turn out quite unexpectedly. When Penfolds Grange Hermitage was first shown to Australian tasters in 1957, it was commented that it "tastes of crushed ants," and that it "would make a good anesthetic for my girlfriend."[7] A similar reception greeted Sassicaia, the prototype of modern Tuscan Cabernet Sauvignons, when first tried in the late 1940s. Both these wines are now accorded international acclaim.

Because, in practice if not always in theory, the criterion in comparative blind tastings is actuality and not potential, wines whose commerical future depends on doing well in a tasting have to be made to be as forward as possible. In Australia, wines sell successfully only if they have been awarded medals at one of the sixteen wine shows—basically, public comparative tastings—held each year. These are serious affairs—unlike some of their European equivalents, such as the wine fair in whose jury one Portuguese merchant declined an offer to join when he was told that it was policy to give an award to everyone who entered. In Australia, many producers make wines in order to win medals: the classic example of this is the German expatriate Wolf Blass, whose Cabernet-Shiraz Black Label unprecedentedly won the revered Jimmy Watson Trophy at the Melbourne Show in three successive years in 1974–76. Blass makes his wine in such a way that it will be close to its best when first sold at between three and five years of age. Like many other Australian wine makers, in order to ensure that his wines are perfectly balanced as soon as they are released and offered for tasting, Wolf Blass blends together the produce of different regions of the country, in order to overcome the vagaries of the weather. He says that "blending products together is the art of wine making."[8] For its medal-winning Chardonnay, Penfolds combines grapes from the Clare Valley with those from Coonawarra, two hundred miles away—tantamount, in terms of distance, to blending Châteauneuf-du-Pape with burgundy. In 1984 Mitchelton Winery in Victoria bought grapes in Mount Barker in Western Australia and trucked them two thousand miles across the Nullabor dessert.

In California, Kendall-Jackson makes its Vintners Reserve Chardonnay by blending together wines from grapes grown in six coastal counties, from Santa Barbara to Mendocino, four hundred miles apart—tantamount, in European terms, to blending burgundy with wine from Penedès in Spain. Although in 1989 it produced five million bottles of this wine, making it the best-selling "premium" (it

sells for $13) Chardonnay in the United States, it says that the reason
for the blending is not to have as large a quanity of wine as possible
but rather to maintain consistency from year to year. Thus in 1989,
when rain spoiled the harvest in northern but not in central California, it included a large proportion of wine from Santa Barbara in
the blend than would normally have been the case.

In Australia, wine makers often apply special techniques to the
batches of wines they enter for the Jimmy Watson Trophy, such as
oxidizing them excessively in order that they show their best sooner.
These practices have been described by more than one Australian
wine maker as "cheating." They certainly deceive the judges, who
are tasting the wines blind. If they knew which wines they were
tasting, they would be able to judge them in the light of their track
record, and would be less likely to be conned by producers who have
tinkered with their wines in order that they should show as well as
possible in their youth. In California, as has already been described
in Chapter 2, a number of wineries, including Kendall-Jackson,
produce Chardonnays with residual sugar, making the wine taste
richer and more rounded in its youth. At the beginning of 1989 it
was revealed that 20 percent of the Chardonnays in the previous
year's Orange County Wine Fair, one of the nation's largest wine
competitions, contained at least 0.4 percent (4 grams per liter) residual sugar, and that six of the wines—which had been entered as
dry wines—contained 1 percent residual sugar or more. In the European Community, wines can only be called dry if they contain less
than 0.9 percent residual sugar. As a result of these revelations, the
rules of the Orange County Wine Fair were changed to divide the
Chardonnays into three different categories: those with less than 0.3
percent residual sugar, those with between 0.3 and 0.7 percent, and
those with more than 0.7 percent.

While some California Chardonnays are made actually sweet
by adding concentrated grape juice, others are made to appear sweet
by maturing them in new oak. New oak has many effects on a wine,
of which one is to make the wine sweeter because unfermentable
sugar is extracted from the oak by the action of the alcohol. Some of
the most highly regarded producers of California Chardonnay—
among them Rick Forman, Peter Michael, and Mount Eden—
mature their wines in a majority of new oak casks. Not only do

Chardonnays that have been matured in new oak taste sweet in their youth, but they can be drunk very young because—for reasons that are not properly understood—they seem to suffer much less than other wines from the shock of being put into bottle.

It is partly because they mature sooner that Australian and California wines tend to beat those from Bordeaux and Burgundy in a blind testing. Indeed, it was a blind comparative tasting of California wines against French that put them on the map, both in Europe and in America. Steven Spurrier had organized this tasting, in the American Bicentennial Year, 1976, in order to gain publicity for his Paris wineshop, Caves de la Madeleine, and had rigged it in order that the French wines would win. Against the California Cabernet Sauvignons and Chardonnays he pitted first-growth Bordeaux and *premier cru* and *grand cru* white burgundies, all from good or very good vintages; and all the tasters were French.[9] In fact, Stag's Leap 1973 came out at the top of the Cabernet Sauvignon class, ahead of Mouton-Rothschild 1970; Château Montelena 1973 came out on top among the Chardonnays, ahead of the 1973 Meursault *premier cru* Les Charmes from Guy Roulot. French critics and wine producers were quick to point out that the California wines won not because they were better but because the wines with which they were competing were not yet ready to drink. The Cabernet Sauvignon section of the tasting has been repeated on many occasions since. In 1988, in a tasting of five 1970 California Cabernet Sauvignons and five top 1970 Bordeaux, the top three wines came from California and the bottom four from Bordeaux. This tasting was held in California with largely California tasters. But Edmund Penning-Rowsell, then the wine correspondent of the British national newspaper *The Financial Times*—and the author of a seminal book on the wines of Bordeaux—attended the tasting and his three preferred wines all came from California. The 1970 Bordeaux, he explained, "have remained obstinately closed and tannic."[10]

The tendency of California wines to "beat" their counterparts from Bordeaux and Burgundy has encouraged California wine producers to make use of them in order to promote their wares. The giant Mondavi company does not advertise its wines at all, but promotes them through a ceaseless program of tastings, some of them blind and comparative. In September 1990 Michael Mondavi flew to

London to present a blind tasting of four vintages of Mondavi Reserve Cabernet Sauvignon and first-growth Bordeaux from the same four vintages. The purpose, he said, was to see whether the Mondavi wines were "worthy of being served at the same table as the great wines of France." Along with most of the other wine writers who attended, I thought that Château Lafite 1986 came from California; and, along with nearly all the other tasters, I imagined that the Robert Mondavi Reserve Cabernet Sauvignon 1985 came from France. Mondavi seemed pleased with the result. In the context, he may not have been wise to be. Only one percent of wine imported into Britain comes from California, and the British are unlikely to buy more of it if they are encouraged to think of it simply as a doppelgänger of French wine. Within the United States, however, these blind comparative tastings work brilliantly. It does not even matter if the French wines win. As Frank Prial has explained in *The New York Times*, these are not really comparative tastings, but positioning exercises: the purpose is not to see whether people prefer California Cabernet Sauvignon or classed-growth Bordeaux, but to ensure that they come to associate the two. "It's like those automobile commercials that say: 'More trunk space than the legendary BMW!' Even if the car in question is powered by squirrels on a treadmill, the association has been made."[11]

Unfortunately for California wine makers, their counterparts in Australia—who are continually kept up to the mark by their show system—are even more adept at producing wines to win tastings than they are. Two Quantas Wine Cup competitions between California and Australia have been held, in 1987 and 1988. The first one was held in Australia in 1987 as a companion event to the America's Cup yachting competition. When Australian wines won in most of the categories, the Californians claimed that their wines had suffered from the air journey and had not been allowed to rest for long enough before being tasted. So in 1988 the competition was held in California. Once again it was won convincingly by Australia, with gold medals in six of the eight categories. California commentators pointed out that many of their best wineries had refused to enter, on the grounds that they had nothing to gain by so doing; they also said that the Australian wines had more fruit and less tannins, and were therefore better designed for winning competitions.[12] The Austra-

lians pointed out that this was hypocritical, given the benefit that
California wine makers had gained from similar competitions in the
past. No Quantas Cup has been held since then.

California wine makers smarting from the results of the Quantas
Cup were able to console themselves in the same way as their French
counterparts after their defeat in the Cave de la Madeleine tasting: by
telling themselves that making a wine to win tastings is quite different
from making a wine that people will actually want to drink. Wines
with high levels of acidity—as Bordeaux and burgundies are, or at
least historically were—tend to taste quite unpleasant when young,
particularly if they are not taken with food. Yet, it is the acidity that
makes them digestible and makes them keep. It was, and still is,
unfair to compare California with French (or even Australian with
California) wines in a blind tasting. The former appear to be more
alcoholic, richer, sweeter, and lower in acidity; therefore they show
more impressively in tastings. But if one sits down to eat, the French
wine is likely to be finished first. Wines from different regions are
made in different styles which simply cannot be compared. When
the Spaniard Miguel Torres's Gran Coronas Black Label 1970 "beat"
Château Latour 1970, Château La Mission Haut-Brion 1961 et al.,
in the 1979 *Gault Millau* "Wine Olympics," the manager of Latour
is supposed to have commented that, while the Torres wine might do
"for a bawdy night out," it was hardly the wine to serve "for an
elegant luncheon."

Even if wines from the same region are tasted against one another, they cannot be judged if they come from different vintages. If
wines developed at an even pace, this would be possible, but they do
not. A young vintage will always show more flatteringly than one
which is in the process of aging but has not yet evolved. Of a large
number of 1988 and 1989 red burgundies I tasted in 1991, in general
the 1989s showed better—not because they were better, but because
they were younger. A comparative tasting of wines from different
vintages is only possible if all the wines from all the vintages are fully
mature; and this is never practicable, because not only particular
wines but also individual bottles mature at different rates. If one is to
compare wines from different vintages, it is essential to taste, not
blind, but seen; for in that case one can judge the wine according to
one's experience of its likely state of development.

Whatever comparisons a taster is trying to make, whatever criterion he has decided to apply, his job is frequently made much harder than it should be by his being asked to taste too many wines at once. I believe that the maximum number of wines which can be covered satisfactorily in a single session is about fifteen to twenty. Otherwise, tasters have to taste so fast that they will be able to judge only on superficiality and not on complexity. The need to taste rapidly helps explain why tasters tend to give higher marks to the more obvious flavors of California Chardonnays and Cabernet Sauvignons than to more subtle white burgundies and red Bordeaux. Moreover, when too many wines are tasted at once, tasters are swayed by the order of tasting. If, in a sequence of fifty wines, no. 14 is fair, no. 15 good, no. 16 poor, and no. 17 good, then no. 17 will probably receive a higher mark than no. 15 because it stands out so much from no. 16 and the taster does not have the time to return to no. 15 to compare it with no. 17 directly. And fifty wines is not an unusual number to taste in one go.

Perhaps it does not matter how many wines are tasted in a session, since the same wine tastes different on different occasions—partly because wine does vary from one bottle to another, particularly if it has not been filtered or pasteurized; partly because tasters vary from one day to another; and partly because of various other factors, such as the temperature of the room. There are a number of instances of the same group of tasters rating the same wines quite differently on separate occasions. In Britain in the autumn of 1983, both the *Times* national newspaper and the wine newsletter *Which? Wine Monthly* published results of comparative tastings of non-vintage branded champagnes. Three people took part in both tastings. In the *Times* tasting, Lambert (the label of Peter Dominic, a large chain of liquor stores) came last, and Piper-Heidsieck second last. In the *Which? Wine Monthly* tasting, Lambert came first, and Piper-Heidsieck second from first.

But then there is another reason for the enormous variation of the results of tastings of non-vintage champagnes—so great that almost every house is able to boast of its success in one tasting or another. It all depends on who provides the samples. The question of bottle age is crucial in any tasting of non-vintage champagnes. Mediocre wines which have spent a year longer in bottle will tend to

be rated more highly than better wines which are still a bit green.
This is fair enough, since most people buy champagne for immediate consumption, not for laying down. However, it does mean that
the results of tastings of champagnes which depend on samples sent
in by importers can easily be manipulated. A canny importer will
keep a special case of well-aged non-vintage champagne specifically
for the purpose of sending out for tastings. Bollinger is an excellent
champagne, but it needs longer aging than most. In 1985 Liz and
Mike Berry, owners of the La Vigneronne wine shop in London,
gave up selling it on the grounds that it was being sold too young. A
sales representative from Bollinger's importers visited the shop, noticed the absence of his company's product, and insisted that the
Berrys come around to the office for a tasting. On the way, they
stopped at a liquor store and bought a bottle of Bollinger. In the
ensuing blind tasting, everyone liked the sales representative's nicely
matured sample and disliked the very green wine the Berrys had
bought in the liquor store.

Comparative blind tastings can be very useful. They have served
to demonstrate that professional tasters expect better Pinot Noirs to
come from Oregon than from California, and indeed from Burgundy
than from America, and apparently adjust their judgments according
to the region from which a wine comes. In 1986 the International
Wine Center in New York held a triangular tasting of Pinot Noirs
from California, Oregon, and Burgundy. This was divided into two
parts. In the morning the participants knew which wines they were
tasting. They tried seven burgundies and four Oregon and eight
California Pinot Noirs. They discussed the wines. They put, as a
group, the burgundies first, the Oregon wines second, and the California Pinot Noirs third. In the afternoon, they tasted a similar
number of wines—not the same ones—without knowing what they
were. This time, California came first, Burgundy second, and Oregon third—possibly because the tasters thought the California wines
came from Burgundy, the burgundies from Oregon, and the Oregon
wines from California.

Blind tastings have also served to demonstrate that, at least in
the case of champagnes, higher prices mean a more exclusive image,
not a better product. In December 1990 *The Wine Spectator* published the results of a tasting of 37 *blanc de blancs* champagnes; that

is, champagnes made wholly from the white Chardonnay grape rather than, as usual, from a blend of Chardonnay with the black grapes Pinot Noir and Pinot Meunier. They rated the champagnes with regard solely to quality and without regard to price. Top of the tasting came the Blanc de Blancs from Bruno Paillard, who founded his champagne company as recently as 1981. This wine cost $40 a bottle. Twenty-ninth came the 1982 Clos du Mesnil from Krug, the most prestigious of all champagne companies. The most remarkable feature of this wine was its price: $240 a bottle for only the fourth vintage produced.[13]

Champagne is perhaps an exception: tastings are the right context to which to judge it, because it is intended to be drunk on its own. Most wine, however, is supposed to be taken with food. Tasted with food, it cannot be spat out: it must be swallowed. In such circumstances, it is not really possible to taste more than five or six wines at any one time. Thus, if this principle were carried into practice, those members of the wine trade who regularly taste between thirty and fifty wines a day ought, in theory, to eat eight dinners a day. Most of them are fat enough as it is, not to mention the state of their livers. However, this is an argument which appears to be favored by Jean Delmas, the manager of the Bordeaux first growth Château Haut-Brion. When told by someone who had drunk Château Haut-Brion with Château Lafite that he had found the Lafite rather better, Delmas simply replied that he had made the Haut-Brion to be drunk with meals, not with Château Lafite.[14]

PART TWO

Introduction: Art and Agriculture

THE SECOND HALF of the book is concerned with the response of producers to those consumer demands which have been described in the first half. This is not the usual way of looking at wine production. Marketing—finding out what the consumer wants and then giving it to him—is a dirty word among fine-wine importers, whose members tend to regard wine as a production, rather than a market-led commodity; as something whose intrinsic character cannot be altered to suit the demands of the market. Consumers are offered wine on a take-it-or-leave-it basis. They are not given the option of asking for what they want.

Certainly, such an enormous variety of wine is made that there is quite likely to be something for every taste. Certainly, wine appears, and is said to be, an agricultural product dependent on the vagaries of the climate. It differs in this respect from such manufactured drinks as beer or whiskey or gin. But is this correct? The agricultural product is not the wine itself but the grapes from which it is made; wine is a processed food product, like bread. Fermentation, in which yeasts excrete alcohol as a by-product of their growth and accidentally cause grape juice to be converted into wine, is a process of controlled decay. The character of the wine is determined by the way in which control over the decay is exercised. The most important person, the wine maker, did not, in many cases, grow the grapes himself.

Wine production has always been market led. In the late Middle Ages, the greatest of French wines was red burgundy, which growers in other regions tried to copy by planting the Burgundy grape, Pinot Noir. Champagne, however, enjoys a colder climate than Burgundy, so the Pinot Noir grapes planted there did not ripen fully: the resulting wine was pink, not red. The young aristocrats who owned vineyards in Champagne succeeded in persuading the French Court that pink wine was the thing to drink. By the early eighteenth century, the tables had been turned and growers in Burgundy were trying to copy champagne, devising various means of obtaining less color in their wines. They interplanted white grapevines among the black-grape vineyards and placed alternate layers of straw and grapes on the press in order to prevent too much red color from being taken up from the skins during the pressing.[1]

This transformation was repeated recently by California wine makers, using the Zinfandel grape. The success of White Zinfandel has already been referred to in Chapter 2. It had its origin in the planting of a large number of Zinfandel vineyards in California during the early 1970s, in anticipation of a boom in red-wine drinking to coincide with an increased interest in food. By the time, however, that these vines came into production three years later, fashion had swung around, and what people wanted was white, not red, wine. To turn a vine from the production of red to the production of white grapes of similar quality and in equal quantity by field-grafting would have taken five years. Following the example of Bob Trinchero at Sutter Home, California wine makers refused to be fazed by this surfeit of black grapes. They simply vinified the black grapes as though they were white ones, separating the must as soon as possible from the skins of the grapes. Unfortunately, the resultant wines were just as much a failure as eighteenth-century Champenois copies of red burgundy: they were pink, not white—and pink wines were even more unfashionable than red. The wine makers remained unfazed. They rechristened these pink wines "blush wines," and a new boom was born.

The original blush wine, White Zinfandel, has proven such a success that it has threatened to destroy itself. The success of White

Zinfandel was founded on its being an inexpensive wine, but its popularity during the 1980s forced Zinfandel grape prices up to a level at which it seemed it might price itself out of the market. The Canandaigua Wine Company in New York State, determined to continue giving its customers what they wanted, discovered how to keep the price of its Marcus James White Zinfandel down to $4 a bottle. This wine comes from the Aurora Valley; it is only if you read the small print on the label that you will discover that the Aurora Valley is in Brazil. Paul Hetterich of Canandaigua sought to justify his position by saying: "The White Zinfandel drinker is not a sophisticated consumer. He's not someone who is interested in whether it came from California or Brazil." California grape growers have alleged, however, that some of the grapes going into the Marcus James White Zinfandel could not in fact be Zinfandel because Brazil simply does not grow enough Zinfandel grapes.[2] Even in California, "White Zinfandels" have been produced which contain less than the legal requirement of 75 percent Zinfandel grapes. In 1992 the Delicato winery in the Cental Valley was fined $1 million for altering their computer records in order to show that wines they had made in the 1988 and 1989 vintages contained a higher proportion of Zinfandel grapes than they actually did.[3]

At Sutter Home, Bob Trinchero confesses himself to being amused by the wine industry's reaction to White Zinfandel. "At first a lot of wine makers dismissed it: they called it soda pop. Now more than fifty wineries make White Zinfandel. Suddenly, it's become a respectable varietal, since it can make people a lot of money. White Zinfandel proves that, if you give people what they want, you'll be successful. That's a lesson a lot of people still haven't learned in this industry."[4]

This said, the history of White Zinfandel serves to demonstrate that, even today, the forces of nature cannot entirely be overcome. The following chapters look at how easily producers are able to give consumers what they want to drink: how far they are able to succeed in overcoming nature's desire to ensure that wine is a predominantly agricultural product.

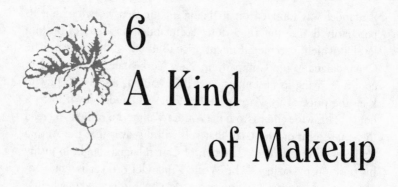

6
A Kind
of Makeup

OUR FUNDAMENTAL taste is a liking for sweetness. This has not always been easy to supply.

Much is made of the phenomenon of noble rot, to which are attributed the world's most celebrated sweet wines, those of Sauternes in France and the Auslesen, Beerenauslesen and Trockenbeerenauslesen of Germany. Noble rot is well publicized because it makes a good story. The grapes look decidedly unpleasant. When, in 1967, federal inspectors found Louis Martini processing Semillon grapes affected with noble rot at his winery in California, they ordered them to be destroyed as unfit to be made into wine: the law stipulated that any wine that was offered for sale had to be made from "clean" and "healthy" grapes.[1] Noble rot is produced by the action of the same fungus, *botrytis cinerea*, which causes gray rot, destroying the aromatic substances contained in the grape skins, imparting an unpleasant taste of its own, and causing the wine made from the affected grapes to oxidize. But, given suitable climatic conditions at the end of the growing season, with mists in the morning and sunshine in the afternoon—as is common in the autumn in the Sauternes region because of the interaction of the cold, spring-fed River Ciron with the warmer River Garonne—botrytis proves beneficial, and contributes a unique taste to a wine by degrading tartaric acid into glycerine and gluconic acid and by secreting a number of other substances which have not yet been identified.

The "discovery" of noble rot is a romantic and frequently retold story. Schloss Johannisberg in the Rheingau in Germany was owned in the eighteenth century by the Bishop of Fulda, whose permission was needed before the harvest could begin. In 1775, as the grapes were reaching ripeness, a messenger was sent from the estate to Fulda, a hundred miles away; but for some reason his return was delayed by a matter of weeks. In the meantime, the grapes had become affected with noble rot. This story is not, it must be said, unique. The use of nobly rotten grapes in the production of Tokay in what is now Hungary is supposed to have been "discovered" a century earlier, when Prince Rákóczi, the ruler of Transylvania, delayed the harvest on his estate at Oremui until late November because a war was going on.

Supposedly, the miracle of notably rotten grapes was not known in Sauternes until the middle of the nineteenth century. The knowledge may have been brought from Germany, or it may have been discovered by chance, at Château d'Yquem. In 1860 a thunderstorm at harvest time stripped the grapes off the vines before they could be picked. The owner was heartbroken, and only after a few days could he face gathering the grapes that had been lying in the sun.

These stories are all nonsense. Sweet wine had been made in France and Germany from nobly rotten grapes since the Middle Ages; it was, however, drunk when taking the sacrament in church, and clerics would have regarded it as heretical to have admitted that their sacramental wine was made from diseased grapes. Instead they described it as *crème de tête*, the cream off the top. It would be hard to explain why the story of the discovery of noble rot at Schloss Johannisberg was not known by Thomas Jefferson in the late eighteenth century without knowing that it was made up half a century after the event, after the estate had passed into the hands of a secular owner, Prince Metternich. He devised the legend to justify his continuing use of nobly rotten grapes.[2]

Likewise, the use of nobly rotten grapes in Sauternes was not made public until the nineteenth century, after the Revolution, when France had been secularized. But if Sauternes had not previously been made in this way, then what were the *vins pourris* (rotten wines) for which the region was already esteemed in the seventeenth century? The story about the thunderstorm at Château d'Yquem in 1860 gives the game away. Inducing noble rot in grapes after they have been removed from the vines does not produce a wine of comparable quality. This is what Alice and Myron Nightingale, who subsequently made wine for Beringer in California, tried to do in the 1950s. Believing that California conditions were not suitable for the natural development of noble rot, they induced it artificially, indoors, after the grapes had been picked. Their method was to lay bunches of grapes in trays, spray on the botrytis spores, wrap the bunches in plastic, and blow alternate blasts of warm and cool air over them for two weeks, in order to replicate the alternate conditions of mist and sun in the vineyard.[3] The problem with this method is that grapes go into a state of shock after picking and so botrytis does not affect them in the same way. Moreover, even if scientists understood the biochemical effects of botrytis sufficiently well to enable them to outperform nature, would conservative European wine makers ever embrace a practice that runs counter to their insistence that the superiority of their produce derives from the particular autumn weather they enjoy?

It is often said that one of the advantages of botrytis is that it contains an antibiotic called botrycine which causes the wine to stop fermenting when it has reached between 13 and 14 percent alcohol, leaving some unfermented sugar in the wine. But naturally occurring German wine yeasts are incapable of fermenting a wine beyond 13.5 percent alcohol, anyway. If the must is very sweet, yeasts find great difficulty in working, which is why German Beerenauslesen and Trockenbeerenauslesen usually contain only about 8.5 percent alcohol. So much for botrycine, whose antibiotic properties would scarcely appear to be esteemed very highly by the Sauternes, judging from the amount of sulphur many of them add to their wines to stop their re-fermenting in bottle. Sometimes even heavily sulphured Sauternes start fermenting again, the most notorious example being the 1983 vintage from Château Raymond-Lafon, an unclassified but highly rated property owned by the manager of Château d'Yquem. This vintage tasted delicious in its youth, but after a few years developed a tendency to re-ferment in bottle. In 1992 it tasted bizarre, citrussy, and largely oxidized.

The most significant feature of botrytis is that, by both concentrating and metabolizing acids, it produces sweet wines that are high
in acidity and therefore not cloying. It is consequently more useful
in the warmer climates of California and Australia than in France
and Germany. Sauternes, Auslesen, Beerenauslesen, and Trockenbeerenauslesen are not necessarily made from nobly rotten grapes.
Usually, only a certain proportion of the grapes is affected with
botrytis, and sometimes none at all. The new German wine law of
1971 introduced a provision that Beerenaulesen and Trockenbeerenauslesen could be made from grapes which were merely overripe,
and not nobly rotten, in order to cover the produce of very warm
autumns, such as 1959, in which the requisite conditions for the
development of noble rot did not occur. The year 1983 was similar.
I cannot recall having tasted any 1983 Auslesen which tasted of
botrytis other than the great Fritz Haag's Brauneberger Juffer-
Sonnenhur Gold Capsule, from the Middle Mosel. Those 1983
Auslesen which do not taste of noble rot are not the worse for its
absence.

Largely because they can be made in years in which noble rot
does not occur, Eisweine have recently become very fashionable
among German vine growers. They are produced by allowing the
grapes to dry on the vines, and then picking them as soon as they
freeze. As the water is frozen, the juice drawn off is more concentrated. The grower picks the grapes at four o'clock on the first winter
morning on which the temperature has dropped to 20°F or below. In
the Mosel in 1986, that happened to be Christmas morning. In the
Rheingau, growers protect the grapes against rain damage during the
wait for a sufficiently hard frost by enclosing them in small plastic
bags; doubtless they would prefer to harvest the grapes in more clem-
ent conditions and then freeze them in their cellars, but they are
forbidden to do so by German wine-making regulations. In New
Zealand, it is the manufacture of sweet wines from highly botrytized
grapes which is effectively forbidden by laws that impose a lower
maximum level of volatile acidity than naturally arises from their
use; as a consequence, most sweet wines are made from artificially
"freeze concentrated" grapes. [4] At Bonny Doon in Santa Cruz in
California, the celebrated eccentric Randall Graham stores grapes
for his Vin de Glacière in a freezer for several months until he has

finished making all his other wines, then he brings them into his winery which would otherwise be lying idle.[5] In Sauternes, producers often now freeze botrytized grapes after rain in order to concentrate them. This method of "cryo-extraction" has caused a great deal of controversy because it is feared that it may lead some less quality-conscious producers not to bother to wait for noble rot to develop.

Even more so than noble rot, the attraction of the Eiswein technique to wine makers lies in its difficulty and prestige. Eisweine are not an economic proposition, nor do they necessarily taste particularly good. I have tasted some very concentrated young Eisweine, but no one has any idea how they will turn out when mature. In his book on dessert wines, *Liquid Gold*, Stephen Brook says that many Eisweine strike him as "overaggressive and one-dimensional."[6] As they are deliberately made as monuments, intended to last longer than the men who made them, it will be well into the next century before we know if Brook is right.

Though they owe nothing to modern technology (other than alarm clocks), Eisweine are a recent invention. Rather than resort to such an elaborate procedure, for many centuries vine growers have found drying the grapes after picking to be the most effective means of concentrating their sugar content in order to produce sweet wine. This method was certainly used by both the Greeks and Romans, but it predates them. It is still very widely employed in Italy, where the wines thus made are described as *passiti*, except in Valpolicella and Soave, where the term *recioto* is used. Muscat (*Moscato* in Italian) is one of the varieties treated in this way, and the wonderful Moscato *passito* made in Strevi in Piedmont by Domenico Ivaldi is a lamentable reminder of how the best French Muscat wines used to taste when they were made by this method. *Passiti* wines are, however, made from all sorts of grape varieties: I have even tasted a really good *passito* Pinot Noir from Umbria. They are also made dry as well as sweet. In the case of *recioti* Valpolicelle, the dry version is probably superior; in the case of the little known but not inferior Sagrantino di Montefalco *passito*, both are equally good. The best examples I have tried are those made by Fratelli Adanti in Perugia, which they sell under the name Sagrantino d'Arquata.

All these *passiti* wines are expensive. From a commercial point of view, the drawback of drying grapes lies in a 50 percent loss in bulk as a result of evaporation. That is why Domenico Ivaldi's Moscato *passito* costs twice as much as the best Muscat de Beaumes de Venise, that of Domaine des Bernardins. It was by drying grapes on straw mats that Muscat de Beaumes de Venise used to be made last century. But when the wine was granted its *appellation contrôlée* in 1945, one of the conditions was that it must achieve a minimum of 21.5 percent "total" alcohol (the result of adding together the fermented and unfermented sugar contents). To be sure of achieving this level, the wines had to be fortified like port—and that is how they are made today. Fermentation is usually stopped when the wine has reached an alcohol content of 15 percent, leaving about 110 grams per liter of residual sugar.

Stopping fermentation with alcohol is suited, however, only to such substantial wines as port and the various Muscat wines of the south of France. The most effective and economical means of sweetening more delicate wines is to add sugar. This was not, however, a widespread method in Europe until the sugar beet industry took off in the 1840s; before that, sugar was neither readily available nor inexpensive. The option had been to add "sugar of lead" (lead oxide), a method which had been known to the Greeks and Romans but was not widely used because lead oxide produces lead acetate, a fungicide, in the wine; it kills cells and is therefore poisonous. In Nancy in 1696, wine sweetened with lead oxide caused the death by convulsion of more than fifty people. The merchants concerned were prosecuted, but only one was fined.

Following the introduction of beet sugar, liquid sugar—a solution of sugar in water—started to be used in Germany in order to improve Mosel wines from poor vintages in the 1840s and 1850s. This practice was disapproved of by Rhine growers, who did not have the same problems. In 1886 the legality of liquid sugar was tested in the courts when a vine grower in the Mosel was charged with adulteration. He defended himself by saying that he had done no more than any other grower in the Mosel. As a result of this case, it was accepted that growers in the Mosel might reasonably add sugared water up to a quarter of the volume of the wine; this permission was eventually overturned by the new German wine laws of 1971. By then, producers had adopted another method of sweetening: the addition of unfermented, or partly fermented, grape juice (Süssreserve) to a finished wine.

Sweetening a wine with Süssreserve is not a new method, though some authorities have reacted to it as though it is. In their book on the Mosel published in 1972, Otto Loeb and Terence Prittie describe the method of sweetening wine with Süssreserve as highly suspect. "Unlike the discriminating addition of sugar, [Süssreserve] can change the intrinsic nature of the wine and reduce [its] alcoholic strength. The growers who made use of [Süssreserve] in the early years after the Second World War were well aware of the dangers. They kept quiet, even though they were not breaking any wine laws."[7] In the eighteenth century the pioneers of stopping the fermentation of port by adding brandy had kept quiet, too, for at the time this was considered to be highly suspect. In a famous exchange of letters in 1754, English wine merchants resident in Oporto wrote to their agents up the Douro Valley to complain of the growers' "diabolical" practice of adding brandy to the wine before it had finished fermenting; they had no objection to the addition of brandy *after* fermentation. Their agents replied that they only fortified the ports they sent them because "The English merchants wished the wine to exceed the limits which Nature had assigned to it, and that when drunk, it . . . should be like the sugar of Brazil in sweetness. . . ."[8]

Both stopping fermentation with brandy and sweetening a wine with Süssreserve in fact enjoy a long history. When ports were first being fortified during fermentation—a practice that did not become general until the nineteenth century—this method had already been common in France for the production of sweet white wines (*Vins des Liqueurs*) for more than fifty years.[9] The term *Vin des Liqueurs* was also in the seventeenth century applied to unfermented grape must—that is to say, Süssreserve, which was then drunk straight. Under the name of Rhenish in the Must, it was very popular with English women and children,[10] but it did not necessarily come from Germany. Most of the wine sold in England as Rhenish in the Must was in fact cheap table wine from the Cognac region to which sugar or honey had been added, and sometimes essence of clary seeds, in order "to give this mixture a delicate flavour."[11] The real thing was difficult to make. Unfermented grape must was prevented from fermenting by being put in a cask which was pitched on the inside, or in which sulphur matches had been burned, or which had, we are told, been rubbed on the inside with cheese. The cask was then sealed and the must chilled by placing the vessel in a well or river for a month. The must then kept fresh for a year or more. Increasingly it was not drunk on its own but added by wine merchants to tired wines or to the acidic produce of poor vintages, sometimes causing the wine thus treated to re-ferment.[12] In the midnineteenth century a large business developed in the South of France involving the production of unfermented grape must for export to the Rheingau, where merchants "used it to great advantage in the manufacture of their wines."[13] No wonder they did not express the same need for beet sugar as producers in the Mosel.

So why did Süssreserve hit the market with such a shock after the Second World War? In part, it was a matter of technology. The then-celebrated Seitz factory at Bad Kreuznach developed filters that were fine enough to remove yeasts, thus ensuring that the addition of Süssreserve to a wine before bottling did not cause it to re-ferment. But the revolution in its use was impelled by demand from a new generation of wine drinkers. According to Wolfgang Siben of Weingut Georg Siben in Deidesheim in the Palatinate, the demand for sweet wines came first from American soldiers stationed in Germany who had been brought up on the sweet taste of Coca-Cola.[14] Fritz Hallgarten, a British importer of German wines, said that this was "quite wrong" and that North Germans had never liked German wine but had preferred Sauternes: it was in order to conquer this market that Germans produced Sauternes-style German wines.[15] In the Mosel Valley, according to the wine producer Dirk Richter, it was the flooding of the river in the winter of 1947 that led to the taste for sweet wines. The river flooded the cellars and stopped the fermentation. When the 1947s were released they were snapped up by people who had made money on the black market at the end of the war and wanted to take up wine drinking to match their newly enhanced social status.[16] Certainly, most people who take up wine drinking for the first time want an inexpensive sweet wine that is low in alcohol. The wine boom in Britain in the last generation can substantially be attributed to basic German wines, which account for one bottle in every four drunk there. In the United States, where the demand for sweet, low-alcohol wines has more effectively been satisfied by Italian Lambrusco and California White Zinfandel, German wine imports, even at their peak in 1984, accounted for no more than 3 percent of total wine consumption. Of the 80 million bottles of German wines then imported, 12 million were of Blue Nun Liebfraumilch. Since then sales of all mass-market German wines, including Blue Nun, have declined dramatically.[17]

Süssreserve was necessary because, naturally and traditionally, the majority of German wines were dry. This fact surprises the majority of wine drinkers. I must admit that, when I visited the Mosel in 1985 I did not at the time believe those producers who assured me that, before the Second World War, German wines were dry. To a certain degree, German wine producers who say that their wines were historically dry *are* trying to mislead us. They have invented a tradition in order to justify their recent conversion to the production of dry wines in order to satisfy the demands of the home market. They also want to overturn the down-market image of German wines overseas as inexpensive sweet wines for novice drinkers. Peter M. F. Sichel, a New York–based wine importer who was born in 1922 and in the 1940s tasted German wines that had been made before the war, says that they were no drier then than they are today. He says that the idea that German wines used to be dry has been propounded in order to give a historical underpinning to the creation of dry German wines intended to accompany food.[18] Some wine makers agree with him. According to Manfred Voepel, the chief wine maker for Deinhard, in reference to the group of leading Rheingau producers who have formed the Association of Charta Estates in order to promote the consumption of dry German wines with food, "Charta is not an old style; it is a new invention." Though these new dry wines have proved very successful in Germany, they have not taken off overseas, where they are frequently condemned as "doughnut" wines—wines with no body in the middle. It was rash of the most forceful exponent of this style, Erwin Graf Matuschka-Griffenclau of Schloss Vollrads in the Rheingau, to have forecast in 1981 that by 1986 almost all the wine produced in Germany would be dry.[19]

Historically, however, German wines *were* dry. If consumers wanted to drink them sweet, they had to add sugar. In his *London*

Journal, the chronicler James Boswell described a supper in July 1763 at which "every man drank his bottle of Rhenish with sugar."[20] In the 1820s, the two British pioneers of modern wine writing, Cyrus Redding and Alexander Henderson, stated that German wines were dry. Redding said that they averaged 12 percent alcohol, much the same as dry Auslesen today.[21] Henderson said: "In general [the wines of the Rhine] are drier than the French white wines."[22] The same could be said of dry (*trocken*) German wines made today: they appear to be drier than French wines, in part because they contain less glycerine, which is a by-product of the malolactic fermentation that white burgundies usually undergo but German wines do not.

Not only were German wines dry in the 1820s, but most of them remained so until the 1960s. As late as 1964, the British wine merchant Allan Sichel wrote: "The majority of German wines are dry or medium dry and can be drunk throughout the whole meal with pleasure."[23] In that sense, Charta and similar wines are not a new invention but a return to tradition after the fad of a generation. If sweet wines have held sway for a while, it is partly because the development of the modern form of Süssreserve brought what had once been rare and expensive wines within the reach of ordinary consumers for the first time—and partly because the new German wine law of 1971, by laying down the minimum potential alcohol content for Spätlesen and Auslesen, has encouraged producers to make sweet wines bearing these names from any grapes which attain the requisite potential alcohol content. In the past they might well have allowed these grapes to ferment out naturally, and restricted their use of the term *Spätlese* to the produce of genuinely late-picked grapes, and of *Auslese* to wine made from the ripest bunches.

There is no reason why Auslesen should necessarily be sweet. The only legal criteria for their manufacture are that all the grapes used must be fully ripe and they must contain at least enough sugar to produce a wine of between 10.4 percent (for Riesling in the Mosel) and 12.5 percent (for grapes other than Riesling in the Rhein-gau). The upper figure is a normal strength for French dry wines. The purpose behind the introduction of the selective picking of grapes in order to produce Auslesen in the second half of the last century was not to produce wines with a residual sugar content, but to produce wines that were low in acidity. Writing at that time,

Johann Thudichum and August Dupré described the growth of selective picking of grapes in order to produce Auslese wines as a recent advance that had made it possible to produce wines for drinking younger than thitherto.[24] A similar explanation lay behind the development of sweet wines using Süssreserve in the 1950s and 1960s. People wanted wines that could be drunk young. Allan Sichel said that, if the wines of the Rheingau were not as good as in the past, it was because they were being made "less austere and less dry than they used to be, in the attempt to meet the heavy demand from the public for younger and fresher wines."[25]

In the past, Auslesen were not necessarily intended to be sweet, but they often turned out that way. When they did, they were looked upon as something abnormal. Ernst Loosen, wine maker at Weingut St. Johannishof in Bernkastel in the Middle Mosel, says that his grandfather would have thought it a fault deliberately to make sweet wines. Thudichum and Dupré wrote than an Auslese "easily loses the character of Rhine wine and becomes a sweet liquorous product resembling Muscat or Sauternes."[26]

There are a number of reasons why an Auslese should have turned out sweet. According to Bernhard Breuer, who makes some excellent dry wines at his estate (Weingut Georg Breuer) in Rüdesheim in the Rheingau, the term *Auslese* historically applied to wines which were sweet because they had stopped fermenting by accident. Fermentation was brought to a halt by the failure of yeasts to work properly, by the onset of an exceptionally cold winter, or by a barrel catching cold from being placed too close to the cellar door. Auselsen were thus, he says, the produce of selected barrels rather than of selected, fully ripe grapes.[27]

It is true that, before the war, individual barrels of the best German wines were bottled separately, rather than being "equalized" by blending them together, as has always been the practice in, say, Bordeaux. The barrels often differed significantly from one another, and doubtless some Auslesen were sweeter than others. Certainly, there is a difference in sweetness today between the barrels of Auslesen which are still bottled separately by some of the best producers in the Mosel-Saar-Ruwer, such as Forstmeister Geltz in Saarburg—but then the wine maker here, Hans-Joachim Zilliken, stops fermentation in individual barrels at different stages. Bernhard Breuer is wrong, however, to deny that, before the war, the term *Auslese* applied to the selection of bunches of fully ripe grapes.

Auselsen sometimes ended up sweet because, depending on the temperature of the cellar, German wines generally stop fermenting at anything between 10 and 13.5 percent alcohol. If some unfermented sugar remains in the must, then the wine is sweet. It is possible to ferment a German wine beyond 13.5 percent alcohol, but it is usually necessary to use yeasts imported from France in order to do so. Several estates, including Weingut J. B. Becker in the Rheingau, Weingut Carl Finkenauer in the Nahe, Koehler-Ruprecht in Rheinpfalz, and Heymann-Lowenstein in the Mosel, have succeeded in producing dry Beerenauslesen, but their fruit flavors are overwhelmed by an alcohol content of about 15–16 percent. I am intrigued to know how the Wehlener Sonnenhur Trockenbeerenauslese 1959, which Michael Broadbent recorded in his *Great Vintage Wine Book* as having tasted in 1965, could possibly have reached the 20 percent alcohol he states. Unfortunately, he failed to note either the name of the grower or how the wine tasted.[28]

Whereas Auslesen are made from selectively picked bunches of grapes, Beerenauslesen and Trockenbeerenauslesen are produced from selectively picked, individual grapes (*beere* means "berry"). The musts are so high in sugar that yeasts find it very hard to work and exhaust themselves easily. Beerenauslesen and Trockenbeerenauslesen have on occasions refused stubbornly to ferment at all, and often ferment very slowly. Most wines usually take about a week to ferment, but in 1959 the celebrated estate of J. J. Prüm at Wehlen on the Middle Mosel made a Trockenbeerenauslese which went on fermenting for two years. Normally, a Beerenauslese will contain between 100 and 150 grams per liter of residual sugar, and about 8.5 percent alcohol. This phenomenon of a naturally sweet, low-alcohol wine continued to amaze wine connoisseurs even as late as the 1950s when the popular explanation of why they had stopped fermenting was the vague assertion that "sugar and alcohol have 'balanced' each other."[29]

Such a "balancing" act, however, only occurs to the produce of exceptionally warm vintages. Today, below the heights of Beerenaus-

lesen and Trockenbeerenauslesen, it is the wine maker who "balanc-
es" the wine, in one of two ways. Either he allows the wine to ferment
out naturally and then adds Süssreserve—as is the most general practice in the Rhine Valley—or he stops fermentation. The latter is the
most common method of producing sweet wines in the Mosel, where
delicate wines low in alcohol are desired. Fermentation can be
stopped in one of a number of ways. Some less sophisticated producers
simply add large amounts of sulphur, which causes the wine to stink
in its youth and forces the purchaser to keep it for many years before
drinking it, while waiting for the sulphur to wear off. More advanced
wine makers stop fermentation by centrifuging or filtering out the
yeasts. It is sometimes suggested that these procedures diminish a
wine's potential quality. When, in researching *Liquid Gold*, Stephen
Brook asked Pierre Dubourdieu, the wine maker at Château Doisy-
Daëne in Sauternes, and possibly the only producer in the region to
use a centrifuge, what he thought of the observation of some enologists that this method was overly brutal, Dubourdieu replied: "The
only thing brutal about the centrifuge is its cost."[30] Dubourdieu also
subjects his wine to a number of filtrations. I believe that these treatments do affect a wine's quality: I shall explain why in Chapter 14.
Even if a wine is not treated brutally and fermentation is stopped simply by chilling it, it still has to be either filtered or well-sulphured
afterwards to prevent its re-fermenting. After all, the fermentation of
champagne was stopped last century by transferring the casks to a
cooler cellar—and the wine re-fermented in bottle in the spring without the addition of any more yeast or sugar.

Does this then mean that using Süssreserve is less adulterous
than stopping fermentation? Or are Loeb and Prittie correct in their
condemnation? They say that Süssreserve is worse than sugar because, by adding Süssreserve to a wine, its alcohol content is reduced: the wine is diluted. A wine is allowed to contain up to 10
percent of unfermented grape juice in the form of Süssreserve. Dilution is not a criticism that can be leveled at the addition of dry
sugar, though it does apply to liquid sugar, the use of which is
prohibited throughout the European Community precisely because
it involves adding water to wine. In time, this problem may be solved
by concentrating the Süssreserve by freezing.

The major defect of Süssreserve lies in its misapplication. It does not have to come from the same vineyard or village, merely from the same region—but if it does not come from the same vineyard, the addition of Süssreserve alters the character of the wine. One reason why different wines made by the same producer in Germany often taste more alike than wines from the same vineyard made by different producers is that the wine maker has used the same Süssreserve for all his wines. Even as quality conscious a firm as Deinhard use Süssreserve, not from each vineyard, but from each village. They have carried out experiments, and they say that there is no difference in taste. But this is tantamount to saying that there is no difference in taste between the wines from the different vineyards in the first case. If Deinhard's Bernkasteler Doctor and Bernkasteler Bratenhöfchen are made with the same Süssreserve, of course they are going to taste more alike than they otherwise would.

Frequently, Süssreserve is not even made from the same grape variety as the wine to which it is added. Many producers of Riesling wines make their Süssreserve from a less noble but earlier ripening variety—one which attains higher sugar levels, such as Müller-Thurgau. A Riesling wine may comprise up to 15 percent of Müller-Thurgau grapes without losing the legal right to describe itself as being made from Riesling. Admittedly, in order to produce a wine of a given level of sweetness, it is not necessary to add so much of a sweeter Müller-Thurgau Süssreserve as of a less sweet Riesling one. But patently the wine's quality is diminished thereby.

These misuses of Süssreserve blunt the principal distinction between its application and the addition of sugar to a finished wine. Whereas the sugar in Süssreserve is grape sugar, added sugar owes nothing to the vine or to the soil in which it grows but is the produce of a vegetable (beet) or a grass (cane). The addition of non-grape sugar in any form after fermentation is prohibited in Germany. But it is permitted elsewhere within the European Community, as long as the sugar is not mixed with water.[31] Two of France's most celebrated drinks are adulterated in this manner.

Sugar is added to cognac as a substitute for proper aging. Properly aged cognac does not need added sugar, partly because it does not have harsh edges which need to be rounded off, and partly because it has absorbed sugars from the hemicellulose in the wooden casks in which it has been matured. For this, up to twenty years' aging is necessary, an expensive procedure, not least because a quarter of the spirit evaporates in this time.

The laws permit up to 8 grams per liter (o.8 percent) of sugar to be added to cognac. Much more than this is added to most champagnes. Champagne is allowed to contain up to 15 grams of sugar per liter and still call itself *brut* (bone dry), and up to 20 and still be called *extra sec* (extra dry)—whereas, under European Community regulations, other wines can only be called "dry" if they contain less than 9 grams of sugar per liter. Under the new Austrian wine laws—introduced in the wake of the diethylene glycol scandal—wines with more than 10 grams per liter of residual sugar have to be labeled "sweet." Many of the *bruts* produced by leading houses sail close to the maximum permitted sugar content: samples of Lanson, Laurent Perrier, Louis Roederer, and Taittinger have been analyzed and found to contain *around* 15 grams per liter. Though the sugar can certainly be tasted, champagnes do not appear, when drinking them, to contain as much sugar as they do because carbon dioxide gas and what is, by French standards, a relatively high level of acidity diminish the taste of sweetness.

This all makes nonsense of Patrick Forbes's attempt, in his book on the region, to justify the addition of sugar to champagne by arguing that, because it ferments not once but twice (the second fermentation producing the sparkle), all the sugar in a bottle of champagne is converted into alcohol, making it drier than other wines. [32] Indeed, one might wonder why the addition of so much sugar—enough to produce an extra 1 percent alcohol—does not cause champagne to ferment a third time. Champagne houses used to add brandy to their wines to stop this from happening, but the last two to do so, de Castellane and Louis Roederer, gave up in 1972, since the process of yeast decomposition during the secondary fermentation in bottle probably absorbs yeast nutrients necessary for fermentation.

The addition of sugar to champagne has been described by Alain de Polignac, Pommery's wine maker, as "a kind of makeup." [33] The fact that they do not need to tart themselves up in this way is the strongest argument in the wardrobe of those sparkling-wine producers in Italy, California, and Australia who seek to emulate champagne. This said, we would probably not be able to afford to drink champagne—so long would it have to be aged before sale, and so much would it have to cost as a result—were it not sweetened with substantial amounts of sugar in order to make it prematurely drinkable.

7
The Sun
in Sacks

T HE PRINCIPLE that German Beerenauslesen and Trockenbeerenauslesen should be very high in sugar, and very low in alcohol, is being challenged by a new generation of wine makers who argue that these wines are unbalanced. Bernhard Breuer, who in 1989 made a Trockenbeerenauslese with 12.5 percent alcohol (compared with a traditional 8.5 percent or less), points out that, with this level of alcohol, there is no need to have a traditionally high level of residual sugar in the wine, because the alcohol helps bring out the sweetness.[1]

Where not satisfied by sugar itself, our taste for sweetness is satisfied by alcohol. Whereas some wines are sweetened with sugar after fermentation, to others sugar is added before and/or during fermentation. The process is called chaptalization, after Jean-Louis Chaptal, Napoleon's Home Secretary, who suggested the method in a book written in 1801. Sugar is added to the grape must in order to increase the alcohol content of the finished wine. In many wine regions of France, such as Burgundy and the Loire Valley, it is standard procedure to add 7.5 kilograms of sugar to a barrel of wine, thus increasing the alcoholic degree by 2 percent. It has been said[2] that 25,000 tons of beet sugar (I have no idea how much cane) are used for chaptalization in France each year. This is a pretty substantial adulteration. Is it really necessary?

Alcohol, like sugar, helps preserve the wine. There are other preservatives—acidity, tannin, and sulphur—but in order to satisfy popular taste, it is important to keep the levels of these as low as possible. We want to be able to drink wines young nowadays, and wines with high levels of acidity, tannin, or sulphur taste unpleasant in their youth. Alcohol, on the other hand, makes a young wine seem riper and more appealing. Wine makers who do not chaptalize as much as their competitors lose out in blind tastings, for example Hubert de Montille, who makes outstanding Volnays and Pommards. His wines contain 12 percent alcohol compared with the 13 percent normal in Burgundy; he relies on a balance of acidity and tannin to preserve them. So they are hard to taste in their youth. As the wine merchant and wine writer Thomas George Shaw was told more than a century ago, red burgundies were chaptalized in order to give them an appearance of richness.[3]

Shaw and other wine merchants who traveled in Burgundy in the middle of last century were shocked to discover that chaptalization was practiced. Certainly, the chaptalization of fine wines is a modern phenomenon. The treatment was invented only in the seventeenth century, when wine makers discovered that what happened during fermentation was sugar turning to alcohol. It was known in both Bordeaux and Burgundy in the eighteenth century, but hardly used before the nineteenth. Even then it did not become common— because sugar was a scarce commodity in Europe before the development of the sugar-beet industry in the 1840s, and because this was the heyday of fortification. It was estimated that at this time three-quarters of all wine exported from France had alcohol added. The best of wines made in this way had the alcohol added at the start of fermentation, just like sugar for chaptalization.[4] (For a fuller discussion of fortification, see the beginning of the next chapter.)

It was feared that chaptalization affected the quality of a wine. In 1816, Lamothe, the manager of Château Latour, increased the alcohol content of the wine by chaptalizing by only 0.5 percent; yet he found that the wine tasted tainted and concluded: "When nature fails to provide the basic elements of a good quality wine, man cannot make up the loss; he will never achieve anything greater than mediocrity."[5] In Burgundy in the 1840s a committee of growers and merchants was set up to find a way to restore burgundy to its ancient prosperity; they came out against sugaring, which, they said, took away a wine's bouquet, its delicacy, and its individuality.[6] The same was said of those Mosel wines of the same period which were improved by the addition of liquid sugar. Growers in the Rhine expressed their disapproval on the grounds that sugaring took away a wine's individual characteristics.

Certainly, excess chaptalization makes all wines similar. Some wine writers believe that they can tell if a wine has been chaptalized. Either cane or beet sugar can be used; on the whole, cane sugar is added to white wines and either cane or beet sugar to red. Among British wine writers, Edmund Penning-Rowsell says that alcohol from cane sugar is likely to taste different from that produced from grape sugar; cane sugar produces a sweetish glyceriny taste if over-done.[7] Pamela Vandyke Price claims that she can tell when a wine has been chaptalized, because the wine smells of beet from the beet sugar used.[8] The smell of beet, or of boiled beetroot, is used by many people as a mnemonic for the smell of Pinot Noir, the grape variety from which most red burgundies are made. Are we in fact identifying red burgundies by their "boiled beetroot" smell because that is the smell, not of Pinot Noir, but of chaptalization? Certainly, red burgundy is the lightest and most shamelessly chaptalized of French red wines. I have identified wines from their beetrooty smell as burgundies which have turned out to be heavily chaptalized Bordeaux from a light year. I remember being one of a tasting group where we all unhesitatingly identified a 1968 Bordeaux, Domaine de Chevalier, as burgundy.

Burgundies are frequently chaptalized beyond the limits permitted by law. For example, sugar is added so as to increase a wine's alcohol content from 10 percent to 13 percent. Legally, burgundies cannot be chaptalized unless they attain a minimum potential alcohol content of 10.5 percent (for a commune wine) or 11 percent (for a *premier cru*). Moreover, the alcohol content is not permitted to be increased by chaptalization by more than 2 percent, nor to be raised by chaptalization to more than 12.5 percent alcohol. In his book on Burgundy published in 1982, Anthony Hanson stated that the Fraud

Squad turned a blind eye to such practices. "The time has come," he said, "to enforce the laws."[9] The time came in 1989, when Claude and Jean-François Bouchard, the directors of the Burgundy merchants Bouchard Père et Fils, were arrested and charged with adding an excessive amount of sugar to some of their 1987 red burgundies. They were released on bail of about $700,000, which was said to have been the value of the wines in question. At the time of writing, this case has not yet come to court, nor is it clear that it will ever do so. If the purpose in prosecuting Bouchard was to make an example of one of the most respectable merchant companies in Burgundy—in order to dissuade other wine makers from continuing to overchaptalize their wines—it has not worked. As Charles Tovey wrote last century: "These mixtures of sugar are almost poison to some constitutions. Men of sedentary habits and the victims of indigestion should avoid these compounds, as they irritate the stomach. How frequently do we hear the observation, 'I cannot drink burgundy; it invariably upsets me.' This would not be the case were the wine unsugared."[10]

Overchaptalized wines taste unbalanced. Just as sugar is said, nutritionally, to provide "empty calories," so chaptalization produces "empty alcohol"; more alcohol from the added sugar but no more extract to balance it. There is no reason why very alcoholic wines should taste particularly alcoholic—but heavily chaptalized wines always do, even if they contain less alcohol. An overchaptalized red burgundy of 13 percent alcohol will taste far more alcoholic than a Châteauneuf-du-Pape that has naturally obtained 15 percent.

Chaptalization does not disastrously affect the balance of a wine if only a little sugar is added—enough to increase the alcohol level by 0.5 percent or at most 1 percent. Such wines may not have enough alcohol to keep well, but there is no reason why a red burgundy should have to be cellared for years, especially not if it comes from a bad vintage. Gérard Potel, who makes benchmark red burgundies at the Domaine de la Pousse d'Or in Volnay, chaptalized his 1975s only to 11.5 percent alcohol and instructed all those to whom he sold them to drink them young. The problem lies with those consumers who still expect red burgundies to be rich, full-bodied wines when they are, in fact, more often light wines to be drunk young and cool—like Beaujolais. As the production of what is expected lies in most years beyond the abilities of nature, it is provided by man out of sugar bags. For the Burgundians, these bags of sugar are "the sun in sacks."

Chaptalization has always been used in Burgundy in poor vintages. The climate of Burgundy is similar to that of Bordeaux in terms of average sunshine, rainfall, and humidity, but the average temperature is lower and—above all—it varies more from year to year. There are more bad vintages in which the wines need chaptalizing. But in fact burgundies are chaptalized not only in poor years but in all vintages, bad and good, with the exception of occasional very hot years like 1985 and 1990.

In Bordeaux, chaptalization was rarely practiced before 1925, when it saved the vintage. It was not legalized until 1938. It has been allowed every year since 1962, although many of the top *châteaux* did not start chaptalizing until the late 1960s. Château Latour, for example, did not chaptalize the terrible vintage of 1963. Nowadays, as in Burgundy, all the estates always chaptalize except in very hot vintages such as 1989.

Now this is very odd. Grapes are picked later, with a higher sugar content, than they used to be. Last century, when red Bordeaux were not chaptalized, grapes were picked before they were ripe in order to avoid possibly cold and damp autumn weather. Until the end of the century, first-growth Bordeaux, when analyzed, were found to contain an average of only 7–9 percent alcohol. Today they achieve a natural 11–12 percent, before chaptalization. Since overripeness is regarded as a virtue, the grapes are left on the vines after they are ripe, resulting in high levels of sugar and low levels of acidity—and in wines that can be drunk young but whose ability to age remains a matter of dispute. In Bordeaux, the average date of starting the harvest between 1945 and 1987 was five days later than the average date between 1869 and 1914. Moreover, in the nineteenth century different varieties were planted higgledy-piggledy, rather than in separate plots, and therefore unripe grapes were picked along with ripe. (This still happens in Rioja in Spain and in the Douro in Portugal, where port is produced.) Even where one plot is planted in only one grape variety, not all the grapes in a bunch ripen at the same time. Away from the light, fruit does not take on color, so a tightly knit bunch will have paler berries on the inside. Between 10 and 30 percent of the grapes in any given bunch will be unripe; it is to give these berries time to improve that many wine makers recommend delaying the vintage.

This delay has been made possible by the introduction, in some regions, of harvesting machines. It used to be necessary to begin the harvest before the grapes were ripe and finish when they were over-ripe. Since he invested in a harvesting machine in 1979, Georges Vigoroux of Château de Haute Serre in Cahors in southwest France has cut his harvesting time from one month to ten days. The machine allows him to wait for ripeness, even for the best time of day. It shakes the vine: the green, unripe grapes don't drop off. Today, in Bordeaux, the majority of the harvest is machine picked. A machine often makes a better job of selecting ripe grapes than pickers would. At Château Sénéjac in Bordeaux in 1976 the young New Zealand–born wine maker Jenny Bailey carefully explained to the pickers at the beginning of the harvest that she wanted them to gather only the ripest bunches. They ignored her—presumably because she was both foreign and female—and picked all the bunches, regardless of their state of ripeness. So, at the end of the first day of the harvest, she sacked them, and finished the job by machine.[11]

So why this sudden adoption of chaptalization? I do not think it is a coincidence that the adoption of wholesale chaptalization in Bordeaux and Burgundy coincides with a vast increase in yields—in the quantity of wine produced per vine—since the 1950s. Yields in Bordeaux remained very much at their nineteenth-century level until the end of the 1950s, since when they have doubled. Chaptalization compensates for overproduction. Sometimes, this is quite necessary. Only with chaptalization are wine producers in the South Tyrol and Friuli in northeast Italy able to overcome the economic necessity of overproducing, on the grounds that they cannot get a fair return for their wines. Only by chaptalizing illegally have growers been able to produce serious dry white wines at remarkably low prices.

The Italian methanol scandal of 1986 occurred because wine makers tried to boost the alcohol content of thin, overproduced wine with a cheaper and more readily available means than sugar. In 1985 heavy fines were imposed by Piedmontese magistrates on sugar producers for selling sugar to wineries, which made the sugar business riskier. Adding alcohol (ethanol) was not an alternative, not just because this is illegal too, but because ethanol is taxed and therefore its movement around Italy is controlled. Since 1984, however, methanol had been untaxed and its movement uncontrolled. So methanol was used instead of ethanol. So twenty-one people died.

A more valid justification of chaptalization lies in the necessity, on some occasions, of picking grapes before they are fully ripe and have reached their optimum sugar content. This is true for white wines, particularly if produced in warm climates. Whereas it is not always required that red wines should taste of the grapes from which they are made (and they can very well be dominated by "secondary" aromas produced during fermentation), in white wines fresh fruit flavors are always desired—that is, "primary" aromas from the grape. These aromas are localized in the skin and underlying cells and appear very early, long before complete maturity, so that early picking can result in finer wines than late picking.

This will not serve, however, as an explanation for the wholesale chaptalizing of white burgundies. Whereas the chaptalization of red burgundies is much talked of, that of white burgundies is not. Yet it is far more culpable. Producers of white burgundies need not worry too much about losing acidity if they wait for the grapes to achieve better levels of sugar, since they can always prevent the malolactic fermentation, which converts malic acid into lactic acid and carbon dioxide. This method is used, for example, by Jacques Lardière, the wine maker for the best of the merchant houses, Maison Louis Jadot. Lardière does not use this method for his red wines, because a red wine with high levels of malic acid can taste rather strange. Moreover, most white burgundies are drunk so young nowadays that lack of acidity is irrelevant as regards keeping qualities. Whereas black grapes do not always ripen in Burgundy—and therefore genuinely require chaptalization—white grapes almost always ripen. Chardonnay grapes usually achieve between 12 and 13 percent alcohol naturally, so why chaptalize? Is it that, as white burgundies have become so expensive that no one can afford to drink more than a half a bottle, they are being made more alcoholic so that it is possible to get drunk on this small quantity? The alcoholic content is raised gratuitously to between 13.5 and 14 percent. Percival Brown of the British burgundy importers Heyman Brothers believes that the alcohol levels of white burgundies are about 1–1.5 percent higher than they were ten or twenty years ago.[12]

Nor is it possible to justify the chaptalization of sweet white wines when the vine grower is not prepared to wait for the grapes to achieve the necessarily high sugar content. Many leading Sauternes *châteaux* chaptalize their wines in order to ensure that when fermentation stops, the wine is sweet. Because they do not want—or cannot afford—to risk the loss of their grapes because of bad weather in the autumn, they do not wait until the grapes contain enough sugar to produce a potential 18 percent alcohol—enough sugar to achieve the legal minimum alcoholic strength (for the *appellation*) of 13 percent, while leaving 90 grams per liter of unfermented sugar. Whereas dry wines were developed in Sauternes in the 1960s because they could not sell the sweet ones, the cooperative cellars in Jurançon in southwest France introduced a dry wine after the last war on the grounds that this was preferable to the excessive chaptalizing of the sweet version.

The most regularly, and legally, overchaptalized of French wines is champagne. This is ridiculous, considering that making a wine sparkling has been since the last century an *alternative* to fortification or chaptalization. Sufficient sugar is added before the first fermentation to increase its alcoholic content by 2 percent, and enough before the second fermentation in bottle—which makes the wine sparkle—to increase its alcohol content by a further 1.25 percent. Thus champagne is chaptalized, overall, from a natural 9 percent of potential alcohol to an actual 12.25 percent. Bottle-fermented sparkling wines in Italy, California, and Australia are chaptalized before their second, but not before their first, fermentation—thus supporting the argument of their makers that their wines are more natural, if not better, than champagne.

Advocates of chaptalization argue that it prolongs fermentation. The best Burgundian wine makers add sugar—not all at the beginning of fermentation, but gradually during its course. Michel and Frédéric Lafarge, who make outstanding Volnays and a particularly good-value Bourgogne Rouge from vineyards outside the *appellation*, chaptalize their wines gradually by between 0.5 and 1 percent in order to prolong fermentation to about ten days and to improve

keeping qualities thereby. There are, however, other means of pro-
longing the period the wine spends in contact with the grape skins,
in order to extract as much flavor from them as possible. Because
extending fermentation by gradual chaptalization is not an option for
producers of wine from the Burgundy grape variety Pinot Noir in
California, where chaptalization is forbidden, many of them have
adopted the method of leaving the wine in the fermentation vat, with
the grape skins, after fermentation has finished. A number of the
wine makers who use this method say that macerating the skins in
the wine for between one and two weeks after the end of fermentation does not make the wines taste more tannic, as one might expect,
but makes them softer and rounder. On the other hand, Joe Cafaro,
consultant wine maker at Sinskey in the Napa Valley, says that he
has tried this method for both Pinot Noir and Cabernet Sauvignon
but has given up on it. He believes that the wines taste smoother
during the six months after bottling, but that the smoothness goes
away after a couple of years. The method therefore does not interest
him, because he makes wine for long-term aging.

The most obvious difference between burgundies and Chardonnays and Pinot Noirs made in California is that the California wines
are made from ripe grapes. Why do vine growers in Burgundy not
follow the example of their California counterparts and wait until the
grapes are ripe—adding acidity, if necessary, to compensate? The
reason for burgundy's reputation lies in the length of the growing
season. Chaptalization can never provide the taste that would have
been achieved had the grapes been picked later.

The big difficulty with delaying a harvest is risking the weather.
Sometimes, fortune favors the brave; sometimes it does not. But this
is not the point. If their gamble pays off, those vine growers who wait
are able to make a better wine; whereas those who risk nothing only
ever achieve a mediocre one.

Bordeaux in 1985 suffered from drought in August and September, which retarded the ripening process so much that in mid-
September, Cabernet Sauvignon grapes contained enough sugar to
produce only 10.5 percent potential alcohol. This was reduced by
dew and mists in late September to 9.5 percent. Rain was predicted
for the first weekend in October, so some picked at this point; others
picked swollen berries after the rain; only those who had the courage

to wait until dry weather returned harvested a crop with good alcoholic degree and fair concentration. The weather held up throughout October; the best wines were picked in mid-October. Though the
best 1985s are the Saint-Emilions and Pomerols—where the early
ripening Merlot grape did not stop ripening on the cooler soils and
was picked before the bad weather—there are some very good late-
picked Médocs, such as Château Lynch-Bages and its second wine
Haut-Bages-Averous.

We should not, however, be misled by those recent vintages in
Bordeaux (in which victory has been snatched from the jaws of
defeat) into imagining that waiting longer always brings happy results. More so than 1985, 1983 and 1978 before it were last-minute
successes. Two weeks before the harvest in 1983, Michel Delon, the
owner of Château Léoville–Las Cases, said to his cellarmaster:
"We've lost the vintage. We have a 1972 on our hands."[13] The year
1964 was a last-minute failure. It was a wonderful summer, and in
August, Edgard Pisani, the Minister of Agriculture, proclaimed that
it was going to be the "vintage of the century." A number of merchants bought wines *sur souche*—while the grapes were still ripening
on the vines—in anticipation of demand exceeding supply after the
vintage. Some very good wines were made—notably at Château
Latour, who finished picking before October 8, when it began to rain
and did not stop for two weeks. Those who had waited for a late
harvest saw their wines ruined, most famously at Lafite and most
disastrously at Mouton-Rothschild.

Late picking, however, can be taken to excess. The most celebrated estate in Burgundy, the Domaine de la Romanée-Conti,
which has holdings in six *grand cru* vineyards, including the entirety
of Romanée-Conti itself, is one of the most fervent advocates of this
philosophy. When he bought the Domaine (as it is often simply
called) in 1869, M. Duvault-Blochet published a book in which he
stated that, except when bad weather or rot threatens to ruin the
harvest, the grapes should never be picked until they have reached
between 13 and 13.5 percent potential alcohol. In recent years the
Domaine has been criticized for its practice of picking between one
and two weeks later than other growers. In 1982, in his book on
Burgundy, Anthony Hanson said that, partly as a result of the Domaine's policy of late picking, the wines were "made with a heavy

hand."[14] In 1984, in a report on a tasting of the Domaine's wines published in *Decanter* magazine, Serena Sutcliffe said that her "overriding feeling" was: "The grapes are picked too late."[15] In 1986, in an article on the Domaine in his booklet *The Vine*, Clive Coates commented that the wines sometimes suffered from "a lack of delicacy" as a result of delaying harvesting too long.[16]

The wines appear to have become more delicate beginning with the 1985 vintage, which was when the manager of the Domaine, André Noblet, died and was succeeded by his son Bernard. According to local gossip, Bernard has abandoned his father's practice of late picking and now gathers the grapes at the same time as everyone else. Lalou Bize-Leroy, one of the owners of the Domaine, denies this, however. She says that the Domaine follows the same policy as it always has: it harvests the grapes "when they are ripe." She points out that in the 1960s and 1970s there were a lot of wet summers, which meant they often picked late. However, there has been a run of good vintages since 1985, so late picking has not been necessary. She also suggests that other vine growers imagine that the Domaine harvests earlier than it used to only because they now harvest later than was previously their practice.

Bize-Leroy is unrealistic, however, to believe that, by dint of late picking, the Domaine is immune to the forces of nature and is able to make wines worth the amazingly high prices asked even for off vintages like 1963 and 1975. It is not. After Serena Sutcliffe criticized the 1975s, she was—according to her *Pocket Guide to Burgundy*—forbidden entry to the Domaine; certainly, she provoked a firm response from Bize-Leroy, who recruited teams of tasters in order to refute her criticism. Bize-Leroy argued in the defense of her wines that, whereas the wines made by the Domaine in good vintages need to be kept for at least fifteen years before drinking, the lesser vintages should be kept even longer.[17] This is an unusual opinion to hold. When I visited the Domaine in 1991, Bize-Leroy was kind enough to open for me to taste a bottle of the 1975 La Tâche, the vineyard which is reputed to perform more consistently across the vintages than any other of the Domaine's wines. The wine was not bad, but it was not worthy of *grand cru* status—let alone the reputation of La Tâche as the second greatest vineyard in Burgundy, after Romanée-Conti itself. In 1981 Serena Sutcliffe wrote to *De-*

canter to say that she had seen the 1963 Romanée-Conti on sale at the Carrefour supermarket at Chalon-sur-Saône, scarcely an outlet which normally would have been allowed to stock so prestigious a wine. If Bize-Leroy is right about the slower maturation of lesser vintages, then how much longer would the purchaser have had to wait for this particular eighteen-year-old wine to blossom?

It is not in the worst vintages that waiting pays off (the grapes simply rot on the vines), nor, indeed, in the best (the result is overripeness and dangerously low acid levels) but in run-of-the-mill vintages such as 1986. This had begun well in Burgundy, but it rained in mid-September, causing a great deal of rot. A lot of vine growers were panicked by the rot into picking early, when the grapes were still swelled by the rain. Only those who waited until the end of the month made fine wine. Sugar levels fell by 1 percent, as a result of dilution of the grapes by the rain, to reach a low point of 9 percent in mid-September. But then they gained 2 percent potential alcohol over the next two weeks. André Pernin, a grower in Vosne-Romanée, picked even later in 1986 than the Domaine de la Romanée-Conti; he ended up producing a wine that was better than the one he had made in the generally outstanding 1985 vintage.

Traditionally, Burgundian wine makers were said to equate acidity with bones and sugar with flesh, and to point out that it is easier to put on more flesh than alter bone structure. In other words, it is better to pick early to safeguard acid levels than to pick late and acidify. This view has now been challenged by the new generation of Young Turks who have done a great deal to restore red burgundy to its former glory. They believe that the balance of a wine is less affected by adding acidity than by adding sugar. Gérard Chave, the leading producer of Hermitage, agrees that it is better to pick on ripeness—and acidify if necessary—than to pick on acidity and then chaptalize. In 1986 the other growers in Hermitage began picking on September 20; he picked between October 2 and 12, after everyone else had finished. Perhaps the Domaine de Romanée-Conti is right after all.

"Old-fashioned" Burgundian wine makers have a problem today if they are not willing to improve the bone structure of the monster they create. It used to be said that red burgundy was a more acidic wine than red Bordeaux. This is no longer true. Pinot Noir grapes suffer today from disastrously low levels of acidity, the consequence of the heavy administration of potassium fertilizer in the 1960s—and of the planting, in the same period, of particular clones of Pinot Noir called Pinots Droits, which naturally produce grapes low in acidity. As a result, in Burgundy in most vintages, most growers both chaptalize and add acidity. This is illegal, but the authorities did not do anything about it until the Bouchards were charged in 1989—not just with overchaptalizing some of their 1987s, but with adding acidity to wines they had already chaptalized. Wine makers have argued in their defense that it is necessary to add acidity in order to restore to the wine the balance it has lost as a result of their having added sugar. They call this the "rule of 1 percent"; for every kilogram of sugar they add, they add a hundred grams of acid. Max Léglise, who was for many years the director of the Station Oenologique in Beaune, describes the "rule of 1 percent" as "completely stupid"; he says that there is no relationship between the acidity and the alcohol. He believes that wine makers ought to be allowed to add both, but that there is no reason for them to add one in order to "balance" the other. Certainly, there are alternatives to adding acidity. Ken Wright, the wine maker at Panther Creek in Oregon, says that he manipulates his wines by using different yeast strains: that in 1987 his grapes had very low acidity, so he used more of a Bordeaux strain which enhanced the structure and thus gave a sense of acidity that was not really there. This technique could not be adopted in Burgundy, however, since wine makers believe that much of the character of their wines is derived from the naturally occurring yeast strains with which they are fermented. Very few of them add cultured yeasts, which is the standard practice in the United States. (This question will be discussed in more detail in Chapter 14.)

Not only are wine makers in Burgundy prohibited by law from adding acid to wines they have already chaptalized, but (in those instances where they have not chaptalized the wine) the law does not permit the acid which they add to be tartaric acid, the type of which is produced by grapes and no other fruit. Evidently, they do add it, because laboratories have hundreds of pounds of tartaric acid at harvesttime and none afterward. But what they are supposed to add is citric acid. The reason why very few wine makers use citric acid is that, if the acidity that is added is of a different type from that produced naturally by the grapes, it can be tasted separately in the wine. Moreover, citric acid is unstable and can decompose under the influence of malolactic bacteria to produce a diacetyl (buttery) odor. Another type, sorbic acid, is said to produce a "geranium" taste if given time in the bottle. British tasters have often observed that some Australian wines taste as though acid has been added to them: since it is in fact impossible to distinguish organoleptically between added and naturally occurring acidity, what they are tasting is either sorbic or citric acid—or, in the case of red wines, unexpected malic acid, the result of preventing the malolactic fermentation from taking place.

Even if the option is not available of picking late and then adding acidity, other alternatives to chaptalization present themselves. Concentration by heating merely replicates the natural process of overripening under a hot sun. When it has achieved its maximum sugar content, the grape ceases to receive substances from the plant and begins to lose water. In other words, the grape receives nothing more from the plant. The same effect can be achieved by heating grapes for twenty-four hours at 105°F, causing a fall in the content of the harsh malic acids (but not the tartaric, which break down only at 135°F), slight concentration by evaporation of water, and an increase in the wine's alcohol content of 1 percent. This method, however, produces a loss in bulk, which would have to be compensated by increased prices; and, like pasteurization, it alters a wine's chemical structure and thus affects its ability to age.

A less harmful process is concentration by freezing. At 32°F ice crystals form, composed of water: alcohol does not solidify at this temperature. By law, concentration by freezing must not produce a greater reduction than 25 percent in volume or a greater increase than 2 percent in alcoholic strength. A process similar to concentration by freezing has recently been introduced in Sauternes—except that, in this case, it is not the wine that is frozen, but the grapes. Called cryo-extraction, it is based on the principle that sugar-rich juices in ripe grapes freeze at a lower temperature than the more acidic juices in unripe grapes; if the grapes are frozen to between 12°F and 20°F and then pressed, only the juice from ripe grapes will be extracted. This method has been criticized by European wine collectors on the grounds that it "denaturizes" Sauternes, but in fact it was used with great success in 1987, enabling vine growers to pick their grapes in the rain without fear of making a diluted wine as a result. Certainly cryo-extraction is preferable to the abomination of chaptalized Sauternes.

The latest advance in developing alternatives to chaptalization is reverse osmosis, filtering a wine under pressure against a filter that has been engineered so as to allow only the water molecules to pass through. This technique is currently being tested in both Bordeaux and Burgundy. It is exceedingly expensive—a machine for reverse osmosis costs about $500,000—but this is not the only reason why wine producers have their doubts about it. Reverse osmosis, like cryo-extraction and concentration by freezing or heating, concentrates the wine by reducing its volume. Chaptalization does not.

Nevertheless, these alternative methods are important because the European Community is thinking of abolishing chaptalization. In order to drain the wine lake—at present 10,000 million liters deep and growing—chaptalization with sugar will be replaced (as it has already been, at least in theory, in Italy) by enrichment with concentrated grape must, produced by heating the must in a vacuum.[18] This would be fine were it not that concentrated grape must inflicts an undesirable taste on the wine. Even if produced from the same vineyard, if concentrated to more than 26 percent potential alcohol it tastes "cooked." Commercially available musts have been concentrated to between 28 and 36 percent potential alcohol. Certainly, must can be "rectified." Indeed, this is obligatory in some regions of Italy, if not in others. But rectification of a must by passing it through an ion exchanger, though it can remove heavy metals and mineral salts, does not take away all its taste elements. Much of the grape-must concentrate used in northern Italy very substantially affects the taste of the wines to which it has been applied, because it is imported from the south. Moreover, even locally produced concentrate, even if kept to below 26 percent potential alcohol, is effectively the same thing as liquid sugar. On the one hand, the use of liquid sugar is illegal, as it adds water to wine. On the other, depending on the region, it is permitted to use concentrate to increase the wine's volume by between 6.5 and 11 percent.

Even those Italian wine makers who care nothing for quality use sugar illegally rather than concentrate legally, though not because it produces superior wine. Concentrate costs more. To chaptalize one bottle's worth of wine—even with the cheapest and nastiest form of unrectified grape-juice concentrate available—in order to increase its alcoholic degree by 2 percent costs 75 lire (about five cents) more than doing the same thing with sugar. Five cents can make a lot of difference to your profit margin when you are selling wine at seventy cents a bottle. But then methanol was cheaper still. . . .

8
The
Champagne
Game

AT THE SAME TIME that chaptalization was becoming common in France, another method of fortifying light wines was very popular: adding stronger wines to them. It has been said that, in the middle of the nineteenth century, virtually the entire harvest of Hermitage was added to red Bordeaux, and practically the whole yield of Châteauneuf-du-Pape to burgundies.[1]

Bordeaux and burgundies were adulterated in order to satisfy the palates of overseas wine drinkers who had acquired a taste during the eighteenth century for wines which had been fortified with brandy, such as port and madeira. While English gentlemen drank port, the most popular imported wine in colonial America was madeira. This was the result of a quirk of political history. An ordinance of the English King Charles II in 1663 declared that nothing produced in Europe might be shipped to the colonies except in "English bottoms" and from English ports. Madeira was not in Europe, but was an island off the coast of Africa, so wine could be exported directly from there to America without passing via England or being subject to English taxes. An attempt by the government of colonial America to impose a tax on madeira in 1764—in order to persuade people to turn to port, shipped to them via England—simply provoked the colonists into boycotting madeira. Customs officials tried to use this new tax as an excuse to run out of business a troublemaker, the Boston merchant John Hancock. They accused him of smuggling madeira in his ship *The Liberty*, and attempted to seize both him and the ship. A Boston mob roughed up the customs men and freed both Hancock and his vessel. In 1773 they were, in a similar incident, to throw tea into the sea; but in this case they drank the madeira.

Madeira was so fashionable, and of such good quality, in eighteenth-century America that the best sort to be shipped to England was known as "American madeira." In New York and the other major cities, each family of repute used to purchase its own pipe (110 gallons) of madeira once a year. George Washington is said to have drunk a pint of madeira at dinner every day.[2]

The taste for madeira, as well as the doubtful quality of such native grape varieties as Alexander and Catawba, encouraged producers of wine from these varieties to fortify them with brandy in the same way as was done with madeira, only to a considerably greater extent. The normal alcoholic strength of madeiras today is between 18 and 22 percent; most of the wines produced in the eastern part of America in the eighteenth and early nineteenth centuries contained 25 percent alcohol, and some of them as much as 40 percent—the same as present-day spirits.

The other reason for the fortification of light French wines was that it was commonly believed that adulteration was necessary in order to enable the wines to survive a journey overseas. The sufferings of modern-day burgundies suggest that this belief was not unreasonable. The California wine importer Kermit Lynch started shipping wines from France in temperature-controlled containers called "reefers" in the mid-1970s, after finding that his first shipment of burgundies from Hubert de Montille in Volnay had lost all its character and flavor on the journey.[3] Transportation problems are much more acute when wine is being shipped from Europe to the West Coast (a journey which takes more than three weeks and involves spending twenty-four hours or more passing through the tropical conditions of the Panama Canal) than if wine is being shipped to the East Coast, a journey which takes only half as long. Many shippers nevertheless refuse to use reefers to transport fine wines from France to California, arguing that it adds an unnecessary expense: it costs them an extra thirty cents a bottle, which means an extra dollar by the time the wine reaches the consumer.

Even those importers who store their wines in refrigerated containers do not necessarily treat them as they should. In 1986 three editors of *The Wine Spectator* tasted five 1983 red burgundies from the Domaine de la Romanée-Conti in San Francisco and marked them between 52 and 66 out of 100, condemning them as being "moldy," "muddy," and "smelling of garbage."[4] Not surprisingly, these observations caused a good deal of controversy—especially since some of the members of staff retasted the wines in London a few months later and changed their minds. According to Lalou Bize-Leroy—one of the owners of the Domaine—the explanation for the discrepancy lay in the handling of the wines by her American agents Wilson Daniels: they had put them in cold storage—but without humidification—and the cold air had dried out the corks. Admittedly, this explanation seems a surprising one. Why should corks have dried out rapidly in the cold? It is more likely that the wines in the San Francisco and London tastings came from different barrels. At the time, the Domaine de la Romanée-Conti bottled the barrels individually: some would have contained wine made from grapes spoiled by hail or rot, and some would not. Nevertheless, Burgundian vine growers remained convinced that the occasional poor performance of their wines in the United States should be attributed to problems of transportation or storage. In the opinion of Gérard Potel, the manager of another of the most celebrated estates in Burgundy, the Domaine de la Pousse d'Or in Volnay: "The way our clients keep our wine is as important as the work we do here. The number-one problem today is that people don't keep the wine properly."

The adulteration of red burgundies—whether in order to satisfy the taste of overseas consumers for full-bodied wines or in order to ensure that the wine can withstand the rigors of transportation—is often spoken of as though it were something historic that ceased as soon as *appellation contrôlée* laws were introduced to prohibit it. In fact, those merchants in Burgundy who used to add wine from Algeria or the South of France to their red burgundies have not stopped doing so. As Hanson has pointed out, giving up is pretty much impossible; once a merchant starts adding bolstering wine in off-vintages, he has to do so in good ones as well, or else they lack the richness of his lesser years.[5]

The illegal addition of a hefty dollop of blending wine from the south is the easiest and most effective means of producing full-bodied red burgundies. Table wine from the south is always at hand; Burgundy merchants already handle it. The practice of selling branded table wine that is produced in the south but bottled in Burgundy in burgundy bottles and sent on its way with a nudge and a wink about including some "declassified" red burgundy (of which there has in fact been no such thing since 1974) has been explained on the grounds that the quantity of wine available for trading in Burgundy is small, so merchants fill up the empty spaces in their business calendars by selling table wines. But is the explanation not the other way around? If Burgundy merchants have become involved in the business of selling branded table wines, might it not be because they were already involved in importing wine from the south for blending into their red burgundies? They only had to invent these branded wines in the 1920s, when the introduction of *appellation contrôlée* laws meant that they could no longer sell these wines under famous Burgundian names.

Certainly, Burgundy merchants have a problem on their hands. Whereas the climate is perfect for the production of white wine, it is frequently too cold for the production of red. The deep-colored and full-bodied burgundies of popular imagination are produced only three or four times a decade—the vintages in the 1980s to seek out are 1983, 1985, 1988, and 1989. Adulteration is the best means of supplying these in lesser years; the Burgundians do not have open to them the option available to the Bordelais, of planting a number of grape varieties—all of which ripen at different times—as a hedge against the climate. They rely on a single black grape variety, Pinot Noir. It is true that a certain amount of Gamay, the Beaujolais grape, is interplanted in the vineyards, and that, blended with Pinot Noir—usually in the proportion of two-thirds Gamay to one-third Pinot Noir—it makes a wine called Passe-Tout-Grains. But the result usually bears more resemblance to an earthy sort of Beaujolais than to a red burgundy. The Gamay is too coarse and too overbearing a grape—and the Pinot Noir too delicate—for the character of the principal grape to dominate the blend, which is the purpose of such combinations.

In the Médoc region of Bordeaux, wines made principally from Cabernet Sauvignon—the main grape variety—are given richness by blending with Merlot. This latter variety has long been cultivated in Saint-Emilion; and in last century wine from Saint-Emilion, which did not yet enjoy a reputation of its own, was blended into wine from the Médoc because, whereas Cabernet Sauvignon in the Médoc naturally achieved only 7 to 9 percent alcohol, the earlier ripening Merlot grape in Saint-Emilion reached 11 percent. It was obviously a small step to introducing Merlot vines into the Médoc and carrying out the blending in the vineyard. Because Merlot ripens earlier than Cabernet, it will produce a good crop even if Cabernet is spoiled by bad autumn weather, as happened in 1964. On the other hand, Merlot ripens earlier than Cabernet because it flowers earlier and is therefore susceptible to bad weather in early summer. The weather was bad in June 1984; the Merlot buds failed to set properly and dropped off; the later ripening Cabernet was not affected. The *châteaux* of Saint-Emilion and Pomerol, where far more Merlot is planted than in the Médoc, having produced generally far better wines than those of the Médoc in 1964, made much inferior, and much less, wine in 1984. Those *châteaux* with the most equal balance of the two varieties escaped the worst excesses of either: for example, Vieux Château Certan, which cultivates 45 percent of the Cabernets Sauvignon and Franc—a relatively high proportion for Pomerol—made an outstanding 1964 but also a very good 1984.

Blending as a hedge against the weather explains one of the great mysteries of Bordeaux: why Cabernet Franc is grown alongside Cabernet Sauvignon. The wine they produce is so similar that experts have trouble in telling them apart. They think they can, but that is because Cabernet Franc ripens earlier and therefore is favored by vine growers in relatively cool climates, such as the Loire Valley. The taste that people think is typical of Cabernet Franc would in fact be equally typical of Cabernet Sauvignon if it were cultivated in similarly cool climates. In the South Tyrol, Herbert Tiefenbrunner unusually cultivates Cabernet Sauvignon rather than Cabernet Franc, but I doubt if many people could identify blind the wine he makes as the produce of the former rather than the latter. Cabernet

Franc is planted in Bordeaux because it ripens a little earlier, and so, even if the Cabernet Sauvignon crop is damaged by bad autumn weather, its relative Cabernet Franc will ensure that the wine retains a Cabernet character.

But is this blending economically necessary? The leading *châteaux* of Bordeaux are now charging enormous sums of money for their wines and making huge profits every year: the break-even point for them would be achieved by selling their wines at a mere 30 francs a bottle. They can afford the occasional failure of their Cabernet Sauvignon vines to produce healthy grapes. Burgundians rely for their red wine entirely on Pinot Noir, which is more susceptible to disease than Cabernet; given bad weather, they just have to make the best of a bad job. Yet, they can still afford to drive around in smart cars—if not in public. There is a story current in Burgundy of a grower in Gevrey-Chambertin who is making much more money than he wants the tax authorities to know about. He has bought himself a Maserati, which he garages fifty miles away. He drives around Gevrey-Chambertin in an old Citroën DCV, but every weekend drives up to the place where he has garaged his Maserati and takes it for a spin around Beaune, where no one recognizes him.

It would not bankrupt the Bordelais if they pulled out all their other vines and cultivated only their best variety, Cabernet Sauvignon. Certainly, this was what, a century ago, Auguste Petit-Lafitte, Professor of Agriculture in the Department of the Gironde, thought they should do. He believed that it was right for the makers of ordinary wines to plant a mixture of varieties to insure themselves against the vagaries of the weather. They depended economically on producing a good quantity of wine each year, as they were unable to charge premium prices for their products. The producers of fine wines, on the other hand, had no need to mix different varieties of vine in their vineyards, because they were able to charge high prices. For them, the aim had to be to produce the best possible wine. Petit-Lafitte cited Deuteronomy XXII, 9: "Thou shalt not sow thy vineyard with divers seeds: lest the fruit of thy seed which thou hast sown, and the fruit of the vineyard, be defiled."[6]

There is, however, a very good reason why the Bordelais will never pull out their other vines and cultivate only Cabernet Sauvignon. In an interview in 1963, Ronald Barton, the late, highly respected proprietor of Château Léoville-Barton—in explaining why red Bordeaux were not as good as they used to be—gave four main reasons why most Bordeaux are made from a blend of grape varieties. Even in the Good Old Days before the Second World War, the best Bordeaux were blended wines. Quality-conscious vineyards contained 70–80 percent Cabernet Sauvignon with 20–30 percent of the other four species: Cabernet Franc, Merlot, Petit Verdot, and Malbec. "Some vineyards favored one and some another and this gave each its own character."[7] That is to say, each *château* cultivated the secondary varieties in different proportions in order to create a house style for itself. What individuality would they have if they all cultivated 100 percent Cabernet Sauvignon?

Admittedly, one estate's Cabernet Sauvignon is not the same as another's. Different clones are planted in different vineyards, and they produce slightly different wine. Equally, wines differ according to the strains of yeast used, the temperature at which they are vinified, the proportion of the oak barrels used for their cask aging, and the length of time they are kept in these barrels. Nevertheless, each *château* of Bordeaux—each brand—cultivates a different mixture of grapes in order to be able to offer an individual product. For example, the two leading *châteaux* in the village of Saint-Julien are Léoville–Las Cases and Ducru-Beaucaillou. The wines are not made in precisely the same way: Ducru tends to be more oaky because it spends a bit longer in cask. The principal distinction between them, however, is that Las Cases is a more austere wine than Ducru, and it takes longer to develop. The reason for this is that it contains a higher proportion of Cabernets Sauvignon and Franc and a lesser proportion of Merlot. Las Cases is 80 percent Cabernets and 15 percent Merlot; Ducru 70 percent Cabernets and 25 percent Merlot.

So important is this uniqueness of taste that, in years when one particular grape variety suffers from adverse weather conditions and therefore produces very little wine, many *châteaux* prefer to maintain their usual balance of varieties, even though this necessitates a drastic reduction in the amount of wine they are able to commercialize. One-third of the vineyard area of Château Pichon-Lalande is planted in Merlot. In 1984, one-third of their Merlot crop failed. This would, in the natural way of things, have produced a much harder wine, with only one-fifth Merlot. In order to maintain a normal balance, the *château* "declassified" one-third of its cabernet; that is, included it, not in the wine commercialized under the Pichon-Lalande label, but in the second-string wine of the *château*, Réserve de la Comtesse. As a result, Château Pichon-Lalande 1984 was very typical of Pichon-Lalande, and not at all typical of the generally unsatisfactory 1984 vintage.

Producing wine in this way, regardless of vintage conditions, reduces wine to the level of beer. For a brewer, the great challenge is to produce a consistent end product from continually changing raw materials. For a wine maker, one might have thought, the challenge is to give expression to a natural product. One leading Italian wine maker, Emidio Pepe—who makes an outstanding Montepulciano d'Abruzzo—has described consistency in wines from year to year as not only undesirable but actually dishonest.[8]

In Valencia in eastern Spain, all the wine which is exported is produced by merchants who buy and blend the same wine from the same cooperatives. Vinival's top wine, Torre de Serranos, is made by blending in 10 percent Rioja. (Ironically, the wine tastes tired and overoaked as a result.) Carlos Garrigos, the son of the owner, explained: "If this wasn't allowed, everybody's wines would taste the same." The same is true of Dão in Portugal. Only one estate-bottled wine is commercially available; the majority of Dãos are bottled and marketed by merchants who are not allowed to make wine from grapes which they have not themselves grown. All the merchants buy most of their wine from the same ten cooperatives. The results would taste more alike than they do if it were not common practice to blend in wine from Bairrada. That is why the Bairrada region was not demarcated until 1979: merchants needed the wine for their "Dãos."

In fact, most Bordelais *châteaux* do their best to give expression to the character of individual vintages within the confines of the requirement to maintain their house styles. Only occasionally do they indulge in the blending of vintages. A number of Bordelais *châteaux* overproduced Merlot in 1983, which came in very handy when much of the Merlot crop failed in 1984. Bernadette Villars of Château Chasse-Spleen has admitted that she added some 1983 press wine—made by pressing the residue of skins left over after fermentation and therefore very rich in extract, color, and tannin—to her 1984. Others did likewise, but are more cagey about disclosing the fact. After all, it is illegal. All French *appellation contrôlée* wines bearing a vintage date must have been produced solely from the fruit of that vintage.

Champagne houses, however, make no effort to give expression to the character of individual vineyards or vintages. Like the Bordelais, they each combine the same grapes in different proportions, in order to create—in theory—a unique and individual taste. Thus, Bollinger, which contains 70 percent Pinot Noir and 20 percent Chardonnay, is altogether "bigger" than Lanson, which contains 45 percent Pinot Noir and 45 percent Chardonnay. But here we are talking, not about the planting of different varieties in the same vineyard, but the blending of wines from different regions—as though classed-growth clarets were still produced by blending Cabernet Sauvignon from the Médoc with Merlot from Saint-Emilion. In Champagne, the house styles are not expressed in the context of different vintages and villages.

Vintages are irrelevant in Champagne. Classed-growth Bordeaux are sold to be laid down, not to be drunk at once, so vintage dates are important. Champagne, however, is sold to be drunk immediately, on the spur of the moment, for a celebration. It is sold, theoretically, ready-aged: non-vintage champagne tends to be three years old at time of sale, and vintage champagne five or six. Apart from a few connoisseurs, no one lays it down, and therefore vintage dates are irrelevant. Vintage champagne, it is true, does taste of the vintage in question, as well as the house style of the producer. But, as far as most consumers are concerned, it is simply a smarter, more expensive version of non-vintage champagne. We do not buy a champagne because it comes from a particularly good vintage. We buy a bottle because it has a—any—vintage date on it. We simply buy whatever vintage is currently available.

At the beginning of the century, virtually all champagne bore a vintage date. Today, 80–90 percent is non-vintage: that is, a blend of vintages. For champagne producers, a vintage label is more of a hindrance than an advantage, because it detracts from their purpose of ensuring that, everytime someone buys a bottle of their particular product, it tastes the same as it did on the previous occasion. What they seek to produce is a consistent and reliable product. Therefore they blend wines together in order to overcome their natural variability, in order to dampen the character of the individual vineyards, villages, and vintages. As Remi Krug has put it, "Champagne bears the stamp not of geography but of its maker."[9] The maker's mark is usually a bland and characterless wine that is offensive to as few people as possible, and that therefore can be sold to as many people as possible.

We are often told that blended champagnes are superior to champagnes made from single grape varieties in single villages. It may have been necessary in the past to blend together different grape varieties; but the reasons for doing so no longer exist. In the seventeenth century, champagnes from different vineyards were blended together in order to make them drinkable in poor vintages. But in those days champagne was a still wine. The climate of the Champagne region, though frequently too cold for still-wine production, is perfect for the production of the considerably more acid grapes needed to produce sparkling wine. There is no vintage so bad in Champagne that excellent sparkling wine cannot be produced.

In the eighteenth century, when sparkling champagne became fashionable, it was found that the addition of white grapes to a wine hitherto made only from black grapes made it sparkle better. But in those days champagne was made sparkling by a method different from the one used today. It fermented only once, and its degree of effervescence depended on how much of the fermentation was incomplete when the wine was bottled in the spring. Today champagne is fermented not once but twice, and the bubbles are produced by adding yeast and sugar before the second fermentation. The type of grapes used does not affect how much the wine sparkles.

The blend of black and white grapes which had been found to produce the best bubbles also, however, established a particular taste. People came to imagine that good champagne *had* to taste the way it usually did. Champagne as a whole became a brand; just like the individual houses, it developed a "house style"—at the expense of the individuality of the wines produced within it. Even champagnes made entirely from white Chardonnay grapes were looked down upon a generation ago as being "too light."[10] Today they are highly esteemed and sought after, partly as a consequence of the fashion for white burgundy, which is made 100 percent from Chardonnay, and partly because they do not taste any different from—in other words, taste equally bland as—most standard blends. But champagne made 100 percent from black grapes does have an individual taste: too individual to be acceptable to all consumers. Therefore very little is produced—except by those growers who cultivate only black-grape vines and therefore have no option. Even pink champagne is usually made, not by fermenting black grapes briefly in contact with their skins, but by blending red and white grapes in the usual way and then adding a little red wine. Yet, for anyone interested in drinking champagne for its taste rather than solely for its image, the great virtue of champagne made 100 percent from black grapes is that it does actually taste of something. A number of outstanding good pure Pinot Noir champagnes are made by growers in *grand cru* villages on the Montagne de Reims, among them Michel Arnould in Verzenay and Henri Billiot in Ambonnay. They are not expensive, either.

The produce of different vineyards also once needed to be blended together in order to ensure that the wine bubbled consistently. A hundred and fifty years ago, sparkling champagne cost twice as much as a white burgundy such as Meursault, whereas today it costs two-thirds as much. It was expensive because the method of making it effervesce—bottling it before the first fermentation had finished—was hit-and-miss. Between 10 and 40 percent of any particular batch of bottles exploded; probably just as many failed to sparkle properly. No wonder at this time the majority of champagne made was still. The problem of inconsistency was gradually solved during the course of the nineteenth century, in a number of ways. One solution was found by Mumm, who imported from Germany some colossal three-thousand-gallon tuns in which to ferment the wine. These huge vats produced wine that sparkled consistently, and were rapidly taken up by other producers as a result. They also produced wines that tasted consistent, and it was this new consistency which made possible the mass marketing of sparkling champagne.

The people who tell us that blended champagnes are superior to champagnes made from single-grape varieties in single villages are interested parties. The big champagne houses, who seek by means of vast public relations expenditure to indoctrinate us with this belief, began as, and still are, merchants, who buy in grapes or wine from various groups and blend them together. Only two of them, Bollinger and Louis Roederer, grow themselves more than 50 percent of the grapes they need; several houses, including Alfred Gratien and Piper-Heidsieck, own no vineyards at all. Thus, if these merchants say champagne is a blended product, it is because their business lies in selling blended products. To sell champagne under the names of individual vineyards or villages would weaken the brand image that they have worked so hard to promote.

Much the same is true in California. Brice Jones, a former Air Force jet pilot and Vietnam veteran who owns Sonoma-Cutrer in Sonoma County, suggests that the reason why wine producers in California have sold their wines almost exclusively under brand names rather than under the names of vineyards—as is the theory in Bordeaux and the practice in Burgundy—is that, in 85–90 percent of instances, the vineyards are owned by someone else. Wine producers have promoted their own brand name because that is all that they own. La Crema in Sonoma County is best known for its Point Noir, of which it produces a quarter of a million bottles a year. It owns no vineyards, but buys in fruit from the whole length of the California coast, from Santa Barbara in the south to Mendocino in the north, often changing its sources of supply from one vintage to the next. In 1990 Gregory Graziano, the wine maker, explained that he fermented the grapes from each region separately, then blended the finished wines together. He claimed: "We are trying to make a complex wine by taking different qualities; on tasting we find that the blends are better than the original wines." But then he would say that, wouldn't he? The most substantial justification for his argument is that, by taking a lot of unbalanced, one-dimensional wines and blending them together, Graziano cancels out their defects and makes an acceptable Pinot Noir.

With port, too, similar principles are applied. Blended, branded port achieved its apotheosis when Cockburns failed to declare the 1977 vintage, as they needed the grapes to improve the quality of their non-vintage ruby port, Special Reserve. This was an act of folly, especially considering that their 1983 and 1985 vintage ports are perhaps the finest of those years and serve greatly to enhance the image of the company and its products as a whole. But even classic vintage ports such as these are a blend of wine from several different vineyards. Need they be? So we are told by Cockburns and other leading British shippers of port. But then, until recently, they had no vineyards in the Douro. The first port-shipping house to start buying vineyards upriver was Offley in the middle of last century. Although in the last ten years or so some of the shipping houses, such as Taylors, have tried to maneuver themselves into a position in which all the grapes for their vintage port at least are produced in their own vineyards, it is too late: the belief that vintage port must be blended from vineyards in different places already runs in their blood. More-over, for the shippers to countenance single-estate vintage port would be to encourage farmers to set themselves up in rivalry. Export regulations prevented farmers who lacked offices in Oporto from exporting their own vintage port before the 1982 vintage. Now an increasing number of single-estate vintage ports from growers are becoming available. The best I have tried is the 1982 Quinta do Cotto from Miguel Champalimaud; mysteriously, he has not re-leased a vintage since then.

Vintage ports, like vintage champagnes, are produced on aver-age only three or four times a decade. In lesser years the produce of the best vineyards has hitherto been used by merchants to improve the quality of their standard blends. In middling years the port houses, having purchased all these new vineyards, have started to commercialize their produce under the name of single-*quinta* ports. In theory these are the produce of single estates (*quintas*) but here, as elsewhere in the port trade, the absence of strict regulations en-ables the shipping houses to do what they like. Unlike in France—where to call a wine Château Quelque Chose there has to be a *château*—nothing in the Portuguese wine laws compels them to use only the produce of a single *quinta* in a so-called single-*quinta* port. Only the vintage port and not the other qualities marketed by the port firm Quinta do Noval are made from the produce of the estate from which the company takes its name. More confusing still, Gra-ham's Malvedos is not a single-*quinta* port but simply the same sort of blend as their vintage port from a less good year. Malvedos is a band name; it is purely coincidental that Graham's owns a *quinta* called Malvedos. Graham's Malvedos has, however, often been listed by wine retailers as Quinta do Malvedos, and is twice described by the British wine writer Robin Young in his *Really Useful Wine*

Guide as a single-*quinta* port,[11] so clearly someone is getting confused. Are Graham's bothered? Or do they, along with all the other
houses who release "single-*quinta*" ports in years which are not quite
good enough to declare as a vintage, want us to believe that in these
years the best wine they can produce is the unblended produce of a
single farm? If so, this conflicts with the doctrine that the best vintage
ports are a blend of wine from several different vineyards.[12]

Likewise, the best champagne is the unblended produce of the
best vineyards. Though they do not admit as much by word, the
champagne houses confess this by deed. In 1984 Krug launched Clos
Du Mesnil 1979, at the top of their range. It was twice the price of
"ordinary" vintage Krug, a ridiculous $100 a bottle retail, despite the
vines' being only six years old. By this act they gave the lie to their
and their colleagues' protestations. Here was the most esteemed firm
of champagne blenders admitting that the best wine they could produce came from a single-grape variety in a single vineyard in a single
year.

A priori, the best champagnes must be those made from single-
grape varieties in single vineyards in single years. To argue otherwise
would be to suggest that the best burgundies should be made, not
only from a blend of vineyards or vintages—as is currently the case
only for lesser burgundies—but from a blend of red and white grapes.
For the grape varieties in Champagne are the same as those in
Burgundy; indeed, they were introduced into Champagne from Burgundy, probably in the fifteenth century. The idea of making pink
burgundies from three-quarters red and one-quarter white grapes
went out in the eighteenth century. No one nowadays produces a
burgundy comprising 60 percent Macon Rouge (half Gamay and
half Pinot Noir), 30 percent Macon Blanc, 5 percent Gevrey-
Chambertin, and 5 percent Meursault—and then sells it at the price
of Gevrey-Chambertin or Meursault. Yet this is precisely what happens in Champagne. It is patently absurd that tasteless blended
champagnes, containing a great deal of indifferent grapes, should
retail in this country for $30 a bottle—more than it costs to buy
champagnes made by growers from the best grapes in the best vineyards.

One of the many reasons why the superiority of single-variety
over blended champagnes is not appreciated is that champagnes are

drunk young, and champagnes made solely from Chardonnay or Pinot Noir do not start to develop their complexity until they are six or seven years old. Most champagnes on sale in 1992 are made predominantly from the 1989 or 1990 vintages. One purpose of blending is to render wines ready for drinking earlier than they might otherwise be. In his interview in 1963, Ronald Barton said that, as a result of the increased proportion of Merlot, red Bordeaux are ready to drink earlier than they used to be. Before the development of modern means of controlling fermentation temperatures, and of extracting color and flavor without tannin, one of the best means of satisfying popular demands for wine to drink young was blending the main variety of the region with something softer: in Bordeaux, softening Cabernet Sauvignon with Merlot.

Blending for this reason is carried out in many other regions. The "traditional" mix of grapes which go into Chianti was invented by Baron Ricasoli, who took over his family estate at Brolio in Chianti Classico in the 1830s. He developed a blend of 80 percent Sangiovese, 15 percent Canaiolo, and 5 percent of the white grape Trebbiano, with the explicit purpose of satisfying the demands of Tuscan consumers for a wine which could be drunk young. Even when Florence briefly became the capital of Italy in the late 1860s, the wines served in polite society were French ones, not Chianti, which continued to be thought of as an everyday wine for drinking young, not a fine wine to keep. It is perhaps surprising that Ricasoli should have thought it necessary to develop this new blend, when historically Chianti had been made principally from Canaiolo, a grape which produces a much less tannic wine than Sangiovese; and in fact, in the 1930s, his family firm was producing Chianti from 40 percent Sangiovese, 40 percent Canaiolo, and 20 percent white grapes. But the introduction of white grapes into red Chianti had been Ricasoli's idea, and was fossilized when, in 1963, *denominazione* regulations were drawn up, making it obligatory for growers to plant a minimum of 10 percent white grapes in their black grape vineyards, while failing to create a *denominazione* for white Chianti. In 1984 the minimum of white grapes was reduced to 2 percent. Those Chianti producers who have been trying to create the reputation of their region as a source of fine wine for aging have steadfastly ignored these requirements. Franco Bernabei, the dynamic, innovative consulting wine maker for Fontodi, Fattoria Selvapiana, and Fattoria di Felsina Berardenga, freely admits that he does not use any white grapes at all.

What happened in Chianti was not unique. In several regions of France white grapes were in the past included in the red wine, but in most cases this ceased last century when consumers became willing to buy wines that needed time to mature. Nevertheless, Burgundian wine makers are still allowed to include up to 15 percent of the white Pinot Blanc and Pinot Gris grapes in their red wine; and producers in the Northern Rhône are still permitted to introduce up to 15 percent of the white grapes Marsanne and Roussanne into red Hermitage—and up to 20 percent of Viognier, the grape variety responsible for Condrieu, into Côte Rôtie. Though white grapes are rarely added to red burgundies—which tend to be pale enough as it is—or to red Hermitage—which is usually considered to be a big, tough wine—they are frequently included in the blend for Côte Rôtie, particularly by vine growers with holdings on the "blonde" side of the slope, in order to give their wines delicacy. René Rostaing's Côte Blonde *cuvée* includes 15 percent Viognier; Guigal's La Mouline, a vineyard in the Côte Blonde, contains between 10 and 12 percent, though no one would describe this as a light wine.

A blended wine is usually ready for drinking sooner than a single varietal. One might expect it to be the other way around, and that a blended wine needed longer to marry. In fact, using a mixture of varieties gives a complex flavor much more rapidly—the different tastes of the different varieties—whereas wine made from a single variety will be no more than fresh and fruity when young. Only as it ages will complexity develop. Few of the chemical reactions that occur during bottle aging have as yet been identified. It is, however, believed that it is the tannins in red wines that are principally responsible for the virtues of maturity. Since tannins are found in the skins of the grapes, the eventual quality of a bottled-aged wine clearly depends on the quality of the grape variety. In each particular region, the best grape variety produces the best wine—if you are prepared to wait for it to develop.

Those Bordeaux which, last century, had a little Hermitage added to them (to make them fuller and richer), lived a much shorter time than pure Bordeaux, even though the latter were lighter and lower in alcohol. It was said that the practice of "hermitaging" clarets "gave the appearance of body but deadened the flavor; and after a few years in bottle, the wine became of a brownish hue, hard and flavorless."[13] Much the same happens to those red burgundies which are today produced by blending different vintages. This would be legal if the wines did not boast a vintage date; but they do, so it is illegal. Both 1976 and 1983 were abnormally hot years, producing grapes with very high sugar and tannin levels. Sensibly enough, many wines in both vintages were blended with the produce of lighter years—1982, in the case of the 1983s. This blending was successful when carried out during fermentation, but not when done afterward. That is why some 1976s have already fallen apart without ever coming around.

The use of softer varieties to make a wine ready to drink sooner necessarily implies blending with higher-yielding varieties in order to increase the size of the crop. One reason why, in Bordeaux, Merlot is softer than Cabernet is precisely that it gives a higher yield and therefore is less concentrated. As Ronald Barton said in his interview in 1963: "Since the War, the Merlot has come into favor because in certain years it produces more." Even those producers who achieve sufficiently high prices to justify making wine entirely from a top-quality but low-yielding variety have recourse to high-yielding varieties which have no real taste of their own but can serve as a cheap, neutral base for a better variety. Whereas Merlot in Bordeaux imposes a definite character of its own on the wine, Pinot Meunier—the little-discussed third grape in Champagne—does not.

The most pervasive of these neutral, high-yielding blending varieties is Trebbiano, known in France as Ugni Blanc. It comes in very useful in central Italy. Since Frascati is not generally considered to be the sort of wine for which it is worth forking over $10 or $15 a bottle, it is not really economic to make it from Malvasia, which yields only half as much juice per hectare as Trebbiano. So Malvasia is blended with Trebbiano. In many cases, the blend is something like 10 percent Malvasia and 90 percent Trebbiano, which probably explains why most Frascatis bear a marked resemblance to a solution of 12 percent ethanol in water. The only mass-produced Frascati which I know to be made solely from Malvasia is the one sold by Colli di Catone in unattractively frosted bottles; it is good, but hardly cheap. Trebbiano serves a similar purpose in Umbria, where it composes up to 65 percent and the relatively low-yielding Grechetto no more than 30 percent of any wine bearing the Orvieto *denominazione*. The best white wines of Umbria are consequently not Orvieti but 100 percent Grechetto *vini da tavola*, such as Bigi's remarkable "Marrano," which is fermented and matured in new oak casks; and, from Perugia, thirty miles northeast of Orvieto, the Grechetti of Fratelli Adanti and Arnaldo Caprai.

The alternative to blending with higher yielding varieties in order to increase the size of the crop is blending with wine from elsewhere. In some instances, this is permitted by the laws. For instance, in Burgundy, a 1990 Vosne-Romanée les Malconsorts must be 100 percent Pinot Noir, 100 percent from the 1990 vintage and 100 percent from the Malconsorts vineyard—and similar rules apply throughout France. In the Mosel, however, a 1990 Wehlener Sonnenhur Riesling Kabinett may be only 85 percent Riesling, may contain 15 percent from another vintage, and 15 percent from other vineyards, not merely from other parts of the village of Wehlen, but from anywhere within the Mosel-Saar-Ruwer region.[14]

In Italy, the position is more complicated. Spanna in the Novara-Vercelli hills in northern Piedmont is not a DOC—*denominazione d'origine controllata*, the Italian equivalent of *appellation contrôlée*—but it is the local name for the Nebbiolo grape and therefore, under European Community regulations, any wine sold as Spanna must comprise at least 85 percent of that grape variety. This requirement is frequently ignored. Spanna on its own can be rather thin, and some of the finest wines of the region are produced by blending in an unspecified quantity of Aglianico from Basilicata, five hundred miles to the south. The once wonderful Spannas of Antonio Vallana were rumored to have been produced by just such judicious blending; have they fallen off since the early 1970s because he now makes them solely or largely from local grapes?[15] On the other hand, Barolo, the most celebrated Nebbiolo wine of Piedmont, is a DOCG—*denominazione d'origine controllata e garantita*—one step up on DOC, with a compulsory tasting test; and local regulations do not permit any blending at all. A number of "very distinguished" Barolo producers nevertheless use Gaglioppo grapes from Ciro in Calabria for the same reason as Spanna producers use Aglianico from Basilicata. But unlike the Spanna makers, who are allowed their 15 percent, Barolo producers have to do it in secret.[16]

Until it was elevated from DOC to DOCG in 1984, the 85/15 percent rule applied also in Chianti. Now wines from Chanti Classico and two of the other six officially recognized subzones must comprise solely locally grown grapes. They are no less in need of beefing up with a quantity of Montepulciano from the Abruzzi than before, but it is now illegal. In four of the seven subzones, however, not only is it still permitted to blend in 15 percent of wine from elsewhere, but also concentrated grape must, which often contributes a "cooked" taste. This is usually produced in the south of Italy, but not from the noble Aglianico or Gaglioppo grapes. The use of concentrate in Chianti has *increased* in recent years as a result of the general abandonment of the traditional *governo* process whereby wine growers dried grapes on trays and added their concentrated juice to the finished wine at the end of the year, causing it to re-ferment and produce a richer, slightly sparkling wine. Growers say that they have given up the *governo* because wines thus produced do not have the ability to age. Nonsense. Fabrizio Bianchi of Monsanto, who makes one of the best and longest-lived Chiantis, used the *governo* until 1968; many of the wines he made by this method are still very much alive. In a surprising move, Franco Bernabei has recently revived the *governo* at Fontodi, where the intense, age-worthy yet accessible 1990 Chianti Classico contains about 6 percent of wine made from dried grapes. He says that, in his opinion, using the *governo* produces wines which are capable of aging *better*, with more rounded tannins and higher levels of acidity. He believes that his contemporaries do not use this method because drying grapes requires a lot of space, and people prefer to use the space they have for drying white grapes to make the dessert wine Vin Santo. The wine writers Sheldon and Pauline Wasserman add that producers have abandoned the *governo* because of the extra labor costs involved: adding concentrate from the south instead is so much cheaper.[17] Thus, in Chianti at least, most blending, legal or otherwise, worsens the quality of the wine.

9

The Law
Is a Ass

WHY DO WINE LAWS not prohibit adulterations such as those described in the previous chapter? Essentially, adulteration is permitted if the most powerful wine producers in a particular region want it to be. Looking at the differing views on adulteration taken by the wine laws of various countries, it is clear that what they do is impose the practices of the majority of producers on the rest, whether they like it or not. For example, the addition of sugar to fully fermented wine is allowed in France but not in Germany. It was legal in Germany between 1886 and 1971, but because it was no longer used by the majority of wine makers, who had adopted Süssreserve instead, it was made illegal by the new wine laws of 1971. Thus the "sugar scandals" of the early 1980s, in which 2,500 wine makers were prosecuted for adding liquid sugar to their wines, are a consequence of a change in the law, not of any change in the methods used by wine makers. On the other hand, chaptalization, the addition of sugar to must before fermentation in order to increase the wine's eventual alcohol degree, is permitted in Germany for wines below Kabinett quality and in the northern half of France but not in Italy. In Italy, political lobbying of vine growers in the south has enshrined in law their insistence that growers in the north who chaptalize their wine should do so with concentrated grape must produced in the south.

Likewise, wine laws prohibit a number of seasonings while permitting others that are no less adulterous but that the majority of producers want to use. In Europe in the Middle Ages, table wines used to be flavored with herbs and spices; though this is no longer permitted, herbs and spices are still used to preserve unsuccessful wines—it is just that the result is now called vermouth. The up-market French vermouth Lillet, which is produced in the Sauternes region, began, late last century, as an attempt to do something with Sauternes from a bad harvest. Today, except in the case of the Greek wine retsina, pitch and pine resin may no longer be added to wines. In Roman times, they were widely employed; Pliny waxes lyrical about the different varieties used, saying that the best resin comes from Cyprus and the best pitch from Brutii—just as a wine writer today might express his preference for oak from Limoges and Nevers.[1]

Not all wine producers whose wines taste of oak, however, have derived that flavor from cask-aging. For a cask to bestow a remark-able taste of oak, it has to be new—but new casks cost $400 apiece for the sixty-gallon size they use in Bordeaux and Burgundy. Allow-ing for interest charges, profit margins, transport costs, and taxes, this means that aging a wine in new oak casks can add an extra $4 or $5 a bottle to the price of a bottle of wine on a shop shelf. Wine producers who cannot afford to put wine in oak therefore resort to alternative methods, such as putting oak in wine. Wines in Rioja tend to be aged in relatively old oak casks; however long they spend in them, the casks are really too old to give them much oak flavor. There is all too often a lack of correspondence between the oaky flavor of a Rioja and the proportion of new casks used in its matu-ration. There is no doubt that many wineries in Rioja add oak chips, though they are not candid about it. In Portugal, many companies are much more open about their practices: the large firm of Caves Aliança has freely admitted to treating its best Dão wines with oak strips.[2] In Australia, a substance called Oakmore—a powder made from toasted oak shavings—is currently fashionable. It is both cheap and efficient, but gives a wine a slightly different taste from oak casks or oak chips: a green, diffused oak taste, with a hint of coconut.

With recourse to Oakmore, large Australian wineries are able to produce convincingly oaky Chardonnays for no more than $5 or $6 a bottle. If the back label of a bottle of Australian Chardonnay states, not that it has been matured in oak casks, but simply that it tastes of oak, then Oakmore has probably been added. It is perfectly legal, but wineries do not like to admit using it because they know that a higher status is attached to a wine that consumers believe has been lovingly matured in small oak casks.

With cognac, another method is used. Since it take twenty years or more to age cognacs in oak, it is obviously far more cost-effective to sweeten a young cognac with sugar in order to conceal its rough edges and to add *boisé* in order to give an appearance of age. *Boisé* is a tannin solution made by adding wood chips to boiling water, straining it, and adding the liquid to young cognacs. *Boisé* has been used in Cognac for many years, but the Federal Bureau of Alcohol, Tobacco and Firearms (BATF), which controls the contents and labeling of wines and spirits sold in the United States, was unaware of its existence until 1988. At that time, an American brandy manufacturer applied for permission to add wood extract to his product, justifying his request by saying that cognac houses used it. The BATF then declared that if, by adding *boisé*, the taste of cognac was altered, the fact of its addition would have to be stated on the label. Obviously, adding *boisé* does alter the taste, for otherwise there would be no reason for cognac producers to add it. The BATF was, however, dissuaded from requiring that the addition of *boisé* be declared on labels after two years' determined lobbying by the French government, the European Community, and the cognac companies.

This was an incorrect decision. Adding a wood infusion to a spirit is no replacement for maturing the spirit in a wooden cask. Reactions occur during cask aging—involving, among other things, the lignin in the wood—that actually improve the taste of the spirits. It is no coincidence that many consumers prefer whiskey to cognac on the grounds that an excess of cognac produces a terrible headache the morning after the night before. The headache is caused by the higher alcohols, also called fusel oils (*fusel* in German means, colloquially, "rotgut"), and it is the purpose of long cask aging to break these down. No cognac is required to undergo long cask aging. Even VSOP cognac need only be four and a half years old. Attempts have been made to "mature" whiskey and brandy with carbon to remove the fusel oil, but without complete success. The carbon removes not only the bad but also the good tastes. It absorbs everything; that is why it is used in gas masks. That is why vodka is passed through carbon, so that the result is as close as possible to a solution of pure ethanol in water.

Boisé is perhaps the least surprising of the various substances that are added to brandies. It is alleged that some cognac houses add artificial flavors which they have purchased from Dutch cognac manufacturers.[3] Early last century, much of the brandy sold as "cognac" derived its character from having almond cake kept in it for a long time—which was considered even then to be adulteration. Yet, almonds are widely used to flavor Spanish and Portuguese brandy today. In Jerez, Terry, who are owned by Harveys, steep each 30,000 liters of brandy in 1,000 kilos of almonds for six months.[4] Prunes are also used. Can these adulterations be justified on the grounds that flavor is thereby improved?

A product is adulterated if the consumer is thereby deceived into believing that it is different, or of another quality, from what it actually is. The flavoring of brandy with fruit and nuts is certainly adulteration—we expect brandy to be distilled *wine*—but not, perhaps, a very serious one, as there is no evidence of an intention to deceive, as there was, for example, in the minds of those producers who, early last century, kept chili peppers in the brandy for a month to give it a hot, pungent flavor and therefore an appearance of strength.

By this criterion, the addition of caramel to brandies and whiskeys is a very serious adulteration, because the consumer is thereby deceived. Since long cask aging turns a spirit dark in color—because of the oxidation of the tannins—a dark color is associated with a longer-matured, and thus superior, spirit. Producers of whiskey and cognac who color these spirits with caramel might well defend their practice on the grounds that consumers want this color but do not necessarily want—or at least cannot afford—to pay for a product that has acquired this color naturally. But this argument can hardly be pressed by port producers who add caramel to tawny port, since the raw product to which this treatment is applied is sometimes table wine from the Dāo region. With a bit of judicious coloring and sweetening with caramel, this can very successfully be passed off as tawny port. It is not possible to put an end to this practice by passing a law against the addition of caramel to port—because such a law already exists. Moreover, the lawmakers themselves are partially to blame for the present situation. It is difficult, by tasting, to differentiate a mixture of Dão wine and caramel from a legal tawny port. Only the very best tawny ports acquire their color from long aging in cask. Most of them are made by blending together young red and white ports.

Not only does its use deceive the consumer, but caramel is not necessarily safe. Burnt sugar is fine, but commercial caramel is not made by burning sugar. Certain caramels have been found to include 4-methylimidazole, which is toxic to mice, rabbits, and chickens. Some forms of caramel are banned in some countries.

Like darkness in spirits, a deep color in a red wine is considered to be a positive feature, since we associate it with the produce of a hot summer and with a product that offers a concentrated flavor. Frequently nature fails to provide this color, and it has to be added. In the days before industrial technology, vegetable dyes such as logwood, beetroot, or elderberry juice were used. England's monastic vineyards in the Middle Ages found it easier to produce white than red wine; they then colored this with elderberry juice to produce the blood-red wine that was required for their religious services. Many of the ports of the first half of the eighteenth century owed their vibrant purple color also to the virtues of elderberry juice. In this case, however, the blending was carried out surreptitiously; and, after the 1750s, it became a felony punishable by transportation for life to have an elder tree growing on a property within the port region. Nevertheless, the use of elderberry juice did continue, if not to the extent alleged by Mr. Lytton, the Secretary to the British Legation at Lisbon, when he said that, up until 1865, all the port exported to England was "composed almost quite as much of elderberries as of grapes."[5]

The claim that port had been colored with elderberry juice was taken up again in the 1980s by those critics of Miguel Champalimaud who were unable to understand how his 1982 Quinta do Cotto vintage port could be so deep in color and so "jammy" in taste compared with the 1982 vintage ports from other companies.[6] In France, wine makers may not be accused of using elderberry juice, but the irony has often been remarked upon that Burgundy is a center for the production both of blackcurrants and of black grapes that are notorious for their inability to produce deep-colored wine, even in run-of-the mill vintages. One wine maker in Gevrey-Chambertin, who worked in the mid-1980s for a laboratory that carried out analyses of growers' wines, remembers that it was sometimes necessary to filter out blackcurrant pips from the wines before they could be analyzed.

This said, it is preferable that wines should be colored with fruit juice than that artificial coal tar dyes should be used. These were first produced in the 1850s, when their vibrant, permanent colors transformed the textile industry. One of the first of them was magenta (originally called fuchsine), produced by the action of arsenic acid on aniline. This came into use in the 1870s, when the phylloxera louse devastated the French vineyards, and *piquettes* and raisin wines had to be commercialized. *Piquettes* were made by adding water to the residue left over after making wine and fermenting the result; raisin wines, by adding water to raisins imported from abroad and fermenting this. Neither looked very pretty: *piquettes* were a dirty pink, raisin wines a dirty white, color. Red coloring therefore had to be added. The exposure of this practice caused a big scare in Britain, not least because it was stated by an authority that "all the French wines are suspicious."[7] Quite apart from its arsenic content, fuchsine, like all coal-tar dyes, is a suspected carcinogen and mutagen. It is no longer used in foodstuffs. In Europe, its role has been taken over by amaranth, also derived from coal tar, and also possibly unsafe. This is widely used in sweets and soft drinks. It is not a permitted additive to wine, but I would not be surprised if it were sometimes used. Amaranth is banned in the States—but the yellow coal-tar dye tartrazine is permitted, and some cider and brandy producers may add it to their products.

Pink champagne is a fad that comes and goes. Ironically, though much champagne, which is made from red grapes, is naturally a pink wine, it is difficult to produce a pink champagne to order. The degree of pigmentation of the grapes varies according to the warmth of the summer; and in any case, most of the color falls out during the double fermentation that champagne undergoes to make it sparkling.

Whenever there is a fad for pink champagne, therefore, two versions
tend to be available: pink champagne made properly by the maceration method—that is, by leaving the juice in contact with the skins
of the black grapes for a while to pick up some red color from them;
and pink champagne made by adding red coloring. In the early
nineteenth century there was *vin de Fimes,* colored with elderberry
liqueur; in the middle of the century, pink champagne was colored
with cochineal. In the second half of the last century, it was replaced
by synthetic dyestuffs, whose color lasted better. (In any case, cochineal is made from cactus beetles and is therefore too expensive to
be used widely today.) Today most pink champagne is made by
adding 10–12 percent of the still red wine of the region to white
champagne. It is the only *appellation contrôlée* wine in France permitted to be made from a blend of red and white wine. Yet it costs
more than white champagne. Patently, a pink champagne made in
this way is a rip-off; but the method whereby the champagne has
been colored is not indicated on the label. Only on tasting can you
tell if a pink champagne has been made from black Pinot Noir
grapes, vinified briefly on their skins. By then it may be too late.

The attitude of wine laws to seasoning and adulteration can
only be understood if it is appreciated that they were introduced to
protect wine producers against the adulteration of their products by
unscrupulous rivals—not to protect consumers against the adulteration, by wine makers, of their own products. Wines have always
been adulterated, but the development of technology in the Industrial Revolution made methods of doing so more sophisticated. Fac-
tories were set up for the faking of wine. It was said that, at the port
of Sète in the Languedoc, "All the wines in the world are made. You
only have to give an order for Johannisberg or Tokay—nay, for all I
know, for the Falernian of the Romans or the nectar of the gods—
and the Sète manufacturers will promptly supply you. . . . The great
trade of the place is not so much adulterating as concocting wine;
they will doctor you up bad Bordeaux with violet powders and rough
cider, color it with cochineal and turnsole, and outswear creation
that it is precious Château Margaux, vintage of '25."[8]

Adulteration became the order of the day after the French vineyards were devastated by the phylloxera louse in the 1870s. In Paris

in 1905, out of six hundred samples tested at random in various warehouses, 80 percent had been adulterated. It was said that it was as rare to find pure wine in the city as a virgin of twenty-one. In 1882 the *Pall Mall Gazette* stated that most of the "cognac" entering England "comes out of potatoes and not out of grapes."[9] No wonder the English upper classes turned to whiskey instead.

As demand increased—and adulteration with it—reliance on the reputation of a brand name became increasingly important. But the brand name needed to be protected in law. By 1819 Le Chambertin was "producing" three thousand casks a year, of which only a hundred were genuine. As a result of this and similar adulterations, pressure was brought to bear by the political representatives of fine-wine districts, resulting in the introduction, in 1845, of legal protection for brand and place names. The establishment in the second half of the nineteenth century of today's brands of scotch, cognac, champagne, port, and sherry would not have been possible without the legal enforcement of the exclusive use of brand names. The registration of trademarks and brand names was introduced in France in 1857, in Britain in 1875, and internationally in 1890 (though not by the Germans until they were forced to in 1919). The present century has seen the gradual introduction in France of *appellation contrôlée*, which is intended to safeguard the reputation of wine regions as a whole.

But has *appellation contrôlée* succeeded in preventing the abuse of famous names? Not until the 1970s did wines have to be tasted before being allowed to bear the name of their *appellation*. A wine produced within the *appellation contrôlée* rules therefore had the right to a famous name, regardless of how disgusting it tasted. As a tasting test now applies to all wines from regions entitled to the *appellation contrôlée*, all wines should, in theory, be at the very least typical of their region. But patently they are not. How else could red wine still be coming out of Burgundy and tasting as though it has been bolstered with wine from the South of France? Is that how the official tasters think burgundy ought to taste? Or are they simply not doing their job? An enormous amount of tasting has to be done in growers' cellars in the few months after the vintage; in most cases, only one wine is tasted. There is no control of what merchants do with the wines they buy from the growers. It is impossible that the authorities should be unaware that certain merchants adulterate the wines in their cellars. But no one seems to mind.

Control is even more lax in Germany. Ninety-five percent of wines applying for an AP (*Amtliche Prüfung*) number are awarded it. This indicates that the wine has passed an official blind tasting and chemical analysis. Patently, undeserving wines are passed: the liquid sugar scandals revealed that. So did the diethylene glycol scandal, when German wines were contaminated by their makers' illegally blending in substantial quantities of Austrian wine. Apparently, a wine needs only to be awarded one and a half marks out of five by the tasting board in order to be passed.

Moreover (at least until 1989), it was very easy to fake an AP number. In 1984 it was reported that a wine producer from Franconia was being investigated for the suspected illegal labeling of unexamined wine as quality wine; that he had used fake AP numbers on his labels from 1979 until 1983; but that "the investigators are having a difficult time."[10] They were having problems because, as the law then stood, once a sample of wine had been passed and given its AP number, the grower could print as many labels as he liked; there was no limit on the amount of wine he was allowed to produce. When, in 1989, maximum yields were introduced, this particular problem went away. There is still no reason, however, to treat Germany's wine laws with respect, when, despite its irregular and often excessively cold climate, 95 percent of its wines—all those in receipt of an AP number—are entitled to the designation "quality wine." In Italy—which enjoys a much more favorable climate—the figure is 10–12 percent. In England, which does not enjoy a much worse climate, the figure is zero.

But then, in France, the *appellation contrôlée* regime, though it successfully ensures that no more wine is sold than has been produced, does not make certain that the wine sold with the *appellation contrôlée* label is the same wine as that which is produced under the *appellation contrôlée* regulations and which was submitted for the tasting test. One may wonder why merchants were so frightened when compulsory bottling in the area of production was introduced in Alsace in 1972. It was feared that this was the thin end of the wedge—but it has not proved to be, despite the support of growers throughout France. I doubt that the reputation which Alsace enjoys throughout the wine trade for offering sound, reliable wines—the sort you might order in a restaurant, even if you had not heard of the producer—is a coincidence.

Bottling a wine in the region of production has always been an effective means of preventing adulteration. Chianti had become very popular in England by the beginning of the eighteenth century. As it was exported in cask, merchants found little difficulty, in 1710, in supplying particularly large orders by blending it with other, inferior wines, so the decision was taken by a number of producers to ship the wine in flasks which could not be tampered with in the same way.[11] In the early nineteenth century, when Lafite was so much the snob name that even Latour was being passed off as Lafite in England, Goudal, the manager of the *château*, suggested that Lafite should bottle all its wine itself in good vintages. In fact, *château* bottling was not adapted by the five first-growth Bordeaux until the 1920s, and then only for part of their production. Since the 1972 vintage it has been compulsory for all the classed-growth *châteaux* of the Médoc, which may help to explain why they are no longer adulterated to the same degree as burgundies.

The estate bottling of burgundies by growers began as a result of their adulteration by merchants. The proto–*appellation contrôlée* law of 1919 required, for the first time, that if a bottle of wine bore a name of origin on the label, then the wine had to come from the place in question. This in fact encouraged abuse. Pommard, for instance, had previously, except in cases of outright fraud, been applied only to fine wines, whether they came from the village of Pommard or that of Chassagne-Montrachet. But now any wine from Pommard enjoyed the right to use that name, even if it was produced, not from the noble Pinot Noir, but from the ignoble Gamay grape, and overcropped to 10 tons per acre or more. The law did not specify the permitted grape varieties, nor place a limit on the yield. But it did enable court cases to be brought to establish precisely how far the land entitled to claim a famous name extended. Certain vine growers, including the Marquis d'Angerville from Volnay and Henri Gouges from Nuits-Saint-Georges, took local merchants to court for selling wine which they did not believe was of a quality to be entitled to the *appellation* it boasted. As a result, no local merchants would purchase their wines, so they had to start bottling themselves. The wines that they made then, and that are made today by d'Angerville's son, Gouges's grandsons, and an ever-increasing number of their vine-grower colleagues, have succeeded in establishing a general conviction that estate-bottled wines from growers are superior to the blends produced by merchants.

This conviction can encourage others to mislead us. If an estate name helps sell a wine, and at a higher price, then regardless of whether it is the produce of a single estate, it is likely to be given that dignity. In Germany, Liebfraumilch produced by cooperatives announces that it is "estate-bottled." In France, cooperatives in Chablis and Cahors vinify in communal vats the grapes sold to them by their members and then commercialize the product under the names of various members of the cooperative. One should beware of confusing the Chablis produced by the growers Gérard Tremblay and René Dauvissat with those bearing the names of Suzanne Tremblay and Jean-Claude Dauvissat, which are cooperative blends. They are perfectly good wines, but that is not the point. You can discover if you are being had by looking on the corner of the label for the bottling number "emb 8906," which the cooperative uses. In Champagne, growers sell their grapes to a cooperative and then buy back the cooperative's wine. This they then sell from their farm door—with a domaine name—as though they had made it themselves. Depending on whose estimate you accept, anything between 15 percent and 50 percent of "growers' " champagnes are the product of a cooperative's blending vat. This patently contravenes *appellation contrôlée* laws for champagne, which state that, if a grower uses the terms *propriétaire* or *viticulteur* on the label, then the wine must come from grapes grown in his own vineyards. If the "grower's" champagne has been bottled in 1991 or later, it is possible to tell whether it has been made by him or by a cooperative, because in the first case it will carry the letters RM (*Récoltant-Manipulant*) on the label, and in the latter instance RC (*Récolant-Coopérateur*).

The extent to which mass-produced wines are passed off as the product of a single, small estate did not become common knowledge until 1989, when twenty-five people were arrested in France and charged with passing off hundreds of thousands of bottles of Bergerac as château-bottled Bordeaux. They might have continued concealing their activities had a truck carrying some of the wine, and bearing false papers, not been stopped by the police because the driver was speeding. This particular incident illuminates a theme that runs through the majority of wine scandals: they only come to light by chance. Thus the addition of methanol to cheap Italian wine was exposed in 1986 when a two-liter bottle of wine claiming to have been made from the local Barbera grape was bought in a Milan supermarket and caused the deaths of the three people who drank it. This bottle cost 1,790 lire (about $1.40). It had been an open secret for some time that such wines must have been fraudulent. After all, the production costs alone of a genuine two-liter bottle of Barbera were about 2,000 lire. It was well known that Piedmont sold more than twice as much wine as it produced. It had been pointed out on many occasions that wines could be bought in big stores in Italy at prices which indicated either that the producer was making a loss or that he was doing something illegal. Yet the only reason why the truth about methanol emerged was that the producer of this wine, Giovanni Ciravegna, made the mistake of adding too much methanol to a particular batch of "Barbera." Otherwise, he and his fellow adulterators would probably have gone on selling their wines for years. People might have died from methanol poisoning, but too slowly for it safely to be attributed to any one source.[12]

The Austrian "antifreeze" scandal was revealed only because Siegfried Tschida, a wine producer in Pamhagen, was greedy enough to claim a refund on the sales tax he had paid on the diethylene glycol he had added to his wine.[13] Yet, the most appalling adulterations had been going on in Austria for years before this scandal was exposed, including the production of artificial wine—which owed nothing to the grape—and the addition of dangerous preservatives to stabilize sweeter wines. At the end of 1985, Erwin Klenkhart was arrested and charged with adding gunpowder to his wine to make it sparkle.[14] Wine laws existed, but they were not enforced. Enforcement lay in the hands of the regional governments, who were not willing to pursue matters that might have embarrassed their political supporters. According to an article in the British wine-trade magazine *Wine & Spirit*, in 1981 an inspector was refused permission to instigate a prosecution against one of the country's leading wine houses.[15]

In Germany, the most eminent of the wine makers to be prosecuted in 1983 (for adding liquid sugar to their wines) was General Werner Tyrell, former president of the German Viticultural Association and sole proprietor of the celebrated Eitelsbacher Karthäuserhofberg in the Ruwer. During his trial it was revealed that the official chemist, Brigitte Holbach, had known since 1979 that Tyrell had been sugaring his wine; but she had been prevented by her superiors from informing the public prosecutor of her findings.[16] But then, as long ago as 1975 it had been noted by a German trade paper that more wine of Spätlese quality was being sold than had actually been produced in some vineyards, and that this wine was sold for two marks (about $1.20) a bottle—although genuine Spätlese costs five marks (about $3) to produce. This wine could only have been produced by illegal sugaring.

Adulterations are sometimes brought to light for political reasons. In 1974 the Cruse scandal destroyed public confidence in the integrity of Bordelais merchants and impelled a collapse in the market for fine red Bordeaux. Because of a dramatic rise in the prices of Bordeaux wines, Pierre Bert, a small merchant, had found himself unable, without losing money, to fulfill a contract he had made to supply wine. Therefore he purchased wine from the South of France and altered *appellation contrôlée* documents covering white Bordeaux in order to pass off this wine as red Bordeaux. He sold this wine to the firm owned by the prominent Cruse family. Bert and the Cruses were found out, prosecuted, and given prison sentences. During his trial, Bert told Anthony Terry of the British national newspaper *The Sunday Times* that he could not understand why, on this occasion, "the inspectors did not just ring up as they have done in the past and say they had some information. The matter was then settled with a handshake and a few thousand francs across the table. After all, everyone has been doing it in one way or another for years and the inspectors have learnt to live with the facts of life." The reason why the Fraud Squad did proceed for once, Terry was told by a Bordeaux merchant, was that the Cruse family was related to Jacques Chaban-Delmas, whom Giscard d'Estaing had just defeated in the presidential election. There was no suggestion that Giscard had ordered the Fraud Squad to investigate the Cruses' activities, but rather that the Fraud Squad inspector in charge of the case thought that Giscard would be delighted to get one over on his erstwhile opponent.[17] That would certainly explain why only the Cruses—and none of the other merchants who had bought wine from Pierre Bert—were prosecuted.

Most scandals, however, are brought to light because jealous rivals have ratted on a colleague. In 1989 René-Claude Martin, the owner of the Muscadet firm of Martin-Jarry, was sentenced to eighteen months imprisonment (twelve of them suspended) and fined 30 million francs (about $5.5 million) for having blended table wine from the Entre Deux Mers and Loire Atlantique regions and sold it as *appellation contrôlée* Muscadet. Martin said that he had been exposed by three rival companies who were jealous of his success. Indeed, they had been jealous for years—it was simply that no one had bothered to do anything about it. Martin, like Pierre Bert before him, had juggled *appellation contrôlée* certificates so that he could sell cheaper wines as more expensive ones. As in the Pierre Bert case, no one ever complained about the quality of the wine he was selling.

For Frascati, as for Muscadet, demand exceeds supply, as the expansion of the Roman suburbs puts pressure on land that might otherwise be used for vineyard expansion. No problem: the wine is produced beyond the generous maximum yield of 126 hectoliters per hectare (7.5 tons per acre), and the excess production is attributed to vineyards that are buried under tons of concrete apartment blocks. It has been suggested that this opportunity for deception will be removed by an official census of vineyard sites.[18] Will it? In Soave the *average* harvest of vineyards planted on the plain is 13 tons per acre, nearly double the permitted maximum yield for the denomination. When, in 1988, a local wine critic stood up in front of a magistrate and denounced the cooperatives for overproducing, the police took off in a helicopter and hovered over the plain taking photographs, in order to find out whether land registered as vineyards was actually woodland or planted in wheat. They found no firm evidence of vine growers' trying to pass off their overproduction as coming from non-vineyard land, but they did see some cooperatives pour out untreated waste into the river; they prosecuted them for that. In the Douro region of Portugal, in order to be allowed to turn grapes into port, a producer must possess a *cartão de benefício*—a permit that states the grapes have been produced in a site which is classified for port production; and that indicates the quality of the site and the price paid for the grapes, varying on a scale from A to F. Not all the land classified for port-grape production is still vineyard land. For example, the football pitch at Regua is classified to produce grade A port grapes. Not surprisingly, there is a booming trade in *cartãos de benefício*. Armed with these permits, a producer can go down to the Dão region and buy wine there for use in his "tawny ports."

In the long term, wine laws can only become effective through scientific techniques of detecting adulteration. The technology exists: it is a matter of using it. Diethylene glycol was added to some Austrian wines from 1976 onwards, and its presence could have been detected long before 1984 if anyone had thought of putting the wines through a gas chromatograph in order to analyze their constituent components. Gas chromatography was developed in the 1960s, and does not require particularly expensive equipment, so there can be no excuse for failing to use it.

It may, before too long, prove possible to check a wine's geographical origin and vintage date by analyzing the proportion of different isotopes of the oxygen atoms in the water—which is the principal constituent of wine. These atoms do not all weigh the same, and can be divided into the isotope ^{16}O and the isotope ^{18}O. Since ^{18}O isotopes are lost by evaporation, a wine produced in a region where rain falls will contain more of them than one produced near the coast. They can therefore be examined to determine a wine's region of origin. As different amounts of rain fall each year, it should also be possible to use ^{18}O isotopes in order to test a wine's vintage.

The grape variety from which the wine has been made can then be checked by "fingerprinting." If a wine is put through a gas chromatograph, its aroma can be separated into several hundred individual components and the quantity of each of these can be measured. By comparing the aroma compounds of a suspect wine with the "fingerprints" of one that is known to be genuine, its veracity can be determined. This method still has a long way to go, because only four hundred of wine's approximately eight hundred aroma compounds have so far been identified—and detection is proceeding at a rate of only three or four a year. It is hoped that eventually, by attributing specific aroma compounds to particular trace elements in the soil, it will be possible to identify the vineyard from which a wine originates.

On the other hand, the enologists Amerine and Roessler do not believe that one can differentiate grape varieties by examining the results of fermentation, because the processes which occur during fermentation are not properly understood and are affected in different ways by various strains of yeasts and bacteria.[19]

In any case, consumers would not necessarily be assisted by more effective laws. In 1987 the Italian government spent half a million dollars on its first nuclear resonance spectrometer, and it was predicted that illegal chaptalization with sugar in Italy would become a thing of the past. The instrument is capable of determining whether alcohol has been derived from sugar or from grapes, because alcohol derived from sugar has a different molecular structure from that derived from grapes; and, by means of nuclear magnetic resonance spectroscopy, it is possible to work out a molecule's structure. But forcing wine makers to use concentrated grape must instead of sugar for chaptalization is a political decision, not a qualitative one. The problem for the consumer is not merely that wine laws can readily be avoided or manipulated, but that wine laws exist to protect the interests of producers, who in some cases themselves manipulate consumers.

The yields permitted for the production of quality wine in many wine regions far exceed those which are commensurate with quality. In France, until 1974, the cascade system existed. This permitted a wine marker to sell the same wine under several different *appellations*, as each one set down a different maximum yield. If, say, a grower in the village of Pauillac in Bordeaux produced 80 hectoliters per hectare (about 5 tons per acre) when the maximum permitted crop for a Pauillac was only 40 hectoliters per hectare, he could sell 40 hectoliters per hectare as Pauillac, 5 hectoliters per hectare as Médoc (the limit for this *appellation* being 45 hectoliters per hectare), 5 hectoliters per hectare as plain Bordeaux (for which the limit was 50 hectoliters per hectare), and the other 30 hectoliters per hectare as *vin de table*. Today the excess production over the limit permitted for each *appellation* has to be sold off for distillation. The wine maker can choose between—at one end of the scale—making a Pauillac and sending half his production to be distilled, and—at the other—making a *vin de table* in which he is permitted to include all the wine he has made.

It is remarkable how many members of the wine trade believe that the cascade system is still in operation, and claim that the table wine they are selling is the "excess production" of some appellation or other. In 1989 the well-known British wine merchants Averys of Bristol offered as futures three white wines from the 1988 vintage bearing only the humble *appellation* Bourgogne Blanc but at very high prices—between $200 and $300 a case. They explained that these were "wines from top white vineyards which are in excess of the yields permitted and cannot therefore be sold with their full *appellation*." It is a mystery how Averys managed to find for sale wines which should by law have been sent for distillation—a mystery that will never be solved because, after deliberation, Averys decided not to import the wines after all. This decision may or may not have been related to the investigation of their offer by the British Wine Standards Board. Certainly this was not the first occasion on which Averys had been involved in the sale of "excess production" burgundies. Ten years earlier they had been the British agents for the Beaune-based merchant Roland Remoissenet, who was convicted in the French courts (of mislabeling wines he had exported to Britain) and given a two-year suspended prison sentence.

In 1974 the old maximum yield for each *appellation* became its basic yield (*rendement de base*). This figure could now be renewed annually, to take account of especially bad or especially good vintages. The yield for the year (*rendement annuel*) in question was to be proposed by the local vine-growers' union and determined by the Institut National des Appellations d'Origine. The *rendement annuel* has usually exceeded the *rendement de base*—but it does not represent the maximum yield. No, the actual maximum yield (*plafond limite de classement*, or PLC for short) is 20 percent above the permitted annual yield, providing that growers ask for it before the harvest. This extra 20 percent is defended on the grounds that a vine grower asking for it has to submit his wine to a tasting test, and if it fails, his entire production of that *appellation* has to be declassified into *vin de table*. What casuistry! This tasting test applies to all wines claiming *appellation contrôlée* status, not just to those wanting an extra 20 percent. The result of this new system is that many growers have produced just as much as under the old cascade system—and sold the whole of the crop under the most prestigious *appellation* to which they have been entitled.

Moreover, in Champagne, the new law, though it permits generous enough yields, has been *legally* broken. In 1973 the maximum yield (PLC) was set at 86 hectoliters per hectare. A bumper harvest in 1982 produced an *average* yield of 92 hectoliters per hectare. No one wanted to waste this bounty, even though it was—theoretically—illegal. The Institut National des Appellations d'Origine allowed the Champenois to keep it in reserve, to be used to top up vintages that did not reach the maximum yield. The 1983 harvest was even bigger, so a further quantity of wine was put into reserve. By this point reserve stocks of illegally overproduced wine amounted to 75 million bottles' worth. These were used to top up the rather smaller vintages of 1984 and 1985. This system of "blocking" stocks was one of the scandals about Bordeaux revealed by Pierre Bert in his book *In Vino Veritas*: that growers who exceeded the legal maximum yield of 40 hectoliters per hectare simply kept their excess production in reserve and declared it as a part of the next harvest if that turned out to be a small one.[20]

A similar system has recently been introduced in Germany. Ironically, it results from a belated attempt on the part of the authorities to impose a brake on overproduction. Until the end of the 1980s, growers were allowed to produce as much wine as they wanted. The reason for this was that the Germans do not consider the quality of their wines to relate to their concentration of flavor—which depends on the lowness of the yield. They dismiss years like 1984, when yields were very low and the wines had good depth. They look for a fragrant balance of fruit and acidity, which can be achieved by enormously high yields. In 1983—allegedly a great year—yields were two to three times higher than those achieved in the "mediocre" 1984 vintage. The German authorities were only encouraged to change their minds when their Austrian neighbors brought in a legal maximum yield after the diethylene glycol scandal—which owed its origins to the need to give more body and richness to thin, overcropped wines. Realizing that, without yield control, they would never come to grips with the problem of illegal sugaring or illegal AP numbers, the German authorities introduced maximum yields in the Mosel, the Rheinhessen, and the Rheinpfalz in 1989, and in the Rheingau and Baden in 1990. The purpose of these maximum yields is not so much to restrict production as to control it. The limit for Riesling in the Mosel has been set at a very generous 120 hectoliters per hectare. A serious grower such as Ernst Loosen in Bernkastel will produce only half that. The limit was established by taking the average yield over the previous decade and reducing it by 10 percent. If a grower exceeds the limit, he is permitted to carry over the excess to the next vintage and declare it as part of that year's harvest. This makes nonsense of the declaration of the German Viticultural Association that the new limits were intended to be absolute.

In some instances, wine laws, instead of trying to make things easier for consumers, help producers to pull the wool over their eyes. In Burgundy, *appellation* laws have officially ennobled lesser wines by allowing them to append the name of the village's most famous site onto the name of the village. Thus the wines produced in the village of Gevrey can bask in the reflected glory of their greatest wine by passing under the *appellation* of Gevrey-Chambertin; those of Chassagne can call themselves Chassagne-Montrachet, and so on. Something similar has also occurred in Bordeaux. By the early 1920s twelve *châteaux* in the Graves had hyphenated the name Haut-Brion onto their own. André Gibert, the new owner of the first-growth Château Haut-Brion, took ten of these *châteaux* to court and in four instances won his action. The court ruled, however, that Haut-Brion was a place and not a brand name, and therefore it might be appended to the names of *châteaux* which shared the Haut-Brion plateau. Larrivet-Haut-Brion, which was not on the plateau, was allowed to continue using the name Haut-Brion on grounds of long usage, but it was forbidden to print "Haut-Brion" in larger type than Larrivet, as it had done previously.

In the Glenlivet case, the court was more generous to the appropriators. Glenlivet had once sarcastically been known as "the longest glen in Scotland." In 1880 George Smith, the owner of the malt whiskey brand The Glenlivet, brought a case to establish that only whiskey made from the water of the Livet burn could bear the name; but he succeeded only in forcing neighboring whiskeys to use a hyphen. Whereas Tamavulin-Glenlivet is situated in Glenlivet, Aberlour-Glenlivet is a Speyside whiskey and does not even taste like a Glenlivet one. Dufftown-Glenlivet is in Glenfiddich; Glenfiddich could call itself Glenfiddich-Glenlivet if it wanted.

At the southern end of Burgundy's Côte d'Or, three little-known villages—Cheilly, Dezize, and Sampigny—have enjoyed the right to add to their names that of their most famous vineyard, Les Maranges. In fact, they are so obscure that the wines have hitherto been sold largely under the generic *appellation* of Côte de Beaune-Villages. But in 1987 a new *appellation* was created; or rather, an existing one was enlarged. All three villages are now able to sell all their wines, not just with the name of their most famous vineyard, Les Maranges, appended, but under that name alone. It is as though all the wine produced in Gevrey could sell itself as Le Chambertin, or all the wine in Chassagne as Le Montrachet—which is precisely what has happened in Germany.

The German wine laws were overhauled in 1971. Famous vineyard names were turned into names covering not just a whole village but a whole district; Scharzberg, hitherto a single site, became a generic name that every single wine produced in the Saar is entitled to use. The single vineyard site Scharzberg no longer exists. It is as though every single red burgundy produced—not merely in the village of Gevrey, but in the whole of the Côte de Nuits (which is about the same size as the Saar)—were allowed to call itself Le Chambertin.

Many other of Germany's most famous sites, though not abused to the same extent, were in 1971 enlarged so far as to lose all meaning. Whereas in Burgundy, the *grand cru* vineyards, however variable as the wine made from them, at least, in most cases, enjoy a unity of potential,[21] in Germany single-site names now encompass a wide variety of soils and exposures. Thus one man's Piesporter Goldtröpfchen or Wehlener Sonnenhur is not merely less well made than another's, but even if it were equally well made, it would not be equally good. That is why it has been suggested that, whereas Burgundy enjoys a classification of the best vineyards into *grands* and *premiers crus*, based on their potential quality, in Germany such a classification would not work. Given the current legalized abuse of

famous site names, the only valid classification would be one of
growers.

All of which is particularly unfortunate, since the law that
applied in Germany before 1971 was considerably less misleading
than that now applying in Burgundy. Any wine grown in the bor-
ough of Piesport could be sold as Piesporter, but only wine from the
Goldtröpfchen vineyard could be called Piesporter Goldtröpfchen.
(Given their practice, mentioned above, of appending the name of
its most famous vineyard on to the name of each village, the Burgundians would have given the name Piesporter-Goldtröpfchen to all
wines produced in Piesport.) It did not matter too much that there
were thirty thousand different site names, because it was indicated
from which village a wine came. But nowadays there is no way of
knowing from which village a wine comes. It may sound ridiculous,
but any wine originating within the same *Grosslage*—a generic denomination covering several villages—can use the name of any village within it.

The French have not deprived themselves of this peculiarly
Germanic form of self-abuse. There are a number of instances of the
enlargement of the area of vineyard entitled to famous names beyond
the soils to which the reputation is due. The wines of Saint-Joseph
in the Northern Rhône have recently become fashionable, following
upon those of Hermitage, Côte Rôtie, and Cornas. Some outstanding wine is produced within the *appellation* of Saint-Joseph, particularly in and around the village of Mauves. Growers such as Pierre
Coursodon, Emile Florentin, and Roger Blanchon produce mini-
Hermitages. But the *appellation* of Saint-Joseph covers a total of
twenty-six villages, few of which contain vineyard sites with the
potential to produce fine wine. Apparently, when the boundaries of
the *appellation* were drawn up, some of the leading growers, com-
placent about the outcome, failed to attend the crucial meeting.

Appellations were first introduced in California at the beginning
of the 1980s, the purpose being to enable the government to prosecute those people who might spuriously label a wine as having
come from a prestigious region such as the Napa Valley. The Napa
Valley was delimited in 1981. Geographically it is defined as the
land contained within the watershed of the Napa River, but the

official delimitation by the BATF extended the Napa Valley to include the Pope, Wooden, and Gorden valleys, on the unsatisfactory grounds that their grapes had traditionally been used to produce wines which bore the words *Napa Valley* on the label. In effect, the Napa Valley appellation includes almost all of Napa County. In 1989 the BATF approved the creation of a separate Stag's Leap appellation within the Napa Valley. Once again, the appellation had been extended far beyond the confines of the district in question. The Stag's Leap area enjoys a particular microclimate, being warmed during the day by afternoon sunlight reflected from the overhanging rocks and cooled at night by fog running north out of San Pablo Bay. But the Stag's Leap appellation was extended far beyond this narrow district in order to include all the land that the group of producers that had proposed the appellation wanted included.

In Madeira, there is a substantial demand for wines made from the noble grape varieties Malmsey (Malvasia), Bual, and Sercial. But consumers are not prepared to pay the necessary price. For example, the ten-year-old Malmseys from Blandys and Rutherford & Miles cost as much as twenty-year-old tawny ports—though even at that price they are undervalued. Therefore the majority of madeiras, though pretending to the names Malmsey, Bual, and Sercial, are made from the less noble Tinta Negra Mole grape. In his book on madeira, Noël Cossart said that when this practice began between the wars, his cousin Sidney Cossart "spat with fury" when he saw an inexpensive madeira labeled "Malmsey." What's wrong with "Rich"?[22] This practice misleads us into thinking that Malmsey, Bual, and Sercial madeiras are everyday wines that it would not be a crime to use in madeira sauce. Following Portugal's accession to the European Community, this practice is supposed to have become illegal—at least for wines produced in the 1992 or subsequent vintages.

On the Portuguese mainland, the wine laws favor producers of branded wines who, in producing their blends, ride roughshod over different regions. After seventy years of discussion, Bairrada was finally demarcated for the production of quality wine only in 1979, the wines having hitherto been used to satisfy the blending needs of merchants in Dão. Yet there is no question that, of the two regions, the future of Bairrada is the brighter.

The vineyards of Dão are planted in a mishmash of grape varieties, many of them bad and most of them diseased. By law, a minimum of 20 percent of each red Dão should be made from Touriga Nacional, the best black grape variety in Portugal and the outstanding constituent of vintage port. But how can this law be observed when plantings of Touriga Nacional in Dão fall far short of 20 percent of the vineyard area and are in decline—and when peasants bring to the cooperatives grapes of different varieties, both black and white, mixed together? On the whole, Dão is being stifled by bureaucrats—a common enough experience in post-Revolutionary Portugal. Wine production is supervised by the Federacão dos Vinicultores do Dão, whose inspectors seal the openings of casks with white tape and red sealing wax. If a merchant wants to draw a sample of wine from a cask to check its progress, he has to notify the Federacão in advance, so that they can send an inspector to break the seal. This requirement is, I suspect, more honored in the breach than in the observance. Wines may not be commercialized until they have passed a tasting test. This would be fine, were it not that tasting panels prevent wines, both red and white, from being put on the market while they are still young and full of fruit; they seem to prefer wines which have spent too long in cask and dried out.

Whereas the vineyards of Dão, an isolated region almost surrounded by mountains, are split up among forty thousand peasants, the Bairrada region runs north from Coimbra. Here, a number of relatively wealthy landowners own substantial vineyards whose produce they commercialize themselves. That of Luis Pato is superb. If the reputation of the table wines of Bairrada have been eclipsed by that of the port wines of the Douro over the last two centuries, it derives only in part from the potential quality of the produce—and partly from the fact that, in the 1750s, the Marques de Pombal, the effective dictator of Portugal, decreed that the majority of Bairrada vineyards be uprooted in order to protect the growing port-wine trade from competition.

Even less well known than Bairrada is Reguengos de Monsaraz in the Alentejo, which was not demarcated until 1989, as it was needed to give richness to *garrafeira* blends. Yet, according to Antonio Franco, president of the merchants J. M. da Fonseca, this region possibly offers greater potential than any other in Portugal. In

1986 his firm sold most of their shares in the company that produces Lancers in order to finance the purchase of the estate of José de Sousa Rosado Fernandes. The red wines produced by this estate are sold at a price which places them among the greatest bargains in the world of wine today, though they do need a few years' aging in bottle to show their best.

Many wine laws protect famous regions against the attempts of other regions in the same country to attain the same status. They do so by restricting the cultivation of grape varieties to which the famous regions have staked a proprietorial claim. In France, for example, growers wishing to enjoy the right to inscribe the words *appellation contrôlée* on their wine labels are usually prohibited, outside Bordeaux, from cultivating Cabernet Sauvignon; and outside Burgundy, from cultivating Chardonnay or Pinot Noir. It is not that these varieties are not "local" elsewhere—until last century Pinot Noir was the dominant black grape variety in the northern half of France—but that the two famous regions wish to enjoy the exclusivity of their use. Vine growers claiming the right to the *appellation* of Châteauneuf-du-Pape may cultivate as many as thirteen different grape varieties, and some producers use all of them. But Jacques Reynaud, the proprietor of Château Rayas—arguably the leading estate of the *appellation*—grows other varieties as well, including Chardonnay and Pinot Noir. His father, Louis Reynaud, who planted the vineyard in 1922, once famously declared: "*appellation contrôlée* is the guarantee of mediocrity."

To a degree, it is right that it should be so. The function of laws is to protect the status quo, not to encourage experimentation. Wine laws exist partly in order to protect the individuality of different regions. I don't think anyone would want all the vine-growing regions of the world to jump on the bandwagon and convert to growing Cabernet Sauvignon or Chardonnay. Protecting the status quo, however, is one thing; looking backward is another. According to Mario Consorte, enologist at Sella e Mosca in Sardinia, "The function of DOC has been to preserve the memory of historic wines, not to reflect the actuality of the market."[23] For example, DOCG laws require Barolo to be aged in oak for a minimum of two years. Many producers consider this to be too long, and quite sensibly ignore the law on this point. Roberto Voerzio, who obeyed the laws until 1982, says that the wines he used to produce now make him sick.[24]

The security of a famous name offers a negative virtue. The most celebrated wine-producing regions acquired their reputation by offering quality; but today a famous name denotes, at best, nothing more than a lack of abuse. Improvement is frequently impossible within the confines of wine legislation. Italian wine laws, by supporting the biggest producers with the most muscle, penalize quality-oriented wine makers. Mario Pojer and Fiorentino Sandri, who make an outstanding Müller-Thurgau and an excellent Chardonnay in Trento in northern Italy, believe that DOC is a disadvantage for producers of top-quality wine, since it enables industrial producers to cash in on officially sanctioned denominations and to lower quality expectations (and hence prices) in consumers' minds.[25]

Their argument is demonstrated by the influence exerted by industrial producers on the laws applying to the two most famous white wine denominations in Italy, Frascati and Soave. Illegal over-production in these regions has already been referred to; but a very high level of production (7½ tons per acre) is itself not merely permitted but encouraged by the law. The three main grape varieties grown in the Frascati region are Malvasia di Candia, Malvasia di Lazio, and the ubiquitous Trebbiano. Of these, Malvasia di Lazio is by far the best. Yet the law requires that at least 70 percent of the blend of any wine sold as Frascati must be made up of Malvasia di Candia and/or Trebbiano. Malvasia di Lazio may make better wine, but it rarely produces more than 3½ tons per acre, which does not endear it to grape growers who are paid by the ton. Its use has therefore been discouraged by the DOC commission, whose members regard it as their role to represent the interests of the growers.

In Soave, the principal grape variety is Garganega, which may seem an odd choice, since it rarely ripens and the wine made from it has an unpleasantly bitter taste—like unripe apples. But there is nothing wrong with growing Garganega in Soave. The only reason why it generally does not ripen is that the growers with vineyards on the fertile plain produce much too big a crop. In the opinion of Leonildo Pieropan, whose vines are planted in the less fertile soil of the hillsides, the whole plain should be declassified and the DOC area limited to the hillsides, since only on these are DOC production limits respected. The plain should be returned to the culture of maize and other cereal crops, which was what it grew before the Second World War. He accepts that the plain will not be declassified, because the strongest political lobby is that of the large cooperatives who control 80 percent of the total production of Soave. Nevertheless, he pleads: "We should try to save Soave before it is too late."[26]

At least Pieropan, like Roberto Anselmi, the other leading producer of Soave, and Antonio Pulcini at Colli di Catone, the most highly reputed grower in Frascati, tries to compete with the cooperatives by selling his wine under the name of its denomination. Many of Italy's finest wine makers have given up on the DOC regime altogether, and sell their produce as humble "table wines"—*vini da tavola*. They include Pojer e Sandri; Silvio Jermann in Friuli; a whole range of producers of Cabernet Sauvignon–based wines in Tuscany (of which the most famous are Tignanello and Sassicaia); and nearly every grower in Tuscany who makes Vin Santo—a semi-madeirized dessert wine made from dried grapes. Yet, unlike such sanctioned wines as Chianti, Vino Nobile di Montepulciano, and Brunello di Montalcino, Vin Santo preserves the taste of the most celebrated wines of Roman Italy.[27]

A similar situation is beginning to emerge in Germany, where serious producers of red wine have come across a problem: the wine makers who make up the official tasting boards that award AP certificates were taught (at the wine-making schools of Geisenheim and Freiburg) that red wine should be produced by heating the mash of skins and grapes to 65–70°C, holding it there for a couple of hours and then pressing. This method produces wines with a lot of color but hardly any tannin or flavor; such wines can only be described as white wines colored red. This method was developed after the Second World War as a response to the problem of gray rot—which itself is the fault of the Geisenheim and Freiburg schools who have developed high-yielding clones of Pinot Noir (locally called Spätburgunder) that are susceptible to rot. There are too many grapes on the bunches: they press each other so hard that they break, the juice runs over them, and they start to rot. Fermenting at a high temperature renders inactive the oxidative enzymes contained in the rot;

and the brevity of the fermentation ensures that the wines avoid a rotten taste or color.

There is no logical reason why vine growers who have harvested healthy grapes should be forced to employ this special vinification process. Rainer Lingenfelder, a grower in Grosskarbach in the Rheinpfalz—who cultivates a rot-resistant clone of Pinot Noir called Maria Feld—has since the 1985 vintage vinified it according to standard red-wine techniques, putting it through its malolactic fermentation and maturing it in small French oak casks. His reputation was made by the AP board's refusal to issue a certificate to his 1985 Spätburgunder, with the consequence that it could not be sold as a quality wine bearing the name of its village and vineyard, but only as table wine (*Tafelwein*). By this time Lingenfelder had already made his 1986, which had chaptalized up to 100° Oeschle (about 13 percent potential alcohol), 5° more than the maximum level to which *Tafelwein* may be chaptalized. If he had also been refused an AP number for his 1986, he would not have been allowed to sell it as wine at all.

Many of the producers of serious red wines prefer not to submit it to the AP board because if at an official quality tasting a wine is rejected as imperfect, it may not even be allowed to be marketed as *Tafelwein*, since the law requires that this, too, must be free from faults. When Thomas Siegrist, a grower in Leinsweiler in the Rheinpfalz, did not put his Spätburgunder forward to the AP board—preferring to sell it as *Tafelwein*—the inspectors came to his cellars and threatened to prosecute him. He said, "Go ahead"—and alerted the press. They replied, "All right, this time we will let you off with a warning." He said, "No, prosecute me." They backed down.

The majority of serious red wines produced in Germany are sold as *Tafelwein*—the principal exception being the best of them all, the Spätburgunder made by August Kesseler in Assmanshausen. Kesseler disapproves of selling serious Spätburgunder as *Tafelwein* because it leads consumers to expect *Tafelwein* to be good, which usually it is not. Most *Tafelwein* is fit only for the European wine lake, to which it contributes in good measure. In order to compensate for overproduction of wine within the European Community, producers of humble table wine—*vin de table, vino da tavola,* or *Tafelwein*—are required to send off the equivalent of one in every three or four bottles to be distilled. Producers of officially recognized "quality wine" are exempt from this imposition. This clearly inconveniences wine makers who have chosen, for whatever reason, to work outside the established quality-wine regulations, especially since they are compensated at a very low rate by the government for the wine they send off for distillation. In Italy a winery such as Sassicaia avoids having to condemn to distillation some of its expensive Cabernet Sauvignon by buying in some cheap wine and sending that off instead.

It should be evident from the chaotic state of the European wine laws that the best interests of neither American consumers nor California vine growers are served by having an appellation system on the European model. The California appellation system that was described earlier in the chapter bears little relation to its European equivalent, because it does not impose quality control or style specification: all it does is seek to establish geographical integrity. A viticultural area may only be named on a wine label if at least 85 percent of the grapes from which the wine was made were grown in the area in question. It is up to the producer to decide whether he thinks that the Stag's Leap appellation is better suited to Riesling or to Cabernet Sauvignon, and whether he wishes to make that Riesling (or indeed that Cabernet) sweet or dry. The main reason for introducing appellations, says Dick Ward, the co-owner of the Saintsbury winery in the Carneros appellation, was that it was important that California wine producers should appear to be just as interested in quality as their European counterparts. "But we don't really want to do what they have done. It is a very American approach: we tell you what is in the bottle but we don't want to tell you what you should think of it."

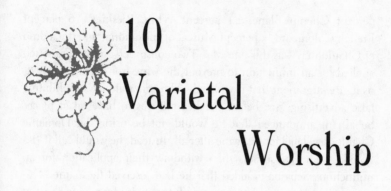

10
Varietal
Worship

WHERE WINE LAWS make no attempt to control the grapes that are planted, then the process by which vine growers decide what varieties they plant is very simple. They plant the black Bordeaux grape Cabernet Sauvignon and the white Burgundy grape Chardonnay. The most famous fine-wine area of the United States, California's Napa Valley, is planted one-quarter with Chardonnay and one-quarter with Cabernet Sauvignon. In 1990, 107 million bottles of California Chardonnay and 65 million bottles of California Cabernet Sauvignon were consumed in the United States, accounting between them for 10 percent of total table-wine consumption. In a wine market that has been in decline since 1985, sales of Cabernet Sauvignon and Chardonnay are growing at 15–20 percent a year.

Chardonnay had become so popular by 1989 that Don Sebastiani, who had taken over the running of Sebastiani Vineyards three years earlier (when his mother, Sylvia, had sacked his brother Sam), announced that he was going to release a wine named Domaine Chardonnay. He had asked for, and received, the permission of the Federal Bureau of Alcohol, Tobacco and Firearms (BATF) for his use of this brand name. It had not, however, given him permission to use the name Domaine Chardonnay for a wine made from 57 percent Chenin Blanc, 24 percent White Riesling, 16 percent French Colombard, 3 percent Muscat of Alexandria, and not a drop of Chardonnay—as this one was. Two consumers in San Francisco applied for an injunction to prevent the wine from being released, using the argument that it violated California state laws prohibiting false advertising; just before the hearing was to have taken place, Sebastiani announced that he would not be using the Domaine Chardonnay label for this wine after all. Instead, he would call it "La Sorella." The consumers then withdraw their application for an injunction. Sebastiani added that he had reserved the name "Domaine Chardonnay" for use at some future point for a wine made at least 75 percent from Chardonnay grapes, as BATF regulations require. It was suggested by some of his competitors that Sebastiani, a former California state assemblyman who had once famously declared that he had no objection to women astronauts "so long as they have a one-way ticket," had engineered the whole episode as an elaborate public relations stunt.[1]

The principal reason for the popularity of Chardonnay and Cabernet Sauvignon is that these are the varieties cultivated in Bordeaux and Burgundy.

It was the fame of Bordeaux that created the reputation of the Cabernet Sauvignon grape, not the other way around. The reputation of the fine wines of Bordeaux was created by wealthy local businessmen who planted their estates in vines largely in the period from 1670 to 1725. In some cases, they uprooted white grapevines and replaced them with black. One of these black grapevines was the Cabernet Sauvignon. It was highly regarded, but yielded little; therefore it spread only slowly. Not until the 1850s and 1860s were the leading estates sufficiently in demand and thus sufficiently profitable to be able to convert a predominance of Cabernet Franc into one of Cabernet Sauvignon.[2] Thus in Bordeaux the fame of the grape derives from the fame of the region, and not vice versa.

It is possible that the growth in the reputation of white burgundy in the course of the last hundred years has owed something to the rise to prominence of Chardonnay. It is not, however, clear when white burgundies began to be made predominantly from Chardonnay rather than Pinot Blanc or Pinot Gris. These varieties have probably been cultivated in the region for longer than Chardonnay, since they are mutations of the Pinot Noir, which is a descendant of a variety of wild vine native to France. Chardonnay is an (admittedly ancient) import from Lebanon. No one knows when Chardonnay replaced the Pinots Blanc and Gris; and no one will admit that it has not yet entirely done so. Vine growers have sought to excuse their "confusion" by claiming that the leaves of Chardonnay vines are indistinguishable from those of Pinot varieties; they are similar but they are not identical. Because Chardonnay today enjoys a better image than Pinot Blanc, vine growers in Burgundy and Champagne claim that their Pinot Blanc vines are Chardonnay. They tell you that they could not have any Pinot Blanc vines because it is not legal to plant them; but they do, and it is. Indeed, *appellation contrôlée* regulations for Champagne name Pinot Blanc as a permitted variety but make no mention of Chardonnay! Certainly, the majority of white grapevines in both regions are Chardonnay; but even an expert would find great difficulty, in a blind tasting, in distinguishing a white burgundy professedly made from Pinot Blanc—such as Lequin-Roussot's Santenay Blanc—from one made from Chardonnay.

In all probability, white-grape vineyards were converted from a predominance of Pinots Blanc and Gris to one of Chardonnay in the middle of last century. But the authorities contradict. In 1816 Jullien stated confidently that the main white-grape variety for fine wines in Burgundy was Chardonnay.[3] Yet forty years later Lavalle described the Pinot Blanc as the fine-wine white grape in Burgundy. He was a botanist, and can hardly have been ignorant of the difference between Pinot Blanc and Chardonnay.[4]

Until the 1940s, no one spoke of grape varieties, of Cabernets and Chardonnays, but of clarets (red Bordeaux) and white burgundies. Wines produced in Australia or California from any type of good-quality grapes were called "white burgundy" or "claret" if they resembled these wines in any respect. This practice led to abuses. In California after Prohibition, producers of ordinary-quality wines appropriated the names champagne, Chablis, burgundy, and claret, thus lessening their image in the eyes of the consumer. When French wine producers complained to the United States government, Congress passed an act that prohibited American wine producers from using French or other European regional names on their labels unless their wine was of the same type. Congress did not, however, determine how narrowly or widely a type should be defined. Since wine produced in Chablis in France is always dry and white, one would have thought that a "California Chablis" would at the very least conform to the original in one of these two respects. In 1965, however, Gallo introduced a "Chablis" from California that was both sweet and pink. According to the current BATF regulations, a "semi-generic" name such as "Chablis" may only be used for an American wine if it appears "in direct conjunction" with the name of the state or district in which it has been produced. In the case of Gallo's "Chablis Blanc," the state of origin—California—appears immediately under the name "Chablis" but in much smaller letters and in much paler print. It is hardly surprising in the circumstances that producers of fine wines have generally avoided these "semi-generic" terms and instead have named their creations after their unique feature—the grapes from which they were made.

The labeling of wines as Chardonnay and Cabernet Sauvignon may have begun fifty years ago as a *faut de mieux* way of saying "white burgundy" or "claret," but today's wine makers sell blended wines as Chardonnay or Cabernet Sauvignon. In California, until 1983, a Cabernet Sauvignon wine need have been produced from no more than 51 percent Cabernet Sauvignon; that figure has now been increased to 75 percent. Ridge's brilliant York Creek Cabernet Sauvignon, for instance, contains between 5 and 15 percent Merlot, depending on the vintage. In Burgundy, Drouhin is one among several major merchant companies to have taken to labeling its basic Bourgogne Blanc with the word *Chardonnay*. This may conflict with Robert Drouhin's protestation that each of his wines reflects unique vineyard characteristics: "I do not make Chardonnay but Meursault, Puligny-Montrachet, and Chassagne-Montrachet." But, as he admits, "Americans do not necessarily know that white burgundy is made from Chardonnay."[5]

The names Cabernet Sauvignon and Chardonnay have become known the world over, partly as a result of the success of California wine makers in their explicit efforts to "beat" red Bordeaux and white burgundy in blind comparative tastings. Initially they were so keen to do this that they did not bother about planting these grapes in the right soils or regions. They planted them in the Napa Valley—which is certainly not the area of California best suited to the cultivation of

Chardonnay, and possibly not to that of Cabernet Sauvignon. According to Jack Stuart, the wine maker for Silverado Vineyards, the
climate of the Napa Valley is more like that of Tuscany than of
France—which is why he decided to plant the principal Chianti
grape, Sangiovese, in 1990.[6] It is possible to find a climate much
more comparable to that of Atlantic France by traveling to the southern end of the Napa Valley, to the Carneros district, which sits on
the northern shore of San Francisco Bay. Because of cooling breezes
from the Bay, summer maximum daytime temperatures are 10°F
lower than in the Napa Valley. Kent Rasmussen, a vine grower who
settled in the region in 1979, says that since they moved there he and
his wife have only been able to sit out and eat dinner three or four
times. Carneros had been planted in vines in the nineteenth century,
but then it was left to the sheep—*los carneros*, in Spanish—until the
1960s. The gap, it has been suggested, came because the first drive
for quality was led by arrogant, didactic academics from the University of California at Davis, who wanted to prove that Cabernet
Sauvignon could produce great wine under California, not quasi-
French, conditions.[7] Certainly, Carneros Cabernet Sauvignons can
be austere and herbaceous for the first few years of their life. It was
with immediately accessible Cabernets and Chardonnays from relatively warm regions that California made its mark on the world wine
map: in the American Bicentennial tasting organized in Paris by
Steven Spurrier in 1976 the top Cabernet came from Stag's Leap
Wine Cellars in the Napa Valley, while the top Chardonnay, Château Montelena, was made from a blend of grapes from the Napa
Valley and from the Alexander Valley in Sonoma County. Before
this tasting, says Warren Winiarski, the owner of Stag's Leap Wine
Cellars, some potential customers had rejected his wine, asking,
"Why should I buy your California wine when I can get good Bor-
deaux?" After the results of the tasting were published, they telephoned him to say that his wine was better.[8]

It is hard to berate California vine growers for cultivating Cabernet and Chardonnay. They have no good native grapes of their
own. The only possible exception to this rule is Zinfandel, which is
both more popular and more successful in California than in Apulia
in Southern Italy, from where it was transplanted in the middle of
the nineteenth century. The status of Zinfandel as a quintessentially

California grape has been enhanced by the suggestion that all the Primitivo vines in Italy were killed a hundred years ago by the phylloxera louse, and that present-day Italian Primitivo is in fact Zinfandel that has been returned to its homeland. Some wonderful, dense, briery red Zinfandels are produced in California, notably by Paul Draper at Ridge Vineyards and by Joel Peterson at Ravenswood, both of whom buy their grapes from old vineyards scattered over the state. In the last ten years, however, Zinfandel has acquired among the majority of American consumers the apparently immutable image of being a sweetish pink wine. A number of restaurants have found great difficulty in persuading their customers that the Zinfandel on their list is in fact red. Commercially speaking, serious red Zinfandel is no more than a curiosity. In practice, therefore, any fine-wine variety that is planted in California has had to be imported from Europe. This actually gives California vine growers an advantage. They do not have gradually to transfer from one vine variety to another, as did growers in Bordeaux and Burgundy in the nineteenth century. They can start with a clean slate; and with only the best variety. The planting of the Napa Valley over the last generation has been compared by Hugh Johnson to the planting of Bordeaux in the period from 1650 to 1750.[9]

Quite apart from Primitivo, the Italians—along with the Spanish and the Portuguese—have great native grapes. Noble black-grape varieties native to Italy include Nebbiolo, Sangiovese, Montepulciano, Gaglioppo, and Aglianico; in Spain they include Grenache, Tempranillo, Mencia, and Graciano. In Portugal they include Touriga Nacional, Barroca, Baga, Ramisco, and Periquita. Noble white-grape varieties are fewer, but still include Aleatico, Greco, Grechetto, Arneis, and Nosiola in Italy; Malvasia and Verdejo in Spain; Arinto, Alvarinho, Louriero, Trajadura, and Fernão Pires in Portugal. The enormous potential of some of the more obscure of these varieties will be evident to anyone who has tried the Arneis delle Langhe from Castello di Neive in Piedmont in northwest Italy or the outstanding Bairrada made from Baga grapes by Luis Pato in central Portugal. For what do vine growers in these countries need Cabernet Sauvignon and Chardonnay?

These local varieties suffer from a negative image. According to Nicolas Belfrage, a London-based wine importer and retailer specializing in Italian wines, in the 1940s and 1950s Italians found themselves having to decide which way they were going to point their wine industry. They decided that, since France had already captured the fine wine sector, Italy's future could only lie in taking up the low and middle ground. This worked well until the early 1970s, when wine consumption began to fall. Because the wines which were no longer wanted were those mass-produced from native Italian grapes—Soave, Valpolicella, Chianti, etc.—other wines made from Italian grapes were caught in a "negative image trap." Vine growers who wanted an upmarket image therefore had to plant grape varieties with an upmarket image: French ones.[10]

Rather like a new pop singer seeking to establish himself by recording "cover versions" of a song made famous by someone else, the planting of French grapes by vine growers in other countries will achieve the desired effect only if—the reputation having been established—the singer/wine maker starts producing his own material. That is the route of long-term fame. It is one reason why the Rolling Stones achieved superstar status in the mid-1960s but the Animals did not.

It is particularly tempting to plant Cabernet Sauvignon and Chardonnay because they are very hardy, disease-resistant vine varieties that even in the hands of a bad wine maker will usually produce an acceptable wine. Moreover, Chardonnay, if not Cabernet Sauvignon, regularly produces large yields. Many of the good native grape varieties in Italy, Spain, and Portugal, on the other hand, have not been clonally selected to produce the best, most disease-free and highest-yielding varieties. Clonal selection involves selecting the single most successful vine in a particular vineyard, testing it in a laboratory to ensure that it is free from disease, then using it as a source of all the new plants of that variety. The problem with clonal selection is that, at present, it takes twenty years to tell if the vines which appear superior really do produce better wine. It is hoped that, in time, by taking chemical "fingerprints" of the aroma compounds of a grape by means of a gas chromatograph, it will be possible to make a judgment about the eventual quality of the wine from which it is made. It should, therefore, no longer be necessary to wait ten years for newly cloned vines to reach maturity—followed by a further ten while the wine made from grapes from ten-year-old vines reaches maturity. A grape from a three-year-old vine would suffice. Clonal selection will also be accelerated by the use of test-tube vines. It the tiniest particle of the growing tip is incubated in a test tube, a healthy baby can be produced from a diseased mother—because, if the mother vine grows fast enough, the virus does not keep up with the growing tip. One day it may even prove possible, through genetic engineering, to alter cell material in order to bring about specific changes in the resulting new vine. But this development is some way off.

It was precisely because of their hardiness and reliability that Cabernet Sauvignon and Chardonnay came to dominate the vine-yards of Bordeaux and Burgundy in the nineteenth century. In the first half of the century, according to Wilhelm Franck's book on the Médoc, the two best varieties were Cabernet Sauvignon and Car-menère, which produced wine of the same quality.[11] In the second half of the century Carmenère lost its popularity. This was not so much, I suspect, because of its susceptibility to floral abortion—Merlot, which is still popular, had the same problem—but because it yielded so little. It was said in 1868 that, whereas Cabernet Sau-vignon (itself a low yielder) produced 1¾ tons per acre, Carmenère grown in the same spot would yield only half as much.[12] Following the devastation of their vineyards by the oidium fungus in the 1850s and by the phylloxera louse in the 1870s, the Bordelais could no longer afford such a voluntary reduction of their crop. At the same time as Carmenère gave way to Cabernet Sauvignon in Bordeaux, Pinot Gris fell out of favor in Burgundy because of its tendency to degenerate and its unwillingness to produce a reliable crop.

In the same period, and for the same reason, vine growers elsewhere in Europe planted Cabernet Sauvignon. In the Ribera del Duero in Spain, Vega Sicilia was planted in 1864 with Cabernet Sauvignon, Merlot, and Malbec cuttings brought from Bordeaux. The owner was disillusioned with local varieties; he wanted varieties that he knew would produce good wine. Today it is the most famous wine in Spain, and is made 40 percent from Bordelais grape varieties and 60 percent from the local Tinto Fino—which, under the name Tempranillo, is also the predominant grape in good-quality Rioja.

According to legend, the better European grape varieties, in-cluding Cabernet Sauvignon, were brought to California in the

1850s by "Count" Agoston Haraszthy, a political exile from Hungary who, after failing to grow vines in Wisconsin, established the Buena Vista vineyard and winery in Sonoma County. But in fact, cuttings of noble French vine varieties had already been brought to California in 1833 by Jean-Louis Vignes (whose name translates as "vines"), a native of Bordeaux who planted them on his El Aliso Vineyard in Los Angeles. The first grower known to have imported superior French varieties to Northern California was Pierre Pellier, who in about 1852 brought vines with him from the Bordeaux region to be planted in his brother's nursery and vineyard near San Jose.[13] In 1857 another Frenchman, Charles Lefranc—unhappy with the quality of the wine he had made from the Spanish Mission grape at his New Almaden Vineyard in Santa Clara County—sent home for some better varieties. In the 1860s and 1870s he made a famous "claret" from these French varieties—mostly Malbec, with some Cabernet Sauvignon mixed in.[14]

With the exception of growers such as Pellier and Lefranc, however, scarcely any French fine wine varieties were grown before the late 1880s. The principal variety for producing fine red wines was Zinfandel, and the main varieties for fine white ones were Chasselas and a type of Riesling. Charles Wetmore, executive officer of the State Board of Viticultural Commissioners, reported in 1884 that Cabernet Sauvignon was only known "experimentally" in California and that Chardonnay was "not practically known" at all. He attributed the failure of the early importations of noble varieties to the old tradition of short pruning, which worked with heavy-cropping Spanish varieties but not with fine French ones.[15]

The second half of the 1880s saw the first wholescale importation of fine-wine varieties. By the end of the nineteenth century a number of prestigious "clarets" were being produced in California. At La Questa in the Santa Cruz Mountains, a wine was made from precisely the same mix of grape varieties as was then planted at Château Margaux, this being the preferred wine of the owner Emmett H. Rixford. At Mira Valle, also in the Santa Cruz Mountains, Pierre Klein, an Alsatian who had come to California in 1875, planted a vineyard with the Bordeaux grapes Cabernet Sauvignon, Cabernet Franc, Merlot, and Petit Verdot; he won a gold medal at the Paris Exposition of 1900.[16] At another place called Miravalle,

this time in the Napa Valley, Tiburcio Parrott, the wealthy illegiti-
mate son of a San Francisco banker, produced an outstanding "Margaux" from Bordeaux grape varieties. At Inglenook, also in the Napa
Valley, the Finnish sea captain Gustav Niebaum invested the fortune he had made from the Alaskan fur-sealing trade in a vineyard
which he planted with vines imported from Bordeaux, Burgundy,
and the Rhine Valley. His winery is now owned by the Heublein
conglomerate; but his house was purchased, and part of his vineyard
replanted, by the film director Francis Ford Coppola.[17]

Since 1979 Coppola has produced an excellent Cabernet
Sauvignon–based blend called Rubicon, made from grapes grown on
his part of the old Inglenook estate. It does not taste like Bordeaux,
however. If you are looking for a copy of a claret or a white burgundy, you will not find it in the warm-climate wines of most of
California. It has already been pointed out in the chapter on wine
tastings that they are made from riper grapes, with lower levels of
acidity, and appear richer and more impressive in their youth.

Climate, however, is not so important a factor as wine-making
technique. This is demonstrated by the history of Chardonnay in
California. The first serious California Chardonnays were made in
the 1950s by Martin Ray (whose vineyard is now called Mount
Eden) in the Santa Cruz Mountains; Fred McCrea at Stony Hill in
the Napa Valley; and by Brad Webb at Hanzell in Sonoma County.
Although Ray and the McCreas fermented their wine in oak casks—
more or less following the Burgundian model—the wine that set the
style for the next generation was that of Hanzell. The vineyard here
had been planted in 1952 by James D. Zellerbach, the former United
States Ambassador to Italy who had developed (not surprisingly) a
taste for Le Montrachet during his time in Europe. He built a winery
modeled on the Château de Clos de Vougeot and filled it with Limousin oak casks from Burgundy. But the wine he poured into the casks
had been fermented in stainless steel tanks. According to Zellerbach's
wine maker Brad Webb, they were using experimental methods to
find the best way to make Chardonnay in California: "confusing the
situation with more variables would have been foolish."

Zellerbach died in 1961 and the wines were made famous by
Joe Heitz, who had bought them at auction. The Hanzell style of
wine making dominated California Chardonnay for the next gener-

ation. It became standard practice to pick the grapes very ripe, ferment them in stainless steel tanks, prevent the wine from going through its malolactic fermentation, then clean it up before transferring it to Limousin oak casks. On the face of it, it seems surprising that California wine makers should have preferred Limousin oak, from the west of France, to oak from central France (Nevers, Alliers, and Tronçais) or from the east (Vosges). In its native country, Limousin oak is used principally for the maturation of top-class cognac, not wine. The oak trees which grow in the Limousin department are probably a different species from those which grow in central and eastern France: they grow out as much as they grow up, so the grains are wider and the wood is more tannic. Wine matured in Limousin casks develops a much more marked oak character than wine matured in wood from the forests of central or eastern France. Alan Phillips, the wine maker at Monticello Cellars in the Napa Valley, matured his first two vintages of Chardonnay, 1980 and 1981, in Limousin oak, but found that it gave the wine "a bourbony-type character," and converted to oak from central and eastern France from the 1982 vintage onwards. Since Burgundy lies in central eastern France, and since white burgundies tend to taste of wine rather than of bourbon, one might have expected the California wine makers of the 1970s to have chosen oak from central or eastern rather than western France for the maturation of their Chardonnays. But they were crucially influenced by an article written by Dick Graff, the owner of Chalone, in which he said that producers of white burgundy used local oak, which was similar to Limousin. Graff had visited France in 1967 because Martin Ray and Douglas Day, the new owner of Hanzell, had refused to tell him where they obtained their barrels or how they treated them. Unfortunately, what he wrote on his return about the type of oak used in Burgundy was wrong.

Largely because of the preference shown by wine makers for Limousin oak, the California Chardonnays of the 1970s were much more oaky—and were ready to drink much sooner—than their Burgundian counterparts. Ironically, it was not this type of California Chardonnay that performed best in the now-legendary Caves de la Madeleine wine tasting of 1976. The top wine, Château Montelena 1973, was cleaner and more austere than its compatriots, only about 7 percent of it having been matured in new Limousin casks. It was described by one of the tasters as "fruity and elegant." Its success encouraged other California Chardonnay producers to try to make a more elegant style of wine than hitherto—using less Limousin oak. They were encouraged in their efforts by a number of French wine makers, who succeeded in talking down the results of the Caves de la Madeleine tasting by saying that they made wines that were meant to be drunk with food, and by a seminal article in *The New York Times* in 1981 by Frank Prial, who criticized California Chardonnays for being clumsy and overpowering, too aggressive and alcoholic to go with food. "They are show-off wines made by vintners who seem to be saying, 'I can outchardonnay any kid on this block,' " he wrote. "There should be a special label warning that says, 'This wine was designed for competition and is not to be used for family dining.' "[18]

In the early 1980s many California wine makers tried to make food wines. The results were disastrous. They had abandoned the naturally ripe style of wine that suited their warmer climate for a thin, anemic imitation of white burgundy. These wines bore more resemblance to Muscadet than to white burgundy and had the critics crying out for the ripe, buttery style of California Chardonnay that they had condemned only a few years earlier.

In 1986 Robert Parker looked back to the heyday of California wines at the end of the 1970s and contrasted it with their decline in the first half of the 1980s. He said that the falloff of interest in California wines had less to do with the stronger dollar and better harvests in Europe than with the attitude of wine makers who had been taught by the University of California at Davis to produce technically perfect wines with just the right amount of acidity and alcohol but very little flavor.[19]

The best California Chardonnay producers have given up trying to use their own methods and have taken up copying Burgundy instead. They have turned their backs on what they were taught at the University of California at Davis—that white burgundies were dirty and defective, and that they should discount what people did elsewhere in the world—and started to apply the wine-making methods they have learned on their visits to France. They have taken to fermenting their wines in barrel and afterward keeping them in contact with the lees (mostly dead yeast cells) left over from fermentation. During fermentation in cask, the yeasts absorb colloids from the tannins in the wood; at the end of fermentation the yeasts digest themselves and liberate the colloids, giving fat to the wine. It might be thought that barrel fermentation would produce more oaky white wines than fermenting a wine in tank and then putting it in barrel afterward. In fact the opposite is true. Red wines have tannins to protect their aromas, white wines do not; they need to be fermented in wood so the yeasts can protect their aromas for them.

The best Chardonnays in California are made by wineries such as Simi, Sonoma-Cutrer, and Saintsbury, using overtly Burgundian techniques. It is not simply for the sake of the pun that the Saintsbury winery T-shirt bears the inscription, "Beaune in the USA." Nor was it through ignorance that, in a blind tasting during a conference on Chardonnay held in Burgundy in 1990, Gérard Boudot, the wine maker at Domaine Etienne Sauzet in Puligny-Montrachet, identified Simi 1985 Reserve Chardonnay as his own wine.

The same predominance of technique over grape variety is evident in the case of red wines. Although thirteen grape varieties are permitted to be used in Châteauneuf-du-Pape, they do not include any of the Bordeaux varieties Cabernet Sauvignon, Merlot, Cabernet Franc, Malbec, and Petit Verdot. Nevertheless, a number of wines made in recent vintages by top Châteauneuf-du-Pape estates such as Château de Mont Redon, Château de la Gardine, and Domaine du Vieux Lazaret have tannin and structure that is reminiscent of red Bordeaux. Whereas growers in Châteauneuf traditionally fermented their wines in contact with their stalks for several weeks and matured them in large old oak barrels for several years—intending that they should be ready for drinking soon after they were bottled—the estates in question are advised by an enologist, Noël Rabot, who has introduced the Bordelais techniques of destalking the grapes and maturing the wines for roughly one year in small new oak casks, intending that they should then mature for a long period in bottle.

Although present-day Rioja does not taste like modern red Bordeaux, it is quite possible that it preserves the taste of the Bordeaux of a hundred years ago by employing wine-making methods that are a fossilization of historic Bordelais practice, such as the long aging of the wines in old 850-gallon oak casks, compared with the eighteen to twenty-four months' storage in a mixture of new and nearly new oak casks which is general in Bordeaux today. During the 1840s, Don Luciano de Murrieta, a refugee from the Carlist Wars, had settled in London and acquired a taste for fine French wines. On his way back to Rioja in 1850, he made a thorough study of the latest practices in Bordeaux and then reorganized the cellars of the Duque de la Victoria on the same lines. The wines, matured in oak casks, won enormous acclaim. In the 1850s and 1860s French merchants turned to Rioja when their own vineyards were devastated by oidium and phylloxera, and the new demand for their products encouraged other Rioja producers to take up Bordelais methods. But very little Cabernet Sauvignon was ever planted in Rioja, because it yielded too little. Bordelais techniques were applied to the produce of the native Tempranillo, Graciano, Carignan, and Grenache grapes.

For most producers and consumers, all these questions of copying—of losing one's national identity—are irrelevant. All that matters is whether Cabernet Sauvignon and Chardonnay produce good wines outside Bordeaux and Burgundy. Indeed, are they as good as—or even better than—red Bordeaux and white burgundies?

There is nothing intrinsically superior about Champagne, Burgundy, and Bordeaux; there is no reason why wines of the same quality cannot be produced elsewhere. If these French wines achieved fame, and others did not, it had much more to do with political geography and superior wine making than with the climate or soil.

Since Roman times, the great wines of France have been produced by the bourgeoisie of the cities. The wines with the greatest reputation under the Romans were those produced by the cities of Vienne, Bordeaux, Autun, and Paris. These remain the great wines of France today: respectively, those of the Northern Rhône (Hermitage, Côte Rôtie, and Condrieu), Bordeaux, Burgundy, and Champagne. The French bourgeoisie derived personal pride from serving their own wines at their tables—and civic pride from the production of wines worthy of export. In the most famous wine law of the Middle Ages, in 1395, Philip the Bold, Duke of Burgundy, ordered the uprooting of Gamay vines, which he considered to be "wicked and disloyal." Plantations of Gamay had increased at the expense of the noble Pinot Noir because the Pinot vine required much more attention and produced many fewer grapes; and there was a shortage of vineyard workers following the Black Death of 1349. This was disastrous to the ambitions of Philip the Bold, who was at the time more powerful than the French king—a point he wanted to rub in by staging magnificent festivities at his palace in Paris. He had to be sure that the wine he offered was up to scratch. When he described Gamay as disloyal, he really meant it. He may have failed to achieve a political position that would enable his grandson to acquire a crown, but he succeeded in creating the reputation of burgundy as the greatest wine of France and the one that, for the next three hundred years, everyone else, including the Champenois, tried to copy.

In medieval France, the cities of Vienne, Bordeaux, Autun, and Paris were not the only ones whose bourgeoisie produced great wine. But these were the cities that enjoyed the easiest access to the wealthy markets of northern Europe, where wine sold at the highest prices. Before the coming of the railways in the midnineteenth century, the only way of reaching these markets was by sea or river—or by one or two land routes suitable for heavy carts. (Burgundy was not too far from Paris and was where Parisians went when their harvest failed.) We have heard of the wines of Sancerre and Saumur, but not of those of Bourges and Oiron. The difference is not one of soil or climate. Sancerre and Saumur exported their wines because they are on the Loire; Bourges and Oiron did not, because they are not. Yet in terms of quality, the red Vin de Thouarsais produced from Cabernet Franc by Michel Gigon, the only vine grower remaining in Oiron, loses nothing to the majority of the red wines of Saumur and Saumur-Champigny.

In establishing a reputation, the quality of a site has not, in most cases, been particularly important. The land around Bordeaux is poor and flat: so much so that the Portuguese who came to Pomerol in the twelfth century, looking for areas to settle, rejected the site of Vieux Château Certan as too arid and dry, and gave it its name— sertão means "desert" in Portuguese. The soil was so poor that its peasants were exempted from paying local taxes. It did not matter that the soil in Bordeaux was not particularly suitable, as wines could be made superior by taking greater care over cultivation and vinification—providing there were consumers willing to pay for them.

After all, that is the principle on which many of the great California wines of the 1970s were produced—in Napa and Sonoma counties, close to the wealthy, wine-drinking market of San Francisco. No one has attributed the differences between these principally to the nature of the soil—so why do so with the wines of Bordeaux?

What can be said is that the climate of Bordeaux and Burgundy ideally suits the grapes that are grown in each of the regions. That is because Cabernet Sauvignon in Bordeaux, and Chardonnay and Pinot Noir in Burgundy, lie at their limits of cultivation; and it is true of all fruits that the longer the growing season, the closer they are grown to their cultivable limits, the better the quality of the product. The longer the growing season, the greater the extraction of nutriments from the soil, the more complex the flavors that are produced. On the whole, Spanish oranges are better than North African, French olives are better than Spanish, and English apples are better than French. The best tea is grown in relatively cold conditions, such as Darjeeling in the foothills of the Himalayas and high-grown Ceylon from the hills in the center of the island. So is the best coffee, such as Jamaican Blue Mountain, Kibo Chagga from the lower slopes of Mount Kilimanjaro in Tanzania, and the Colombian coffee produced on the foothills of the Andes.

Different grape varieties have different limits of cultivation. Mourvèdre used to be cultivated all over Provence, but since being grafted onto American rootstock after the vineyards were devastated by the phylloxera louse a hundred years ago, it ripens later, and can only be grown near the Mediterranean coast, principally in Bandol. The wines produced under this *appellation* must by law comprise a minimum of 50 percent Mourvèdre, which here, at its cultivable limit, produces a superb red wine. Mourvèdre was grown in the region last century but by the time the *appellation* was created in 1941 it had all but died out. Lucien Peyraud, the owner of Domaine Tempier, persuaded the authorities to require people to plant Mourvèdre, as it was on this that the quality of Bandol depended. Today Peyraud's sons make the most expensive, and possibly the best, wines in the region. The whole area maintains very high standards, with the Bandol produced by the La Roque cooperative offering particularly good value. Riesling, on the other hand, does best in the Rhine and Mosel valleys, which in some parts are little warmer

than southern England. Alsatian Riesling lacks the delicacy of the
best German Riesling; it is never of the same quality. Nor is wine
made from Riesling elsewhere (in most cases illegally) in France. It
is just too warm.

If every region is matched to its ideal grape variety, then only in
climates comparable to those of Bordeaux and Burgundy can Cabernet Sauvignon and Chardonnay be regarded as suitable—at least as
challengers to red Bordeaux and white burgundy. Quasi-Burgundian
Chardonnays are produced in those parts of California which enjoy
a climate comparable to that of Burgundy—not in the Napa Valley.

The example of Carneros has already been discussed. This region attracted a lot of attention during the 1980s, but by the end of
the decade many people were looking toward Santa Barbara County,
in part because of the purchase by the large and prestigious Mondavi
company first of the Tepusquet vineyard and then of the Byron
vineyard and winery in the Santa Maria Valley. Michael Mondavi
went so far as to describe Santa Maria as the Burgundy of America.

One might expect Santa Barbara County, which is closer to Los
Angeles than to San Francisco—indeed close enough to Los Angeles
to have a ready-made market there—to be too hot for Cabernet
Sauvignon, let alone Chardonnay or Pinot Noir. But near the coast
the climate is perfect. The coast runs from east to west, as do the
coastal mountains. A westerly wind blows up the Santa Maria and
Santa Ynez valleys, cooling them but itself warming up as it goes.
Only a narrow band of land—between fifteen and thirty miles from
the coast—is ideal for vine growing. Any closer to the coast, and it
is too cool; any farther away, and it is too warm. Certainly the
temperature can reach 100°F during the day in midsummer, but it
falls to half that in the evening. The hot weather never stays, because
the heat brings in fog from the ocean.

Richard Sanford, a geographer by training, says that he looked
all over the West Coast for the right place to grow Chardonnay and
Pinot Noir before settling in the Santa Ynez Valley in 1970. Jim
Clendenen of Au Bon Climat considers this story to be unlikely: how
can Sanford have scoured the United States looking for the best site
to plant Chardonnay and Pinot Noir, given that—after finding his
site—the first grape varieties he planted were Cabernet Sauvignon
and Riesling? Nevertheless, Clendenen considers the vineyard San-

ford planted—up until 1990 called Benedict, but now renamed Talinda Oaks Ranch—to be both the coolest vineyard in California and the best vineyard in California for Chardonnay and Pinot Noir.

It remains a moot point whether Santa Barbara truly deserves the title "Burgundy of America," given its situation at 35° N, compared with Burgundy at 47° N—and therefore a much shorter growing season, with many fewer hours of daylight in the summer. Nevertheless, the Benedict vineyard has, not only in the hands of Jim Clendenen but also in those of Rick Longoria (the wine maker at Gainey), produced some of the finest Chardonnay and Pinot Noir to have come out of the United States.

This said, the argument that the finest wines are made in marginal climates has its detractors—not least among those wine makers who seek to cultivate cool-climate grapes in warm regions. One of these is Miguel Torres, whose firm's Cabernet-based Gran Coronas Black Label shot to fame when it won the 1979 *Gault Millau* "Wine Olympics." He argues that, if it was thought in the past that great wines could be produced only in those areas of Europe which enjoyed an Atlantic (e.g., Bordeaux) or Continental (e.g., Burgundy) climate, this was only because Mediterranean areas were too hot during September and October. The grapes were too warm when brought in to the winery, and fermentation was too rapid, at too high a temperature.[20] Moreover, grapes ripen very fast in hot climates, turning from underripe to overripe in a matter of hours. The problem of fermentation temperatures has been overcome by the introduction of temperature-controlled vats; that of fast ripening of the grapes has been solved by the development of harvesting machines. Torres says that in 1985 his Cabernet Sauvignon grapes were picked by machine in peak condition in three to four days; by hand it would have taken two weeks and the second week's fruit would have been "lousy, totally overripe."[21]

The problem with Torres's argument is that he is prejudiced by his own position. If he cultivates cool-climate grapes in a warm region, then he would say that, wouldn't he? If wine makers prefer warm climates, it is because the risks are less and the rewards at least as great. After all, wines produced from cool-climate grapes in warm regions "win" comparative tastings against red Bordeaux and white burgundies because they have more alcohol and more opulent fruit. This is not to decry Torres's red wines, however, particularly his "ordinary" Gran Coronas, a classic example of a warm-climate wine, and an excellent value for money.

It is possible to find a cool microclimate in a warm region, simply by going uphill. Torres grows Chardonnay and Riesling up in the mountains, at 2,500 feet. In the South of France, Aimé Guibert produces an outstanding, if no longer underpriced, Cabernet Sauvignon–based wine at Mas de Daumas Gassac, twenty miles northwest of Montpellier, in a part of the country which is generally far too hot for the cultivation of Cabernet Sauvignon. But the estate lies at the limits of vine cultivation, just below the moorland, hot by day but cold by night, at seven hundred feet but with the climatic equivalent of 1,600. The grapes are harvested early in October, at the same time as in the Médoc—not least because the vineyard faces not south, as is usual, but northwest. In warm climates it is often necessary to plant cool-climate grapes on north-facing slopes in order to produce fine wine. Angelo Gaja in Barbaresco, Antinori in Orvieto (for their "Cervaro della Sala"), and Jacques Reynaud at Château Rayas in Châteauneuf-du-Pape all cultivate Chardonnay vines on north-facing slopes.

The effect of the climate also depends on the nature of the soil. A warm soil mitigates a cool climate. Dark soil, such as the slate of many Mosel vineyards, absorbs heat more rapidly than light soil and radiates it more rapidly. A cool soil mitigates a warm climate. The ripening of grapes in the Carneros appellation is retarded, not merely by a breeze from San Francisco Bay, but by the cooling effect of a clay soil. One might not think of Pomerol as hot, but its clay soil lengthens the ripening period of the early ripening Merlot grape sufficiently to produce a fine wine.

In order successfully to cultivate Cabernet Sauvignon, the soil has to have the right structure. Many growers in Coteaux d'Aix-en-Provence have planted Cabernet Sauvignon in the belief that a noble grape will automatically produce a good wine. But Cabernet needs unfertile ground; in Coteaux d'Aix-en-Provence there is too much fertile topsoil above the underlying gravel, so Cabernet produces a wine that has deep color and high alcohol but that is thin and harsh.

At Mas de Daumas Gassac, there is a unique outcrop of glacial
debris, 4 to 6 meters deep, covering 20 hectares, which provides the
right soil conditions for Cabernet Sauvignon.

It is a matter of intense dispute whether, beyond physical effects
such as these, the chemical and biological constituents of the soil
greatly affect the nature of the wine made from vines growing on it.
On the one hand, most soils contain all the chemical elements a
vine needs; and, to those that do not, the necessary chemicals can be
added. There is absolutely no difference between nitrogen or phosphorous pre-existing in the soil and the same chemicals added in a
pure form. Of course, if chemical fertilizers are added to excess, the
vine produces too much fruit or vegetation, and the wine suffers; but
one cannot blame the chemicals for a vine grower's abuse of them.

Can one quantify the relative importance of the microclimate
and soil in making a fine wine? It depends on what side of the fence
a wine maker is standing. Whereas many Californians might say that
a fine wine is 10 percent soil, 30 percent climate, and 60 percent
wine making, a Frenchman is just as likely to say the opposite. It is
an American characteristic to consider that everything in life is measurable. Since climate can be measured, and soil cannot, most
American vine growers consider that climate is more important than
soil. It is a French characteristic, on the other hand, to believe that
only those elements that cannot be measured are important. Accordingly, French wine makers uphold the supremacy of soil over climate. They are romantics who believe in their birthright, in the
quasi-mystical qualities of their land. They have spilled so much
blood over it over the centuries that they could hardly think otherwise.

Psychology apart, the French make a great deal of noise about
the uniqueness of the soils of the *grands* and *premiers crus* of Burgundy and the classed-growth *châteaux* of Bordeaux because they
have to. Only by convincing people that their soil somehow endows
their finest wines with unique properties can they justify the prices
they charge—or win the argument as to whether the wines they
produce can be equaled elsewhere. It is, however, a little difficult to
fathom how the soils of the classed-growth *châteaux* of Bordeaux can
be unique when they keep moving. Because the brand names of the
châteaux have been classified—not their vineyards—many of them

have gotten away with swallowing other, lower-rated, or unclassified *châteaux*. There is nothing to prevent the wine from all being made together, with the less good vats sold under the name of the lower-rated *château*. Where this is done, the belief of the classed-growth *châteaux* in the superiority of their soils is patently contradicted; for how can it be said that Château Rausan-Ségla—which heads the second growths in the 1855 classification of the leading *châteaux* of the Médoc—possesses the finest vineyard soil in the commune of Margaux after Château Margaux itself, when it has absorbed the humble *cru bourgeois* Château Lamouroux?

Certainly much of the flavor of wines *does* come from the soil—from mineral substances taken up through the roots of the vine. These form what is called the sugar-free dry extract of the wine. In 1978–79 the University of Piacenza in Lombardy studied wines made from the black Vernatsch grape from nineteen different sites in the South Tyrol. It established that the color, acidity, and aroma substances of the wines were all fundamentally affected by the mineral content of the soil. It is not fanciful, for instance, to taste minerals in the wines made from the Schlossböckelheimer Kupfergrube vineyard by the Nahe State Domain. *Kupfergrube* means "copper mine," though early this century it was reshaped and turned into terraced vineyards by convict labor. Mas de Daumas Gassac is made 80 percent from Cabernet Sauvignon, but it does not taste like claret. Aimé Guibert, the owner, points out that "the *terroir* [soil, more or less] is so strong that it makes Pommard with Cabernet." Actually, it tastes more like a Rhône wine—but his point remains.

The issue of soil is brought to a head by the question of limestone. Vine growers in Burgundy believe that Chardonnay and Pinot Noir can only be grown successfully on limestone. When asked why, they can only reply that it is because, in Burgundy, Chardonnay and Pinot Noir are grown on limestone subsoil. In America, most Chardonnay and Pinot Noir vineyards are not planted on limestone, and therefore vine growers do not believe that limestone is important. There are exceptions, however. When Michael Mondavi described Santa Maria as "the Burgundy of America," it was partly because of its climate and partly because—like the Côte d'Or in Burgundy—it is an old seabed made up of fossil shells—limestone. The most fervent California *terroiristes* (believers in the importance of *terroir*) are Josh Jensen of Calera and Dick Graff of Chalone, two men who have planted vineyards in the inaccessible heights of the Gavilan mountains because that is where they have been able to find limestone. In Graff's opinion, "The point of having limestone is that you can make Burgundian wines. The Burgundian quality comes from the soil." It might not be fanciful to argue that Graff and Jensen are only able to produce top-class Chardonnay and Pinot Noir in what is—at least by Burgundian standards—an inappropriately warm climate because they have planted their vines on appropriate soil. But there is no evidence to suggest that limestone soil gives a "Burgundian quality"—a specific character—to the wine.

It has been suggested that limestone exerts a positive effect on wine quality by controlling vine vigor: that the calcium sequestrates the magnesium needed for photosynthesis, so the plant struggles. This hypothesis would certainly help to explain why Chardonnay grown on limestone tends to produce a small crop of grapes that make a concentrated wine capable of long-term aging, whereas Chardonnay grown on a more fertile soil generally produces a larger crop of grapes which make a simpler, more fruity wine. One reason why some Cabernet Sauvignon, Chardonnay, and Pinot Noir plantations in the United States have failed to produce fine wine is that the soil is too fertile. In most of the great vineyards of Europe the soil is meager, and the vine has to dig its roots deep in search of nutriments. The reason for this is historical: in the past farmers were prohibited from planting vines on fertile soils because they were needed for food crops. The encroachment of vineyards onto arable land was one (but not the only) reason for the famous edict imposed by the Roman emperor Domitian in 92 A.D. prohibiting the planting of any new vines in Italy and requiring that half the vineyards in all the provinces of the Empire (including present-day France) be grubbed up.[22]

A vine planted on overly fertile soil can be forced to dig deeper by planting it close to other vines so that it is forced to compete for nutrition. Close planting is the standard procedure in French vineyards; in California and Australia the vines are usually planted much farther apart, with only one-sixth as many of them to the acre. A vine in California is required to carry six times as much fruit as its counterpart in France simply in order to produce the same yield. Close

planting would not be possible in most of the vine-growing regions
of California or Australia because soil moisture evaporates too rapidly: a grower in a warm climate who close-planted his vines would
have to irrigate them—which would defeat the whole point, since
irrigation encourages the development of a superficial surface root
system. Moreover, close planting on fertile soil unbalances and con-
fuses the vines; it may even cause them to abandon their efforts to set
fruit and to dedicate themselves to producing vegetation. The best
that a vine grower with a fertile soil in a warm climate can do is to
encourage vines to dig deeper by tilling the soil around them in order
to kill off surface roots. Otherwise he just has to wait. Vines in many
parts of America and Australia are too young. As they become older,
they delve deeper, and a wine which initially tasted very much of the
grape variety, but not of much else, comes to taste uniquely of the
soil of the region in which it is made. Or at least that is the theory.
We shall see whether in time it is possible to discern a California
Chardonnay from an Australian one.

Young vines do offer the advantage of producing wine that often
shows prematurely well in its youth. Cabernet Sauvignons and
Chardonnays made from young vines in America and Australia often
"beat" those from Bordeaux and Burgundy in blind tastings for this
reason—the fruit is more immediate. Young vines can produce excellent wine in good vintages, but the produce of old vines is much
better in bad ones. Old vines have deeper roots, particularly if the
soil is porous. In such soil, the roots have to reach down to the water
table to find permanent water supplies. This not only enables them
to better withstand drought, but also makes them less susceptible to
rot. When rain follows drought, vines with only surface root systems—young vines and those planted on overly irrigated or poorly
drained soil—take up water so fast that the skins of the grapes split,
and rot results.

One cannot, however, write off as a consequence of the youth
of vines in other countries the fact that Bordeaux and Burgundy are
still producing wines from Cabernet Sauvignon and Chardonnay
that are the envy of the world. The vines are not necessarily younger.
The coming of prosperity to Bordeaux in the 1970s enabled many
proprietors to replant their vineyards: in 1979, 57 percent of the
Cabernet Sauvignon vines in Bordeaux were less than ten years old.

They produce their best and most concentrated grapes between the ages of twenty and thirty.

The vineyards of Bordeaux and Burgundy have been provided with superior clones of Cabernet Sauvignon and Chardonnay by three hundred years of natural selection. Vine growers in the United States have been prevented from planting these clones by the attitudes of the University of California at Davis and Oregon State University, the only institutions in their respective states that are licensed to import clonal material from Europe. They are licensed to do so, but in general they have not. The University of California at Davis, which pioneered grape-virus detection in the 1950s, has developed its own virus-free clones of Chardonnay and Cabernet Sauvignon—selections which it has made on the grounds of health and productivity, with no regard to quality. The disappointing quality of most Chardonnay produced in Oregon should be attributed principally to the Davis clone (locally called UCD 108) that most growers have planted. UCD 108 sets so much crop that it cannot ripen except in unusually warm vintages. The most that can be said of the wine that has been made from it is that it is boring. It is because of UCD 108 that Craig Broadley, a wine producer in Monroe in central Oregon, says: "We hate Chardonnay and it hates us."

During the 1970s and 1980s the importation of superior clones of Cabernet Sauvignon and Chardonnay into California from Burgundy was prohibited because Dr. Austin Goheen of the Department of Plant Pathology at Davis had developed a theory that the main differences between clonal types were not genetic but were a function of the degree of infection.[23] Growers who have planted vineyards during the last generation have therefore had to choose between planting the easily available Davis selections, scrabbling around old vineyards looking for other plant material, and smuggling in cuttings from Europe in a suitcase. Those who have chosen the latter option have not always found that their selections produce superior wine. It is simply not possible to tell how a clone will mutate once it has been planted on a different training system in a different soil in a different climate. All plants will mutate to suit local climatic conditions. The Chardonnay clones that produce the finest white burgundies will not necessarily produce the finest Chardonnays when they are transplanted to the West Coast of the United States. Certainly that accords with the experience of those American vine growers who have planted contraband cuttings of the red burgundy vine Pinot Noir. The first Pinot Noir vineyards in Oregon were planted by David Lett at Eyrie Vineyards in the Willamette Valley in 1966 in conditions very different from those prevailing in Burgundy: the soil was not limestone but a volcanic clay loam; the vines were not planted close together and trained close to the ground on the Burgundian model but were spaced widely and trained high, in accordance with contemporary California practice. Lett planted principally the Wädenswil clone, from Wädenswil in Switzerland, but he also put in some cuttings from the Domaine de la Romanée-Conti which had "somehow" found their way into California. The Wädenswil clone was responsible for the 1975 Eyrie Vineyards Pinot Noir South Block Reserve which put Oregon on the world viticultural map when it beat a Chambertin-Clos de Bèze 1961 in a tasting organized by the Burgundy merchant Robert Drouhin in 1980. (This will be discussed in more detail in the next chapter.) The Romanée-Conti clone, on the other hand (says Lett), made "shitty wine."

11
Old Wine
in New Bottles

I HAVE ALREADY suggested that young vines produce wine that often shows particularly well in its youth. Does this make wine of this sort especially desirable? Many people have always preferred the taste of young wines: the taste of fruit and the effect of alcohol. Yet, in the past it was often necessary to keep wines for many years before they were ready to drink. The problem that wine makers faced was that they could either make wines which were good to drink young, or ones which were microbiologically stable—but not both.

In order to ensure their stability, wines in the past contained more sulphur, acidity, and tannin than they do today. The great German wines of the past contained up to one gram of sulphur per liter, compared with legal limits today of 350 milligrams per liter for Auslesen and 400 milligrams per liter for Beerenauslesen. They had to be kept for twenty years before drinking, in order that the sulphur content should diminish by 50 percent. Even today German wines and Sauternes continue to be criticized for being "oversulphured"—when actually they are only young.

Last century red Bordeaux was far more acidic a wine than it is today. Much more of the Petit Verdot variety was cultivated, even though this rarely ripened and, even when ripe, contained one and a half times as much malic acid as Cabernet Sauvignon and three times as much as Merlot. Since the last war, plantings of Merlot have greatly increased. On the one hand, the higher levels of acidity used to be necessary so that the wines could withstand long aging in cask until they were sold; on the other, the long cask aging was necessary in order to soften wines that were picked earlier and were therefore more acid than they are today. In the Rheingau in Germany—until the introduction of the selective picking of ripe grapes (Auslesen) in the middle of last century—wines had to be kept in barrel for between ten and twenty years, in order that their acidity should diminish.[1]

In the past, Bordeaux contained a level of tannin found today only in a few traditionally made Barolos. It contained a higher proportion of more tannic grape varieties; the fermentation temperature was not controlled; and the wine was kept in the fermentation vats after fermentation had finished, in contact with the grape skins for three or four weeks, compared with one or two today. The last vintage to have been made generally in the "old-fashioned" way was 1945. By all accounts, neither the Château Latour nor the Château Mouton-Rothschild of that year is yet ready for drinking.

Until the recent introduction of heat exchangers and stainless steel vats (which can be cooled by running water down their sides), there was no means of accurately controlling the fermentation temperature: wine makers simply threw lumps of ice into the vats. Yet it is the length and temperature of fermentation which determine the character of a red wine. Red wine is different from white because of the coloring matter and tannins contained in the skins of the grapes. The longer and higher the temperature of the fermentation, the more substances—both desirable and undesirable—are extracted from the skins of black grapes. Wine makers must choose between a shorter, hotter fermentation—which extracts more tannin—and a longer, cooler one—which produces more aroma molecules. The tannins are responsible for the development of most of the flavors that we consider desirable in a bottle-aged fine wine; only a red wine that is intended to be drunk young is fermented at a relatively cool 75–80°F, at which temperature not too many tannins are extracted.

As a result of the influence of Emile Peynaud, Emeritus Professor of Oenology at Bordeaux University—who now acts as consultant wine maker to a number of Bordelais *châteaux*—fermentations have become longer and cooler in the last twenty years. Peynaud says that for a fine wine, the ideal fermentation temperature is no more than 85°F, irrespective of grape variety. He says that it is dangerous to ferment a wine at a temperature higher than this, because the yeasts work faster, tire more quickly, and are therefore more likely to stop reproducing. This causes fermentation to cease, perhaps with some unfermented sugar left in the wine.[2] Not everyone is prepared to adopt such a defensive attitude to wine making. The red wine at Domaine de Chevalier is vinified at a high 90°F. It used to be lower, but in 1974 one vat was accidentally fermented at 95°F and found to be better than the rest. There are those who find a certain sameness in wines which have been *peynaudisés*. According to one story, a Bordelais proprietor, no lover of Peynaud's methods, was given a glass of wine by a visitor and asked to identify it. He tasted it and said, "I cannot tell you where this wine comes from, but, tell me, was it made by Emile Peynaud?" The wine was Greek, Château Carras. The consultant wine maker to Château Carras is Emile Peynaud.

Certainly, Peynaud's influence has been substantial. After all, wine making is not a process that changes rapidly. A wine maker, unlike a chef or even a brewer, does not get much chance to experiment. A chef cooks at least one meal every day; a brewer produces beer continuously; a wine maker makes a vintage only once a year. Even today, a lifetime encompasses only forty vintages; it was many fewer in the eighteenth and nineteenth centuries, when people died much younger. This may help to explain why there was little in the way of technological or scientific improvements in wine making itself until this century—and why it took so long, for instance, for the temperature-controlled fermentation of white wines (ensuring that they turned out fresh and lively, rather than dull and oxidized) to be introduced. It appears extraordinary that it took wine makers so long to think of doing this when brewers have been using temperature-control mechanisms since the beginning of the nineteenth century. Wine makers, however, are innately conservative: when Château Latour installed stainless steel vats in 1964, there was an outcry. The new English owners were accused of turning the *château* into a dairy.

The most important technological improvement before the present century was the development of bottle making. This enabled wines to be produced that did not need to contain the high levels of sulphur, acidity, and tannin necessary to withstand long aging in cask. Yet even after three hundred years, the full implications of the invention have not been realized.

Although bottles were manufactured from the first century A.D. onwards, until the end of the seventeenth century they were used, for the most part, only as decanters for serving wine, not as vessels for its storage. The late introduction of bottling is often ascribed to the fact that the cork was not "rediscovered" until the end of the seventeenth century. I do not, however, find it credible that a substance native to the Iberian Peninsula can have been an object of mystery to medieval Europeans. If wine was not bottled until the end of the seventeenth century, it was because the glass was too fragile. The origin of the straw-covered Chianti flasks that were so popular in the 1960s lies in the fact that, from the fifteenth century on, flasks containing Chianti were covered with straw to stop their breaking in transport. These bottles were not strong enough to withstand the corking process and were therefore sealed with the oil in the same way that Roman amphorae had been. This did not prove convenient, as foreign customers did not take care nor have the equipment to remove the oil; they often drank the wine mixed with the oil. Nevertheless, at least the Chianti that was exported in flasks at the beginning of the eighteenth century did not go off as previous consignments in cask had done.

The corking of bottles became possible thanks to the introduction of lead-crystal glass in England by Ravenscroft in 1675. This was precipitated by the needs of the navy. Admiral Sir Robert Mansell was concerned at the destruction of forests by glassmakers and persuaded King James I to prohibit the use of wood in glass-works furnaces. Coal was employed instead, and found to be better. It is the invention of lead-crystal bottles which explains the invention of sparkling champagne in England at the end of the seventeenth century. Only the English had bottles strong enough to withstand either the corking process or the pressure of the carbon dioxide.

Champagne was put into bottles because it was too delicate a vine to survive in cask. Bottling enhanced the natural tendency of champagne to sparkle, on account of the high chalk content of the soil. Moreover, champagne did not complete its fermentation in the cold Champenois winter, and therefore refermented when the weather warmed up again in the spring. If put in bottle in March, and corked to prevent the carbon dioxide from escaping, it would become sparkling.

Like the fact that champagne sparkles if it is put in bottles at the start of spring, the fact that wines improve in bottle was discovered quite by accident. By the beginning of the eighteenth century, champagne was valued for having a bit of bottle age: one of the Dutch friends of the English King William III, who was born in Holland, used to keep back some five-year-old champagne for when he came home to visit. As red burgundies, too, began to be aged in bottle, their style changed during the course of the eighteenth century. Deep color and toughness came to be prized rather than despised; and, in order to achieve this result, the white grapevines, which earlier in the century had been interplanted in the black-grape vineyards in order to achieve a lighter style of wine, were pulled out.[3]

Various factors, however, slowed down the development of bottle aging. Traditionally, wine was kept in cask until it was sold. Bottling was carried out by the purchaser—in New York or wherever—not by the producer. Thus, in the early nineteenth century, the first-growth Bordeaux were aged in cask for five years, whereas today they spend only about two years in wood. There are still some producers in the South of France who keep wine in cask until it is sold. I have tasted seven-year-old Châteauneuf-du-Papes and Côtes de Provence that have only just been bottled.

The need, in the past, to preserve wines while waiting for customers influenced the style in which they were produced. In Burgundy the so-called ancient method (*méthode ancienne*) was invented at the end of last century because of a fall in demand. Long skin contact produced rich, tannic wines of which Anthony Hanson famously remarked, "If this is how the ancients did it, I am all for progress."[4] In fact, before this, red burgundies had been light wines. In the early eighteenth century, the best burgundy was considered to be Volnay, which was described as a *vin de primeur*, that is to say, one that lasted only a year. This, like champagne, was a pink wine, the color of a partridge's eye (*oeil de perdrix*).[5]

Madeira may have been first fortified with brandy for the same reason. According to Noël Cossart, madeira was first fortified in the first half of the eighteenth century, when disturbed sea conditions caused ships to call at the island less often; this led to stockpiling; and therefore surplus wine was distilled into brandy, in order to fortify and preserve stocks.[6]

Furthermore, only in the present century has the difference between the chemistry of cask aging and that of bottle aging been realized. Empirically, the distinction is obvious. Compare, for example, a twenty-year-old tawny port, which will have been aged in cask for about twenty years, with a 1970 vintage port, which will have been bottled after two years in cask. If the two ports come from the same shipping house, they will have been produced from the same quality and style of base wine. But last century no one understood exactly what the difference was. Pasteur got it completely wrong when he said, "It is oxygen which makes wine; it is by its influence that wine ages." Certainly it is oxygen which controls the aging of wine in cask. But once the wine has been bottled, any oxygen dissolved in it combines rapidly with other substances. The aging of wine in bottle owes very little to the presence of oxygen, since only an insignificant amount enters through the cork. This is a fact of which a number of members of the wine trade appear to remain unaware: on several occasions I have been assured that all that happens during bottle aging is that the wine breathes through the cork.

Given this degree of scientific ignorance, the only way of finding out whether a better wine was produced by more or less cask aging has been a lengthy process of trial and error. As a result, the swing from aging wine in cask and then bottling it when it is ready to drink, to aging a wine very little if at all in cask (perhaps only enough to give it a bit of extra flavor) and expecting it to do its maturing in bottle, has been very gradual. This transformation is not yet complete. Will fine wines one day spend no time in cask at all? An oak flavor, if it is desired, can perfectly well be provided artificially—so what does cask aging do for a wine?

There is no simple answer to this question. We are told, on the one hand, that wines are aged in new barrels in order to increase their tannin content, and on the other, that wines are matured in cask in order that they should become less tannic. Authorities appear to contradict one another—and even themselves—on this matter. In his book on wine making, Emile Peynaud, quoting from the work of his mentor Jean Ribéreau-Gayon, says that the amount of tannin extracted from a cask is "not negligible," and can be as much as 200 milligrams per liter from a small new oak cask in the first year.[7] Yet in an interview in 1984, he said that it was a mistake to think that the wood of the cask gives tannin to a wine, and that the reason for using new oak casks was not to give more tannin but to give spice to the wine.[8]

Cask aging causes a wine's tannin content both to increase and to decrease. On the one hand, new oak gives tannin to the wine; on the other, oxygen enters the wine through the staves in the cask and oxidizes the tannins in the wine, causing them to bind into longer molecular chains which eventually become too large to remain soluble and so fall out of solution. Often the two processes cancel each other out. Figures given by Pascal Ribéreau-Gayon show that a wine aged in a new wooden barrel contains only 5 percent more tannin than one aged in stainless steel—and that one aged in an old wooden barrel contains the same amount.[9] Is either effect of cask aging necessary? High levels of tannin are no longer needed in order to preserve wines during long barrel storage. A wine's tannin content can be decreased by ensuring the absence of the tannic grape stems from the fermenting vat, by vinifying at a lower temperature, and by draining the wine off the grape skins before fermentation has finished. A wine's tannin content can be increased by doing the opposite.

New oak casks may contain more tannin than old ones, but those red wines which are matured in new oak casks are not put through this treatment in order that they should be more tannic and relatively unapproachable in their youth. The staves of new oak casks are less compact than in old ones, so there is more exchange between the wine and the air outside; because the wine has been oxygenated to a greater extent, it develops more rapidly than if it had been matured in an old cask. At Domaine Armand Girardin in Pommard in Burgundy, some of the wine is matured in a mixture of new and one-year-old casks, in order to fulfill the demands of the American importer Robert Kacher—and some is matured in older casks, in order to satisfy the tastes of British and French wine merchants. When I visited the estate at the end of 1990, I tasted several wines from the 1989 vintage from both new and old casks. In each case, the version of the wine in the new cask was riper, rounder, more fruity, more opulent. It was much more impressive in its youth—which was presumably the reason why its importer had asked that it should be matured in this way for the American market—but that did not mean that it would necessarily be better when it was mature. At Domaine Bruno Clair in the spring of 1991 I tasted from a new oak cask an amazing, explosive Marsannay Les Longeroies 1990 that smelled and tasted of blackcurrants. Clair warned that the aromas of new oak are not stable and that this was just a phase the wine was going through.

The collectible status of the single-vineyard Côte Rôties of Marcel Guigal has been discussed in Chapter 4. These wines are criticized by Guigal's neighbors, partly because he sells them more readily and for much higher prices than they sell their products, and partly because they do not approve of their being matured entirely in new oak, which they believe destroys their character. Marius Gentaz, the owner of Domaine Gentaz-Dervieux, says that he makes his wine exactly the same way as his father-in-law did eighty years ago; the result is a very classy wine that tastes rather dumb in its youth, as wines made from the Syrah grape are inclined to do. When asked what he thinks of Guigal's wines, Gentaz replies that he sells wine, not oak. In his book *Adventures on the Wine Route*, Gentaz's American importer, Kermit Lynch, condemns the popular approbation of Guigal's Côte Rôtie, which he describes as "a very anonymous-tasting wine, easily mistaken for a big, oaky Gigondas or even a Bordeaux. It reminds me of an acquaintance who always seemed to have a new girlfriend. His girlfriends all had two things in common: huge breasts. His choice might be pretty or not, intelligent or not, interesting or not. Nothing seemed to matter to him as long as the breasts were enormous."[10]

As Peynaud says, new oak casks are used, not to give more tannin, but to give spice to the wine—only, in many cases, the end product tastes of spice rather than of wine. The taste of new oak is as pervasive today, and sometimes as destructive to fine wine, as that of resin was in Roman times. Consumers consider new oak to be a mark of quality; wine makers believe that it confers prestige on their product. Those wine makers who mature their white wines in new

oak have founded their convictions on the belief that white burgundy, the world's most prestigious white wine, tastes strongly of new
oak. It is not clear that, originally, they were correct to do so.
According to Thierry Matrot, who makes outstanding white wines at
his family estate in Meursault, the adoption by California wine
makers of the idea that white burgundy tastes of new oak is the result
of a historical accident. In the 1960s, he says, white burgundies
enjoyed a poor reputation and were difficult to sell. A number of
wine makers decided that the principal cause of the problems was
that many of the wines were being ruined by storage in old, badly
maintained casks. And so they made a major investment in new
casks. Because it brought improved hygiene, people linked new oak
with quality. This all happened just at the time that producers of
California Chardonnay started to visit Burgundy. They encountered
an untraditionally oaky style of white burgundy, and—imagining
that that was traditional—went home and tried to copy it.[11] Matrot
himself uses only 10 percent new oak, which he regards as commensurate with the regular renewal of good casks. He accepts that
other producers do sometimes mature their top wines in between 10
and 20 percent new oak if they like them to have smoky, vanilla
tastes, but he considers this comparable to putting *crème de cassis*
(blackcurrant liqueur) into Bourgogne Aligoté. If a wine maker were
to use more new oak than this, he says, all his wines would taste the
same for the first ten years of their life. Many of Matrot's neighbors
do use more new oak than this, however. In Meursault today, the
average is probably one-third new oak—the same amount as is generally used in California. It is possible, but unlikely, that Matrot's
neighbors have been inspired to increase their usage of new oak by
the results of California wine makers' misinterpretation of traditional
Burgundian practice. It is more probable that they have realized of
their own accord that their consumers no longer have the money,
space, or inclination to keep their wines until they are mature but
prefer them to have the sweet, spicy taste of new oak, so that they can
drink them young.

This said, it is not clear that it is the oak which people like.
Perhaps it is simply the Chardonnay. I am not convinced that even
expert tasters can necessarily detect the taste of oak. Jacques Lardière,
the brilliant wine maker for the Burgundy merchant company Louis

Jadot, says that ripe Chardonnay grapes have aromas that resemble new oak—which is why in richer vintages, such as 1983 and 1985, he used only 5 percent new oak. The wines he made in these years do not appear, on tasting them, to be any less "oaky" than usual. Not all the serious producers of Chardonnay in California believe in oak maturation. The Callaway winery in the Temecula district north of San Diego tried maturing its Chardonnay in oak in the 1970s, but without success. As well as American and French oak, it tried German, which, according to the company's president Terrence Clancy, gave the wine "a horrible flavor like ground-up walnuts and pesticide."[12] Then the wine maker visited Chablis—and discovered that not all Chardonnays were aged in oak. In 1981 Callaway started producing an un-oaked Chardonnay, which it sells under the name Calla-lees. Clearly some American consumers like the style, because it sells more than a million bottles a year.

Just as we find difficulty in distinguishing the taste of Chardonnay from that of new oak, so we associate a certain taste with wines that were long aged in old casks. This taste is not the result of cask aging per se but of the "old-fashioned" wine-making methods employed by the sort of people who imagine that it is a good idea to keep their wine in cask for a long time. There are wines made in this style without cask aging at all—Bairrada in Portugal is probably the best example. In *Vino* (which, when it was published in 1980, was the pioneering English-language work on fine Italian wine), the expatriate American wine writer Burton Anderson describes how Luciano Usseglio-Tomasset, Professor of Enology at Alba, having shown that a Piedmontese red wine after barrel aging had its basic elements deteriorate through oxidation and excessive presence of sulphates from cleaning operations, declared that, in his judgment, "Conservation in wood is without doubt detrimental to the quality of great red wines." One maker of top-class red wine who would agree with him is Emidio Pepe from the Abruzzi in central eastern Italy. He ages his outstanding Montepulciano d'Abruzzo in bottles, and decants the wines off their sediment into fresh bottles before sale. Pepe justified his methods to Burton Anderson by saying: "I want to keep my wine young as long as possible."[13] He might not, perhaps, be described as a man of wide experience, since he only drinks his own wine. But he is not alone among the leading wine makers of central and southern Italy in resisting oak aging: others to do so include Duchi di Castelluccio, also in the Abruzzi; and Salvatore Ippolito in Ciro in Calabria, down in the deep south where the hot climate causes wine to evaporate all too rapidly, and to put it in barrels is to invite oxidation. It was in these parts of Italy, not in the north, that the great wines of Roman times were made; and these were never aged in cask, but in earthenware amphorae.

It is, however, easy to dismiss wines that have been aged in old oak casks because, despite the oxidation of the tannins, they can take longer to mature than wines that have spent no time in oak. They are stabilized by cask aging, made resistant to further change. The more a wine has gradually been oxidized by aging in oak, the better it will withstand further oxidation. An oak-aged white wine such as the white Tondonia Rioja from Lopez de Heredia, which spends up to five years in cask, will not go off if left for a week or so recorked and half-consumed in a refrigerator; a "modern," un-oaked white wine that has been fermented at low temperature will sometimes go off within hours, because the shock of a first contact with air is too much for it. The ultimate demonstration of the longevity of barrel-aged wines is given by madeiras, which are aged in cask for up to thirty years—admittedly after having been heated to 105°F for six months. At a tasting in 1985 of old vintage madeiras from Cossart-Gordon, it was clear that none of the wines from 1920 and younger vintages were yet ready for drinking; the 1863 Bual seemed to be just about at its peak. Noël Cossart, however, ascribed the longevity of madeiras to the volcanic soil in which the vines grow rather than to the method of processing the wines.[14]

Wines lose their individuality with age, particularly if they have been aged in oak. After all, similar physical and chemical processes occur in all fine wines, irrespective of grape variety. Old Hermitage and Côte Rôtie can be very similar to old Bordeaux; old Zinfandel can taste like old California Cabernet Sauvignon; old white Rioja can be indistinguishable from old white burgundy. Mature vintages of the white Rioja from Marqués de Murrieta are commercially available, if anyone wants to go to the expense of testing this theory. Yet, it is usually necessary to wait for fine wines to age, because they tend to "close up" for a certain period of their lives. It is not fully understood why this happens: it has been suggested that it may have something to do with the presence of bacteria. This theory would appear to favor those wines which have had all their bacteria eliminated by sterile filtration, therefore would not be expected to suffer from a closed period—but in fact they suffer for some time after bottling from the shock of the filtration itself. As a general rule, the worst time to drink a fine wine is at about five years of age—which tends to be when you think of broaching the first bottle to see how it is getting on. The finer the wine, the longer the period during which it will remain closed up. Having tasted a range of Gérard Chave's white Hermitage back to 1929, I would suggest either drinking most recent vintage or one of at least twenty years earlier—anything in between will be a disappointment.

The Holy Grail of wine making today is to have the best of all possible worlds—to make a wine which tastes good when young, does not go through a dumb phase, and improves with age. This is not undiscoverable. It has been found, for instance, by the Châteauneuf-du-Pape estate of Domaine du Vieux Télégraphe, who, like many other producers in the region, have changed their style in recent years. With the installation of a new winery in 1979, several changes have been made to the vinification and storage, of which the most important is the use of a new pneumatic press. This presses the grapes very lightly without crushing their stalks, so that the wine no longer has an herby taste and green tannins as it did in the past. At a tasting at the domaine's British importers in 1987, the 1978 was still tough and unyielding, whereas *all* the later vintages were attractive to drink.

Other estates in Châteauneuf-du-Pape are producing a lighter, early-drinking wine by the adoption of carbonic maceration. This is a method of vinification in which a certain proportion of the grapes ferment internally while still unbroken, before the alcoholic fermentation. It gets around the problem of drawing out color and flavor from black grapes without extracting too much tannin, and produces wines with a reduced level of acidity. Figures given by Peynaud of an analysis four months after harvesting of a red Bordeaux made from Malbec grapes—some of which had been vinified normally and some by carbonic maceration—show that the wine made by carbonic maceration contains two-thirds the tannins, two-thirds the acidity, and two-thirds the extract of the wine vinified normally.[15] Carbonic maceration is most famous for being used in Beaujolais; but it has been employed to greatest effect in the Midi (the French Deep South), where it has transformed such wines as Minervois. Whereas in Beaujolais, the Gamay grape produces fruity wines, low in tannin and attractive in their youth—whether vinified by carbonic maceration or not—the wines of the Midi have suffered from being made from a grape, Carignan, which is very tannic when young but not worth the effort of aging.

There is, however, nothing new about carbonic maceration. It simply involves the return by modern science to an ancestral process. In the past, grapes were poured into fermentation tanks without being crushed, or else trodden by foot—in which case crushing can hardly have been complete. Until Bordelais methods were introduced in the second half of the nineteenth century, the red wines of the Rioja were made by proto-carbonic maceration. These are still made by small growers in Rioja Alavesa for consumption locally or in Bilbao. Recently, larger producers have adopted modern methods of carbonic maceration. So traditional and modern methods of carbonic maceration are being used side by side. Since small growers in Rioja are not allowed to export their wines, it is only the modern version of carbonic maceration, such as Artadi from Cosecheros Alavesas, that is available abroad.

On the one hand, the return to carbonic maceration is part of a trend toward the unashamed production of red wines for drinking young. On the other, wines made by this method can last. If Beaujolais Nouveau has fallen apart within a year in the past, it was the result of excessive filtration to try to produce a clear and stable wine within a month of the harvest—not because the wine is intrinsically incapable of aging. Patently, it is in the interest of producers of and merchants in Beaujolais to encourage the belief that their wine has to be drunk young: this idea does wonders for their cash flow. Gérard Brisson, who makes an excellent Morgon (not by carbonic maceration) at his Domaine des Peuillets, says that the Beaujolais merchants try to stop him from saying that his wine improves with age. Unless it has been filtered overenthusiastically, Beaujolais Nouveau is no different from other versions of Beaujolais (whether made by carbonic maceration or not), except that the malolactic fermentation is hastened in order to ensure that it has occurred before the wine is bottled in early November.

In Châteauneuf-du-Pape, Domaine de Nalys—who use carbonic maceration—claim that their wines can age; and even Robert Parker, who is not a fan of what is going on in Châteauneuf, admits to tasting a good 1967. I have tasted only the 1985, which seems to have the structure to last. Perhaps, however, it is because of the use of carbonic maceration that Baron le Roy of Châteaux Fortia thinks that Châteauneuf-du-Pape is "going to hell."[16]

The great drawback of carbonic maceration is not so much that wines made by this method are incapable of aging gracefully as that the wine tastes more of the process by which it is produced than of the grapes from which it is made. Beaujolais made by carbonic maceration is more closely comparable to Rhône wines or Rioja made by carbonic maceration than to Beaujolais not made by carbonic maceration. Georges Duboeuf, the most celebrated exponent of carbonic maceration Beaujolais, also produces a Côtes du Rhône that I suspect most people would identify blind as Beaujolais.

Alternative means of extracting good color and fruit flavor from a wine, without too much tannin, include cold maceration, must heating, and the recycling of the pomace of skins in the vat. Cold maceration has received a great deal of publicity in the last few years because it has been advocated by Guy Accad, a Lebanese-born enologist who oversees the wine making at a couple of dozen estates in Burgundy. Accad had shocked his neighbors by producing intensely colored wines from the Pinot Noir grape, which (as has been discussed in Chapter 8) rarely produces wines with much color. Accad's technique is to crush some of the grapes, chill the mass of skins and juice to 50°F or below, add sulphur dioxide, leave it all to stew for a week or so, then warm up the juice to start the fermentation. The cold temperature stops the juice from fermenting; the sulphur dioxide acts as an acid to extract color from the grapes. One of the drawbacks of this method, however, is that the sulphur dioxide blocks the links between the tannins, preventing them from precipitating out of the wine during fermentation; as a result, the wine is harsher and more tannic. Accad's method is a solution to the problem of pale-colored red burgundy, not to the problem of extracting good color and fruit flavor from grapes without also extracting too much tannin.

Before Accad came along with cold maceration, the trendy technique in Burgundy for extracting color from Pinot Noir grapes was must heating. This is simply an extension of the principle that fermenting at a higher temperature produces a wine with better color. By vinifying at normal temperatures, a wine maker extracts only 30 percent of the coloring matter of the grapes (the rest is lost in the pomace); if he heats the whole grapes to 160°F the cells of the skin are killed, so that when the grapes are crushed they rapidly distribute into the juice the substances they contained. Must heating enjoyed its heyday in Burgundy in the 1970s, when it proved an effective method of rapidly extracting color from grapes that were affected by rot. Unfortunately, it was found that this method was unsuitable for wines intended for aging—the colors and aromas that were extracted were not stable—as well as causing different wines to resemble one another. On the other hand, as Anthony Hanson was told by Bernard Drouhin of Domaine Drouhin-Laroze in Gevrey-Chambertin, one of the practitioners of this method, having wines that resembled each other was preferable to having wines that re-sembled nothing on earth.[17]

Recycling the pomace simply speeds up the extraction of color, and is used to great effect by Masi to make their Valpolicella Fresco, which spends only a day in contact with its skins and as a result offers the sort of tannin-free, vibrant fruit that makes one realize why Valpolicella became famous. Like must heating, the recycling of the pomace generally produces wines that are incapable of improving in bottle—which may explain why wines made by these methods are sometimes described in France as *vins putains*—they are seductive when young, but do not age well.

To lighten a wine capable of aging, it is probably best just to add water to the finished product. According to Noël Cossart, the rela-tively light Rainwater style of madeira originated in the eighteenth century when some pipes of Verdelho were left on the beach over-night before shipping to America; by mistake they were left un-bunged, and some water seeped in. The style was very much liked by the purchaser, Andrew Newton, a Scotsman who had settled in

Virginia. In his ignorance, he described the wine as "soft as rain-water," and ordered some more.[18]

Although European Community rules today prohibit the addition of water to wine—which is why the use of liquid sugar in Germany is banned—it is used, both directly and indirectly. In Burgundy in 1983 the grapes came in with very high sugar levels, enough to have produced Meursaults with 16 percent alcohol. Local enologists advised the addition of five gallons of water to each sixty-gallon barrel. I have no idea how many wine makers carried out their advice. In California, a number of leading producers achieve excessively high sugar levels most years, and therefore regularly add water to the grape must before fermentation. But then, many of those who condemn this practice water their wines indirectly, by irrigating the vineyard. The result is the same; it is simply that in the one instance the water is added to the finished wine; and in the other it is taken up into the grapes through the roots. One of the reasons for the excessive yields obtained by the leading Bordeaux *châteaux* at the turn of the century—causing a decline in their reputation—was that, at Château Latour, for instance, the vineyard was irrigated by spraying. This made nonsense of the fact that the quality of the wine derived at least in part from the porosity of the topsoil, which forced the vine's roots to dig deep to find water and thus to extract more mineral flavors from the soil.[19]

Certainly it seems sensible for a vine grower in a dry climate to irrigate his vines in order to ensure that the vine is able to continue to photosynthesize throughout the summer. In Spain, irrigation is illegal for wines which claim a *denominación de origen*—the Spanish equivalent of the French *appellation contrôlée*. As a result, the national average yield is a ludicrously uneconomic 1¼ tons per acre. Sensible wine producers ignore the law. Because he irrigates the Cabernet Sauvignon vines at his Val de Pusa estate on the La Mancha plain near Toledo, the Marqués de Griñon was, in 1979, fined 120,000 pesetas. This was the year of his first vintage, and the fine brought him very necessary publicity.[20] It is, however, a small step from adding enough water to enable vines to continue to grow to adding water to increase the eventual crop. At the vast Raimat estate in the *denominación* Costers del Segre in Catalonia, the vines are also irrigated in contravention of the law; but in this case the authorities turn a blind eye. Their attitude may be related to the "experimental" nature of the grape varieties grown on the estate, or perhaps to the quality of the wines.[21] These are undoubtedly very good, but if, by less enthusiastic watering, the estate were to produce yields lower than the present 6 tons per acre, they might well be even better.

Adding water to a cask of wine before selling it is among the oldest and easiest of adulterations. After all, about 85 percent of wine is water. In some countries, at some periods, strict regulations have been applied to the watering of wine. In 1471 a vintner in South Germany was immured alive for doing this. Elsewhere, the law has been more lax. In France early this century, retailers and bar owners used habitually to "baptize" wine by adding about 20–25 percent of water. This was perfectly legal, as long as the alcohol content of the wine did not fall below 10 percent.[22] Since then, the law has changed; practices, it has seemed, have not. In the autumn of 1987 the satirical magazine *Le Canard enchaîné* published a report sent by the Fraud Squad to the Ministry of Agriculture concerning its tests on the produce of the 1986 vintage. These revealed widespread overchaptalization, and illegal chaptalization in those *appellations* where it was not permitted. Among the illegally chaptalized wines were a pink Côtes du Roussillon and a sweet white Bergerac: having by this means attained an excessive alcoholic degree, they were then diluted with 15 percent and 20 percent of water, respectively.[23]

12
Keeping Up
With the Jayers

I F MANY of us prefer the taste of young wines, how come old vintage dates are so sought after that they have frequently been faked? Rioja shippers, for example, could not, before the 1980s, always be trusted as to the date of the vintage they quoted on their labels. It is said that sales of the 1970 vintage were four times as great as the production of wine in that year; indeed, the date was used with such liberality that the authorities were eventually compelled to ban the export of 1970 vintage-labeled Rioja to a number of markets.[1] During his researches in the 1950s into the wines of Jerez, the British wine writer Julian Jeffs was assured that one of the Rioja shippers had registered "Vintage 1929" as his trademark; but then, according to local barroom gossip, sherry producers who sold dated *soleras* used their telephone numbers.[2]

When, at the end of the last war, the federal government of the United States lifted restrictions on the importation of bottled wine from Portugal, the market was flooded with madeira bearing fictitious dates. One Chicago merchant sold over four hundred cases of 1874 madeira in 1949 and 1950—probably more vintage wine than was ever made in that year, when production was reduced because of the devastation of the vineyards by the phylloxera louse.[3] Spurious vintage dates may not pose a problem today, but dated *soleras* do.

These boast the vintage when wine was first put in the cask, since which time, at regular intervals, between 10 and 25 percent of the wine has been drawn off and replaced with younger wine. Laws have recently been introduced which limit to ten years the period during which it is permitted to "refresh" a dated *solera* with younger wine. *Soleras* began after phylloxera when the shippers simply did not have enough wine to lay down as single-vintage madeiras. In his book on madeira, Noël Cossart sought to justify them on the grounds that otherwise all the pre-phylloxera vintages would by now have been drunk.[4] But are not some consumers misled into thinking that *solera* madeiras are genuine vintage wines?

So-called vintage cognac used to be made by such a *solera* system. How else could Bisquit Dubouché have fulfilled the claim in their advertisements in the 1930s that they were able to supply apparently unlimited quantities of the 1865, 1834, and 1811 vintages?[5] Unless there exists documentary evidence to prove the age of a cask of cognac—which there almost never does—the use of a vintage date on a mature bottle of cognac is today illegal. Vintage cognacs will not appear on the market again until some time next century, since officially controlled production of the vintage product began only with the 1988 harvest. Vintage armagnacs are being sold today, but only a few of the cellars contain enough casks of different sizes of any one vintage to allow for genuine topping-up of old vintages. The British wine writer Nicholas Faith believes that the Armagnaçais illegally practice the sort of *solera* system the Cognaçais used to use.[6]

Once a wine has been provided with a fictitious date, it is possible to try, by heating it, to make it appear as though it has achieved that age of its own accord. The Romans manufactured "smoked wines" by storing their amphorae full of wine above a smoke room from which smoke rose up and heated them. In 1830 the Italian Ulisse Novellucci started experimenting with heating sealed bottles in water, bringing them up to near the level at which alcohol vaporizes for a few minutes and then cooling them down. He said that this procedure gave the wine the same "taste it would have in eight to ten years' time, except for a very tiny difference which the connoisseurs can detect and describe as being 'cooked.' "[7] Aging wine by heating reproduces some of the process of cask aging; the slower it is, the better. Anyone with a cellar at room temperature, rather than the recommended 50°F, will see his wines develop relatively fast. That is why the same wines taste much older in Texas than they do in Scotland. Restaurants that serve fine wines far too young are therefore right to store them at room temperature, not least because this reduces the period of "bottle sickness" (during which the wine is recovering from the shock of being bottled).

Various other methods of aging wine artificially have been tried. In 1890 Cesari Bernardi tried subjecting red wines to electrolysis, and found that, after four to five days, they acquired "a delicate perfume and became fuller-flavored and more velvety."[8] In fact, though electrolysis certainly changes the character of a wine, causing simultaneous oxidation at the cathode and reduction at the anode, the result does not at all resemble the aging process. More recently, irradiation has been tried and found to be even less successful—since it causes chemical decomposition and changes the odor of the treated substances. After all, one of the main uses of ultraviolet light, apart from irradiation, is to deodorize buildings. Experiments carried out in 1986 involving the irradiation of Pilsner beer with gamma radiation not only reduced the color but produced a totally unacceptable smell of bad eggs (hydrogen sulphide). Some years ago, the radiologist William Levett tried irradiating a bottle of Château Latour from a recent vintage. It tasted disgusting—but that may have been because, in his calculations beforehand, he had put a decimal point in the wrong place and thus subjected the wine to ten times as much radiation as he had intended.[9]

One reason why artificial aging has proven so difficult is that red wines contain several hundred flavor components. In 1986, however, Leo McCloskey, a researcher at Ridge Vineyards in the Santa Cruz Mountains, announced that he had identified the most important of these, a substance which he called oenin and which he said represented up to half the flavor of a fine red wine. He also announced that he had developed a means of accelerating the natural development of oenin, which is formed by the grouping together of tannins as a red wine matures. He declared: "We should soon be able to deliver wines that possess this very desirable flavor more often and better, so that fine wines will be more available and cheaper." By using a nuclear magnetic resonance spectrometer, McCloskey produced "fingerprints" of each wine's molecular structure. Paul

Draper, the wine maker at Ridge, was quoted in an article in *The Wall Street Journal* as saying: "Theoretically, you could take a 1961 Château Latour and get its fingerprint, and then work on a 1980 Ridge Monte Bello Cabernet Sauvignon to come up with the same fingerprint, and you would indeed have reproduced most of the quality of a very, very great wine."[10] Draper subsequently declared that this quotation was "apocryphal."

Why should we believe so fervently that old wine is better that we seek to produce it artificially? In the Middle Ages and Renaissance, no one actually chose to drink old wines. But some wines did survive longer in the casks in which they were stored than others. Wines that survived to old age without going off were demonstrably better than wines that had to be drunk young, before they went off. Above all, they showed themselves to be pure and unadulterated, because wines that had been mixed with one another or with other substances soon fell apart. This was the origin of the belief that old wine is good wine. There was never any suggestion that it improved in the aging process.

Had medieval man believed that wine was ameliorated by aging, he could perfectly well have put this belief into practice. His lack of lead-crystal bottles would not have stopped him. Wine can perfectly well be aged in cask. It does not oxidize—providing that the cask is kept filled to the brim and regularly topped up to replace the liquid lost through evaporation. Indeed, a cask is a far better medium for aging than the widemouthed earthenware amphorae used by the Romans. These were ineffectually sealed with wax, and their contents frequently had to be preserved with pitch and resin. Yet, this did not prevent the produce of the first great vintage of Roman times—that of 121 B.C.—from surviving for two hundred years. When today we accuse a poor, oxidized wine of having been kept too long in cask, we may be making the same mistake as those people who connected the fall in the birth rate in Sweden after the Second World War with a corresponding fall in the stork population: confusing statistical with causal correlation. Oxidation is caused by poor wine making and careless storage.

The development of wines intended for aging was, it has been suggested, the consequence of the closure to Bordeaux of its traditional markets when English and Dutch merchant ships were chased away in the second half of the seventeenth century by protectionist French trading policies. At war with France, England developed the vineyards of the Douro in Portugal as an alternative source of wine to that which they had enjoyed for five hundred years. When the English market was again opened to them after the signing of peace in 1713, the Bordelais found that they could not compete on price with port, because they had to pay higher customs duties. Furthermore, the *haut bourgeois* proprietors of the Bordeaux city suburbs were being undercut in their local markets by the produce of the recently drained, newly planted, and more fertile marshland. Their only way out was to convert to quality-wine production—to produce wines which were intended, not for immediate consumption, but for laying down.[11]

The Bordeaux of the late seventeenth and early eighteenth century were the first fine wines, in the modern sense, to be produced. But they were not available to everyone, not even for ready money. Social climbing was not easy in the eighteenth century, since many objects of prestige could only be obtained through personal contacts. Wine was one of these. By the nineteenth century, it had become easier for the *nouveaux riches* to get their hands on the wines hitherto enjoyed only by the aristocracy. At the same time, the Industrial Revolution saw the creation of a new, large, acquisitive middle class who aspired to upper-class tastes even though they could rarely afford to indulge in them. This class placed a premium on one-upmanship and petty snobbery, and its members were quite happy to pay money for artificially aged wines if the genuine article was beyond their means.

The values of this class are dominant today. We pay money principally for exclusivity rather than for taste. Young wines are in plentiful supply because they have not yet been drunk; therefore they are not, on the whole, exclusive. For some people, even the latest vintage of Château Pétrus or Romanée-Conti is neither expensive nor exclusive enough. They are the sort of people who pay $156,450 for a bottle of Château Lafite 1787. This particular bottle was purchased by the New York publisher Malcolm Forbes at an auction at Christie's in London in December 1985.[12] He placed the wine in his museum, under spotlights. These caused the cork to dry out and fall into the wine—so no one will ever know how it tasted.

The wine had fetched such a high price not so much because it was a bottle of 198-year-old Château Lafite, but because it bore what were apparently Thomas Jefferson's initials. No one knows whether Jefferson actually owned the wine—except possibly Hardy Rodenstock, a former pop-group manager who now makes money from selling condoms packaged in hazelnut shells to the Far East, and from buying and selling old wines. Rodenstock says that he found more than a dozen bottles of first-growth Bordeaux from the 1784 and 1787 vintages in an old cellar in the Marais district of Paris, but he has refused to reveal its exact location.[13] The wines' identification with Thomas Jefferson rests on their having the letters "Th.J." engraved on their sides. It is quite possible that they are genuine, since Jefferson did buy wine from the first-growth *châteaux* at this period; but I have seen no firm evidence that Jefferson ever bought any wine from the 1787 vintage or that he bought Château Mouton-Rothschild from any vintage. At the time this was called Bran-Mouton, and it was rated by Jefferson himself as a third growth alongside such little-known *châteaux* as Marquis du Terme.[14] Mouton, which became famous after the Rothschilds bought it in 1853, was only elevated to first-growth status 120 years later, by which time it was better known than any of the four existing first-growth *châteaux* in the United States.

The $156,450 paid for the 1787 Château Lafite remains the record price paid for a single bottle of wine, but it is possible that this would have been exceeded by the sum paid for the 1787 Château Margaux from the same collection, had this come up for sale. It was being offered by the New York wine retailer William Sokolin for $519,750. In April 1989 he took it to the Four Seasons restaurant in New York in order to show it to the present owners of the *château*, who were attending a dinner sponsored by their American importers. In carrying the bottle around to another of the guests, he knocked it against a serving cart. The bottle broke, and most of the wine spilled out onto the carpet. Sokolin went home in distress, but then decided to make the best of a bad experience and tasted the wine. It was not much good.[15]

It would be unreasonable to expect a red Bordeaux to taste good after two centuries. The resinated, deliberately oxidized sweet wines of Roman times may well have been capable of lasting that long, but

only in a few exceptionally tannic vintages—1870, 1928, and 1945—
have Bordeaux *châteaux* produced wines which have taken fifty years
to become ready to drink and have proven capable of lasting for a
hundred years or more. Neither 1784 nor 1787 was a vintage of this
kind. In Jefferson's opinion, the first-growth *châteaux* of these vintages reached their peak at four years of age and started to decline
three years later.[16] The general condition of old red Bordeaux was
demonstrated by a tasting organized in 1988 by Hardy Rodenstock of
fifty-nine wines from the 1937 vintage. This was not a great year, but
it was one of the best vintages in the 1930s. According to James
Suckling of *The Wine Spectator*, who attended the tasting, it was "an
extremely unpleasant experience." Half the wines were totally dead
and many of the rest were hard and acidic, with very little fruit. Yet,
a bottle of 1937 red Bordeaux from one of the first-growth *châteaux*
would cost $400 or $500.[17] The person who purchased one would
clearly not be doing so for the pleasure of the taste. In *The Unofficial
Guide to Wine Snobbery*, Leonard S. Bernstein tells the story of a
young couple having dinner at Lutèce in New York who ordered a
bottle of Château Lafite 1890 for $1,200. André Soltner, the pro-
prietor, suggested that it would be risky to have such an old wine and
recommended that they order a 1961 Lafite ($400) instead. The man
of the couple accepted his suggestion. "We'll have one of each," he
said, "so we can compare."[18]

    In seeking out exclusive products, we are paying money for
what marketers call "added value." "Added value" means conferring
an image on a product that makes it seem worth more than it is. The
"added value" is the extra money a consumer can be persuaded to
pay above the intrinsic worth of a product in order to make a statement about himself: that he is fashionable, has good taste, has lots of
money, or is otherwise desirable. In 1983 two surgeons at St. Mary's
Hospital, Paddington, London, asked eight members of their unit to
try to distinguish, in a blind tasting, between six Scotch whiskies, of
which three were single malts (made from malted barley and distilled
in the traditional manner in a pot still) and three were standard
blended whiskies (made by mixing a small amount of malt whisky
with a large amount of whisky that had been distilled from other
grains in a continuous still). Four of the tasters were regular, expe-
rienced whisky drinkers; the other four were not. However, they all

came out with the same results. Despite—or perhaps because of—trying each sample several times, they were about 50–60 percent successful in distinguishing malt from blended whisky.[19] A group of monkeys would have done just as well. Yet malt whisky is fast becoming the fashionable alternative to cognac. The reason is that people buy malt whisky in order to make personal statements about their status as discriminating, successful, well-traveled people, rather than because of the intrinsic taste of the whisky. Those are not my words. They are the words of the marketing manager of a leading brand of malt whisky, Glenfarclas.[20]

The most obvious example of a drinks product whose high prices can be accounted for only in terms of the added value it offers is champagne. In terms of taste, this offers very poor value for money, but in terms of added value it is positively cheap. A bottle of champagne costs much less than the other elements of a "champagne life-style," such as fast cars, slow yachts, and beautiful women; it even costs less, and lasts a little longer, than an ounce of caviar. Thus, in terms of the added value it confers, champagne is underpriced. That is why, given the tendency toward free spending during the Reagan presidency in America, sales of the cheapest element of conspicuous consumption doubled between 1980 and 1985.

If people will pay more for champagne than for equally good sparkling wines from elsewhere, it is not because they like the taste. In the chapter on wine tastings, I referred to the problem of Bollinger's being sold too young in Britain. In 1989 the famous El Vino wine bar in Fleet Street, London, took Bollinger off its wine list for precisely this reason. The week after it had been delisted, I tested the palates of a number of El Vino's customers—all of them regular champagne drinkers—by serving them glasses of Bollinger. But I told them only that it was some kind of sparkling wine. Only one of them identified it as champagne at all; most of the rest suggested that it was Cava from Spain or sparkling Saumur. Yet, a week earlier, Bollinger had been the second-best-selling champagne at El Vino, after its own house brand.

People pay more for champagne than for other sparkling wines because these other wines lack the association with celebration that champagne producers have promoted so assiduously over the years. Sometimes they have done so by dubious methods. In 1902 George

Kessler, Moët et Chandon's agent in the United States, somehow succeeded in substituting a bottle of Moët for one of the German sparkling wines at the launch, in a New York dockyard, of the German Kaiser's yacht. He also had Moët served at lunch after the ceremony. The resulting publicity for champagne so infuriated the Kaiser that he recalled the German ambassador from Washington. Four years later, Kessler also attempted to associate champagne with commiseration, when he presented a whole railway carriage of Moët to the victims of the San Francisco earthquake.[21]

The enormous investment made by Champagne producers in the creation of an association with celebration—and the added value of a "champagne lifestyle"—helps explain why such producers act with ferocity to protect their propriety over the name of their region. In England in 1975 they obtained an injunction forbidding the makers of a sparkling perry (which is similar to cider, only made from a mixture of apples and pears) called Babycham from describing it as "champagne perry"; and even succeeded in having the use of the name "Babycham" itself prohibited. This latter ruling was reversed by the Court of Appeal on the grounds that the champagne industry had not been able to produce a single witness who was confused by the Babycham label. In 1992 the champagne manufacturers applied for an injunction in the English courts against Thorncroft Vineyard in Surrey, seeking to prevent it from selling a non-alcoholic sparkling elderflower drink as "elderflower champagne." The judge observed that "not even a moron in a hurry would confuse the product with French champagne"—but he granted the injunction all the same.

Within the European Community—and in many other markets, such as Canada and New Zealand—the Champenois have succeeded in preventing the producers of sparkling wines from grapes grown outside the Champagne region from using the name "champagne." Within the European Community, moreover, it will be forbidden after the mid-1990s to use the words *champagne method* or *méthode champenoise* to describe wines made in other regions by the same method that is used in Champagne. In the United States the situation is somewhat different. There is nothing to stop local sparkling wine producers from calling their wines "champagne" or from saying that they are made from the champagne method. Some

of the Champagne companies who have established their own production facilities in California have been quite prepared to describe
them on the label as being made from the "champagne method,"
and also prepared to see them under the name of the Champagne
company, which must surely lead to a certain amount of confusion.
The Champagne companies argue, in their defense, that confusion
is unlikely, because they sell their champagnes at much higher prices
than their California sparkling wines. It is not surprising that they
make this distinction. They wish to give the impression that, even
with Champenois know-how, it is not possible to produce in the
United States sparkling wine that is as fine as champagne. The fact
that it is perfectly possible to produce sparkling wine in the United
States which is at least as fine as champagne will be evident to
anyone who has taken the trouble to compare the excellent Mumm
Cuvée Napa Reserve with the disappointing Mumm Cordon Rouge
champagne. But how many people take the trouble? How many
assume that the Cordon Rouge must be better, because it costs twice
as much?

The champagne producers are well aware that price in itself
creates added value because it makes a product exclusive—or at least
creates an image of exclusivity. By asking and obtaining a high price,
it is possible to persuade consumers that a product is of high quality.
Pommery have greatly increased the sales of their champagne in
France since 1985—not by improving the product, but by the simple
expedient of raising their price.[22] It is not surprising that people think
that, if a wine costs more, it is better. If there do not exist any
objective criteria to distinguish between different wines, if you do not
know anything about the product you are buying, then it is not
ludicrous to take price as a guide to quality. After all, price is a guide
to reputation.

A wine's reputation, however, is created as much by its price as
by its quality. It is only by charging a high price that the image can
be achieved that will bring consumers to accept that the price is
justified by the quality. Certainly, it would be hard on any other
grounds to justify the ludicrous prices that are asked for *cuvée de
prestige* champagnes. These have been introduced by many champagne houses in the last fifteen years, largely because ordinary champagne has become too cheap. When, in the autumn of 1983,

following two enormous harvests, the price of a bottle of champagne fell to under $10, it could be said that for many people even champagne had become an affordable, everyday product. *Cuvées de prestige* are simply champagnes with a fancy image sold in fancy bottles at a fancy price. They exist to fulfill the needs of those who consider that ordinary, non-vintage champagne is no longer expensive or exclusive enough. In the United States, 13 percent of champagne consumption is accounted for by *cuvées de prestige*.

The image of *cuvées de prestige* as exclusive products has to be cultivated assiduously—and at the expense of the truth. Two of the most famous *cuvées de prestige* are Dom Perignon, made by Moët et Chandon, and Comtes de Champagne, made by Taittinger. These are everywhere sold "on allocation," although they are not exactly in short supply. According to my estimates—based on figures provided by Moët et Chandon's London office—more than 1.5 million bottles of Dom Perignon are produced each year. This is equivalent to the entire production of white wines in the village of Puligny-Montrachet in Burgundy. Taittinger produces about 400,000 bottles of Comtes de Champagne each year, accounting for roughly one-tenth of its total sales.

The situation is ridiculous. Champagnes just as good as swanky *cuvées de prestige* sell for one-third the price. The village of Le Mesnil is rated a *grand cru* and is regarded by many people as the finest source of white grapes in Champagne. Half the vineyard area in the village is owned by small growers who take grapes to their local cooperative. Sixty percent of the wine made by the cooperative is sold to the big champagne companies, among them Moët and Taittinger. M. Leboeuf, the director of the cooperative, says that these companies have told him that the wine they buy from Le Mesnil will normally be used in their *cuvées de prestige*. Moët denies that it includes wine from the Le Mesnil cooperative in the blend of Dom Perignon, which it says is produced entirely from grapes grown in its own vineyards, not all of them in *grand cru* villages. Taittinger admits that a quarter of the blend for Comtes de Champagne comes from the Le Mesnil cooperative. The 40 percent of the wine made by the cooperative that is not sold to the big companies is kept by the cooperative, fermented a second time in order to turn it into champagne, and sold under its own label or that of its members. It would be contrary both to human nature and to sound business practice if the cooperative were to sell its best 60 percent to the big houses and keep its worst 40 percent for itself. The champagne produced by the cooperative under the Le Mesnil label is not only quite delicious but costs $25 compared with $80 for Dom Perignon or Comtes de Champagne. The marketing director of a champagne company (who asked not to be identified) once admitted how the prices of *cuvées de prestige* were calculated. "The consumer knows nothing," he declared. "The more a champagne costs, the better he thinks it is. A high price makes him feel secure."

The *châteaux* proprietors of Bordeaux are perfectly open about the fact that the image of higher quality is achieved by charging a higher price. The success of this policy can be seen in the rise to prominence of Château Pétrus in the 1950s—which Edmund Penning-Rowsell ascribes in no small degree to the policy of its proprietress, the late Mme Edmond Loubat. She believed that her wine was the equal of the first growths of the Médoc, and refused to sell her wine for a price any lower than theirs.[23] A similar policy has more recently been applied by the Thienpoint family, Belgian wine merchants and owners of Vieux Château Certan, to another Pomerol made entirely from Merlot grapes and matured in 100 percent new oak casks, Le Pin. Although they only bought the property—a tiny 2½-acre vineyard—in 1979, and only launched the first vintage (the 1981) onto the market as recently as 1983, the Thienpoints sell Le Pin at a higher price, not only than Vieux Château Certan, but than any other Pomerol, with the sole exception of Pétrus. In my experience, and in that of some specialist writers on Bordeaux, Le Pin is inferior in quality not only to Pétrus but also to the Cabernet-based Vieux Château Certan, which has a better structure and a greater length. But it appears that quality is not the principal criterion. Although the Thienpoints deny that they are trying to "do a Pétrus," their success in selling a hitherto unknown wine at a very high price has inspired others to follow them—including another Belgian wine merchant, Mark Schiettekat, who in 1991 launched the first three vintages of another tiny, 100 percent Merlot property in Pomerol, Clos du Vieux Plateau Certan, on to the market at the same price as Le Pin. I have not tasted the wine. The *châtelains* of Bordeaux vie with each other to see who can charge, and obtain, the highest prices, not because they are greedy for money—if they can afford to run a classed-growth *châteaux*, they don't need that—but because they are greedy for prestige. Jean Sanders, the Belgian proprietor of Château Haut-Bailly, describes the pricing policy of "many Bordeaux *châteaux*" as "stupid and very dangerous. It's a *marché de voisinage* [a matter of keeping up with the Joneses] where everyone is far too busy worrying about what his neighbor is getting. Whose are the most fairly priced wines? The ones from *châteaux* which belong to businessmen."[24]

In the 1960s the prices of classed-growth clarets were forced up by the rivalry between Elie de Rothschild—the owner of Château Lafite—and his cousin Philippe de Rothschild—the owner of Château Mouton-Rothschild—who vied with each other to see who could charge the higher price, in the belief that whichever wine fetched the more money was the better one. This competition contributed to the collapse of the market in 1974. The fear is sometimes expressed that a similar rivalry today between the "super seconds," Château Léoville–Las Cases, Ducru-Beaucaillou, and Pichon-Lalande, will lead to a similar collapse.

This is a game the Bordelais have always played. M. de Rauzan, the proprietor in the eighteenth century of the then-united estates of Château Rausan-Ségla and Rauzan-Gassies, became dissatisfied with the price offered for his wine in Bordeaux. Therefore he chartered a ship, which he loaded with casks from good vintages, and sailed for London. Using his ship in the Thames as an office, his initiative won him both publicity and orders. But he still did not consider the price high enough. He announced that, unless he obtained what he considered a fair price, he would throw the casks into the river one by one. After he had thrown away four of the casks, the onlookers could stand it no longer and gave way.[25]

Clearly, the new fine wines that were developed in the late seventeenth and early eighteenth centuries could not be sold in Britain—even to wealthy Londoners rejoicing in the proceeds of a first stock-market boom—unless some effort was put behind their promotion and added value was created in order to justify their price. The first Bordeaux *château* to make a name for itself was Haut-Brion, thanks to the marketing skills of the owner, Arnaud de Pontac, who sent his son François-Auguste to London in 1666 to open a tavern called "The Sign of Pontac's Head," in order to promote his wines. This tavern became the most fashionable meeting place in London. The superior status of Haut-Brion was established by selling it for seven shillings a bottle (sixty cents at present-day exchange rates) when other perfectly good wines could be purchased for a quarter as much. Within a decade, the cost of the wine if purchased direct from the *château* had doubled because rich Englishmen ordered it to be bought at any price. In his book on the wine trade in the eighteenth century, Alan Francis argues that, after 1715, there was no profit in importing anything but expensive Bordeaux wines into England.[26]

Similar methods of adding value are used by wineries in California to promote their new wines today. A major instrument in forcing up prices is the Napa Valley Wine Auction, first held in 1981. The fact that all proceeds are given to local charities encourages bidders to pay quite absurd sums for the wines. The inaugural 1981 auction was chosen by Robert Mondavi and Baron Philippe de Rothschild (the owner of Château Mouton-Rothschild) for the launch of the first vintage of their joint venture, Opus One. They had announced their collaboration the previous year, but at that time no wine existed. The first vintage of Opus One, 1979, was produced *after* the announcement of the collaboration; it was made in 1980 by Lucien Sionneu, the wine maker at Mouton-Rothschild, from a selection of wines that had originally been produced by Mondavi for inclusion in its Napa Valley Cabernet Sauvignon and Reserve Cabernet Sauvignon blends.[27] The first case of Opus One 1979 was sold at the Napa Valley Wine Auction for $24,000. This enabled the price of $50 a bottle—which was asked when the wine was subsequently put on commercial release—to appear less impudent than it actually was. The relationship between the price of the bottle and the quality of the wine it contained appears to have been irrelevant to the equation.

Although the Napa Valley Wine Auction has been held every summer since 1981, the sum paid for the first case of Opus One was not exceeded until 1989, when Robert Woolley of Dallas, founder of the Embassy Suites hotel chain, bid $55,000 for an 18-liter bottle (the size of twenty-four normal bottles) of Stag's Leap Wine Cellars Cask 23 Cabernet Sauvignon 1985 and the same size bottle of two future releases of this wine. At the time of writing, this remains the record price paid for a single lot of wine at the auction. Thanks to this extraordinary bid, Warren Winiarski, the owner of Stag's Leap Wine Cellars, was able subsequently to offer the 1985 Cask 23 for commercial release at a remarkable $75 a bottle—the highest price ever asked for a California wine. According to Joe Heitz who—despite enormous demand for his Martha's Vineyard Cabernet Sauvignon 1985—had kept the release price down to $50 a bottle, the $75 which consumers had paid for the 1985 Cask 23 was not a "real world" price but had been artificially inflated by the sum bid at the Napa Valley Wine Auction.[28] When he released the 1986 Cask 23 a year later, Winiarski returned to the real world—if a price of $50 can be described in that way. Certainly, when Mondavi released the first vintage of Opus One at that price, its purpose was to shock people: the high price made the wine stand out, and enabled it to gain a cachet that other California wines have been unable to attain.[29] The 1979 Opus One was undoubtedly a very good wine, but the principal justification for its very high price was the fact that it was a joint venture with Château Mouton-Rothschild. Mondavi was seeking to take advantage of the popular American belief that French wines enjoy a superior status to their own—and, by giving in to that belief, it was doing a disservice to the California wine industry as a whole. When Opus One was launched, Warren Winiarski, who used to work for Mondavi in the late 1960s, told a reporter: "Robert Mondavi is a wonderful wine maker. Why he needs the Baron to do what he has already been doing all these years is beyond me."[30]

The American consumer's belief that French wines are superior goes back a long way. The success at the 1900 Paris Exposition of the Bordeaux-type blend produced by Pierre Klein at Mira Valle in the Santa Cruz Mountains has been referred to in Chapter 10. Klein had been encouraged to plant his vineyard by his experience of working in the restaurant business in San Francisco—where he was shocked to learn that California wine had to pass under phony French labels in order to be accepted by American wine drinkers. He hoped that, by making his own wine, he would further the idea that California could produce wine good enough to sell under its own name.[31] His policy was supported by the establishment, in 1880, of a State Board of Viticultural Commissioners, itself partly as a result of the denunciation of the adulteration of genuine French wines and the rebaptizing of California ones as French by Charles Wetmore, a San Francisco journalist. Wetmore was made the Board's executive officer. The Board pushed for federal controls on wine labeling, but was powerless to stop retailers in Boston and New York from selling their lesser European wines with California labels—and their better California wines with European ones. Moreover, substantial quantities of California wines were exported to Europe, and it was claimed that some of them were re-exported to America bearing French labels. [32] It was later said that it had been standard practice in San Francisco, in the late nineteenth century, to blend California wine with French wine that had arrived as ballast in ships calling to load California grain for Europe. At first the blend was half and half, but as California wines began to improve, it was increased to 80 percent California and 20 percent French—but always sold under a French label. [33]

American wine makers may no longer pretend that their wines come from Europe, but they still dignify them with French names such as champagne, burgundy, and Chablis. In his history of American wines, Leon D. Adams has sought to defend the appropriation of French names on the grounds that they have been used for a century or more: if the United States were forced to give up these names, he argues, France would reap an overnight monopoly on the vast markets that have been built up by American wine companies for champagne, burgundy, and Chablis. [34] This argument is specious: it is the American wineries who have for many years benefited unfairly from the reputation established by the famous wine-producing regions of France.

It is bad enough that the Champagne houses who have set up facilities in California should describe the sparkling wines they have made there as having been made by "champagne method," but native companies such as Korbel and Schramsberg sell their produce as "champagne." Korbel, which was founded in the Russian River Valley in Sonoma County in 1882, today sells more wine made by the same method as is used in Champagne than any other company in California: 13–14 million bottles of its "champagne" each year. Schramsberg, which was established in the Napa Valley in 1965, has enjoyed an international reputation ever since President Nixon had thirteen cases flown over to Peking in order that they could be served at his historic banquet for Premier Chou En-lai.[35] It is sold as "champagne," explains its owner, Jack Davies, because consumers would not expect a bottle labeled simply "sparkling wine" to be of high quality[36]—which is, of course, the whole point.

Some producers have found ways of identifying their product even more closely with champagne than have Korbel and Schramsberg. The first winery to be established at Hammondsport in the Finger Lakes in New York State was the Pleasant Valley Wine Company; it was founded in 1860. At that time, the sparkling Catawba produced by Nicholas Longworth—with the help of a French wine maker—in Cincinnati, Ohio, was all the rage. The new Hammondsport winery attempted to follow this model by making a sparkling wine in the French style. In order that the French connection should be made as obvious as possible, it obtained the post office address of Rheims, which it used on its letterhead for the next hundred years. The Rheims post office may long since have been closed, but the tiny village of that name still exists. At the beginning of 1991, eleven champagne companies filed suit in the Federal District Court in Rochester in an attempt to stop Philippe Guermonprez from selling the produce of his Finger Lakes winery under the label "Château de Rheims." Guermonprez argued that, because he lived in the village of Rheims, the law was on his side. It wasn't. When the case was decided at the end of the year he was ordered to cease using the name "Château de Rheims" and to destroy all existing labels within six months. Ironically, Guermonprez is a native of France.[37]

Even when they do not use French names, many American wine makers have difficulty in shaking off their belief that the French wines are automatically superior. The majority of the vine growers who have established themselves in Oregon in the last generation are emigrants from California who have rejected the technology-oriented attitudes of the California wine industry. Instead of adopting California wine-making techniques, they have adopted Burgundian ones. Pat Campbell, the wine maker at Elk Cove, planted Pinot Noir and Chardonnay in 1974 because she loved burgundies. She freely admits that she tried to learn "by copying Burgundy techniques." She went to Burgundy in 1976 during the harvest before making her first wine in 1977.

Russ Raney set up Evesham Wood in 1986 after corresponding with Henri Jayer, the most celebrated wine maker in Burgundy. Raney, who describes Jayer as his mentor, even tried fermenting some of his Pinot Noir grapes in the 1989 vintage with the yeast taken from the sediment in a bottle of Jayer's wine—with such success that he released the experimental batch of wine as a separate "Cuvée J" at nearly twice the price of his ordinary Pinot Noir. "I'm not ashamed to admit that we would like to emulate Burgundy," he explains.

Every summer since 1987 Oregonian producers of Pinot Noir have organized a conference at McMinnville (and another, less public one at Steamboat), to which they have paid Burgundian wine makers to fly over. In 1989 Philippe Senard of Domaine Daniel Senard in Aloxe-Corton, one of the wine makers advised by the consultant enologist Guy Accad, came over and spoke about Accad's method of macerating the grapes in their juice at a low temperature before fermentation. (This technique was discussed in more detail in the previous chapter.) Two months later, many Oregon wine makers were trying it out. It can be useful in Burgundy, because it extracts more fruit and color from the grapes, but it is not necessary in Oregon, where Pinot Noirs naturally have good fruit and color. There is no reason why Burgundian methods should be the ideal ones for Oregon, given that the Pinot Noir is made from different clones grown on a different training system in a different climate. "People follow Burgundy," says one Oregonian observer, "because they don't know any better. Americans have no cultural heritage, so they have to have someone to imitate."

If even wine makers in the United States believe that French wines are superior, it is not surprising that their clients feel the same way—and accordingly adjust the prices that they are prepared to pay. Red burgundies are not necessarily superior to Oregon Pinot Noirs—as was first demonstrated in the "Wine Olympics" held in 1979 by the French food and wine magazine *Gault Millau*.[38] The 1975 Eyrie Reserve from Oregon came third in the Pinot Noir class, and in general the red burgundies did not do so well as expected. The Burgundy merchant Robert Drouhin said that the tasting had been unbalanced because the best burgundies had not been chosen. So he organized a rematch in 1980, with wines selected from his cellars.

This time, the Eyrie 1975 Reserve came second, behind Drouhin's Chambolle-Musigny 1959; but the Eyrie was ahead of his *grand cru* Chambertin-Clos de Bèze 1961. In the opinion of David Lett, the owner of Eyrie, this tasting was the turning point for vine-growing Oregon. Certainly it helped persuade Drouhin, some years later, to establish his own vineyard and winery in Oregon. In the best vintages, the Eyrie Pinot Noir Reserve is the most expensive wine in Oregon: the outstanding 1985 sells for $40 a bottle. Other leading Oregon Pinot Noirs sell for between $15 and $30 a bottle, with Robert Drouhin's wine, Domaine Drouhin, at the top end of the scale. Oregon Pinot Noirs have been accused of being overpriced, but these figures compare favorably with the $30–40 charged for the current vintage of Drouhin's Chambolle-Musigny and the $70–80 price tag on his Chambertin-Clos de Bèze. The difference in price can be explained, at least in part, by the fact that vine growers in Burgundy have been cultivating Pinot Noir for nearly two millennia and exporting the wine they have made from it for several centuries, whereas the first Pinot Noir vines were planted in Oregon in 1966. It is principally for reasons of tradition that we pay larger sums of money for wines coming from France than from elsewhere. This much is admitted by Robert Drouhin. "We don't sell wine," he says. "We sell luxury. We sell the image of the cobbled streets of Beaune."

The image and prices of the finest French wines are so successfully supported by tradition that we seem to have trouble believing that certain of the most celebrated French wines, with the noblest history, are no longer worth the sums that are asked. Château Lafite has a great reputation that reached its zenith in the nineteenth century, when it was so much the snob name in Britain that in 1836 the St. James's Club purchased a hundred barriques of Ch. Latour 1831 under the name "Lafite."[39] From the late 1960s until the late 1970s, Lafite was living on that reputation. The 1971—from a good, though not great, vintage—was never much better than plonk, and went over the hill some years go. Yet it sells for about $100 a bottle, retail. Clearly, it has not achieved this price on grounds of quality.

But tradition is not all. If it were, German wines would still attain their historic status. The exception to the rule that wines were drunk young until two hundred years ago can be found in the wines

of the Rhineland, which, from the sixteenth century on, were matured in enormous vats on a *solera* system and kept to a great age. In
the last century the best German wines attained prices higher than
first-growth Bordeaux. A British wine list of 1867 (that of Harveys of
Bristol) quotes Steinberger Auslese 1862 at £9 a case, compared with
£4 14s. for the Château Lafite 1864, a great vintage. (At present-day
exchange rates, the equivalent prices would be $15 and $8.) Today
you can buy wines from the best estates in Germany, such as Lang-
werth von Simmern in the Rheingau, the State Wine Domain in the
Nahe, and Burklin-Wolf in the Rheinpfalz, for $8–13 a bottle. Ger-
man wines suffer partly because, as I have already mentioned, their
system of nomenclature is often confusing, sometimes misleading,
and always open to abuse; and partly because they are not branded.

Burgundies, too, suffer for not being branded. Red burgundies
may seem expensive compared with Oregon Pinot Noirs, but they
are still cheaper than clarets of equivalent quality. In the summer of
1990 the Pacific Wine Company in San Francisco offered as futures
a number of 1989 red Bordeaux and 1988 red burgundies. Each of
the two vintages was a great one in the region in which it was offered.
For a similar price (about $440 a case) a customer could choose
between two wines of equivalent status, the Bordeaux second-growth
Château Cos d'Estournel and Volnay *premier cru* Les Caillerets from
the Domaine de la Pousse d'Or. Yet the total production of Volnay
Caillerets by the Domaine de la Pousse d'Or is only about 5 percent
that of Château Cos d'Estournel. Its scarcity should have made it
much more expensive.

In Burgundy, the Rhine, and Mosel, most vineyards enjoy
multiple ownership. In Burgundy, the noble and monastic estates
were expropriated during the Revolution and divided among a number of smallholders. If the Domaine de la Romanée-Conti can command much higher prices than its rivals—upwards of $100 a
bottle—it is because its holdings were not split up when they were
sold after the Revolution, and it enjoys sole ownership of the two best
grand cru sites in the region. On the other hand, Clos de Vougeot,
whose reputation predates that of the Domaine de la Romanée-Conti
by several centuries, was divided between six purchasers in 1889, and
now—thanks to the French practice of multigeniture—is owned by
more than eighty.

Because the vineyards are divided into a large number of very small holdings, the majority of top-class burgundy and German wine is sold under the names of sites rather than those of estates. In Burgundy, only the Domaine de la Romanée-Conti has been given exemption from the rule that no company may use as part of its name the name of any of the *appellation contrôlée* vineyards in which it owns land; in this case, the *grand cru* Romanée-Conti. The vineyards are brand names in themselves, from Clos de Vougeot and Bernkastel Doktor downward. But this has led to abuse. Whereas in Bordeaux the reputation of the brand—the *château*—depends on one single wine, in Burgundy and Germany, with a few exceptions, the reputation of the brand—the site—depends on many growers, who make wines of varying qualities. In general, the reputation of the sites has been established by dedicated growers, and then abused by unscrupulous growers who share ownership. I cannot imagine that the owner in Piesporter Goldtröpfchen who was reported to have produced an average crop of 30 tons per acre over the four vintages from 1979 to 1982 can have been solicitous of the reputation of the vineyard.

Vineyard sites in Burgundy are classified according to their potential quality. Actually, one man's straight Vosne-Romanée is superior to another's Vosne-Romanée les Beaumonts—a *premier cru*, and therefore theoretically superior; so, too, is one man's Vosne-Romanée les Beaumonts superior to another's Echézeaux—a *grand cru*, and thus in theory at the top of the tree. The classification is only really of use in choosing between wines made by the same wine maker from the produce of different sites. It is certainly possible to see the ascent in quality from plain Vosne-Romanée through Vosne-Romanée les Beaumonts to Echézeaux in the wines made by Etienne Grivot under the label of his father, Domaine Jean Grivot.

The abuse of the reputation of site names, and their misrepresentation of a wine's quality, could be circumvented by producing a classification of growers, were it not that the reputations of wine makers are too volatile to provide a reliable basis for classification. Certainly the leading producers in Bordeaux are classified, but they enjoy a flexibility with their raw material that is not open to vine growers in Germany and Burgundy; and their classification is still wholly unreliable. Officially, the disappointing Château Cantenac-

Brown precedes its celebrated neighbor Château Palmer in the list of third growths. Even if it had not been produced more than 130 years ago (as was that of the Médoc), even if it is updated every now and then (as is that of Saint-Emilion), such a classification will always be out of date by the vintage after its publication, as new stars emerge and old ones fall.

The famous 1855 classification of the Médoc has served to reinforce the reputation of the leading estates. It was only following this classification that most of the *châteaux* began to sell their wine under their own names rather than those of the merchants who sold them. Although it has been suggested that the classification was made by the trade in order to stop price competition between growers,[40] its consequence was both to widen the price between the first and other growths and artificially to elevate the price of lesser growths. A classification of growers will never be introduced officially in Burgundy or in Germany because the less conscientious growers in good sites would recognize its likely consequences and never agree to it.

The survival of the 1855 Bordeaux classification is often justified on the grounds that it rates *châteaux* according to the potential of their soil. Thus, even if a *château* is making bad wine at the moment, when it does pull its socks up, it will be making wine up to the level of its classification. There is some truth in this. From the middle of the nineteenth century until the Depression of the 1930s, Léoville-Poyferré was considered to produce possibly the best wine in Bordeaux after the first growths. The estate then fell into a decline. Though classified as a second growth, it was doubtful whether it was producing wine even of fifth-growth quality. In 1982 the old cellarmaster was knocked over by a car while crossing the main road that separates the vineyards from the cellars. This enabled the son of the owner, Didier Cuvelier, to take charge and to persuade his family to make an overdue investment in improving the equipment. The wine has since the 1982 vintage returned to second-growth quality.

A revindication of the 1855 classification? No. The 1855 classification has nothing to do with the potential of the soil in the vineyards. In the first case, it was based on the prices—not the quality—of the wines in the early 1850s. As A. d'Armailhacq, the proprietor of what is now Château Mouton-Baronne-Philippe, wrote at the

time of the classification, "The brokers and merchants never pay for
a wine according to its real quality, but according to its reputation."[41] Second, it classified the brand names of the *châteaux*, not
their vineyards. Thus *châteaux* are able to keep their classification
even if they have moved or enlarged their vineyards—as most *châteaux* have. The quantity produced under the names of the second
growths has increased from an average of two thousand cases in 1855
to twenty thousand or more today, though yields have only doubled
or at most trebled in that period. Château Siran, an unclassified
château in Margaux, has about 40 percent of its vines on land which
had belonged to classified *châteaux* in 1855, including two-thirds of
the vineyards which in 1855 had belonged to the third-growth Giscours and fifth-growth Dauzac.

The manner in which *châteaux* migrate can be seen in the
reconstruction by the Russian-born American Alexis Lichine of Château Cantenac-Prieuré, a fourth-growth Margaux that he bought in
1951 and renamed Prieuré-Lichine. He has enlarged it from 27 to
145 acres. There are thirty different plots in five communes within
the Margaux *appellation*, some as far as 3 or 4 kilometers away from
the *château*. (In Burgundy a journey of 4 kilometers would also take
you across five different communes: from Gevrey-Chambertin to
Vosne-Romanée.) The vineyards include parcels which previously
belonged to the second growths Dufort-Vivens and Brane-Cantenac,
and to the third growths Palmer, Ferrière, Kirwan, Giscours, Issan,
and Boyd-Cantenac. I would not be surprised if they also include
land which did not belong to classified *châteaux* in 1855; but we are
not told about that. Until his death in 1989, Alexis Lichine continued to try to extend his domaine. He said: "We glean from the best
of the *appellation* of Margaux"[42]—no suggestion of trying to express
the character of an individual site. Château Prieuré-Lichine is basically a (very) upmarket blended Margaux.

In his *Really Useful Wine Guide*, the British wine writer Robin
Young suggests that *châteaux* are even allowed to buy in grapes from
other producers and sell the wine under the *château* name.[43] They
certainly do so, but they are not allowed to, since French *appellation
contrôlée* laws do not permit a *château* name to be used on a label
unless the wine is produced exclusively from grapes grown on the
estate. But it is undoubtedly true that the only restriction on the

brand identity of the classed-growth *châteaux* of the Médoc is the law
of *appellation*, which requires that all the wine sold under the label
of a *château* in a particular village must come from that village—and
that this law, too, is ignored. *Châteaux* have plots of land all over the
place. Three-fifths of the vineyards of Pichon-Lalande are in Pauillac, two-fifths in Saint-Julien. The *château* used to be obliged under
appellation contrôlée regulations to sell three-fifths of the crop as
Pichon-Lalande from the village of Pauillac and two-fifths as Pichon-
Lalande from the village of Saint-Julien. This was patently ridiculous, since the wine was all the same. In the 1960s the *château* was
given permission to use the *appellation*—Pauillac—in which the
majority of the vines lay. Brand names are clearly considered to be
more important than *appellation contrôlée* regulations.

It has been suggested that this process of enlarging vineyards
beyond all recognition could be prevented if each Bordelais vineyard
were given its own *appellation*, as in Burgundy. This would also
prevent the abuse of the names of classed-growth *châteaux*, as is
currently enjoyed by such blended Bordeaux as Mouton-Cadet and
Chevalier de Lascombes. After all, no one is allowed to sell blended
burgundy as Chambertin Cadet, or blended Côtes du Rhône as
Chevalier d'Hermitage.[44] But the Burgundians do abuse famous
names by hyphenating them onto names of villages. Moreover, it is
tempting for a vine grower who owns small patches of vines in a
number of different vineyards and villages to sell as much wine
under the name of his most famous vineyard as his possibly can. If
some of the grapes in his holding in a *grand cru* vineyard happen to
be destroyed by hail, when that year's wine is finally produced the
damage will mysteriously have been transferred to one of his holdings in a less prestigious vineyard. This does not matter, since the
smallness of his holdings may well have led him to vinify the produce of several of them in the same vat, giving the result several
different names—one reason why "different" wines from the same
producer often taste the same. This blending can work to the benefit
of the wise consumer rather than to his disadvantage. After all, if an
Echézeaux and a plain Vosne-Romanée are fermented together in
the same vat, the Echézeaux may not be as good as might have been
expected—but the Vosne-Romanée will be better. It is sometimes
suggested that this is what Jacques Reynaud does at his Châteaueuf-

du-Pape estate of Château Rayas with his Côtes du Rhône from Château de Fonsalette, in theory a separate estate. He has a guaranteed sale of Château Rayas to Michelin three-star restaurants all over France; Château de Fonsalette is sold to (relatively) impoverished wine lovers. Might both wines not emerge from the same vats? Certainly, what is sold as Château de Fonsalette is a remarkable wine; certainly, Jacques Reynaud is a mysterious man.

In 1984 the classification of Saint-Emilion was revised and the imposition introduced that no classed growth was to increase for ten years the declared vineyard area covered by the classification. In 1985 it was decided to declassify Château Beauséjour-Bécot from the top group of twelve *premiers grands crus classés* to the second group of ninety *grands crus*, on the grounds that the proprietor had in 1979 included, without permission, two *grand cru (classé)* vineyards in his property, thereby increasing its size from 50 to 87 acres. Effectively, a new law was being imposed retrospectively, as Michel Bécot had been perfectly entitled to do what he did before 1984. Ironically, the quality of Beauséjour-Bécot has improved since the new vineyards were included.

Producers of champagne find themselves in an even more fortunate position than those of Bordeaux. Not only can they charge higher prices because of the security afforded the consumer by well-known brand names, but they can also increase the production of the wine under those brand names to meet demand. I have already discussed in Chapter 8 how champagne is blended for marketing purposes and not for any qualitative reasons, but that producers have succeeded in persuading consumers to part with extra money for the added value of their skill in blending inferior wines to produce a marvelous one. They can also increase production at the last minute by buying ready-made champagne from the Centre Viticole de la Champagne at Chouilly or from Marne et Champagne in Epernay and slapping their own label on it. It has been calculated that one in every four of the bottles sold by the big champagne companies between 1987 and 1990 was produced in this way.[45] This particular scam is known as the *sur lattes* scandal: *sur lattes* means "on lathes," and applies to those bottles of champagne maturing in other people's cellars which the big houses buy. There is nothing new about it. A hundred years ago, Charles Tovey wrote:

The more the public is enlightened with respect to the growth and manufacture of champagne, the sooner will the absurd delusion as to the superiority of certain brands be dispelled. It is no secret to the well-informed English wine merchant that most of the champagne houses, when their original stock of any year is exhausted, supply themselves from the stock of *speculateurs*, and that identically the same wine so purchased will, when advanced with the brand and the label of the big house, fetch from ten to twelve shillings per dozen more than when introduced into this country under the modest auspices of a smaller shipper. How long will such a system last? Surely the time will come when champagne drinkers will become wise. . . .[46]

Since the 1960s the area under vine in Champagne has doubled and the amount of wine produced has trebled. This is important. Few producers of fine wines can hope to acquire an international reputation without being able to produce enough for people to be able to get their hands on it. Most consumers of fine wines want to be seen drinking a wine which their peer group will know. The principle that a fine wine should seem to be in short supply (in order that it should appear to be exclusive), but in fact be very widely available, is practiced not only by champagne companies but also by the Robert Mondavi winery in California. This assiduously cultivates the image of a small, family-run boutique winery, yet is in fact one of the giants of California, producing (it has been estimated) 6 million bottles a year of Napa Valley varietals—including over a million bottles of Napa Valley and Reserve Cabernet Sauvignon—at its facility in St. Helena, and a further 18 million bottles of generic California wines at Woodbridge in Lodi. When pressed, Michael Mondavi admits: "The reason why we like the image of being smaller [than we are] is that other small wineries have bastardized their quality by growing bigger. We don't want to have the image of being large because Gallo are large."

The importance of making a lot of wine is demonstrated by the history of Greek wines, which, until the end of the first century B.C., enjoyed the same sort of reputation in Italy as French wines do in America today. They were the most sought after, and the most expensive. But from then on, Greek wines fell out of fashion. The reason, Edward Hyams believes, is that the Greeks were unable to change the pattern of their industry, to turn from small-scale to large-quantity production. The Romans wanted a wine which was good and expensive but which was also plentiful.[47] Today, burgundies are expensive partly because they are scarce; but the produce of the best growers might command more of a premium if it were not quite so hard to obtain. The entire vineyard area of the commune of Morey-Saint-Denis is substantially smaller in size than the two branded wines, Château Lafite and Château Mouton-Rothschild; and I know of more than sixty growers in the village, each of whom makes several different wines. Mondavi may produce a relatively small quantity of Pinot Noir compared with its other varieties, but its annual production is still as great as that of all the producers of village, *premier cur*, and *grand cru* wines in Morey-Saint-Denis put together.

Despite the ability of the champagne houses to increase their production to meet demand, the prices of their wines have not increased to the same extent as those of Bordeaux. At the end of the 1960s a bottle of Château Figeac 1962 would have cost you the same as one of non-vintage Moët et Chandon, about $4 or $5. Today a bottle of Château Figeac 1982 would cost you about $60, nearly three times as much as one of Moët. The prices of Bordeaux have outstripped those of champagne because they have become an object of investment. It is possible to invest in wines only if they are branded—that is to say, well known, easily recognizable, and available in commercial quantities. By this criterion, both Bordeaux and champagne qualify. But investment in wines is a long- rather than a short-term commitment. Therefore it is essential that the wines invested in should be perceived, not only to be long-lived but also to improve on keeping. This criterion excludes champagne but includes Bordeaux.[48] According to Hugh Johnson, "Today, the principal virtue of a *vin de garde* [a wine made for keeping] is that it remains a tradeable commodity for longer."[49]

It was investment in Bordeaux as a commodity that caused the collapse of the market in 1974. People were encouraged to invest in Bordeaux because the prices paid for mature wines in the London auction rooms rose steeply in the 1960s. Wine appeared to be a good investment because of the sharp increase in the rate of inflation, which made the return offered by traditional investments much less satisfactory than that obtained by investing in apparently "inflation-proof" luxuries: paintings, postage stamps, or wine. Unsatisfactory vintages in 1968 and 1969 concentrated investors' attention on the much better 1970 and 1971 vintages. Demand exceeded supply; what had been a buyer's market became a seller's one. The growers were encouraged—after a generation of largely poor returns from poor vintages—to increase their prices substantially even for their generally very bad 1972s. Prices peaked in 1973, and then—given a push by the Cruse scandal—collapsed in 1974.

Can such a crash happen again? That now depends much less on what happens in Britain than on what happens in the United States. As has already been described in Chapter 4, large-scale American interest in buying Bordeaux futures began with the 1982 vintage, when the dollar bought twice as much francs as it had when the last outstanding vintage, 1978, had been offered. The wines were not cheap—*The Wine Spectator* counseled its readers against buying them on the grounds that the prices were excessive—but if you had bought almost any of the leading *châteaux* at opening prices in the spring of 1983, you could have made a 100 percent profit if you had sold the wine when it was actually shipped in the autumn of 1985. People were encouraged to buy subsequent vintages, in the hope that the same would happen again.

By 1987, however, it looked as though the market might be about to crash. Retailers had bought the 1985s at high prices because they were still infected by the hysteria that had surrounded the 1982s; but they had not sold them all. Moreover, there was still a lot of wine sitting unsold in Bordeaux, causing some people to remember what Michael Broadbent, the director of Christie's Wine Department in London, had said just before the crash of the 1970s: "There is a hell of a lot of wine in Bordeaux."[50] The latest vintage, 1986, had been an outstandingly good one, and American importers feared that the inflated prices asked for the 1985s would be maintained or even increased when the *châteaux* came out with their prices for the 1986s in the spring of 1987. The American market could not have afforded to pay this much, not least because the dollar had fallen against the franc.

The crisis was averted largely because of the efforts of Abdullah

Simon, the wine buyer for Château & Estate, the fine-wine subsidiary of the Seagram empire. Château & Estate controls 40 percent of American imports of classed-growth Bordeaux; the American market accounts for one-third of the total exports of fine wines from Bordeaux. So Simon is a powerful man. He had been equally powerful within the American market in the early 1970s, when, as the fine-wine buyer for Austin Nichols, he had bought too much of mediocre wines at inflated prices, contributing not only to the collapse of the market but to the downfall of his own company.[51] Seagram took him on to set up a fine-wine division in 1974 because other enterprises were in shambles. In the spring of 1987 Simon exerted greater influence, internationally, than he ever had before. With the support of British wine merchants, and some of the merchants in Bordeaux, he succeeded in persuading the *châteaux* to lower their prices by 15 percent.

Simon believes that the influence of the American market has declined since 1987, with the growth in importance of other markets such as Japan, Germany, and Switzerland. Certainly he had no influence on the prices asked for the 1988s, which were the same as, or a little more than, for the 1986s; nor on the prices of the 1989s. The futures campaign for the 1989s began, not in the spring of 1990, but while the grapes were still being picked, an event shown on television in the United States. The next day, according to Michael Aaron of Sherry-Lehmann, people started telephoning retailers saying that they wanted to buy the wine—which had not been made yet and would not be available for another year. When the 1989s were made available in the spring of 1990, they were 30 percent more expensive than the 1988s had been, but this did not stop people from buying them. Simon had said that he could not see people paying more for the 1989s than they had for the 1988s, but he was proven wrong.

Although many of the British purchasers of Bordeaux futures buy them for the purpose of investment, it is unlikely that this was foremost in the minds of many of the Americans who were so keen to get their hands on the 1989s. This is because of the restrictions on disposing of your purchase that are imposed by the majority of state laws. In Britain, reselling wine is easy: you do not require a liquor license if you are selling a case or more, and if you are trading with another private person the transaction is exempt from sales tax. In most of the United States, resale is practically impossible. In New York, for example, state liquor laws prohibit members of the public from selling wines back to the wine trade. William Sokolin, who specializes in selling wine for investment, claims that it is possible to get around the laws because the New York State Liquor Authority unofficially accepts fine wine as an investment rather than liquor. That is a moot point. In general, unless you live in Washington, D.C.—in which case you can sell to a retailer—or in Illinois or California—where you can submit your wines for auction—the only way you can legally sell your wines is by exporting them to an importer in another state.

The relative rarity of wine investment in the United States compared with Britain is demonstrated by the different types of purchasers who attend auctions. Whereas most of the buyers and sellers at auctions in Britain are involved in the wine business, in Illinois and California most of the customers are private individuals. Bruce Kaiser, a director of Butterfield & Butterfield in San Francisco, believes that very few of its customers buy and sell fine wine purely for speculation. He points out that the wine market in the United States is too "trendy" for investing in fine wines to be anything more than a hobby, and that the price fetched by a wine at auction depends too directly on the rating it was given by Robert Parker.[52]

The probity of investing in fine wines is questionable, to say the least. Someone who had bought 1975 Bordeaux in 1976 and sold them at auction in 1986 would have realized just enough money to replace them with an equivalent quantity of wine of equivalent quality from the 1985 vintage. Having sold his 1975s, it would have proved difficult to justify replacing them with 1985s, when the 1981s were available for 25 percent less and were four years closer to maturity. It would, indeed, have proved very difficult to justify selling the 1975s at all. I can see no economic reason for buying Bordeaux futures at current prices, except for the wines of a few estates in Pomerol which are impossible to get hold of when they are older.

It is likely that the majority of American purchasers of Bordeaux futures buy the wines either because they intend to keep them and drink them at a later date or else in order to put them in their collection. Wine collectors are not going to be dissuaded from buying a vintage just because it offers poor value for money. If they are told that it is the thing to buy, then they will buy it. "The phenomenon of collectibles," says the Boston wine importer Fred Ek, "has caused wines to go up to a price which is not related to their drinking worth. If people have the wines, they are embarrassed to drink them. They sell them. Psychologically they don't want to drink them anymore."

Will the prices of classed-growth Bordeaux ever stop increasing? Will they ever become affordable again? One Bordeaux merchant justified the spiraling prices of the early 1980s on the grounds that, "If you are dying of thirst in the desert and somebody offers you a glass of water [for] ten million francs, the price is a fair one."[53] Has he not read the story of Abe's sardines, which was told by the Bordeaux merchant Peter Sichel in his report on the 1971 and 1972 vintages in Bordeaux? "Abe bought a shipment of sardines that had already been traded many times and each time profitably. Unlike previous buyers, Abe took the trouble of procuring a box of his purchase. The sardines were terrible. He telephoned Joe, from whom he had bought them only to be told, 'But Abe, those sardines are for trading, not eating.' "[54]

13
The Falernian
Syndrome

THE PRICE of wines bears no direct relation to their quality but derives from their image. The "added value" afforded by this image is, however, necessary for quality-wine production, since without first creating a high price for his wines a producer cannot afford to lavish the expense necessary to produce top-class wine. What would seem to be the natural relationship between quality and price is in fact inverted. A wine maker has to create added value in order to be able to afford intrinsic value.

I have already mentioned that, although it is overpriced in relation to its intrinsic worth—given the amount of added value it offers—champagne is cheap. Indeed, it is too cheap. The costs of actually making it and of marketing and advertising are so high that the very important aspect of aging has to be skimped. This aging cannot be carried out by the consumer after he has bought the wine; it has to be carried out in the cellars of the producer while the yeasts are still in the bottle. During the champagne's long period of conditioning in contact with its yeast cells, the yeasts give back to the wine substances—notably amino acids—that they have previously taken from it. The value of this long yeast contact is evident from Bollinger RD, the one *cuvée de prestige* which possibly is aworth the price. This ages for ten years in contact with its yeasts before the yeasts are expelled and the champagne recorked for shipment.

The higher the price a merchant charges for his champagne, the more money he has to give the vine grower from whom he has bought the grapes. This prevents merchants from ripping off growers. But it also prevents them from increasing their price to finance a longer period of aging, since the extra money goes to the grower rather than into investment in stockholding. It has been said that the difference between a peasant in Champagne and a rich Parisien is that the peasant has to wash his own Mercedes. Yet, if champagne is to justify its high price, a longer period of aging is necessary. Currently, most champagne is young, green, and overly sugared. When champagne costs more, greater care could be taken in its production. On his travels in France just before the Revolution, Arthur Young visited Champagne and ascribed much of the fine flavor of the wine to the care taken by pickers in selecting only healthy bunches of grapes.[1] Today, rotten grapes are usually picked and pressed along with healthy ones; the must is then filtered to take away the taste.

The most famous example of a wine which became so uneconomic to produce as—in the case of some estates—to disappear altogether is that of Sauternes, which can only be produced by selectively picking grapes affected by noble rot. Since noble rot does not strike all the grapes in a vineyard at once, the bunches have to be picked individually, by hand, sometimes in several passages through the vines over a period of months. On top of the labor costs, the size of the eventual crop is small. This is the consequence partly of the concentrating of the grapes by noble rot, partly of the fact that not all the grapes are affected, and partly of the need to reject a lot of the grapes that have been picked because the rot turns out to be the gray rather than the noble kind. It is sometimes mentioned as though it were something extraordinary that Château d'Yquem, which produces the most celebrated and expensive wine in Sauternes, yields on average little more than ½ ton per acre, going up to ¾ ton in good years. In fact, all the leading Sauternes *châteaux* achieve similarly low yields, ranging from two-thirds to one and a third tons per acre.

The leading red wine *châteaux* of Bordeaux regularly achieve yields of 3 tons per acre.

Sauternes is not cost-effective to produce unless a high price is charged for it. Though the selective picking of Sauternes was known in the eighteenth century, it was not used—at least not for commercial purposes—until someone could be found who was prepared to pay the price. The first vintage of Château d'Yquem as we know it today was produced because the Russian Grand Duke Constance/ Constantine, brother of the Tsar, paid $1,500—five times the odds— for a *tonneau* (one hundred cases' worth) of the 1847. Château d'Yquem has established a reputation—added value—which today enables it to charge a price two to three times as high as that of its rivals. Therefore it can afford to spend as long as is necessary to pick the grapes: sometimes the pickers make nine or ten passages over three months. It can afford to pick fast when necessary, such as in 1984, in the week of October 15, when it employed 130 pickers at an approximate cost of $25,000 for the week. Its rivals cannot always afford such care. The first-growth Château Suduiraut notoriously produced a 1985 Sauternes lacking in concentration, because they finished picking too early. They finished on November 20, a month before Yquem.

In the decade after the end of the Second World War, Sauternes was profitable to manufacture. Wage costs were low and the wines sold for prices that took into account the fact that it cost three times as much to harvest a white-grape vineyard in Sauternes as a black-grape one in the Médoc. First- and second-growth Sauternes sold for the same prices as first- and second-growth red wine *châteaux*. The change came, it has been suggested, when Europe finally recovered from the aftereffects of the war and people's diets returned to normal. Consumers, particularly in France, no longer craved the sugar that sweet wines provided, and indeed rejected Sauternes as being a reminder of their past sufferings.[2] Many of the top *châteaux*, unable to afford the indulgence of several selective pickings of nobly rotten grapes, started making dry white wines instead. Even Château d'Yquem did so, starting in 1959. Comte Alexandre de Lur-Saluces, who took over at Yquem in 1968 (and who sold only six cases of wine during the whole of 1974), described his early vintages as "desperate, debilitating years" during which he thought noble rot had disappeared altogether, perhaps because it had been killed by pollution.[3] Some *châteaux* pulled up their white grapevines and planted red. Max de Pontac, heir to the family which invented fine red Bordeaux at Château Haut-Brion in the late seventeenth century, plowed up the vineyard at the second-growth Château Myrat in 1976. He had taken his decision purely on economic grounds. He explained that, before the Second World War, he could pay the wages of five men by selling the same quantity of wine that now enabled him to pay for one man.[4]

Sauternes might have gone the way of Monbazillac, fifty miles away, which earlier this century used to produce wines equal to those of Sauternes. Today, most producers can no longer afford selective picking. Yields, at 2½ tons per acre, are far too high to make good sweet wine. *Appellation* regulations in Monbazillac forbid mechanical harvesting, since the wine is supposed to be made by a selection of nobly rotten or at least overripe grapes. In fact, a number of growers harvest by machine, and they say that officials turn a blind eye to the practice.[5]

The turning point for Sauternes came with the 1983 vintage. An excellent harvest of nobly rotten grapes coincided with popular interest in buying Bordeaux futures, encouraged by the enormous success of the red wines in 1982. For the first time in a generation, producers of Sauternes were able to sell their wines profitably, for twice the price they had achieved in the rare good vintages of the 1970s. The wines they made in 1983 were not uniformly wonderful, but the money they made enabled them to invest in new equipment, so that—when the next good vintage came along in 1986—they managed to produce consistently outstanding wines. The equipment that they were now able to afford helped them make better wine— not only in good vintages but also in years when it rained during the harvest, thus ensuring that the depression of the 1960s and 1970s would never return. A number of leading Sauternes *châteaux* each spent 1.5 million francs (about a quarter of a million dollars) on equipping themselves for cryo-extraction—the method of freezing the grapes in order to draw off only the richest juices that has been described in Chapter 7. Cryo-extraction enabled many Sauternes *châteaux* to make much better wine in the 1987 vintage than they would otherwise have produced.

By 1988 the manufacture of Sauternes had become sufficiently profitable for the sons of Max de Pontac to replant Château Myrat. This was symbolic, but it did not mean that Sauternes sold for prices as high as the red wines of the region. For this, *château* owners had to rely on the added value of an Act of God. The 1988 vintage was also excellent in Sauternes, but when the wines were first offered as futures in the spring of 1989, they were not significantly more expensive than the 1986s had been. Then, during the summer, the region was struck by a hailstorm. It was reported that some top Sauternes estates—including Château d'Yquem—had lost up to 50 percent of their crop. Suddenly, Sauternes prices took off. Château Rieussec, which was being offered for well under $300 a case retail before the storm was reported, cost nearly $500 soon afterward. When the grapes were harvested in the autumn, it transpired that the damage had been much less than had been feared; but this did not cause prices to fall. Today, the leading Sauternes sell for a price between that of the second- and first-growth red wine *châteaux*, and Yquem costs more than anything except for Pétrus.

In Sauternes it is, by and large, the good vintages that are cheap and the bad vintages that are expensive. In 1983 the grapes all become nobly rotten at once: at Château Raymond-Lafon the pickers made only four or five passages through the vines, and 90 percent of the crop was bottled under the *château's* own label.[6] In bad vintages, the pickers have to make more passages: at Raymond-Lafon in 1974 they made ten of them, but the *château* still had to sell off the entire crop to merchants as generic Sauternes.

The same is true of the red wines of the region: bad vintages are more expensive to produce. How is this expense to be financed? By what is commonly referred to in the British wine trade as "blackmail."[7] If a merchant, importer, retailer, or consumer wants to buy a sought-after wine in a good vintage, he has to buy it also in bad vintages: 1984, for example. Opening prices, both in Bordeaux and in Burgundy, were about 10 to 15 percent higher than for the far superior 1983s. In order to justify asking more for their 1984s than they had for their 1983s, the Bordelais piled on the excuses: the need for a lot of expensive spraying; the loss of Merlot grapes through floral abortion; etc. But the only way they persuaded merchants to buy their 1984s was by "blackmail."

Up until the 1974 crash, stocks of wine were held by merchants in Bordeaux. Since then, everything has changed. The merchants no longer have the capital (nor could they afford the interest involved in borrowing the money) required to finance every vintage. Instead of being stockholders, as formerly, they have become dependent on selling recent vintages on a commission basis; they have been transformed from merchants into brokers. They are interested in quick sales, however they are achieved. They want to pass on the tins of sardines as fast as possible.

The "blackmail" travels down a chain until it reaches the eventual consumer. It stops here. As with other versions of blackmail, the consumer is perfectly at liberty to resist the blandishments of his wine merchant; but if he does, there will be a price to pay. Many consumers refused to buy the 1984s when they were originally offered, forcing retailers to reduce their prices. Today the 1984s sit on liquor-store shelves bearing price tags lower than those of any other recent vintage; but for the most part they remain lean, mean wines that would not offer good value for money at any price. The 1985s are quite a different matter, however. This was a great vintage, and one might normally have expected the *châteaux* proprietors to have raised their prices compared with 1984, arguing that this was justified by their far superior quality. They did not, however. American wine importers, led by Abdullah Simon of Château & Estate, persuaded them to keep their prices at the 1984 level. The *châteaux* owners agreed—on the understanding that American allocations of the big 1985 vintage would remain at the same level as for the small 1984 one. As a result, those consumers who had not bought any 1984s found that their wine merchants were unable to supply them with any 1985s.

In Burgundy and the Northern Rhône, "blackmail" is the essential consequence of the domaine-bottling movement, for peasant vine growers cannot afford to finance the poor vintages. We consumers cannot have it both ways. If we believe that we should buy our burgundies and Northern Rhônes direct from the growers rather than indirectly through the blends made up by merchants, then we have to finance them. If we won't do so willingly, then their alternative is either to "blackmail" us—or to go back to selling to merchants who will mix up their wine with the produce of other growers in a blending vat. It is very tempting, however, for growers who resort to "blackmail" out of necessity to become greedy when the market turns in their favor—as happened with certain white-wine producers in Burgundy's Côte d'Or, where prices doubled between the 1982 and 1985 vintages. The British wine retailer Corney & Barrow, which supplies the cellars of the Queen, the Queen Mother, and the Prince of Wales, enjoys a good relationship with a number of estates in the region, but no longer with any in Chassagne-Montrachet. In one of their wine lists they described how they used to buy wine from Ramonet-Prudhon, but stopped doing so after it had taken two years, and the dispatch of solicitors' letters, to deliver the 1976s they had ordered. In 1979 they started to buy wine from Bachelet-Ramonet instead, but in 1984, when prices were rising by the day, they discovered that 250 cases they had ordered had already been sold *twice* to other purchasers.

Bordelais proprietors justify the system of "blackmail" by looking at it the other way around. In certain good vintages, demand exceeds supply, so it is necessary to make an allocation. How to choose to whom to allocate the wines? "Blackmail," the proprietors argue, is preferable to selling to the highest bidder, or to operating on a basis of "first come, first served." But shouldn't they, rather than their customers, bear the loss in bad vintages? It is they, after all, who make the profit in good ones. Even if Bordelais *châteaux* had cut their prices in 1984, they would not exactly have suffered a loss. It has been estimated that the maximum possible cost of making a bottle of classed-growth Bordeaux is 30 francs, so *châteaux* who were selling their product for 100 francs or more were hardly in danger of suffering economic damage.

This said, to a certain degree, the lesser quality and higher prices of the top wines in bad vintages is offset by the fact that the gap between wines from the best estates and those from lesser producers is much greater in bad than in good vintages. It may well be worth buying wines from less celebrated properties in Bordeaux and Burgundy in good vintages like 1985, 1988, and 1990, when even careless wine makers would have had to make an effort if they wanted to produce bad wines; but, if you feel the need to buy in lesser years, it really is worth sticking with the big names. Whereas, in Bordeaux, the leading *châteaux* reject the majority of their vats as not up to scratch, in Burgundy, the *premier* and *grand cru* sites lie on the better-drained hillsides and are therefore not as vulnerable to the effects of too much rain as those vineyards at the bottom of the slope which are entitled only to the plain communal *appellations* (straight Nuits-Saint-Georges, etc.).

In Bordeaux, even in a good vintage, it is necessary to eliminate less good vats in order to ensure that the quality is up to scratch. It is often pointed out that this is enormously expensive. In 1985 the second-growth Château Ducru-Beaucaillou sold for 100 francs and its second wine La Croix—the repository of its less good vats—for 40 francs a bottle. By rejecting 40 percent of the harvest from the first wine, the owners lost a potential 6 million francs. But then the wine wouldn't sell for the price it does if these steps were not taken to ensure quality. Moreover, one might wonder why a Bordelais chatelain should need to eliminate 40 percent of the harvest in a good vintage.

The Bordelais use vat elimination as their standard method for reducing excess yields. They effectively operate the cascade system (already explained in Chapter 9), which permitted a wine maker to sell the same wine under various different *appellations*, up to the maximum production permitted for each. It was outlawed in 1974. Today the excess production over the limit permitted for each *appellation* has to be sold off for distillation. A disincentive for producing a big crop, one might have thought. In fact, the redrafting of the laws and the introduction of *rendements annuels* and *plafonds limites de classement* have ensured that a producer with a big crop does not suffer—and that a châtelain can produce 80 hectoliters per hectare (5 tons per acre) and still be allowed to sell the whole lot as Pauillac. Of course, the resultant wine won't be worthy of a classed-growth *château*. No matter, the châtelain eliminates his thinner vats. "Elimination" should not be taken too literally: in many instances, the producer doesn't throw the wine away or even sell it off to merchants as part of a Pauillac, Médoc, or Bordeaux blend; like Jean-Eugène Borie at Château Ducru-Beaucaillou, he releases it under a "second label" and at a price which would seem healthy to all but the greediest producers of classed-growth Bordeaux. Still, vat elimination does at least ensure that the wine will be good, despite the excess production.

Vat elimination is a procedure that is only possible for big properties with a large production which is all sold under a single label. Therefore it is not an option which is open to the smallholders of Burgundy, most of whom own vines in various different vineyards from which they make wine which they commercialize under various different labels. If they think a crop is likely to be too large a one to be commensurate with good quality, they cut off some of the bunches of grapes in midsummer. This allows the remaining grapes to achieve better ripeness and concentration of flavor.

The only problem with this method is that the vine growers don't really know as early as midsummer whether the harvest is likely to be a large one or not. They sometimes guess wrong. In midsummer in 1982 they considered eliminating some grapes but did not do so because they remembered that the 1981 harvest had been small. The resulting wines were so dilute that they had to resort to the desperate means of running off between 10 and 20 percent of the juice before fermentation in order to produce red wines with any degree of color or concentration. In July 1983 they remembered the problems of 1982 and therefore did eliminate some grapes. As a result, the grapes were too concentrated, their sugar levels too high, and some of the resultant wines had excessive levels of acetic acid (vinegar). Others had to be diluted—illegally—with water.[8]

Quite apart from the smaller size of their holdings, the Burgundians had to resort to these risky and often desperate means because their black grape, Pinot Noir, is denatured by high yields. Thus they could not overcrop and then eliminate vats in the summer of the Bordelais. It is usually held that Pinot Noir cannot produce good wine if allowed to produce more than 3 tons per acre. There are, it must be admitted, those who disagree. Scott Henry, a former aerospace engineer who returned to his family farm in the Umpqua Valley in Oregon to grow grapes in 1972, has made experimental batches of wine from grapes cropped at every level between 2 and 12 tons per acre. He has settled on cropping about 6 tons per acre, because he says that the best wine is produced at this level. The reason why he is able to crop his Pinot Noir vines much more heavily than growers in Burgundy is that he has planted his vines in fertile alluvial soil where they are naturally much more vigorous. Also, it is warmer in the Umpqua Valley than in Burgundy—or,

indeed, than in the Willamette Valley, the main region for Pinot
Noir in Oregon, 150 miles to the north—so it is possible to ripen a
larger crop. In theory, a warm climate and a fertile soil are preju-
dicial to the quality of Pinot Noir—but Henry's 1985 and 1987
Reserve Pinot Noirs are excellent.

Like Pinot Noir, Merlot—the grape cultivated on Bordeaux's
right bank, in Pomerol and Saint-Emilion—can be denatured by
high yields. This can be demonstrated by tasting a cheap Italian
Merlot which is unlikely to bear any resemblance to the versions
produced in Bordeaux. In Saint-Emilion and Pomerol, bunches of
grapes are sometimes cut off in midsummer, as in Burgundy. It was
particularly important in 1986, when some estates in Saint-Emilion
achieved 7 tons per acre—far more than the permitted maximum
yield. In Pomerol, Vieux Château Certan cut off 50 percent of their
bunches of grapes. In 1982, considered at the time an enormous
vintage, at Château Pétrus one bunch in four was removed once the
size of the potential harvest was apparent. As the full-time vineyard
workers would have considered this to be sacrilege, the task was
carried out by a few students.

Cabernet Sauvignon, which predominates on Bordeaux's left
bank, is not denatured by high yields to anything like the same
degree. Its quality may be much diminished, but it still tastes like
Cabernet Sauvignon. This is partly, I suspect, a consequence of its
thick skins and high tannin content. That is why overcropping followed by the elimination of thinner vats is possible in the Médoc.
Thus, whereas the top Burgundian estates yield 2 tons per acre, or
less, for their red grapes, top Bordeaux *châteaux* yield twice as much
and then sell off up to half. For example, at Château Latour the
average yield in the 1970s was 3 tons per acre, but on average only
57 percent of total production was sold under the principal Château
Latour label—which, by a stroke of casuistry, produces, in Bordelais
eyes, a yield of 1¾ tons per acre.

But do the Bordelais, by their peculiar method of overproduction, cause quality to suffer? Certainly it is facile to believe that there
exists a simple equation: the smaller the yield, the better the wine. If
lowness of yield in itself indicated superior quality, we would have to
assume that no wines are as good as they used to be. We would have
to agree that Château Latour 1970 cannot possibly be as good as the

1870 because the yield was twice as large. It all depends on what causes the yield to be low. In Dão in Portugal, the low average yield of 1⅔ tons per acre is largely the consequence of the vineyard's infestation with the fan-leaf virus. In Priorato in Catalonia in eastern Spain, the ludicrously low average yield of ¼ ton per acre can best be explained by a lack of water reaching the vines on the rocky hillsides. In California, too, the yields on unirrigated hillside vineyards can be absurdly low—as, particularly, in the drought years of the late 1980s. In the Santa Cruz Mountains, the crop at Mount Eden (the descendant of a vineyard originally planted at the bottom of the mountain with cuttings brought from Burgundy by Paul Masson, an immigrant from France at the end of the nineteenth century) averages ½ ton per acre; at the Santa Cruz Mountain Vineyard the harvest has ranged from 1¼ tons per acre in 1983 to a ¼ ton per acre in 1988. Its owner, Ken Burnap, makes a Pinot Noir and a Cabernet Sauvignon that have great length and intensity but which are not exactly elegant. The most celebrated producer of red burgundy, Henri Jayer, replies to questions about his crop level by saying that he does not go to ridiculous lengths to reduce it—2 tons per acre or so is fine.

This said, excessive yields do produce poor wines. All over Europe, grape varieties are reviled because they are normally set to work producing as much juice as they can manage. In Germany, the grape responsible for the mass of Liebfraumilch is Müller-Thurgau; but it only produces poor wine, the emptiness of which needs to be concealed by the addition of substantial quantities of unfermented sweet grape juice because it is made to crop at 15 tons per acre. In his holding in the Bernkastel Schlossberg vineyard in the Middle Mosel, which he cultivates by "organic" methods, Ernst Loosen yields about 2½ tons per acre from his Müller-Thurgau vines, less than from the Riesling he cultivates elsewhere, and produces a remarkable wine as a result.

The relationship between yield and quality has best been explained by the late British philosopher, polymath, and wine writer, Edward Hyams. A given area of vineyard can be understood as having a certain amount of goodness. A vine grower has the option of dividing this goodness among a small quantity of wine—and thus producing fine wine—or between a lot of wine, and thus diluting it. [9]

When vines are overcropped, the leaves simply cannot produce enough sugar by photosynthesis to enable the grapes to ripen properly and develop normal flavor. Moreover, as the yield per vine increases, the nitrogen content decreases. It is nitrogen which during fermentation helps the formation of esters and higher alcohols, producing more intense flavors and aromas; and it is possibly these which react during bottle aging, producing a fine wine.

The best wines are produced from low yields. Strictly speaking, this does not prove a causal connection—it may simply be that producers who take the care to produce good wines are also those who crop the least. Nevertheless, it is strong circumstantial evidence. The most expensive and, I believe, best Châteauneuf-du-Pape, Château Rayas, yields slightly less than 1 ton per acre. The second most expensive and, I believe, second best estate in the region, Château de Beaucastel, crops on average just about 1 ton per acre. Yet, the average yield in Châteauneuf-du-Pape is twice as large.

It is possibly the excessive yields which explain why so many German dry wines taste thin when historically they were rated so highly: at the end of the last century London wine merchants sold top dry Rheingau wines for more than first-growth red Bordeaux. But in those days the yield of German wines was lower than that of French ones, which were busy being overmanured in order to overcome the effect of phylloxera. In Germany today, high yields are seen as a sign of a healthy vineyard. This is not unique: the same is true for white grapes in Burgundy, where it is commonly said that, whereas too many black grapes make a bad wine, for white grapes quantity and quality go hand in hand. Some excellent, elegant wines were made by producers of white burgundy who cropped 6 tons per acre in the prolific vintages of 1988 and 1990. The legal limits on production which oblige them, at least in theory, to send half of their wine off for distillation may serve to explain why vine growers in the Côte d'Or have not confessed to the size of their crops; but in Chablis in 1990, William Fèvre, the head of one of two competing vine growers' unions, urged the government to increase the maximum yield of 60 hectoliters per hectare (3½ tons per acre), pointing out that it was absurd to have required producers to distill one quarter of their crop in the outstanding 1988 vintage. In Germany, the average yield had reached 6 tons per acre by the 1970s, and culminated in an average of 10 tons per acre in 1982. The most quality conscious estates, however, achieve yields only one-third to one-half this size.

Why are yields today so much higher than they used to be? Many vine growers would say that yields were lower in the past because the vine stock was less healthy and because their predecessors lacked the modern chemical sprays that exist to deal with disease and rot. Rot was certainly a problem in the past—that was why grapes were picked earlier—but it was *less* of a problem because lower yields meant that the bunches of grapes were less tightly packed and therefore more easily able to dry out after rain, and so less susceptible to the spread of rot. Moreover, excessive use of nitrogenous fertilizers has produced an excess of vegetation, which causes increased humidity around the vine and makes rot more likely. Until recently, the vine growers relied on Bordeaux mixture as a prophylactic against fungal diseases. This copper sulphate solution burned the hands of those who used it and hardened the skins of the grapes, rendering them less liable to rot than they are today. Modern anti-rot sprays are, at best, a short-term solution, and have in some instances made the problem worse. There was substantial rot among Pinot Noir grapes in Burgundy in 1983 because the rot fungi had developed resistance to the anti-rot sprays. The produce of certain great estates, including Domaine Armand Rousseau and possibly the Domaine de la Romanee-Conti, was tainted with rot. If the sorting out of rotten grapes by hand has only fairly recently become common practice in Bordeaux, then it can only be because it has only recently become necessary. According to the British wine merchant and wine writer David Peppercorn, it was adopted because of the disastrous results of 1963; it enabled much more successful wines to be made in 1968, despite similar weather conditions.[10]

Disease is an undying problem. Five hundred years ago, many of the vines in the Côte de Beaune were destroyed by a plague of beetles. As human efforts were of no avail, the Burgundians concluded that the plague was the work of the Devil, and sought God's assistance. A public religious procession was organized; each man was instructed to go to general confession and to abstain from swearing. When similar measures proved ineffective against another sort of beetle which attacked the vines in the 1540s, the insects were excommunicated.[11] The dangers facing vines have, however, become more serious since the appearance in Europe of the oidium fungus in the middle of the nineteenth century and of the phylloxera louse and mildew fungus twenty years later. These diseases have not been conquered; their march has merely been halted. Grapes are sprayed with sulphur to prevent the onset of oidium and with Bordeaux mixture against mildew. The ravages of phylloxera were stemmed in Europe at the turn of the century by grafting European wine-producing vines onto the roots of American wild vines, which are resistant to phylloxera because they are too tough for the louse to penetrate.

Today, vines are grafted in most European wine-producing areas, with the exception of regions such as the Mosel Valley, where phylloxera is unable to burrow into the slate soil. In Oregon, however, 90 percent of the vines are planted on their own roots, which may serve to explain why phylloxera was found in a number of vineyards in 1989. In California, most vines are grafted, but generally onto the rootstock AxR 1. Growers chose this rootstock partly because vines take well to grafting onto it, and principally because it produces large crops. Unfortunately, it is not very resistant to phylloxera, which is the reason why it is not used in Europe. When a new mutant strain of phylloxera, Biotype B, appeared in the Napa Valley in the early 1980s, it had little trouble in munching through the apparently phylloxera-resistant roots of American vines. It is thought that three-quarters of the vineyards in Napa Valley and Sonoma County will have to be replanted, at an estimated cost of between $500 million and $1 billion. In 1987 George Ordish, the author of the standard work on phylloxera, expressed the fear that the world's vineyards could "soon be in the position they were in just over a century ago—threatened with extinction by this tiny insect."[12]

The principal vine-growing regions of France have other problems to contend with. In the 1960s and 1970s the disease most talked about was fan-leaf (also called infectious degeneration), provoked by a microscopic root-sucking worm which lives in the soil and causes vines to degenerate and die at fifteen years of age, just when they ought to be producing their best and most concentrated wine. Fan-leaf cannot be treated except by grubbing up and disinfecting the infected vineyard. At the beginning of the 1970s it was already causing the loss of 20 percent of the production of Le Montrachet.[13]

Fan-leaf was joined in the 1980s by another disease, eutypiose, which is caused by a fungus which enters the vine through a pruning wound. It is difficult to detect, because an infected vine can seem healthy for several years before showing signs of the illness. The only known treatment is amputation of the infected arm; if the fungus has reached the trunk, the vine will die. Eutypiose may well have existed in all the major vineyard areas of France for a long time, but it was only discovered in 1977 in Cognac. It spread rapidly during the 1980s and now affects 20 percent of the vines in Cognac and a significant proportion in Bordeaux; it may or may not be present in Burgundy.

Whether or not eutypiose has yet become a factor, it is evident that degenerative diseases are the principal explanation for the relatively low yields achieved from Pinot Noir grapes in Burgundy, which in many cases do not exceed 2 tons per acre. In any given vineyard it is likely that there will be a mixture of healthy vines producing a good crop of grapes and diseased vines producing a small crop or none at all. Joseph Voillot, who makes some of the best, and most elegant, wines in Volnay, believes that the problem is likely to get worse. He points out that vine growers pay much less attention to care of the soil than they used to, and that they no longer leave the vineyard to rest for three or four years after pulling out vines and replanting new ones, so the disease-bearing worms remain in the soil. He believes that "the problem of Burgundy" should be taken in hand by the government; that the vineyards should be considered as a national treasure and therefore a national problem.

If yields have doubled in France on average since last century, it has less to do with the conquest of disease than with the selection of productive clones and the introduction of fertilizing. Both these changes have proven to a certain degree detrimental to quality.

In Burgundy in the middle of last century the question of fertilizers was much discussed. A committee of growers and merchants convened in order to decide upon the means of restoring the trade in the wines of Burgundy to its former prosperity—and of restoring the quality and reputation of its great wines. The committee concluded that it was necessary to stop applying nitrogenous fertilizers. Burgundy was losing its reputation because some vine growers were adding excessive amounts of manure to their fine wines. Nobody

objected to the manuring of wines of ordinary quality. A question-
naire sent our around the wine-producing villages of the Côte d'Or,
asking whether manuring was desirable, received the reply: "It is
helpful to manure the common varieties [Gamay, etc.], for with
them the object is to produce quantity. On the other hand, it would
be a mistake to manure the noble varieties [Pinots] because the
increase in quantity would not compensate for the loss in quality."[14]
Whereas Pinot Noir yielded on average one ton per acre, a vineyard
planted with Gamay and manured was capable of achieving eight
times as much.

Attitudes to the manuring of fine wines changed when the
vineyards were devastated by mildew and phylloxera in the second
half of the last century. At Château Latour, these caused the average
crop to fall by 50 percent. So, from the 1880s on, the vineyard was
fertilized heavily. Following a very large crop in 1899, 516 tons of
manure and 12,750 tons of the new, untested chemical fertilizers
were added. As a result, in 1900 the yield of the wine sold under the
Château Latour label was 2¼ tons per acre, more than twice the
average achieved in the thirty years from mid-century. (I have no
idea how much extra wine was produced but "declassified.") In
Bordeaux, 1899 and 1900 are reputed as great vintage years. The
British wine writer Nicholas Faith has argued that the wines produced in these vintages demonstrate that "contrary to received opinion (and to the regulations surrounding the production of fine wines
in France) the lavish use of fertilizer does not necessarily dilute the
quality of the wine produced."[15] But do they? In his *Great Vintage
Wine Book*, Michael Broadbent says that he found the Latour 1900
on tasting not to be as full-bodied as he had expected.[16] Monsieur de
Braquessac, proprietor of the Voisin restaurant in Paris, was, in
1905, more explicit. He said that there were no longer any *grands
vins* in France; that Château Latour, which used to be delicious, was
no better than the stuff the peasants drank; and that matters were
getting worse, not better. He spoke in response to the investigations
which the Comte de Beaumont, the *château's* director, was carrying
out in order to discover why the price and reputation of his wine had
fallen. In the first decade of this century, prices for the leading
Bordeaux fell, on average, by over 25 percent. How far this was the
result of overproduction—supply exceeding demand—and how far

the consequence of a fall in quality, actual or perceived, is a moot point. Nevertheless, in 1907, several *châteaux* found it necessary to grant the exclusive distribution of their wines to brokers on a long-term basis; the contract which brokers made with Château Latour stipulated that chemical fertilizers were not to be used, and that manuring was not to be carried out to excess. [17]

The effects of clonal selection are equally contentious. One of the reasons for the very high yields in Germany today is that they were developing more productive clones of the Riesling grape long before similar work was begun in France. Work on clonal selection began at the vine-breeding institute at Geisenheim in the Rheingau at the end of the nineteenth century; and yields took off from the 1930s as a result. By the outbreak of the Second World War, the average yield in Germany had reached 2¼ tons per acre, at a time when the average yields of the top wines in Bordeaux and Burgundy had fallen back to their historic figure of just over one ton per acre. There was a very good reason to increase the yields in Germany: people were complaining about the price. It is ironic in these days—when fine German wines do not fetch a fair return—to read the book on German wine written by Hugh Rudd in the 1930s in which he seeks to justify the high prices of German wines by pointing to the need for expensive manuring every year—and to the need to prune the vines hard in the spring to achieve quality. [18]

The average yield in Bordeaux in the 1950s was 1¾ tons per acre, no higher than it had been in the first decade of the century and only 50 percent up from the amount produced in the early nineteenth century. Yields in Bordeaux only took off in the 1960s, because—it has been said—of the introduction of massal selection in the 1950s: choosing the healthiest vines in the vineyard and using these as the source of all new cuttings. [19] Massal selection is not such a sophisticated method as clonal selection: in the former case the new vines are descended from a group of healthy-looking, but not necessarily virus-free plants; whereas in the latter they are the children of a *single* mother who has been demonstrated to be free of disease by testing in a laboratory. Massal selection is an obvious procedure that *must* have been adopted in Bordeaux long before the 1950s. If average yields increased by one-third between the 1950s and 1960s, it was partly because many old and unproductive vines were pulled out after the frosts of 1956—and partly because mineral fertilizers were added less discriminately. The increase of yields from 1962 on brought prosperity to the Médoc.

According to Julian Jeffs, the purpose of clonal selection has been to propagate disease-free vines, and increased yield is incidental.[20] It is not possible to separate the two issues, however. It may well be the case that disease can serve a positive purpose in restricting yield to reasonable levels. The degree to which the inferior quality of many California and Oregonian Chardonnays should be attributed to the selection of high-yielding, virus-free clones by the University of California at Davis has already been discussed in Chapter 10. The same has been true for Pinot Noir. Francis Mahoney, an importer of burgundies, bought land in Carneros in the early 1970s because he thought it would prove a suitable area for growing Pinot Noir. At the time, three standard clones of Pinot Noir were available. The University of California at Davis, which had selected them, said that they were superior. According to Mahoney, what was superior about them was the size of their crop, not the quality of wine they produced. They yielded between 5 and 6 tons per acre and were, says Mahoney, the reason why Pinot Noir had fallen out of fashion in California. Mahoney went out and took cuttings from a number of old vineyards that had originally been planted before Prohibition with selections brought directly from Burgundy—among them Mount Eden in the Santa Cruz Mountains and Chalone in the Gavilan Mountains. He planted twenty different selections in an experimental plot, intermingling them so that none had better soil than others. For ten years he observed the growth of the plants and made different wines from each of the selections. Finally he concluded that six of the selections were superior. They yielded between 1½ a half and 4 tons per acre, and were all infected with virus.[21]

In several regions of France, officially sanctioned clonal selections has resulted in vines that produce an illegally high yield. The principal grape variety in Châteauneuf-du-Pape is the Grenache. This is generally said to produce wine that is inferior to that made from the other main grape varieties, Syrah and Mourvèdre, but this has less to do with any intrinsic inferiority than with the high yield of new clones. The finest Châteauneuf-du-Pape, Château Rayas, is made almost entirely from old, low-yielding Grenache vines. Modern, clonally selected Grenache vines produce 5 tons per acre, double the legal limit for the *appellation* (42 hectoliters per hectare, about 2½ tons per acre). Growers cannot propagate a massal selection of the best old Grenache plants in their own vineyards because they are widely infected with the fan-leaf virus. Instead, they try to keep their old, low-yielding vines in production as long as possible—many vineyards in Châteauneuf-du-Pape are seventy or eighty years old—or, if they have had to plant new vines, they pray that there will be bad weather in the early summer, preventing the flowers from setting properly and thus reducing the eventual crop. They had even tried to make the blossom fall off by applying copper during flowering, but it is much too delicate an operation to be relied upon.

Clonal selection of black grape varieties can particularly be criticized where it has led to an increase in the yield, not because the vines have produced more grapes, but because the grapes are larger. An increase in a size of the grapes means a corresponding decrease in the ratio of skin to juice in the fermentation tank; and it is the tannins and other substances that are extracted from the skins during fermentation that provide almost all the flavors in red wines. In *The Wines of the Rhône*, John Livingstone-Learmonth says that the nature of the Syrah grape (the principal variety grown in the Northern Rhône) was altered in the 1970s by clonal selection: the new strain of Syrah better resists floral abortion, but a number of growers are concerned that the new Syrah vine produces larger grapes, which dilute the plant's fruit.[22] Similar reservations have been expressed about the Pinot Droit clone of Pinot Noir, which was widely planted in Burgundy between the 1930s and the 1970s. Because it produces larger grapes than traditional Pinot Noir clones, it may well bear some responsibility for the long-term decline in the reputation of red burgundy. But then we are demanding less concentrated wine which matures sooner than it used to, and we should not shy away from admitting that, as a result of altering viticulture to suit this public demand, wines are no longer as good as they used to be.

There is another reason why yields have increased in recent years. Harry Waugh, who joined the British wine trade in 1934, says that before the Second World War red burgundy was every bit as popular as red Bordeaux, and the good vintages were laid down for the future as eagerly as were the Bordeaux vintages; but that since the war—perhaps on account of the small production and increasing world demand—the quality of red burgundy has been allowed to deteriorate with an inevitable depressing effect on its reputation.[23] In the 1970s red burgundies became lighter and thinner, culminating in the rosés of 1982, a vintage which led consumers to yearn for the Algerian blends of yesteryear.

Burgundy is not alone in this. The reputations of all the most famous wine regions of the world are being damaged by overcropping. The average yield per acre in Champagne has increased from 3 tons in the 1960s to 5 tons in the 1980s. Of course, excess yields do not really matter in Champagne. The wine is usually drunk on its own and therefore doesn't need to have the depth or body to stand up to food. In any case, how many people buy champagne for the taste?

On the whole, consumers pay for added value and not for intrinsic quality. Once a wine has established a reputation for quality—quite possibly without making a profit—then is the time to cash in. Wine makers are farmers, not wine lovers. The wines they produce will not necessarily remain fashionable for very long. I cannot imagine, for example, that such ordinary wines as Sancerre and Pouilly-Fumé can go on obtaining the prices they do forever. At their best they express the appetizing but rather simple flavors of the Sauvignon grape—flavors that can equally well be produced by Sauvignon grapes grown in similarly cool climates elsewhere in the world. And how often are they found at their best? Already British consumers are passing them over in favor of Sauvignons from New Zealand; regardless of whether this particular change in fashion spreads to the United States, the pattern is set: in a natural progression, high quality is followed by a good reputation, which leads to abuse and consequently to downfall. Rioja has progressed rapidly from the second to the third stage. It is not as good as it used to be, not least because the best black grape, Graciano, and the best white grape, Malvasia, yield very little and so are disappearing fast. There were once good stocks of old wines in the region, but as the continuing efforts to stretch the 1970 vintage have shown, they have all but dried out. Because the growth in international demand was not matched by a commensurate increase in the size of the harvest, grape prices—and thus wine prices—increased markedly in the 1980s without any corresponding improvement in quality. At an extensive tasting early in 1992 of several dozen of the Riojas that were imported into Britain, there were a few good wines, but they were not cheap, and there were a few cheap wines, but they were not good. Rioja was a boom region in the 1970s—but who will still be drinking its wines in 2010? Looking at the Bordeaux boom of 1675, the British author Sir Edward Barry pointed out in 1775 that the popularity of the wine caused it to be overproduced and adulterated. Spanish and other wines were added to Bordeaux, causing the wine to re-ferment. "By these arts we have been almost entirely deprived of any genuine claret [Bordeaux] wines . . . it is therefore no wonder that the port wines are now universally preferred to French claret."[24]

Where possible, famous wines have always been overproduced throughout history. As Pliny said of the most celebrated of Roman wines, Falernian, "The reputation of this district is passing out of vogue through the fault of paying more attention to quantity than to quality."[25] Château Haut-Brion lost its reputation in the early nineteenth century, and was overtaken by Lafite, because—according to a contemporary authority—"Too much manure is used."[26] Like Falernian before it, Haut-Brion was cashing in on its reputation.

It could be argued that the only economic incentive for the production of good-quality wine is the hope, in future, of establishing the sort of reputation that will enable you to rip off consumers. In many regions, vine cultivation is uneconomic: in the Mosel, for instance. In the 1970s the income from wine of the average grower in the Mosel-Saar-Ruwer region was calculated as being only one-third of that of his counterpart in other regions.[27] Ernst Loosen, a leading producer of wines from the Riesling grape in the Middle Mosel—particularly from the Erdener Prälat vineyard—says that because he keeps his yields down to 3½ tons per acre, he spends the equivalent of 4.50 marks a bottle on labor costs alone—although, if his grapes have only attained a sufficient level of ripeness to be sold as Kabinett (rather than Spätlese or Auslese) quality, he will only be able to sell the wine he makes from them for 5 marks (the equivalent of $3 at current exchange rates).[28] This situation is being partially relieved by a reorganization of vineyard (*Flurbereinigung*). Vineyard holdings used to be so diverse that growers could spend longer getting to their plots than working on them. As a result of *Flurbereinigung*, growers have exchanged plots of land with each other to make access easier, and production costs have halved. But still the production of ordinary QbAs (*Qualitätsweine bestimmter Anbaugebiete*) is uneconomic. Good-quality QbAs made from the superior Riesling grape grown on steep hillside sites in the Mosel-Saar-Ruwer can be bought for $5–6 a bottle, the same price as Blue Nun Liebfraumilch, which is made mostly from higher-cropping Müller-Thurgau and Silvaner grapes grown on relatively flat land in the Rheinhessen.

The Mosel vineyards require four times as many man-hours of labor per acre as those of Bordeaux. The base costs are so high that cheap wine can *never* be made profitably; and therefore, although it is currently uneconomic, the only hope for a long-term improvement in the economic condition of vine growers in the Mosel lies in selling top-quality wines for a high price. Such wines in the Mosel can only be made from Riesling; but Riesling wines cannot always be sold for a profit. To make a profit, a grower needs sufficiently ripe grapes to sell his wine as Spätlesen. Growers have therefore converted from the noble Riesling to the fairly ignoble Müller-Thurgau grape, because Spätlesen can be made more easily from this. In 1950 over 90 percent of vineyards in the Mosel-Saar-Ruwer were planted in Riesling; the proportion today is less than 60 percent. The vine growers have signed their own death warrant.

Producers in the Northern Rhône have faced similar problems. In the Northern Rhône, one man can work 5 acres; in the Southern Rhône, 25. In 1983, John Livingstone-Learmonth quoted the well-known local wine merchant Max Chapoutier as saying that he had lost money in Côte Rôtie every year since 1973.[29] In the 1890s, Côte Rôtie enjoyed as high a reputation as Hermitage, but it fell in the middle of this century because no one was prepared to work the slopes. Farmers found it more profitable to grow fruits and vegetables in the fertile Rhône Valley for sale to the inhabitants of Lyons. Côte Rôtie came to be sold for less than it cost to make it. The region was revived in the 1960s by Alfred Gérin, the mayor of the local town of Ampuis, who had roads built into the hillsides, which had hitherto been inaccessible to vehicles. He encouraged the plantation of vines on the plateau above the hillside, because this was easier to work. Thanks to Gérin's initiative, the vineyard area has been extended from 150 acres in the 1960s to 375 acres today, of which two-thirds are on the hillside and one-third on the plateau above. On the one hand, it is the opening up of the plateau that has encouraged the young people of Ampuis to start to take up vine growing again; on the other, the wine made from vines grown on the plateau can never achieve the quality of that produced from vines on the hillside. One of the results of the opening up of the plateau, however, has been to draw attention to the produce of the best hillside vineyards; with the hyping of the 1985, 1988, and 1989 vintages—and particularly of the single-vineyard wines made by Marcel Guigal—vine growers have finally begun to receive a fair return for their labors. So it can be done.

On the whole, however, the production of the world's best-value fine wines can better be explained by the fanaticism of a few hobbyists than by the prospect of economic advantage. This certainly seems to be the case in California. The ridiculously low yield achieved by Ken Burnap, a self-styled former "wine groupie" who replanted an old vineyard in the Santa Cruz Mountains in 1969, has already been referred to. Burnap has calculated that it costs him about $50 to make a wine which he sells for $20 or $25. He could increase the crop by irrigating the vineyard, but this would not improve the wine, as it would promote the development of a superficial root system that is less well able to withstand the effects of drought—and thus it would effectively tie the vineyard into a vicious circle. In Burnap's opinion, his 1988 Pinot Noir, made from a crop of 1/4 ton per acre, is the best wine he has ever made.

Even those vine growers who achieve more realistic yields have difficulty balancing their books. The current price of raw grazing land in Carneros is $50,000 an acre. A vine grower who took out a mortgage in order to purchase land at this price would have to earn $5,000 per acre each year, or $1,250 per ton of grapes, simply in order to meet the interest payments on his loan. Kent Rasmussen—a former librarian who decided to switch to vine growing because he did not enjoy being indoors so much—was able to buy his vineyard in 1978 for $8,000 because the previous owner had defaulted on his loan payments. Prices were forced up in the 1980s by Champagne companies who wanted land for sparkling-wine production. Rasmussen could not afford to buy land in Carneros today. He believes that, if you pay more than $25,000 per acre, you can never recoup your land costs. At least Rasmussen—who is possibly the leading producer of Pinot Noir in Carneros and certainly the only small vine grower on the Burgundian model—is able, by selling his wine for $18 a bottle, to make a living. Other wine producers are not. In 1990 Vic Motto, an accountant specializing in the wine industry, calculated that, while the average selling price of top-of-the-range California Cabernet Sauvignons was $17 a bottle, the wineries that produced them needed to sell them for $20 in order to make a profit.[30]

The leading wine producer in the Abruzzi in central Italy is the dropout lawyer Edoardo Valentini, who makes a remarkable red Montepulciano and an even more remarkable white Trebbiano— not in fact the much-derided Trebbiano of Tuscany but quite another grape which few people can afford to cultivate anymore because of its susceptibility to rot. Valentini declared his philosophy to Burton Anderson: "I could have a profitable operation if I chose to mass-produce wine from my grapes. But no thanks. You've got to love it to get through what I do to make my kind of wine, but I just wouldn't have it any other way. It's hard work, and it doesn't pay, but wine is my way of committing myself."[31]

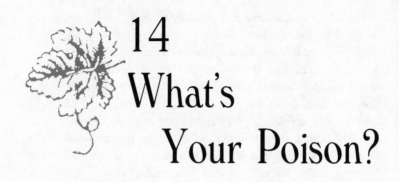

14
What's
Your Poison?

SOME VINE GROWERS deliberately make things harder and more expensive for themselves by adopting so-called organic methods of cultivation and vinification.

Why? Is it a con, designed to make us pay higher prices? In Britain in April 1989, an opinion poll found that one person in four would pay up to 25 percent more for "environmentally friendly" goods. In May the Environment Secretary, Nicholas Ridley, drew farmers' attention to the increasing demand for organically grown foodstuffs and told them: "I personally view it as a way for you to rip the customers off by charging more for identical produce."[1]

Levels of misinformation about organic wines are considerable. One British wine retailer, The Organic Wine Company, claimed in one of its newsletters that the scandal in Burgundy—involving the prosecution of Bouchard Père et Fils for overchaptalizing their wines—was a reason for buying organic wines. We should buy organic wines, it said, because organic producers do not chaptalize their wines (by adding sugar to them before fermentation). First, this is wrong. In a region such as Burgundy, everyone chaptalizes his wines, organic producers included. Second, even if organic wine makers did not chaptalize their wines, are we supposed to regard sugar as poison? Another British retailer of organic wines, Lavinia

Gibbs-Smith, claimed in her fact sheet that "Wine produced organically has more taste than wine produced in other ways. . . . Chemical additives reduce taste considerably, as anyone who has eaten monosodium glutamate in food must know."

Does she really imagine that chemicals are used in wine making as a "taste enhancer," as monosodium glutamate is in food production? It is sometimes hard to tell which is the more pernicious additives industry—that of adding extraneous substances to food products, or that of separating incorrect "scare" stories about their effects.

Wines are often described as "organic" when they are not. Within the European Community, the term *organic* is applied to wines that are made in a conventional manner from organically produced grapes. When one looks at the matter more closely, one finds that even the grapes have not been grown organically—in the strict sense of the word. Virtually all professedly organic wine makers use sulphur sprays against the oidium fungus and a copper sulphate solution (Bordeaux mixture) against mildew. Bordeaux mixture is certainly necessary, even in a dry climate. Some Riojanos thought they were safe in their dry climate, so they did not spray—until their 1971 and 1972 crops were destroyed by mildew. But confidence in its wholesomeness is not engendered by looking at how this was discovered. Last century, at harvesttime in Bordeaux, it was necessary to protect vines near the road from the depradations of grape thieves. At Château Latour two workmen stood on guard with shotguns. Less wealthy châtelains sprayed the vines nearest the road with well-known poisons. First, they employed verdigris (copper acetate), but this became expensive when it started to be used in the insecticide Paris Green (acetoarsenite of copper). So some châtelains took up spraying the vines with blue vitriol, a copper sulphate solution that looked like verdigris. This was the method employed at Château Saint Pierre-Sevaistre. In 1882, Pierre Millardet, Professor of Botany at Bordeaux University, noticed that the vines along the edge of the road—those that had been sprayed—were not suffering from mildew, whereas unsprayed vines were. So copper sulphate began to be used as a specific against mildew. Not everyone approved of its administration. It was widely believed that the copper got into the vine and affected the quality of the grapes. At the beginning of this century, Dr. Robin, an eminent Parisian stomach specialist, forbade his patients wine because, he said, copper sulphate produced potassium sulphate crystals, which are corrosive.[2]

Before this year, the term *organic* had no legal status within the European Community, so each vine grower was able to define "organic" in the way that he wished. There was nothing to stop a grower from producing so-called organic wine by using chemically dependent viticulture. The Listel wine company in the South of France planted barley and rye between their rows of vines in order to protect the soil during the winter, and encouraged them to grow with artificial fertilizers. Listel nevertheless claimed that its wines were organic—partly because it avoided any chemical treatments of the vines during the summer, and partly because there were no chemical residues in its wines. According to Listel, because it is impossible to watch a vine grower all the time, it was the unofficial view of the French Fraud Squad that you should define organic wine, not by reference to the methods used, but by analysis of the end product. Listel said that the Fraud Squad had analyzed professedly organic wines and found them to contain substantial residues of nitrates and pesticides.[3]

In theory at least, the meaning of the term *organic* within the European Community has been standardized by regulations introduced in 1991 and 1992, which are expected to have come into full effect by July 1993. The new law has neither codified prevailing practice nor ended it. Producers are still allowed to label their wines "organic" (or *biologique* in French or *ökologisch*—"ecological"—in German), but only if they explain elsewhere on the label that "organic wine" means "wine produced from organically grown grapes." This rule applies equally to the vast majority of professedly "organic" vine growers who make their wine by conventional methods from organically grown grapes, and to the few genuinely organic wine producers—such as Domaine Saint-Apollinaire in the Côtes du Rhône—who do not use any chemicals in their wine making, either. The European Community has failed to make any distinction between partially and wholly organic wine because it has determined that the term *organic* refers to the system of viticulture and not to the method of wine making.

In the United States, on the other hand, the regulations do distinguish between partially and wholly organic wine. Sulphur sprays and Bordeaux mixture may be used in the vineyard, but no wine may be described as "organic" if it has had sulphur dioxide added to it. The American regulations take us back to Roman times, and to the practices advocated by Columella, who, after discussing the use of pitch and resin to preserve wines, said: "We regard as the best wine any kind which can keep without any preservative . . . for that wine is most excellent which has given pleasure by its own natural quality."[4] The only drawback from such a strict definition of "organic wine" is that, in the state of technology that exists nearly two thousand years after Columella, it is virtually impossible to produce wines that are stable without adding sulphur dioxide at some point during their manufacture—usually a little at the beginning of vinification, to prevent the wine's being spoiled by bacteria, and rather more at bottling, to guard against oxidation.

A new German method which employs excimer lasers might in time serve as an alternative to sulphur dioxide for cheap wines, but it affects the chemical constituents of the product and therefore could not be used on fine wines intended to age. Certainly some organic wines are produced in California without adding sulphur dioxide, but their stability is suspect, to say the least. John Schumacher, who makes organic wines at Hallcrest Vineyards in the Santa Cruz Mountains, goes so far as to suggest that organic wines should be "an entirely different category of beverages, more like perishable fruit and produce, to be consumed while they're still fresh."[5] Moreover, even a wine that qualifies as organic by virtue of having had no sulphur dioxide added to it may well contain a certain amount of sulphites (the salts of sulphurous acid, which is formed by the dissolution of sulphur dioxide in wine), since this is produced as a by-product of yeast metabolism during fermentation. I have tasted organic wines that stink of naturally produced sulphur. In the 1989 vintage Jonathan Frey, the wine maker at Frey Vineyards in Mendocino County, managed to produce organic white wines that contained only the smallest trace (1 part per million) of sulphites, but only by using a new type of genetically engineered yeast. For a wine to be regarded as "organic," at least in the colloquial sense of the word, it should surely be fermented by the naturally occurring vineyard yeasts. Manipulating the sulphite levels with yeast strains is not organics but techno-organics.

In 1989 a group called the Organic Grapes into Wine Alliance (OGWA) was formed in order to pressure the California state legislature into allowing locally produced organic wines to contain up to 100 milligrams per liter/parts per million of sulphites, the maximum level then permitted by organic groups in Europe, but it was rebuffed by legislators who were unwilling to open a Pandora's box that creating organic standards for processed, as opposed to simple, food products would involve. The majority of organic vine growers in California must therefore content themselves with making ordinary wine from organically grown grapes—and describing that as "wine made from organically grown grapes."

Ought the state legislature to have acceded to the OGWA's requests? Is consumption of wine containing more than 100 parts per million of sulphites harmful? In 1973 the World Health Organization set the acceptable maximum daily intake at 0.7 milligrams per kilogram of body weight, equivalent to 49 milligrams for a 150-pound adult. So, even drinking wines that meet the OGWA's standards, a bottle-a-day man exceeds that limit. Many regular wine drinkers certainly take in more sulphites than is recommended. If they are doing themselves any harm, however, it is because of the alcohol, not because of the sulphites. Experiments on animals have shown that large doses of sulphites are acutely toxic but that low long-term doses have no adverse effects. We all form endogenously an average of 1,680 milligrams of sulphites every day, all of which is excreted in urine. There are, however, always a few people who are allergic to particular naturally occurring substances such as sulphites. Between half a million and one million Americans are sensitive to sulphites, and in recent years a number of deaths have been linked to ingestion of the chemical. The Food and Drug Administration has reacted to this problem by banning sulphite preservatives in fresh food and vegetables. In 1987 the drinks industry agreed with the Bureau of Alcohol, Tobacco and Firearms to introduce sulphite labeling before such labeling became mandatory. By taking the first step, drinks producers only bear the slight imposition of having to state that a product "contains sulphites"—

there is no need to give the quantity—and this statement can be made on the back label.[6]

The question of sulphite labeling has been treated separately from that of general ingredient labeling of drinks product, which is not compulsory, as it is for packaged foods. Regulations requiring that beer, wine, and spirits bottles carry labels listing all their ingredients have been proposed on several occasions but have never been enacted as law. In the 1970s such a proposal was introduced by the Carter administration—but it was canceled by the Reagan administration. Will ingredient labeling of such products ever be introduced in the United States? The European Community is currently discussing the possibility of introducing just such a requirement in 1994. In Australia, wine labels must already show the World Health Organization's antioxidant and preservative numbers.

It is unlikely, however, that the compulsory ingredient labeling of wines would work effectively. Producers who are adding illegal substances to their wine—for example, burgundy producers who illegally add acid—are unlikely to advertise the fact on their labels. Neither are producers who add water. The authorities in wine-producing countries have enough trouble in administering the law as it is.

Furthermore, wine makers employ a great number of processing aids such as casein, bentonite, and potassium ferrocyanide; these are not additives and therefore would not have to be declared on the label. Casein and bentonite are both supposed, in theory, to precipitate out of the wine, taking with them substances which cause cloudiness and discoloration. But what if they do not? A quarter of a million Americans are allergic to casein, the principal protein occurring in milk. Bentonite is a clay, a compound of aluminum, the ingestion of which may well be a cause of senile dementia. It is added in very large quantities: one part per thousand. If tests on beers in Britain conducted by the Campaign for Real Ale (CAMRA) are anything to go by, aluminum from bentonite fining probably does sometimes remain in the wine. CAMRA found very high concentrations of aluminum in a number of the beers they tested. One beer contained six times the recommended European Community limit for the aluminum content of drinking water. The presence of aluminum was just as likely the consequence of fining of the water with aluminum sulphate (alum) before the beer was made as of bentonite fining of the finished beer. But this does not affect the issue: some residue remained in the beer.[7] The use of bentonite in wine making could be avoided by heating the must or by adding gum arabic instead. Apart from clarifying the wine, however, bentonite removes histamine and tyramine, substances which are produced when the malolactic fermentation is provoked by undesirable strains of lactic acid bacteria—and which may possibly be the origin of headaches in people who consume red wine. (See Chapter 2.)

Potassium ferrocyanide is used in Germany to resolve discoloration of the wine by a combination of iron and tannin. When it was introduced in the 1920s, it was hailed as a great advance because it produced wine that was crystal-clear—so hock glasses no longer had to be colored. The process is called "blue fining" because it forms a blue precipitate—the dye Prussian blue—that is usually removed by filtration. If the filtration is not carried out properly, some of the blue precipitate may get into the bottle; and, in time, this decomposes to form hydrogen cyanide—cyanide gas—which gives the wine a bitter almond odor. To check that this has not happened, the wine maker needs a laboratory equipped with an atomic adsorption spectrometer. This is not an item frequently to be found in the establishment of German vine growers. In Britain in 1986 the Wine Standards Board investigated two instances of wine to which the process of clarification with potassium ferrocyanide had been incorrectly applied. Thankfully, hydrogen cyanide in wines has never been found to be above the toxic level. Nevertheless, its use is prohibited in America. Other treatments exist, such as the addition of citric acid or calcium phytate. Unlike potassium ferrocyanide, these do not diminish a wine's ability to improve in bottle. If German wine makers could afford to invest in modern equipment, the problem would not occur in the first place.

Third, labeling of the sulphur content—as opposed to merely stating that the wine in question, like all others, contained sulphites—would not be practicable. The free sulphur dioxide content varies from one week to another; the proportion of bound sulphur dioxide is more stable. But it is the free sulphur that is offensive, and it does not always form the same proportion of the total sulphur content.[8] Existing regulations are based on the total sulphur content.

If the free sulphur dioxide content were labeled at time of bottling, it would undoubtedly have changed by the time the consumer came to drink the product.

It is certainly common sense not to add an excessive quantity of sulphur dioxide to a wine. It smells unpleasant. It also destroys vitamins, particularly thiamine (B_1), of which the average concentration in wine is 8.7 milligrams per liter. This means that a glass of wine contains more thiamine than a bowl of oat-bran cereal. We do not, however, drink wine for its vitamin content.

Sulphur has not merely a negative, protective function—which might well be substituted by other methods—but a positive role as well. In Europe, many organic wines, produced with a minimum of sulphur dioxide, are kept clean by vinifying away from air, under a blanket of nitrogen. But a wine destined for bottle-aging needs to have contact with air during vinification. Sulphur dioxide allows this to happen without the wine's oxidizing. To this, a sophisticated organic wine maker might reply that the must should certainly be oxygenated, but in the *absence* of sulphur dioxide. This way, the tannins oxidize and bind together into long chains that are too heavy to remain in solution—and so they precipitate out. They are not liable to oxidize in the bottled wine, because they are not there. If, on the other hand, sulphur dioxide is added to the must, it combines with those tannins most liable to oxidize; these tannins remain in small units rather than forming heavy chains and therefore are not precipitated out during fermentation or fining; they stay in the wine where they later evolve, turning it brown.

More harmful than sulphur dioxide is the danger that the current obsession with sulphur dioxide levels will have a deleterious effect on the quality of wines produced. A consumer survey in Bavaria in 1987 found that 44 percent of respondents would prefer sulphur-free wines, even if they were more expensive than sulphured wines. The quantity of sulphur dioxide that needs to be added at the start of vinification can be reduced if the microbial population of the grapes is kept as low as possible by spraying regularly against rot and other infections. But if modern chemical sprays are used, this may introduce a harmful substance into the wine and possibly cause long-term ecological damage. Sprays may also harm the people who use them. Jacques Beaufort, who makes an excellent champagne in the *grand cru* village of Ambonnay, went organic when his son inhaled a chemical spray he was using. One of the boy's lungs ceased functioning, and he was temporarily paralyzed.

Since the late 1980s an increasing number of California vine growers—among them such large companies as Gallo and Mondavi—have started to take up organic cultivation. They have done so not because they believe that organically grown grapes, or organically produced wines, are superior but because they are concerned about the effects of chemical sprays on people living near or working in the vineyards. Tony Soter of Spottswoode converted to organic methods in 1985 because he did not want to risk spraying anything that might land on his neighbors' homes.[9] Fetzer Vineyards in Mendocino County, which are usually (but mistakenly) described as cultivating the largest organic vineyard in California, went organic at least partly in order to avoid liability claims from any farm workers who might have been affected by chemical sprays. That is why Rusty Eddy, the founder of the OGWA, says that eventually everyone in the wine industry is going to have to go organic. His prophecy has been made more likely by the passage of Proposition 65—California's Safe Water and Toxic Enforcement Act of 1986, which obliges producers to warn consumers about the presence of potentially toxic substances in their wines.

It is clear that the wholesale conversion to organic cultivation of vineyards in California is not consumer-led. How could it be, when the wines made from the vineyards cannot generally be labeled as "organic"? In any case, popular interest in produce that *can* be labeled as "organic" has faded. Organic foodstuffs became very fashionable in 1989, largely because of a scare over Alar, a systemic product sprayed on apples. Suggestions that Alar might be likely to cause cancer—allegations that were never conclusively proven—led the Environmental Protection Agency (EPA) to ban the product. The ban came not so much because the EPA thought Alar was dangerous, as in order to calm public disquiet. Within a year, however, most consumers had lost interest in organic produce and shops were cutting back their selections.

It is not clear that the conversion to organic methods is industry-led, either. Vine growers who convert to organic methods for fear of liability proceedings are effectively giving in to the antialcohol lobby.

The movement to organic viticulture may, on the face of it, seem laudable; but its effect is to help the enemies of wine in promoting the idea that wine is unhealthful. This is certainly what they are trying to do, and they are succeeding. Their latest attack on wine has been directed at its content of lead, the substance that is popularly believed to have brought the fall of the Roman Empire. The wine attackers were given their opportunity in 1991 when it was revealed in *The Wall Street Journal* that FDA tests on lead content in five hundred domestic and imported wines demonstrated levels ranging from 50 to 700 parts per billion. Although no tolerance level for lead in wine had yet been established in the United States, the recommended level for drinking water had recently been reduced from 50 to 15 parts per billion. In further tests, the FDA announced that the lead levels were greatly increased when wine was poured out of bottles that had been sealed with lead-foil capsules. The FDA proposed a ban on these capsules, saying that although the levels found in wine did not represent an immediate health hazard, they could represent long-term risks for children and pregnant women. Given that the legal minimum drinking age in virtually all states is twenty-one, and that enormous pressure is already put on pregnant women, by means of warning labels, to prevent their drinking, this was a rather odd statement. John De Luca, the president of the California Wine Institute, said that he had been assured by FDA officials that lead levels in domestic (as opposed to imported) wines were not a problem, and blamed antiwine health groups for forcing the release of data without any explanation as to its health significance. He pointed out that FDA tests had shown lead present in many other foods: the average concentration of lead in apples is the same as that in California wine, and the concentration in canned tuna is seven times as high.[10] Nevertheless, the FDA's findings were sufficient to enable a San Diego law firm to file a class-action lawsuit against a number of major wineries—alleging that they had violated Proposition 65—and for the wineries to react by agreeing to abandon the use of lead-foil capsules on all wines intended for sale in California after the beginning of 1992.

Whatever the reasons for taking up organic cultivation, wine drinkers should be thankful that wine producers are doing so. The London Food Commission has released figures to the effect that the sprays used by some conventional wine makers in Europe contain forty-nine potentially carcinogenic compounds and sixty-one that can cause birth defects. We are always being assured by wine makers who depend on the use of pesticides and insecticides that there is no danger of such substances getting into the wine we drink. If so, how come Xavier Gardinier, the new owner of Château Phélan-Ségur, had in 1987 to buy back the 1986 vintage from merchants and destroy all the bottles of the 1984 and 1985 vintages stored at the *château* because—he said—the wine (made by his predecessors) had a disagreeable odor caused by the use of the systemic insecticide acephate? (This substance, which was sold under the brand name Orthene 50, is unpleasant rather than poisonous.) It has long been known that systemic insecticides—which act on both the outside and inside of grapes, through the sap of the vine—do leave a residue in the eventual product. Gardinier sued the manufacturers of Orthene 50, the Chevron Chemical Company, claiming damages of $7 million for ruined stock, and punitive damages of $50 for the prejudice that he felt his company had suffered. Initially, Chevron claimed that the bad smells in the Phélan-Ségur were simply the result of poor wine-making techniques. Later in the year, however, it admitted that a number of lawsuits had been brought against it by German vine growers whose 1984 and 1985 vintages had developed similar offensive odors, and that as a result of all the complaints it had stopped selling Orthene 50 in Europe. It has been suggested that the problem with Orthene 50 was that, if it remained in a sufficient concentration in the wine, it decomposed and formed mercaptans (an advanced stabilized form of hydrogen sulphide), which have variously been described as smelling of rubber, of rotting cabbage, and of sweaty socks. [11] Chevron has never admitted liability, however. None of the lawsuits against it has been tried in court so far. What can be said is that it is ironic in the circumstances that Gardinier made his fortune in the field of chemical fertilizers.

In order to reduce the risk of there being residues in the finished wine, it had been recommended that Orthene 50 should not be sprayed on vines fewer than three weeks before the harvest. The time when chemical sprays (whether systemic or otherwise) are most likely to get into the wine is when they are used close to the harvest. If no rain falls in between the administration of the spray and the harvest, then there will most probably be some pesticide residue in the eventual wine. Yet the very time when modern antirot treatments are most necessary is fairly soon before the harvest—for example, after a fall of rain has swollen the grapes, reduced their sugar content, and therefore caused an imminent harvest to be delayed. The controversy over acephate in 1987 was followed in 1990 by another over procymidone. This is the active ingredient in Sumisclex, a systemic antirot treatment used in Burgundy and Bordeaux. Sumitomo, its manufacturers, had not registered procymidone for use in the United States because there is not enough of a rot problem in the principal American vineyard areas to warrant its sale there. In March 1990 the FDA discovered procymidone in wines imported from France while carrying out a random check for illegal additives. Because procymidone was not registered as a drug in the United States, no tolerance level has been established. Therefore any quantity was illegal. Imports of Bordeaux and Burgundy were held up while the EPA established an interim tolerance level (7 parts per million). This applied retrospectively to wines from the 1989 or earlier vintages. The FDA warned that any wine made from the 1990 or subsequent vintages which was found to contain procymidone might be seized by Customs. This observation encouraged growers in Burgundy to give up using Sumislex—which, in any case, had not proven wholly effective because, like all systemic products, it creates resistant plants.

In the long term, we simply have not idea what ecological damage we may be causing by the administration of pesticides and insecticides, nor what sort of super-bugs we are creating. A fear for the future of the ecosystem justifies organic methods of growing grapes or, indeed, of any other form of fruit or vegetable.

It is not usually difficult for a conscientious vine grower to rid himself of vineyard pests without recourse to chemical insecticides. He merely introduces other insects to feed on the pests in question. Since he introduced the killer mite to his vineyards in the late 1970s, Peter von Weymarn of Weingut Freiherr Heyl zu Herrnsheim in the Rheinhessen in Germany has not needed to spray against red spider because the killer mite does the job for him. Another method—adopted by the Ott family at Château de Selle in Provence—is to use substances that red spiders and other insects find unpleasant to smell.

Organic manure is quite a different matter. It is not necessary. How can organic wine makers, without hypocrisy, spray a copper sulphate solution on their grapes yet declare their opposition to chemical fertilizers—which are simply natural materials obtained in a pure form as the result of a chemical process? If a soil is deficient in nitrogen, phosphorous, or magnesium, why not add it in a pure form, rather than going out of your way to find a shepherd with time on his hands who is prepared to drive his sheep your way? There is no difference between the nitrogen contained in manure and nitrogen administered in pure form. Certainly, mineral fertilizers act more rapidly when added in pure form than when administered as manure, but the prudent vine grower will add small amounts at various times, not all at once. The harmful effects of the addition of chemical fertilizers on both the environment and the wine derive from their excessive use, not from their use in preference to sheep's droppings, horse manure, or dead cats.

Ironically, it has been suggested that chemical weed killing is less destructive to the soil than turning it over mechanically, a process that destroys the surface roots of the vine so that they cannot feed on the surface soil. The nutriments in the topsoil are very important to the vines, because this is where 80 percent of their root system is found. Also, if vineyards are not tilled, worms are not killed, and these ventilate the soil. [12]

Most of the wine produced by growers who cultivate their vineyards according to organic principles is mediocre, to say the least. Much of it is undrinkable. There are significant exceptions, however. They include:

> Clos de l'Arbalestrier, Saint Joseph
> Château de Beaucastel, Châteauneuf-du-Pape (Its nearby Côtes-du-Rhône estate, Cru de Coudoulet, is also organic, and considerably cheaper.)
> Guy Bossard, Muscadet
> Domaine Cauhapué, Jurançon
> Gérard Chave, Hermitage
> Auguste Clape, Cornas
> Domaine de Chevalier, Graves

Domenico Clerico, Barolo
Coulée de Serrant, Savennières
Mas de Daumas Gassac, Vin de Pays de l'Hérault
Freiherr Heyl zu Herrnsheim, Rheinhessen
Gaston Huet, Vouvray
Domaine Leroy, Vosne-Romanée
Castello di Luzzano, Lombardy
Château Montelena, Napa Valley
Poderi Montenidoli, Vernaccia di San Gimignano
Château Musar, Lebanon
Leonlido Pieropan, Soave
Spottswoode, Napa Valley
Domaine Tempier, Bandol
Terres Blanches, Côteaux des Baux en Provence
Domaine de Trévallon, Côteaux des Baux en Provence
Aubert de Villaine, Burgundy
Castello di Volpaia, Chianti

Few of these producers belong to an organic association; in many cases they did not consciously adopt organic principles but simply applied what struck them as being the best system of viticulture, then found that this happened to be organic. Maybe they would not have realized that they were organic had someone not told them so. They can be compared to Monsieur Jourdain in Molière's play *Le Bourgeois Gentilhomme*, who discovered that he had been speaking prose for more than forty years without knowing it.[13] It is a general tendency of proselytizing organic vine growers and particularly the importers and retailers of their products to claim as their own techniques that are in common use in quality-conscious vineyards the world over. The planting between rows of vines of leguminous plants, to act as fertilizer, is not peculiar to organic viticulture: it was reintroduced by the Austrian Dr. Lenz Moser in the 1920s.

Modern chemical antirot treatments have been abandoned by a number of vine growers, not just organic ones. The Moueix estate—farmers of a number of leading Saint-Emilion and Pomerol properties from Château Pétrus downward—experimented with modern chemical antirot treatments, but gave them up in 1978 on the grounds that they delayed fermentation.

Nor is a preference for natural over cultured yeasts peculiar to organic wine production. Although in the United States the restriction on the presence of sulphites in organic wines has encouraged the use of specially engineered strains of yeasts—in order to ensure that sulphur compounds are not produced during fermentation—most organic wine makers in Europe (as well as some of the American producers of wine from organically grown grapes) argue that the character of the wine depends on the yeasts that occur naturally on the skins of the grapes in the vineyard and that cultured yeasts produce formulaic wines, smelling of pineapple and tasting of fruit salad. Certainly, this is the predominant character of Australian Chardonnays, whose uniformity has been attributed to the fact that many of them have been fermented by the same yeast strain, R 2, which was originally selected in 1979 at Château Rahoul in the Graves in Bordeaux by its Danish wine maker Peter Vinding-Dyers.

It is not, however, clear that the most important yeasts are those which live in the upper layer of the soil and are carried by insects onto the skins of the grapes. It may be that the most important yeasts are to be found in the cellar. If so, questions of organic cultivation and avoidance of chemical sprays are largely irrelevant. According to Peter Vinding-Dyers—who now runs Château de Landiras (whose wine is also seen under the label Domaine la Grave)—every wine cellar has its own group of yeasts. That is why, he says, Léoville–Las Cases tastes different from Léoville-Poyferré, which is made only 10 meters away; and why grapes produced in the vineyards of one and vinified in the cellars of the other will have the character of the estate in whose cellars it is made. If Vinding-Dyers is right, then this would help explain why wines made by the same wine maker from the produce of different, often very disparate, vineyards in Burgundy, the Rhine, and Mosel so closely resemble one another. They are all made with the same yeasts. (But it does not explain why merchants' burgundies—blended from wine they have bought in—taste so similar. In some instances, this similarity can have been achieved only by the illegal inclusion of wine from elsewhere.)

It is unusual for wines in California or Australia to be fermented by naturally occurring vineyard yeasts because in general the vineyard has not been cultivated for long enough to allow a benevolent yeast population to build up. An exception is Ken Burnap's Santa Cruz Mountain Vineyard in the Santa Cruz Mountains, which has been in continuous cultivation since 1863. Burnap believes that the wine derives complexity from being fermented by a whole bunch of different cultures. It is similarly unusual for wines in California or Australia to be fermented by naturally occurring cellar yeasts. The most celebrated exception to this rule is Tyrrell in the Hunter Valley in New South Wales in Australia, where Murray and Bruce Tyrrell make their wine in a winery that was built in 1864. Tyrrell makes wines that are rather volatile by Australian standards; but, as Bruce Tyrrell explains, "Volatility makes a wine exciting."

If most Australian wine makers prefer to use selected yeast strains rather than rely on those which occur naturally in their cellars, it is, according to Dr. Terry Lee, director of the Australian Wine Research Institute, because this "eliminates much of the element of chance in wine making." It is hardly surprising that Peter Vinding-Dyers should have said, in a lecture to candidates for the Master of Wine examination: "The day we arrive [at this sort of uniformity in Bordeaux], Bordeaux is finished."

The contrast between wine made using cultured yeasts and wine made using natural yeasts is as great as that between pasteurized and unpasteurized cheese. Pasteurization of milk kills fault-producing microorganisms but also destroys most of the enzymes—some of which are responsible for the development of flavor as the cheese ripens. Commercial cheese makers who pasteurize have to add starter cultures, so all their cheeses taste the same. Unpasteurized cheeses, where the naturally occurring enzymes and bacteria are allowed to work, are different every time. Certainly, pasteurized cheeses are more reliable than unpasteurized, and sometimes they are just as good. But no one would claim that the pasteurized versions of soft cheeses such as Camembert or Brie bear any relationship to the unpasteurized versions. Moreover, pasteurized cheeses are never as interesting as unpasteurized. Do we want wines that all taste the same, or that taste different from every wine maker and every vintage?

The advantage of cultured yeasts is that they start fermenting faster than natural ones. That is why some wine makers, who would not dream of sterilizing or pasteurizing the must and then adding a cultured yeast strain, nevertheless add a starter yeast to get fermentation going. The locally adapted, naturally occurring yeasts then take over during fermentation. In his book on German wines, Fritz Hallgarten said that he had not found the use of a starter yeast to affect the flavor of the eventual wine, with one exception: a Steinberger Trockenbeerenauslese which was so difficult to bring to fermentation that as a last resort sherry yeast was used. Nobody was told about this, but at the first public tasting, experts considered that the Steinberger Trockenbeerenauslese had a special, unusual character.[14]

A further aspect of wine making to which organic vine growers claim propriety is an opposition to filtration. Certainly, few organic vine growers filter their wines. But the rules of European organic associations such as "Terre et Vie" permit it. An opposition to filtration has nothing at all to do with organic viticulture and everything to do with the making of top-quality wine.

In the early days of filtration after the Second World War, it was a dangerous procedure because asbestos filters were used. These were banned in the United States only in the 1980s; in other parts of the world they are still used. Jim Roberts, a wine maker in New South Wales who died in 1986 of mesothelioma, a lung disease caused by exposure to asbestos, had won not long before his death substantial damages against the manufacturers of the asbestos filter pads he had been using for the previous twenty years. His family says that the same pads are still used by other wine makers.

Any dispute over the effect of filtration today concerns the taste of the wine. In his book on wine making, Emile Peynaud argues that the purely mechanical (as opposed to chemical) action of filtration cannot possibly have a negative effect on the quality of wines, because the foreign substances in suspension and the impurities that form the lees do not have a favorable taste function.[15] How can Peynaud say what he does, when the character of champagne depends on what is in the lees? The base wine for champagne is usually neutral-tasting, and the final product only has any flavor at all because of the breakdown of yeast cells during the second fermentation. Muscadet, too, is a neutral-tasting wine—unless it has spent some months in contact with its lees, without being racked from one cask to another. The unfiltered Muscadets *sur lie* made by the

Chereau and Carré families from their five estates actually improve
in bottle: Château de Chasseloir, Grand Fief de la Commeraie,
Moulin de la Gravelle, Château du Coing à Saint Fiacre, and Château l'Oiselinière de la Ramée. Nor is it any coincidence that the top
producers of Meursault—François Jobard, Domaine des Comtes
Lafon, and Jean-François Coche(-Dury)—are those who keep their
wines in contact with their lees for a long period. In the course of two
years' aging in cask, the Lafons do not rack their wine off its lees at
all, even though this brings an increased danger of spoilage.

Wine makers who believe in lees contact before bottling do not,
however, necessarily disbelieve in filtration. In Western Australia,
Moss Wood, who make a brilliant Semillon, filter the wine before
bottling, after long lees contact. Unfiltered white wines are very rare,
largely because consumers who are bothered if they find sediment in
a bottle of red wine are going to be totally fazed if they discover
sediment in one of white. After all, white wines are rejected if they
have tartaric acid crystals in the bottom of the bottle. These tend to
form in cold weather unless the wine has already been chilled in the
winery to encourage their precipitation before bottling. I have bought
from various wine merchants at ridiculously low "bin-end" prices a
number of white wines which have formed tartaric acid crystals. One
or two merchants, however, are canny enough to persuade their
customers that, because the tartaric acid has precipitated out, the
wine is less acidic and therefore a better, not a worse, buy.

Filtration is carried out for purely commercial reasons. Why
should restaurants bother with a wine that has deposits in it, when
few of their staff will have the time or ability to decant a bottle of
wine off its dregs, and, if they present their customers with a bottle
which has sediment in it, it will be sent back? Moreover, an unfiltered wine is more likely to go off, because it contains impurities that
may cause an unfavorable chemical reaction. Unfiltered wines contain yeasts which, if the wine contains any unfermented sugar, can
spring to life in warm temperatures and cause a refermentation.
Robert Parker says he knows sommeliers in France who remove
certain unfiltered wines from the list in summer because they come
alive and taste "spritzy."[16]

How can anyone argue that filtration takes nothing out of the

wine, when Beaujolais Nouveau lacks aroma and flavor because it
has been heavily filtered so that it can be drunk in a stable condition
within two months of the harvest? Filtered "vintage character" port
never achieves the same quality as unfiltered crusting port. The
former is sold for drinking young; the latter is intended to mature for
a few years in the bottle. Churchill's Crusting Port, made, they say,
from the same quality of grapes as their Vintage Character, is, even
two years after bottling, in another class. Unfiltered wines will develop greater complexity with age than filtered ones because a greater
number of different chemical reactions are likely to occur during
bottle aging. This is because essential constituents have not been
removed from the wine—even if no one knows what constituents
these are.

There is a patent difference in taste between filtered and unfiltered versions of the same wine. At Domaine du Vieux Télégraphe
in Châteauneuf-du-Pape, Daniel Brunier filters all his wine after the
end of its malolactic fermentation and most of it before bottling. One
cuvée escapes the second filtration: that which is exported to Kermit
Lynch in Berkeley, California. Since the 1982 vintage Lynch has
insisted that his wine be sent to him unfiltered. He proved his point
in 1985 when, on a visit to the Domaine, he and all the Brunier
family tasted both cuvées of the 1983 and all of them found the
unfiltered version to be superior.[17] Robert Parker has also tasted the
two cuvées, in both the 1983 and 1984 vintages, and in each case
preferred the one that had not been subjected to the second filtration.[18] This led Daniel Brunier to accuse Parker of wanting to cause
controversy, to claim that the difference between the two cuvées only
lasted for one month while the filtered wine recovered from the
shock of the filtering process; he also suggested that the only reason
Lynch insisted on having an unfiltered cuvée was that Parker had
created a demand for unfiltered wines.

Brunier may have overstated his case, but he does have a point.
Sometimes Parker takes his advocacy of unfiltered wines a little too
far. He has a tendency to point to the adoption or abandonment of
filtration by a producer as an explanation for a sudden decline or
improvement in the quality of his wines—when in fact the explanation for the change is usually more complex. In some instances
Parker probably acquires an exaggerated view of the significance of

filtration because he has tasted the wine or wines in question soon after they have been bottled, when those wines that have been filtered are still suffering from shock. In his book on Burgundy, Parker stated that the wines of Domaine Lucien Boillot et Fils in Gevrey-Chambertin had much improved since the two sons who run it stopped filtering beginning with the 1987 vintage.[19] In January 1989 I visited the estate and tasted two samples of Gevrey-Chambertin, one of which had been filtered and the other not. The filtered wine was more aromatic, but the unfiltered one had far greater depth and profundity. But, since these wines had only recently been bottled, the comparison proved nothing. Parker has also criticized Gérard Potel, the wine maker at the prestigious Domaine de la Pousse d'Or in Volnay, for filtering his wines.[20] Potel started doing this in 1980, after carrying out an experiment on the 1966 vintage. He filtered the half of the wine he made in 1966 that he sent for export but not the half he sold in France. He says that he has held regular blind tastings to compare the two bottlings, and has found that there was a difference for the first eighteen months after bottling but not afterward.

One problem with trying to judge the effect of filtration is that the term itself is meaningless. It all depends what sort of filter is used. A filter with very large pores lets through all sorts of yeast and bacteria. One with very small pores lets no bacteria through at all, and is therefore described as a "sterile" filter. In the opinion of Michel Dupuy—an enologist who has turned Château de Fieuzal into the most fashionable white-wine *château* in Bordeaux—bacteria have an important part to play in the bottle maturation of a fine wine: bacterial action explains why wine ages faster at a higher temperature. According to Dupuy, harmful bacteria are very big and useful bacteria are very small, so a light filtration is positive but a sterile filtration is not.

The distinction between sensible and sterile filtration, and the part played by bacteria in bottle maturation, demonstrate the absurdity of the arguments used by the burgundy merchant Louis Latour in defense of his company's use of pasteurization. He has sought to justify the practice by saying that to use sterile filtration instead would be to adopt a "more brutal process" that removes color and flavor from the wine at the same time as rendering it stable. In fact, even sterile filtration is preferable to pasteurization, which was invented as a desperate remedy for diseases of wine which are, thanks to an improved understanding of the process of vinification, no longer much of a problem. In 1863 Emperor Napoleon III asked Louis Pasteur to find a solution to the diseases of wine. Pasteur discovered that the principal disorders which afflicted wines were the result of the activity of microorganisms, and that they could be killed by heating. He argued that it would be easier to destroy microbes after fermentation than to prevent their entrance. Unusually for a wine producer, the present Louis Latour's grandfather took a scientific degree at the end of the nineteenth century, at which time Pasteur's discoveries were all the rage. That is why Maison Louis Latour pasteurize their wines today. But Pasteur did not understand how wine matured. He thought that wine matured only through the action of air, and that therefore bottle maturation involved nothing more than slow oxidation through the cork. As I have already pointed out, bottle aging, though it involves a number of chemical and physical changes—the full extent of which is not yet understood—owes little, if anything, to the effect of oxygen. Louis Latour pasteurize their red burgundies by heating them to 158°F, which causes both chemical and physical change.[21] How can it be argued that this does not affect the taste of a wine when even the purely physical changes caused by filtration—or by chilling a wine to below 32°F in order that tartaric acid salts should precipitate out—emasculate the end product? Admittedly, the difference in taste may become evident only after chemical reactions have occurred during bottle maturation. Because it causes similar chemical changes in different products, pasteurization makes these products more alike than they might otherwise have been.

Pasteurization is suitable for cheap, everyday wines that are not intended to mature. Indeed, it is essential for the stability of sweet, low-alcohol, low-acid, virtually tannin-free wines such as Lambrusco and Asti Spumante. According to Nicolas Belfrage, it was the introduction of hot-bottling in the 1960s that was largely responsible for Italian success in selling reliable, high-volume lines. This method involves heating the wine to between 137° and 147°F and bottling it at this temperature, either chilling the bottles afterward or allowing them to cool down of their own accord. Hot-bottling became unfashionable in the 1970s, and is no longer much used outside Sicily.[22]

In his book on burgundy published in 1982, Anthony Hanson revealed the fact that Maison Louis Latour pasteurized their red wines, and said that this was known in Burgundy, "But no more talked about than if the King were walking about with no clothes on."[23] Louis Latour defended himself in print. Pasteurization, he said, was necessary to protect red burgundies against acetification, particularly in hot years with low acidity. He made this rather extraordinary statement: "Scientific and technical progress has always been beneficial to wine."[24] Yet, the scientific progress achieved by Louis Pasteur occurred at the same time as less quality conscious producers were discovering the benefits of the new azo dye magenta to give pale wines a bright red color. This may have helped the wine, but it certainly did not help the people who drank it.

On the other hand, we should not follow organic wine makers in dismissing scientific and technical progress. What is old is not necessarily good. John Locke, on a visit to France in the 1760s, described how wine was made at Montpellier in the Languedoc: how the grapes went into the vat rotten and full of spiders; that "They often put salt, dung, and other filthiness in their wines to help, as they think, its purging"; and that "The very sight of their treading and making their wine (walking without any scruple out of the grapes into the dirt, and out of the dirt into the grapes they are treading) were enough to set one's stomach ever against this sort of liquor."[25] Wine drinkers, like many other classes of society, have a tendency to invent a fantastic past for themselves. Among the more recent fantasies conjured up by this way of thinking are industrial heritage museums—which create an image of a healthy working society, to counteract today's high levels of unemployment; which present poverty as something wholesome, warm, and welcoming; and which create a nostalgic longing for non-existent better days.

Organic wine makers suffered badly from *la nostalgie de la boue*. Some organic producers are actually living in that lost past: they have not made a conscious decision to "go organic"; they have simply not yet got around to using modern chemical sprays and additives. Paul Bouron at Château de Chavrignac in Bordeaux lives a life straight out of *Madame Bovary*, going around in wooden clogs, without socks, even in the depths of winter. Other organic wine makers have readopted the cosmic view of their medieval ancestors.

In the cultivation of Coulée de Serrant in Savennières in the middle Loire, Nicolas Joly follows the biodynamic methods created by Rudolf Steiner in Germany at the beginning of the century—which take us back into a world dominated by lunar cycles. Joly only works the earth when the moon is in Leo, Aries, or Sagittarius. Remarkably, he produces the best wine in *appellation*.

CONCLUSION

15
A Plea
for Flavor

T ASTE IS NO LONGER a factor in food production," argues James Boudreau of the University of Texas at Houston. "Fruits and vegetables are grown for yield and ease in transportation and are ripened by artificial means." He says that the reliance on a few fertilizers with a high nitrogen content produces foods with a different chemical composition; and that the use of other chemicals has not merely destroyed good tastes but produced bad ones. For instance, the chemicals used to loosen oranges for mechanical picking have been found to introduce new chemicals with off tastes into the orange. "Many of the foods selected over millennia for flavor have, in the last twenty or thirty years, because of changes in chemical composition, become bland or even objectionable in flavor."[1]

If organic foods are necessary, and organic wines unnecessary, it is because there is no quality market for the best varieties of tomatoes or potatoes, cropped to the sort of low yields that will produce the best flavor. The only way better-tasting vegetables can be marketed at a price which makes them economic is by adopting the "organic" tag. Wine production, on the other hand, is geared to quality. A wine maker does not have to call his produce "organic" in order to charge, and obtain, a fancy price. Therefore, from the point of view of quality, there is no need for wine to be produced by organic methods.

The significance of the adoption of organic methods of vine growing and wine making in the United States is a cultural one. It stands in stark contrast to the technically driven sterility of modern American vinification techniques, which produce wines that are technically perfect but wholly without flavor.

Nearly all the white wines produced in the United States are fermented at a low temperature, a method that was originally introduced as an antidote to the problems facing white-wine production in California. One of the reasons why consumption of table wine did not take off as had been expected after Prohibition was that many California white wines, which had been fermented at much too high a temperature, tasted dull and heavy or even oxidized. It was Ernest & Julio Gallo who found the solution by introducing "cold" fermentation in stainless-steel tanks in order to produce their "Chablis," which rapidly became the largest-selling white wine in the United States. Cold-fermented wines certainly smell and taste fresher than warm-fermented ones. Twenty-five percent more fatty-acid esters— which contribute to a fruity aroma—are found in a wine that has been vinified at 70°F than in one that has been fermented at 85°F.[2] There are even some outstandingly aromatic white wines that are made by this process, such as the single-vineyard Frascati, *vigneto* Colle Gaio, from Colli di Catone, which is fermented for six months at 53°F. (This may seem absurd, but the Malvasia grape from which it is made oxidizes very easily.)

On the whole, however, fermenting a wine at a temperature such as this produces a clean but tasteless product whose main characteristic is an aroma of bananas. Certain of the leading instigators of cold fermentation in Europe have realized that it is time to take a step backwards. Giacomo Tachis, the wine maker for Antinori in Tuscany, who helped at the end of the 1970s to invent Galestro, one of the most tasteless of all cold-fermented white wines (as a means of getting rid of the white grapes which had previously been added to Chianti), has now been experimenting with fermentation temperatures up to 77°F. Cold fermentation is a means of avoiding faults rather than of achieving quality. According to the Australian Murray Tyrrell, "Fifty degrees over six months is a load of bloody nonsense."[3]

If many people find pleasure in cold-fermented white wines, it is because they are more interested in the absence of negative than in the presence of positive attributes of taste. It is sad to say so, but most of us have very little interest in the taste of what we drink. As long as it is not objectionable, it does not matter if a drink does not taste particularly good.

Our general lack of interest in the taste of a wine is demonstrated by our lack of interest in its smell. Most of what we think of as taste is in fact smell. If you smell a wine in the glass, you inhale only those substances which become volatile at the temperature of the wine, which ought to be between 55° and 65°F. If you take a wine in your mouth—and particularly if you hold it there for a second or two—it very rapidly warms up to approach the temperature of your tongue (101°F), and many more substances become volatile and are inhaled up the back of your nose from the inside. Our lack of interest in how a wine smells is epitomized by one of my favorite wine-snob stories, an apparently genuine incident retold by a Canadian correspondent to *Decanter* magazine. At a dinner party, he took a sip of wine, turned to the woman next to him, and said, "I just love the smell of Chardonnay." She replied with all sincerity that she was wearing Chanel No. 10.[4]

If we were interested in smelling wine, we would not use the glasses we do. It is one thing to employ standard "Paris goblets," or even tumblers, for everyday wine, which is for glugging, not sniffing. But what about a wine for whose superior quality you have paid a more substantial sum? How can you swirl a wine around in the glass, in order to encourage its contents to become odoriferous and to enable you to smell them before they dissipate, if the glass is not a large one, with a big bowl and tapered at the top? Virtually all wineglasses on the market are far too small; the exceptions are the fine wineglasses designed by the Riedel company, some of which go to the other extreme, being capable of holding the contents of an entire bottle of wine and being far too big for any practical use.

Sight has become a much more important sense than smell when apes rose from all fours and began walking on two legs. Our sense of smell has been deteriorating ever since. Unlike many other mammals, our major instrument of sexual selection is now sight rather than smell, perhaps because in humans vision acts at a distance, whereas smell does not. We have not lost our ability to secrete pheromones—hormones to which members of the opposite sex re-act—but we are gradually losing our ability to detect and respond to them.

Our greater interest in appearance than in smell or taste is demonstrated by the popularity of sparkling wines, whose appeal lies principally in display. This is demonstrated by their being served in tall, thin "flûte" glasses, which are very narrow and are usually filled to the brim, making them quite inappropriate for smelling the stuff but ideal for showing off the bubbles. It was expressly with the intention of displaying the bubbles that flûte glasses were developed in the first half of the seventeenth century. They were initially used to serve sparkling beer, which was invented before champagne, but were popularized at the court of the English King Charles II by the Marquis de Saint-Evremond, one of the four young noble property owners in Champagne who had created the fashion at the French court for the wines of the region. When, in 1662, Saint-Evremond fell out of favor in France and was exiled to England, he took the fashion for champagne with him.

The champagne Saint-Evremond had drunk in France was a still wine. As has been described in Chapter 11, sparkling cham-pagne was an English invention, which was popularized—along with flûte glasses—at the English royal court. The fashion for spar-kling champagne soon spread back to France. When, however, the Maréchal de Montesquiou d'Artagnan, thitherto a regular purchaser of still champagne, asked his wine merchant Bertin de Rocheret for sparkling champagne because "It is a fashion which rules every-where, but more particularly among the younger generation," De Rocheret replied that sparkling champagne was an "abominable drink," that the bubbles destroyed the flavor of the individual growths, and that "effervescence, I believe, is a merit in an inferior wine, and the property of beer, chocolate, and whipped cream." The condemnation of sparking wine by connoisseurs as a drink suitable only for the uneducated rabble has continued into the present cen-tury. In the 1920s, the British wine writer Morton Shand wrote: "The outstanding example of the menace to the survival of wine is the *champagnisation* of all kinds of wine, quite irrespective of their suitability for gaseous treatment. Our spendthrift generation is con-vinced that the sparkling variety of any given wine must needs be its highest, because its costliest, expression. It would seem that in the United States, wine, in common parlance, always implies a sparkling wine of sorts. It is arguable whether sparkling wine is really wine at all."[5]

The problem of the champagnization of unsuitable raw material remains today. The ideal climate for producing sparkling wine is one similar to Champagne, which Tom Stevenson has described in his book on the region as a "viticultural twilight zone."[6] Champagne is 150 miles north of Burgundy, and its climate is influenced by the Atlantic, which has a cooling effect in the summer. Grape varieties which ripen fully in Burgundy do not achieve full ripeness in Champagne. They are therefore ideally suited to sparkling wine production. To make a sparkling wine by a double fermentation, you need a base wine that is low in alcohol and high in acidity. That is because the addition of sugar before the second fermentation increases the alcoholic degree and the process of fermentation reduces the acid level by the precipitation of tartaric acid crystals and the degradation of some of the malic acid by the action of yeasts. A base wine with 10.7 percent alcohol produces a champagne with 12 percent, and with acid levels between a quarter and a third lower.[7]

Champagne may provide the ideal climate, but two-thirds of the sparkling wines drunk in the United States have been produced in California, where most of the grapes for bottle-fermented sparkling wines are grown in climates more comparable to that of Burgundy than to that of Champagne—for example, the Anderson Valley in Medocino County. This is a relatively young viticultural region which only attracted the spotlight in 1985 when the champagne company Louis Roederer decided, after looking all over the United States, to site its American sparkling wine facility there. Hans Kobler, who produces delicious still Pinot Noir and Gewürztraminer at Lazy Creek Vineyards, believes that the valley will be taken over for sparkling wine production. He doubts the wisdom of this. He believes that the Anderson Valley is really too warm for sparkling wine, for which people start picking the grapes at the end of July. He points out: "If an area is right for still wine, it is too warm for sparkling." Certainly the sparkling *grand cru* red burgundies that were produced at the end of the nineteenth century (and which have been described in Chapter 2) were a sad waste of fine wine, and one of the factors that impelled Morton Shand into his attack on the champagnization of unsuitable raw material.[8]

The most important region in California for grapes for bottle-fermented sparkling wines is Carneros, at the bottom of the Napa and Sonoma valleys. This is warmer than the Anderson Valley, and warmer than Burgundy. Nevertheless, three-quarters of the Pinot Noir grapes grown here go into sparkling wine. They are cropped to a level (12–14 tons per acre) which would make even the extravagant yields achieved in Champagne look pathetic—and picked early, before they are fully ripe, in order to maintain the right level of acidity. Not surprisingly, the wines that are made from them do not have a great deal of flavor. According to Dick Ward, co-owner of Saintsbury, one of the leading still-wine companies in Carneros, and an occasional producer of uncommercial quantities of rich, tasty sparkling wine, "One of the biggest mistakes of sparkling wine producers in California is that they are intent on making tasteless wine."

Taste is irrelevant in sparkling wines because, in America, they are served so cold as to numb them into submission. The same is true of beer. Anheuser-Busch, the manufacturer of Budweiser, the biggest-selling beer in the world, recommended that it be dispensed at 42°F. Budweiser was originally modeled on European Pilsner beers such as the Czech beer Budweiser,[9] which are generally served at 48°F. The reason why the American beer is served colder is simply that it has less taste. Whereas the best European Pilsners are made solely from malted barley, hops, yeast, and water, in America the malt tends to be cut with rice or corn, producing a much lighter drink. Anheuser-Busch is actually proud of its use of rice in brewing Budweiser, and says that it contributes to the "snappy taste, clarity, and brilliance of the beverage." Josef Tolar, the production manager of the Czech Budweiser brewery, has described the American Budweiser as "soda water with a dash of color."[10]

In recent years most American beers have become more rather than less tasteless. According to Joseph Owades, director of the Center for Brewing Studies in Boston, during the 1970s the major American breweries modified their products in order to make them more "drinkable," a term used by the brewing industry to describe beers that are less bitter on the palate and lighter in body. The level of bitterness has been reduced by adding fewer hops and "the whole flavor level has come down" as a result of reducing the malt content.[11]

If most American beers are bland, it is because most American beer drinkers like it that way. After all, Anheuser-Busch sells 2,500 million gallons of beer every year. When convened to judge American against European beers, American beer drinkers tend to prefer the American ones. At one tasting held by the *Philadelphia Inquirer*, the panel happened to prefer the "clean-tasting" Schmidt's—brewed in Philadelphia—in preference to such superior European beers as Heineken and Becks. Some microbreweries do make decent Pilsner beers, but they tend not to set themselves up in competition with the big breweries, preferring to produce darker beers in the British style. The one nationally distributed, serious Pilsner beer is Samuel Adams Boston Lager.

Likewise, American wines, even if they have not been cold-fermented, are dull by comparison with their European equivalents. This can be demonstrated by the distinction between California Chardonnay and white burgundy. The development of California Chardonnays in becoming more Burgundian—adopting such methods as barrel fermentation and lees contact—has already been discussed in Chapter 10. It has been pointed out in Chapter 14, however, that California wine makers have not adopted the Burgundian method of allowing the wines to be fermented by the yeasts that occur naturally in the vineyard or in the cellar, but instead add selected yeast strains to the wine, producing cleaner but less individual wines.

Moreover, the raw material is also different. John Hawley—now the wine maker at Kendall-Jackson but then at Clos du Bois—remembers that in 1983 there was a surprisingly large number of rotten grapes in their Chardonnay vineyards. He asked a French girl who was working for them, "Do you ever see grapes like this in Burgundy?" She said, "No, we have much more rot." When questioned on this subject, Burgundian vine growers like to claim that the rot in their vineyards is noble rot, the fungus that is responsible for producing sweet wines in Sauternes, Germany, and the Loire Valley. In 1983, when it managed to be hot and humid at the same time, noble rot did develop in Burgundy. But most years, there is nothing noble about the rot other than the fact that it has been produced in Burgundy. It is gray rot, the fungus responsible for ruining many vintages of red burgundy.[12] If it does not ruin the white wines as it does the red, it is because white grapes are not fermented in contact with their skins. The year 1975 was a disastrous vintage for red wines, but some of the white wines—which had just as much rot—were very good. They were fragile, but the rot gave them a lot of fat and made them very soft. Gray rot also contributed an exotic aspect to the bouquet of many 1986 white burgundies, a vintage which was acclaimed in its youth but whose potential for maturation is doubtful.

Because of the strange aromas that are produced by allowing rot-infected grapes to be fermented by naturally occurring yeast strains, many California and Australian wine makers condemn white burgundies as defective. James Halliday is not only Australia's most prominent wine writer and a leading wine-show judge, but he also makes an excellent Chardonnay at his Coldstream Hills vineyard in the Yarra Valley in Victoria. He has collected a large range of white burgundies over the years, but now—he says—he is selling them off. Much of his life has been devoted to criticizing wines and seeking out their defects. He can no longer drink white burgundies without noticing the defects, and being upset by them.

Perhaps white burgundies do, from a technical point of view, taste defective in their youth—but they can be wonderfully complex and aromatic when they are mature. Burgundian wine makers have a tendency to attribute these distinctive flavors to the soil of their region, but they would probably be more correct to link them with the fact that they have introduced defects into their wines. Sometimes they introduce too many defects and the wines are ruined. But on other occasions the defects are small enough to ensure that they add complexity rather than destruction. Clean, technically perfect white wines are boring. White burgundies may have defects—which sometimes destroy them—but these defects are what make them exciting. To make great wine, you have to live dangerously.

Wheras white burgundies mature, and develop, in dramatic and exciting (and often disappointing) ways, California Chardonnays have a tendency, as they mature, to enter a state of cryogenic suspension: they do not improve, they are preserved. This can be demonstrated by anyone who is prepared to purchase, for example, a bottle of Trefethen Chardonnay and hold it in his cellar for five or ten years.

Cryogenic suspension seems to be a deliberately sought-after state. When I referred to the American obsession with refrigeration in Chapter 2, I suggested that it was linked with the reverence that is accorded to the role of technology in the development of the United States. Keith Botsford, a widely traveled food writer for the British daily newspaper *The Independent*, has extended the technology argument by suggesting that the American obsession with refrigeration is linked with a corresponding obsession with freshness and hygiene; that food, like people, should strive for immortality; that life should ideally be a state of cryogenic suspension.[13] Certainly, American visitors to food stores in Europe are horrified to have meat cut for them from a joint that has been sitting on the counter, exposed to the germs of the people who handle it; to see fruits and vegetables lying loose in boxes, to be picked over by potential purchasers; to discover that game that has started to become rancid is prized rather than thrown away.

The American obsession with freshness and hygiene is similarly demonstrated by restrictions that are placed on wine-making procedures, restrictions which ensure that, even if wine makers wanted to make their Chardonnays and Pinot Noirs by traditional Burgundian techniques, they would not be allowed to. The greatest burgundies are produced in small, dank cellars with mold on the walls and gravel on the floor. If you taste the wine direct from the barrel, you spit it out afterward onto the floor, helping to maintain the humidity level. In such an atmosphere, native strains of yeasts—to carry out the alcoholic and malolactic fermentations—are kept going for many years. In America, in general, wineries have tiled floors that can be hosed down regularly, rather than gravel; and wine makers prohibit visitors from spitting on the floor, saying that it is illegal. In such an atmosphere, new yeast strains have to be added every year. Wineries that attempt to follow the Burgundian model and therefore reject the regulations run the danger of being closed down. Adelsheim, one of the most prestigious wineries in Oregon, was once closed down for not having a clean cellar.

At another Oregon winery, Panther Creek, the owner and wine maker Ken Wright defies convention in order to extend the fermentation of his Pinot Noir to two weeks—by climbing naked into the vats in order to disperse the hot spots where the solids have packed and where it is about 25°C warmer. He explains that it is much better to use your body for this than to use the normal method of punching down the fermenting mass with a tool from the top of the vat: punching down does not deal with the hot spots, so it shortens the fermentation. This technique is certainly effective—Panther Creek Pinot Noir is a soft, rich wine—but it is likely to remind more conventional American wine makers of the method that was practiced at the then-monastic vineyard of Clos de Vougeot in Burgundy before the French Revolution. The monks used to jump naked into the vats three times during the vinification in order to ensure that the skins mixed properly with the juice. This exertion was (and is) called *pigeage*. This was the only occasion in the year when the monks had a bath, and it was said that a real burgundy expert could declare by the taste whether a wine was pre- or post-*pigeage*.[14]

Wright's method of near-total immersion is still employed by a number of wine makers in Burgundy, but not by any of his colleagues or competitors in the United States. "Most wine makers in America," he explains, "think only of efficiency, when their whole effort should be directed at getting better wine into the glass." According to Patrick Glynn, the coeditor of the *Journal of Contemporary Studies*, "In America, technology is understood to be the ultimate supplier and limiter of human opinions."[15] The exaggerated lengths to which technology can take its users is demonstrated by the discovery of oenin, which has been described in Chapter 12. When Leo McCloskey declared to the newspapers that he had discovered a substance which represented up to half the flavor of red wine, he had not realized that what would interest them most was the question of whether it was, or would become, possible to synthesize oenin—in order to artificially produce fine wines. In the opinion of Paul Draper, the wine maker at Ridge Vineyards—where McCloskey conducted his experiments—synthesis is impossible because wine is much too complex a substance, a mess of polymers (long chains of tannins) which simply cannot be analyzed.

Draper and McCloskey did, however, discuss what would happen if it ever did become possible to synthesize fine wines. Would there still be a place for Ridge? They concluded that there would. In

Draper's opinion, "People drink wine as a corrective to the high technology of today, as a link with the seasons and the soil. Wine naturally made is the foremost symbol of transformation: that is why it has been part of so many religions."

Draper is right. Only a desire to maintain a link with the seasons could explain the popularity each November of Beaujolais Nouveau—generally a feeble, overpriced wine—of which Americans consumed 5 million bottles a year during the second half of the 1980s. Only its role as a symbol of transformation and its part in the offering of the Eucharist can explain why the manufacture of sweet wine from rotten grapes was once concealed from its consumers. This required the invention of the stories, accounting for the sudden "discovery" of wine made by this method in the dechristianized Europe of the nineteenth century, which have been described in Chapter 6.

The agricultural and transubstantiational aspects of wine appear not to be properly understood in the United States, and not just because it is more of a Protestant than a Catholic country. Wine may be a processed product, but only in being the transformation of an agricultural one. The sooner that American wine companies start looking on wine as an agricultural rather than a manufactured product—and start talking about vine growing rather than "the wine industry"—the better. The French belief in the relative importance of viticulture over that of vinification is well expressed by Frédéric Mugnier, the owner of Château de Chambolle-Musigny in Burgundy. He believes: "All you can do in wine making is transform the grape. In fact, you can't do that—you can only take part of what is in the grape. You make a choice; take a certain route. You can't add anything to the grape—you can only take away as little as possible. If you go into the vineyards and taste the grapes, they taste of their *appellation*."

When *appellations* were established in Burgundy in the 1930s, they codified the experience of several hundred years. Vine growing in California is too new for it to be possible to establish appellations that control the choice of grape varieties and the application of wine-making techniques in the same manner. But it is important that appellations should be established, because they give a wine a geographical identity in the way that the name of a winery or wine maker does not. We drink wine only partly (if at all) for the taste, and partly in order to be able to travel in our minds: to associate ourselves, however briefly, with an exotic foreign land. This is one major reason why American consumers are prepared to pay so much more for French wines than for equally good American ones.

The names that have been given to fine American wines have only rarely identified them with their origin. Some vine growers in the early Republic did name their wines after the place of production, such as Nicholas Herbemont of Columbia, South Carolina, who called his white wine "Palmyra," the name of the farm where he grew the grapes.[16] But he did not succeed in establishing a precedent. As has been described in Chapter 12, most wine producers preferred to usurp European names, and therefore producers of fine wines after the Second World War had no option but to adopt varietal names.

In Chapter 8 I have cited the observation of Brice Jones, the owner of Sonoma-Cutrer, that wine producers in California have sold their wines almost exclusively under varietal and brand names rather than under the names of vineyards—because in 85–90 percent of instances, the vineyards are owned by someone else. There is no reason, however, why a vineyard should not be made famous by the man who makes the wine from it, even if he is not its proprietor. Joe Heitz does not own Martha's Vineyard in the Napa Valley, yet it is possibly the most famous source of Cabernet Sauvignon in the whole of America; Jim Clendenen of Au Bon Climat does not own the Benedict vineyard in the Santa Ynez Valley in Santa Barbara County from which he has made outstanding Chardonnays and Pinot Noirs; Burt Williams of William Selyem does not own the Rochioli vineyard in the Russian River Valley in Sonoma County, from which he makes America's most expensive and most sought-after Pinot Noir. The most famous producer of red burgundy in the 1980s, Henri Jayer, did not own the parcels of vines in the *premiers crus* Nuits-Saint-Georges Les Murgers and Vosne-Romanée Les Brulées and Cros Parantoux and the *grand cru* Richebourg from which he made his wines, but rented them from Domaine Méo-Camuzet, to whom he returned them in 1988. It has nevertheless been suggested that it is to the quality of the wines made by Jayer that the reputation of the Les Brulées and Cros Parantoux vineyards is due.[17]

In California, the most prestigious wines, in general, do not bear the names of the vineyard from which their fruit was made but are fantasy names which in themselves correspond to no geographical reality. Obviously this was a sensible choice in the case of Opus One, which began as a marketing concept in 1980, with neither a vineyard nor wine to its name. Not until the 1988 vintage has any of the fruit for Opus One come from its own vineyards in Oakville, and then only one-third of the blend. But why is Dominus, another joint venture between a celebrated French wine maker—in this case Christian Moueix of Château Pétrus—and a California vine grower—in this instance Robin Lail and Marcia Smith—not named instead after Lail and Smith's Napanook vineyard, from whose fruit it is made? This vineyard is hardly an obscure one: Lail and Smith are the daughters of John Daniel, who ran Inglenook from 1939 until his death in 1970, and who used Napanook as one of the two principal sources of Inglenook's Cask Selection Cabernet Sauvignon. Moreover, Napanook produces wine with a very particular character, quite different from other Napa Valley Cabernet Sauvignons, very hard and tannic in its youth but capable of aging superbly.[18]

The preference of wine makers for fantasy names will perhaps be counterbalanced by the introduction of more specific appellations, along the lines of the ones that exist in Burgundy. The creation of the Napa Valley appellation and of regional appellations within it has already been discussed in Chapter 9. In 1989 a number of vine growers and wine makers applied to the Federal Bureau of Alcohol, Tobacco and Firearms (BATF) to create two village appellations, Rutherford and Oakville, and within them two superior appellations, Rutherford Bench and Oakville Bench, for vineyards on the west side of the Napa River. These were the most controversial appellation proposals so far, because they envisaged the introduction of a hierarchical element into the California appellation system for the first time. It was proposed that the Rutherford Bench appellation should include some of the most historic vineyards in California, among them Beaulieu, Inglenook, and Niebaum-Coppola, and that the Oakville Bench appellation should include Martha's Vineyard, among others. One might have expected Joe Heitz, the man who made Martha's Vineyard famous, to support the proposals. Instead, he described them as "just farting around." He added that, in his opinion, the balkanization of the Napa Valley would simply serve to dilute all the efforts made by local vine growers and wine makers in creating the reputation of the Napa Valley as a whole.[19]

Certainly it is important that the Napa Valley, the most famous wine-producing region in America, should retain its identity. It is in the nature of the majority of city dwellers to want to imagine that we are farmers, and therefore to seek to identify as closely as possible with the produce of our local farming community. Those of us who cannot afford to fulfill our fantasies by throwing away millions of dollars on building our own wineries can at least visit our local wineries and consume their produce. It is local patriotism which explains why, in general, in Australia, consumers do not care from where ordinary wines come, but will only drink the fine wines produced in their own state. If they live in Sydney in New South Wales, they drink wine from the Hunter Valley; if they live in Melbourne in Victoria, their wine comes from the Yarra Valley; if they live in Adelaide in South Australia, it comes from the Barossa. It is not just their local wine: they actually imagine that it is their own wine. These attitudes take us back to the historical geography of medieval France, described in Chapter 12: the reputation of the most famous vineyard regions was created by the bourgeoisie of the local cities, who took pride in serving the wines at their tables.

The local patriotism of the inhabitants of the cities of the Bay Area requires that the Napa Valley remains at the top of the tree. It was difficult to see how the proposed new appellations would weaken this position, however. Surely the introduction of a hierarchical element into the Napa Valley would serve to enhance, rather than lessen, its status—just as the existence of *grands crus* and *premiers crus* enhances the status of all the ordinary wines produced in Burgundy? Moreover, the linking of status to the supposed virtues of a particular type of soil—in the case of the Rutherford Bench a fan of soil on the valley floor that was created by the merging of a small creek with the Napa River—would serve to introduce an element of French mysticism to American wine making for the first time. Nevertheless, perhaps partly because of a fear of French mysticism, the BATF decided in 1992 that, while it would probably sanction the introduction of the village appellations Rutherford and Oakville, it was not prepared to introduce the superior appellations Rutherford Bench and Oakville Bench. Not only had the applicants failed to demonstrate that the grapes grown in their "bench" areas were intrinsically superior to grapes grown opposite them, on the east side of the Napa River, but they had been unable to show any historical precedent that would justify these names being enshrined in law: there was no evidence for the use of the term *Rutherford Bench* before the 1970s, while the term *Oakville Bench* was created as part of the appellation proposals.

The rejection of the proposed "bench" appellations marked a victory for reason over vision, and thus a fundamental difference between American and French attitudes to wine. The contrast between the American belief in the greater importance of things that are measurable (such as climate) and the attachment of French wine makers to whatever is most magical and least measurable (such as soil) has already been referred to in Chapter 10. The attitude of the French may seem absurd to rational beings, but it has its advantages. According to Comte Henri de Vaucelles, the owner of Château Filhot in Sauternes, "A luxury product must never say that it is manufactured: it must be a miracle of climate and soil." That is why, he says, each region has invented its own legend: this enhances the miraculous, and thus inimitable, nature of its wines.

It is said, for example, that Côte Rôtie in the Northern Rhône came to be divided into two slopes, the Côte Brune and the Côte Blonde, because the nobleman who owned the hillside in the Middle Ages had two daughters, a blonde and a brunette, and he divided the vineyard between them. The slope inherited by the blonde produced wine that was pretty in its youth but faded quickly; wine from the slope inherited by the brunette was shy at first but developed splendidly. Marcel Guigal has made use of the popular belief in the legend of the two hillsides in the marketing of his three single-vineyard Côte Rôties. He describes La Mouline as quintessential Côte Blonde, La Landonne as classic Côte Brune, and La Turque as a Brune with Blonde characteristics. In fact, La Mouline and La Turque are brand names which Guigal owns. La Mouline is certainly a vineyard on the Côte Blonde and La Turque a vineyard on the Côte Brune, but Guigal can put wine into them from wherever in Côte Rôtie he wants. La Landonne is not a vineyard on the Côte

Brune but a separate hillside called La Landonne; it is not even next to the Côte Brune, because Côte des Moutonnes lies in between. The brunette and blonde characteristics of Guigal's wines may be a matter of dispute, but they certainly help him to attain stratospherically high prices for them.

Champagne has the legend of Dom Perignon, allegedly a blind monk who invented sparkling champagne. In fact, as has already been described, sparkling champagne was invented in England before Dom Perignon exerted any influence in Champagne. As Nicholas Faith has pointed out in *The Story of Champagne*, the main achievement of Dom Perignon—who could see perfectly well—was to produce white wine from black grapes. The Dom Perignon legend has proved very convenient for champagne producers, however. "Its apparently holy origins greatly help legitimize a drink originally associated exclusively with dissipation and seduction."[20]

The Dom Perignon story points out two essential distinctions between the American and French approaches to wine. First, American wine has no legends to render it miraculous. In part, this is the consequence of the attitude of American wine makers, who have concentrated too hard on manufacturing their wines and not hard enough on creating a world of fantasy around them. In part, it is simply a product of the novelty of American fine wine, which existed at the end of the nineteenth century but then not again in any quantity until the 1960s. It was this novelty—the lack of a long-term history of the superiority of certain areas—which killed off the Rutherford Bench and Oakville Bench appellation proposals.

Second, Americans would never have thought of associating a fine wine with dissipation and seduction. One of the principal legacies both of seventeenth-century Puritanism and, more significantly, of nineteenth-century Protestant non-conformism is a tendency not to show overt pleasure in food or drink. That is why the Americans, like the British, tend to look upon wine as an intellectual pleasure, to be written about at great length, to be made an object of study rather than a gastronomic indulgence—whereas the French regard wine as being indelibly linked with food, and find difficulty in separating them when they write, eat, drink, or make love. This distinction is certainly a major reason why the habit of enjoying fine wine and fine food together has not taken off in the United States.

Another principal legacy of nineteenth-century Protestant non-conformism is of course the belief that the consumption of alcoholic drinks should be prohibited altogether. It is for this reason that it is especially important for American wine producers, deprived of the permanent support of legends or of a popular belief in the natural alliance of food and wine, to emphasize the connection, real or imaginary, between the wine that they are trying to sell and the soil in which the grapes have grown. On the one hand, the more magical and less precisely measurable the origins of wine become, the harder it will be for the antialcohol lobby to destroy it. On the other, the more a wine can be identified with its origin, and the less with its manufacture, the stronger the wine business will be. The further that wine drinking is separated from the consumption of beer and spirits, the less likely it is that increasingly severe restrictions on wine drinking will be introduced. The role of Leon D. Adams in persuading a number of states to pass farm winery laws—thus encouraging the idea that wine drinking is a pleasurable pastoral pastime rather than a shameful urban sin—was described in Chapter 1. Adams, who lived through national Prohibition, knows the power of the temperance lobby, but he remains confident. "What makes the wine business strong these days is the fact that agriculture is behind it. Agriculture is what gets the farm winery bills through opposition from liquor retailers and other groups. Wine growing is agriculture, and agriculture is always stronger than liquor."[21]

Conversion Tables

ALCOHOL CONTENT

I have expressed alcohol content throughout this book in percent of alcohol by volume, since this is the form in which it appears on labels. Various other forms of measurement are encountered, however. Brewers talk about original gravity (OG), German vine growers about ° Oeschle, and California wine makers about ° Brix. These are in fact measurements of the sugar content of the must, i.e., the *potential* alcohol content. The alcohol level actually achieved depends on how much of the sugar turns to alcohol. Rough equivalences are:

SUGAR CONTENT (GRAMS PER LITER)	° BRIX	° OESCHLE	OG	POTENTIAL ALCOHOL (PERCENT)
70	7	30	1030	4
110	11	50	1050	6
145	14.5	65	1065	8
180	18	80	1080	10
215	21.5	95	1095	12
250	25	110	1110	14
290	29	130	1130	16

YIELDS

Similar difficulties apply when trying to correlate different methods of measuring the size of the harvest. In this book the figures that have been given are the grape yields—in tons per acre—as that is the system used by vine growers in the United States. In France, however, growers talk about hectoliters per hectare—the yield in terms of wine. It is impossible to precisely correlate the two systems, because the quantity of wine made from a given quantity of grapes depends on how hard they are pressed and on how much liquid is lost during fermentation. As a general rule, a conscientious wine maker will produce roughly 3 tons per acre, which is the equivalent of 45–50 hectoliters per hectare, or 2,400–2,700 bottles from each acre.

Wine Book and Magazine Snobbery

BOOKS

This is a review of the most important drinks books to have appeared in the last few years. Importance is a subjective criterion: the list does not include all the standard works which one would probably want to have in a representative collection of wine books.

Burton Anderson, *The Wine Atlas of Italy and The Traveler's Guide to the Vineyards* (Simon & Schuster, 1991). A disappointment. Although it is full of information, it is satisfactory neither as an atlas nor as a work of prose. It updates, but does not supersede, Anderson's outstanding pioneering work, *Vino: the Wines and Winemakers of Italy* (Little, Brown & Co., 1980). The problem Anderson has been unable to overcome is that Italian wine is simply too big a subject to encompass in any depth in a single volume. It is no more feasible than trying to say all that needs to be said about French wine in one book. The future for books on Italian wine lies in the publication of works on individual regions. This has begun with the enlightening *Barolo: Tar and Roses, a Study of the Wines of Alba* (Century, London, 1990) by two British wine importers, Michael Garner and Paul Merritt; a forthcoming book on Chianti by another (in this case Canadian-born) British wine importer, David Gleave, is also likely to be excellent.

Oz Clark's *New Classic Wines* (Simon & Schuster, 1991). Oz Clarke, a former actor, is the most outlandish, the most exaggerated, and the least British of British wine writers. His enthusiasm is genuine; his honesty is fundamental. Other British wine writers have tried to copy his hyperactive prose style, but have fallen flat on their faces. This, his first *real* book, is principally a collection of profiles of wine producers in California and Australasia. It is exhausting to read, but it is worth it.

James Conaway, *Napa: the Story of an American Eden* (Houghton Mifflin, 1990). There is some interesting history in there, if you can be bothered to wade through all the gush.

Hugh Johnson, *Vintage: The Story of Wine* (Simon & Schuster,

1989). A fascinating and beautifully written book which was, however, overrated at the time of its publication. Johnson is a wine writer, not a historian, but that does not excuse his failure to place wine in its historical, sociological, and gastronomic context. The predecessor to this book—William Younger, *Gods, Men and Wine* (Michael Joseph, London, 1966)—was much more satisfactory, even though it concentrated largely on Britain. Johnson's best and most useful book remains his *World Atlas of Wine*, first published in 1971 but updated at regular intervals.

Matt Kramer, *Making Sense of Burgundy* (William Morrow, 1990). I prefer this to Parker's book (see below), because Kramer has a better feel for the region. It is not comprehensive—Kramer omits a number of important producers, as well as the Hautes Côtes, the Côte Chalonnaise, and the Maconnais, the sources of the best-value burgundy—but it will remain the best introduction to the region until the British wine retailer Anthony Hanson publishes the second edition of his brilliant and seminal *Burgundy* (Faber & Faber, London, 1982), which he is currently in the process of writing.

Kermit Lynch, *Adventures on the Wine Route: A Wine Buyer's Tour of France* (Farrar Straus & Giroux, 1988). This is a homily to those small French growers whose wines Lynch imports through his company in Berkeley, California. It is both an expression of his wine-buying and wine-drinking philosophy—he is vehemently opposed to growers who filter or otherwise denature their wines—and a marketing exercise. It is passionate, instructive, unremittingly entertaining, and probably my favorite wine book. I recommend reading it in conjunction with its British equivalent: Simon Loftus, *Anatomy of the Wine Trade: Abe's Sardines and Other Stories* (Sidgwick & Jackson, London, 1985). Loftus is the influential ex-hippie wine buyer for the wine retailing business of Adnams, a medium-sized, high-quality brewery in Southwold, Suffolk. Most recently he has published a delightful (if not particularly useful) account of everyday life in one of Burgundy's most famous villages: *Puligny-Montrachet* (Ebury Press, London, 1992).

Edmund Penning-Rowsell, *The Wines of Bordeaux* (6th ed., Viking Penguin, 1990). A quintessentially British approach to the most Anglophile of French wine-producing regions. Penning-Rowsell, who takes himself terribly seriously, is precisely the sort of British wine writer who is lampooned in the annual April Fool issue of *The Wine Spectator* (for which see below), but the fact remains that this is the best book written on Bordeaux. It is, of course, more a work of history than a consumer-friendly guide to the best *châteaux* to follow today.

Jancis Robinson, *The Great Wine Book* (Sidgwick & Jackson, London, 1982); *Vines, Grapes, and Wines* (Knopf, 1986). Jancis Robinson is a charismatic television presenter and a brilliant journalist, but she has published some disappointing books. These are the best of them. *The Great Wine Book* manages to combine a glossy, coffee-table approach with a great deal of insight, although it is now clearly dated; *Vines, Grapes, and Wines* is a brave, pioneering attempt to produce a standard work on grape varieties which is actually readable.

Robert M. Parker, *Bordeaux: the Definitive Guide* (Simon & Schuster, 1985; revised edition, 1991); *The Wines of the Rhône Valley and Provence* (Simon & Schuster, 1987); *Burgundy: A Comprehensive Guide to the Producers, Appellations and Wines* (Simon & Schuster, 1990). Nobody reads Parker in order to acquire an in-depth understanding of French fine wine or for sheer enjoyment of his prose. People read him for the relentless energy of his tasting notes: for his ability to deconstruct the most complex of wine regions by reducing them to their essentials—the taste and quality of the wines. Because they represent a victory for American pragmatism over French mysticism, these books offer a slightly distorted view of the regions with which they deal. Certainly, Parker's approach works much better in Bordeaux than in Burgundy. Since books of tasting notes go out of date more rapidly than any other kind, these should be supplemented by a reading of Parker's bi-monthly newsletter *The Wine Advocate* (for which see below).

Tom Stevenson, *Champagne* (Sotheby's Publications, 1986); Nicholas Faith, *The Story of Champagne* (Facts on File, 1989); Patrick Forbes, *Champagne* (Victor Gollancz, London, 1967). No wholly satisfactory modern work has been published on Champagne. Tom Stevenson's book is exceedingly useful but rather dull. Nicholas Faith's is very well written but concentrates on the history and is of little use as a guide to the villages or producers. The best book on the subject remains that of Patrick Forbes, written more than a generation ago. Forbes worked for Moët, and was not only biased toward the big merchants but was the person principally responsible for creating the legend of Dom Perignon. Nevertheless, it is the one book on the subject which can be approached as champagne should be—self-indulgently.

Jay Stuller and Glen Martin, *Through the Grapevine: The Business of Wine in America* (Wynwood Press, 1989). Supposedly an exposé, but it is no more hard hitting than one would expect from two people who have worked in the public relations business.

James Suckling, *Vintage Port: The Wine Spectator's Ultimate Guide for Consumers, Collectors and Investors* (Wine Spectator Press, San Francisco, 1990). This is the best of the three *Wine Spectator* guides so far published, the other two being *California's Great Cabernets* and *California's Great Chardonnays*, by James Laube. It is basically a collection of profiles of all the producers of vintage port. It does not fill the gap in the market for an honest, authoritative book about port in general.

MAGAZINES

For people who can afford to drink it, the two indispensable guides to fine wine are *The Wine Advocate*, P.O. Box 311, Monkton, Maryland 21111 (Robert Parker), and *The Vine*, Lamerton House, 27 High Street, Ealing, London W5 5DF (Clive Coates). I more often agree with Coates than with Parker, but that may have more to do with the fact that British wine tasters generally prefer leaner, more elegant wines than Americans than with any question of correctness. The main difference between the two has nothing to do with reliability—nor indeed with the much-discussed topic of marking systems—but is the fact that Coates gives off through his writing an image of pomposity and self-importance, whereas Parker gives the impression of being an ordinary (if informed) consumer writing for other, like-minded people.

The wine magazine is *The Wine Spectator*, 387 Park Avenue South, New York, New York 10016. I find many—too many—of its tasting judgments to be way off beam, but its stories are lively, readable, and always to the point. Its hyping of certain producers can sometimes go too far, but if its aim is to make wine exciting and dynamic, to make more people want to drink the stuff, then it succeeds. Stuller and Martin (see above) cite a vine grower in Sonoma County, California, who compares *The Wine Spectator* to *The National Enquirer*: "The vinous equivalent of ax murderers and aliens from outer space." Perhaps so. But it is prepared to go digging for stories, unlike the British magazines *Wine* and *Decanter*. These are simply too oriented toward the wine trade to justify their claim to be consumer magazines. At least *Wine* is interesting; *Decanter* is so boring and so full of puffs that I cannot understand why anyone should ever want to read it. I cannot imagine either being capable of producing wine journalism as brilliant as the First Annual Swimsuit Issue published by *The Wine Spectator* on April 1, 1989.

The best newspaper wine column may no longer be the one written by Frank Prial every Wednesday in *The New York Times*, but it is still the most important and most readable. Because he is a journalist first and a wine writer second, Prial is able to detach himself from the hype with which he is surrounded and simply write about what he finds most interesting. He has exerted great influence on the development of wine consumption and production in the States since he began writing about wine in 1972. At one point his column was syndicated in seventy-five newspapers around the country. He has attempted on several occasions to resign, but each time has been brought back "by popular demand." It is anyone's guess whether he will still be writing his column in 1993.

Notes

Foreword: The British Edition

1. *The Financial Times*, December 17, 1988.
2. *Wine*, December 1988, pp. 63–65.
3. Press release from German Wine Institute, July 31, 1985.

PART ONE

1. Prohibition and the Wine Boom

1. *American Farmer*, October 1, 1819, quoted in Thomas Pinney, A *History of Wine in America from the Beginnings to Prohibition*, University of California Press, 1989, pp. 149–50.
2. The two French wines mentioned are single-village wines from Champagne.
3. Captain Thomas Hamilton, *Men and Manners in America*, 1833, pp. 118–21.
4. Frank Schoonmaker and Tom Marvel, *American Wines*, 1941, pp. 4, 13.
5. Roper survey, quoted in Jay Stuller and Glen Martin, *Through the Grapevine: The Business of Wine in America*, Wynwood Press, 1989, p. 68.
6. *The Wine Spectator*, February 28, 1991, pp. 23–28.
7. *The New York Times*, December 1, 1986.
8. Stuller and Martin, *Through the Grapevine*, p. 63.
9. Leon D. Adams, *The Wines of America*, 3rd ed., McGraw-Hill, 1985, p. 114.
10. Eric B. Rimm et al., "Prospective study of alcohol consumption and

risk of coronary disease in men," *The Lancet*, August 24, 1991, pp. 464–68. This survey found that, the more men drank, the less likely they were to suffer from heart disease. Other surveys have found that, while moderate drinkers are less likely to suffer from heart disease than teetotalers, heavy drinkers run a considerably greater risk. It has recently been suggested that this distinction may be related to the effect of alcohol consumption on the body's sensitivity to insulin and on the quantity of triglycerides (fats) in the blood: G. Razay et al., "Alcohol consumption and its relation to cardiovascular risk factors in British women," *The British Medical Journal*, February 11, 1992, pp. 80–83. Scientific surveys about the effects of alcohol consumption contradict one another because many people lie about the amount of alcohol they consume. The results of such surveys should therefore always be approached with a certain degree of caution.

11. *The Wine Spectator*, May 31, 1992.
12. Of course, wine is recommended in the Bible—despite the attempts of members of the nineteenth-century temperance movement to prove that, where wine was mentioned in the Bible, what was actually referred to was unfermented grape juice. The authors of *The Temperance Bible Commentary* rewrote 493 references to drink in the Old Testament and 144 in the New Testament, such as changing "Stay me with flagons" (Song of Solomon 2:5) to "Sustain me with a cake of grapes." See Norman Longmate, *The Waterdrinkers*, Hamish Hamilton, 1968, pp. 182–91.
13. *The Independent*, June 9, 1991.
14. *The Wine Spectator*, September 15, 1991.
15. *The New York Times*, May 23, 1990, and January 1, 1991.

2. THE AMERICAN SWEET TOOTH

1. *The New York Times*, March 6, 1985.
2. James Conaway, *Napa*, Houghton Mifflin, 1990, p. 267.
3. Cyril Ray, *Ray on Wine*, J. M. Dent & Sons, 1979, p. 24.
4. Robert Masyczeck and C. S. Ough, "The 'Red Wine Reaction' Syndrome," *American Journal of Enology and Viticulture*, vol. 34, 1983, pp. 260–64.
5. Julia T. Littlewood et al., "Red wine as a cause of migraine," *The Lancet*, March 12, 1988, pp. 558–59.
6. It is not difficult to rapidly alter the temperature of a wine as long as you remember that it changes very rapidly when immersed in water in a kitchen sink or an ice bucket, but very slowly when left to change temperature in the surrounding air. To bring a red wine up to "room" temperature of 65°F from a cellar temperature of 52°F in a room heated to 70°F takes two and three-quarter hours. To do so in a bucket of water at 70°F takes fourteen minutes. To cool a white wine down to 55°F from a room temperature of 70°F in a fridge at 40°F takes 1 hour 40 minutes. To do so in a bucket of iced water at 40°F takes eight minutes.
7. Simon Hoggart, *America: A User's Guide*, Collins, 1990, pp. 68–70, 127. It has been calculated that two-thirds of all American homes have

air-conditioning: *Newsweek*, June 10, 1991, p. 42. In Europe, air-conditioning is rare.

8. *Wine*, April 1990, p. 9.
9. Quoted in Jay Stuller and Glen Martin, *Through the Grapevine: The Business of Wine in America*, Wynwood Press, 1989, pp. 105–6.
10. Julian Jeffs, *Sherry*, 3rd ed., Faber & Faber, 1982, pp. 51–52.
11. *American Farmer*, December 21, 1832, quoted in Thomas Pinney, *A History of Wine in America from the Beginnings to Prohibition*, University of California Press, 1988, p. 129.
12. John L. Hess and Karen Hess, *The Taste of America*, 3rd ed., University of South Carolina Press, 1989, pp. 64–65.
13. See Thomas Oliver, *The Real Coke, The Real Story*, Random House, 1986.
14. *Wine & Spirit*, July 1987, pp. 51–52.
15. He also added some Scuppernong juice from North Carolina because he knew that people liked its muscadine flavor.
16. Denzil Batchelor, "The Sparklers" in Anthony Hogg (ed.), *WineMine: A First Anthology*, Souvenir Press, 1970, p. 71.

3. RED WINE IN RESTAURANTS

1. It is also why, it has been suggested, the French stopped drinking Sauternes when their diets returned to normal after the Second World War. See Chapter 13.
2. Giorgio Lulli et al., *Alcohol in Italian Culture*, 1958.
3. *The Wine Spectator*, May 15, 1990, p. 38.
4. *The New York Times*, March 6, 1985.
5. Ibid.
6. Ibid., August 22, 1984.
7. Ibid., July 10, 1991.
8. I am indebted for this story to Faber & Faber's wine editor Julian Keffs.
9. Alexis Bespaloff, *The New Encyclopaedia of Wine*, William Morrow, 1988, p. 142.
10. *The Wine Spectator*, April 15, 1990, pp. 28–37.
11. *Wine*, October 1989, p. 7. Ironically, the substance which is primarily responsible for a corky aroma is 2,4,6-trichloroanisol, which does not occur naturally in cork but is produced as a result of the process of sterilizing it with a chlorine solution: this produces TCP, which is then converted by penicillin molds into 2,4,6-trichloroanisol. The solution is not to leave the corks unsterilized—this exposes the wine to other forms of infection—but to bottle the wines with screw caps. This is done with jug wines, which people drink straight after buying them, but not with "fine" wines, which are intended to be laid down to mature. Producers claim that they could not bottle fine wines with a screw cap, because it would prevent them from maturing in bottle. This is nonsense; wine does not mature by breathing through the cork but by reacting with substances which are dissolved in it. The real reason why fine wines are not bottled with screw caps is that it would detract from the imagery which their manufacturers have labored so hard to create.

Only in Switzerland are fine wines bottled in this way. The most prestigious California wine so far to have borne a screw cap was a 1990 Napa Valley Dolcetto which Glen Ellen put on the market at $10. But this was a onetime event: the purpose of the screw cap was to show that this was a light wine, intended for immediate consumption.

12. *The New York Times*, April 26, 1987.
13. *The Wine Spectator*, September 30, 1991, pp. 29–37.
14. *Wine & Spirit*, September 1989, p. 85.

4. WRITERS AND COLLECTORS

1. *The Sunday Times*, March 9, 1980; *The Daily Post*, February 11, 1982.
2. *The Sunday Telegraph*, August 4, 1991.
3. It must be admitted that, possibly as a result of my condemnation in the British edition of *Wine Snobbery* of its practice of publishing articles by wine importers and retailers, *Decanter* now uses many fewer wine trade contributors than it used to.
4. David Gleave, *The Wines of Italy*, Price Stern, 1990, p. 5
5. The *Los Angeles Times*, August 23, 1987.
6. *The Wine Spectator*, September 30, 1987.
7. Ibid., November 30, 1989, pp. 24–29.
8. *The Wall Street Journal*, February 25, 1988.
9. *The Wine Spectator*, June 15, 1990, p. 7.
10. Ibid., January 31, 1992, pp. 24–43.
11. *The New York Times*, December 6, 1989.
12. The *Los Angeles Times*, August 24, 1987. It is possible that the customer had been right to return the wine in the first place, since Chalone's wines had been spoiled in a number of vintages by a corky smell and taste. See my comments on Heitz.
13. David Peppercorn in *Decanter*, December 1986, p. 99. Many of those people who criticize Parker use a twenty-point system. Parker's system begins at fifty so it is really a fifty-point scale. Tasters who use a twenty-point system allow themselves half marks so it is really a forty-point scale. So what's the difference?
14. *The Sunday Times*, August 10, 1986.
15. *Wine & Spirit*, October 1985, pp. 33–35.
16. *The Wine Advocate*, no. 48, December 1986, p. 36, and no. 76, August 1991, p. 47. The vineyard is called Beaux-Frères (brothers-in-law). Unlike Parker, *The Wine Spectator* has permitted itself a conflict of interest: in November 1990 its European bureau chief, James Suckling, wrote a laudatory report on the Nacional bottling from the port house Quinta do Noval without saying that his wife handles public relations for Quinta do Noval in Britain.
17. Robert Parker, *Burgundy: A Comprehensive Guide to the Producers, Appellations, and Wines,* Simon & Schuster, 1990, pp. 157–58, 868.
18. Robert Parker, *The Wine Buyer's Guide*, 2nd edition, Simon & Schuster, 1989, pp. 550–51.
19. *The Vine*, no. 65, June 1990, pp. 3, 9.
20. *The Wine Spectator*, January 31, 1989, pp. 24–29.

21. Ibid., January 31, 1990, p. 28.
22. Ibid., March 15, 1990, p. 8, and March 15, 1991, p. 12.
23. Ibid., January 31, 1990, p. 31.
24. *The Wine Advocate*, no. 46, August 1986; Robert Parker, *The Wines of the Rhône Valley and Provence*, Simon & Schuster, 1987, p. 54.
25. *The New York Times*, December 6, 1989.
26. *The Wine Advocate*, no. 70, August 1990, p. 35.
27. *The Wine Spectator*, December 15, 1990, p. 112.

5. WINE TASTINGS ARE BUNK

1. *Decanter*, July 1985, p. 31
2. *The Wine Spectator*, October 15, 1989, p. 13, and March 31, 1990, p. 18.
3. Ibid., February 15, 1990, pp. 47–52.
4. Ibid., July 15, 1989, p. 18.
5. Ibid., December 31, 1990, Buying Guide.
6. *Decanter*, September 1983, p. 35.
7. Max Schubert, "The Story of Grange Hermitage," *The Rewards of Patience*, Penfolds, 2nd ed., 1990, p. 81.
8. *Wine & Spirit*, August 1987, p. 49.
9. Simon Loftus, *Anatomy of the Wine Trade: Abe's Sardines and Other Stories*, Sidgwick & Jackson, 1985, p. 120.
10. *The Financial Times*, February 25, 1989.
11. *The New York Times*, February 5, 1986.
12. A more valid criticism was that the three Australian judges who took part in the tasting were interested parties: Len Evans, co-owner of Rothbury Estate in the Hunter Valley in New South Wales, whose wine won the Chardonnay gold medal; James Halliday, owner of Coldstream Hills in the Yarra Valley in Victoria, whose wine won in the Pinot Noir category; Ian McKenzie, chief wine maker for Seppelts in Victoria, whose Salinger Brut was the most successful sparkling wine.
13. *The Wine Spectator*, December 31, 1990, pp. 61–62.
14. I am indebted for this story to the British wine importer Joseph Berkmann.

PART TWO

INTRODUCTION: ART AND AGRICULTURE

1. Claude Arnoux, *Dissertation sur la situation de Bourgogne*, 1728.
2. *The Wine Spectator*, February 15, 1989, p. 9.
3. Ibid., February 15, 1992, p. 8.
4. Jay Stuller and Glen Martin, *Through the Grapevine: The Business of Wine in America*, Wynwood Press, 1989, p. 106.

6. A KIND OF MAKEUP

1. Roy Andries de Groot, *The Wines of California*, 1982, pp. 194–95.

2. I am indebted for this information to Comte Henri de Vaucelles, owner of Château Filhot in Sauternes.

3. Stephen Brook, *Liquid Gold: Dessert Wines of the World*, Beech Tree Books, 1987, pp. 309–10.

4. *Wine & Spirit*, June 1988, p. 16.

5. *The Wine Spectator*, April 15, 1989, p. 24.

6. Brook, *Liquid Gold*, p. 174.

7. Otto Loeb and Terence Prittie, *Moselle*, Faber & Faber, 1972, pp. 117–19.

8. State Papers, 89 series, no. 53, quoted in Sarah Bradford, *The Story of Port*, 2nd ed., Christie's Wine Publications, 1983, p. 35.

9. Martin Lister, "A Journey to Paris in the Year 1698," in John Pinkerton (ed.), *Voyages and Travels*, vol. 4, 1809, pp. 50–53.

10. William Turner, *A New Book of the Natures and Properties of All Wines that Are Commonly Used Here in England*, 1568, p. B 4.

11. Walter Charleton, *The Mystery of Vintners*, published in *Two Discourses*, 1669, pp. 195–98.

12. Such a re-fermentation is still sometimes provoked in Chianti, as will be described in Chapter 8. Charles Estienne, *Maison Rustique*, 1572, p. 210; Christopher Merret, *Some Observations Concerning the Ordering of Wines*, published in *Two Discourses*, 1669, pp. 221–22, 226–27; *L'Encyclopédie*, 1765, vol. 17, pp. 300–1, art: "Vin muet."

13. M.-A. Puvis, *De la culture de la vigne et de la fabrication du vin*, 1848, pp. 205–6, 240–41.

14. Stuart Pigott, *Life Beyond Liebfraumilch*, Sidgwick & Jackson, 1988, p. 9.

15. *Wine & Spirit*, November 1988, p. 17.

16. *Wine*, November 1989, p. 42.

17. *The Wine Spectator*, November 15, 1989, pp. 89–90.

18. *Decanter*, September 1985, p. 25.

19. Jancis Robinson, *The Great Wine Book*, Sidgwick & Jackson, 1982, p. 149.

20. Frederick A. Pottle (ed.), *Boswell's London Journal*, Heinemann, 1950, p. 297.

21. Cyrus Redding, *A History and Description of Modern Wines*, 1833, p. 202.

22. A. Henderson, *History of Ancient and Modern Wines*, 1824, pp. 220–21.

23. Allan Sichel, *The Penguin Book of Wines*, 2nd ed., Penguin, 1971, p. 191.

24. J. L. W. Thudichum and August Dupré, *A Treatise on the Origin, Nature and Varieties of Wine*, 1872, pp. 281–304, 548, 556–57.

25. Sichel, *Book of Wines*, p. 186.

26. J. L. W. Thudichum and August Dupré, *A Treatise on Wine, its Origin, Nature and Varieties*, 1894, p. 201.

27. Brook, *Liquid Gold*, p. 154.

28. Michael Broadbent, *The Great Vintage Wine Book*, Knopf, 1980, p. 316.

29. Alfred Langenbach, *The Wines of Germany*, Harper & Co., 1951, p. 80.

30. Brook, *Liquid Gold*, p. 57.
31. The addition of sugar to wine is not permitted in California. The sweetening of Chardonnays, which has already been described in Chapters 2 and 5, is therefore effected with concentrated grape must.
32. Patrick Forbes, *Champagne*, Victor Gollancz, 1967, p. 329.
33. *Wine & Spirit*, March 1987, p. 49.

7. THE SUN IN SACKS

1. *Wine*, March 1991, p. 24.
2. Fritz Hallgarten, *Wine Scandal*, Weidenfeld & Nicolson, 1986, p. 63.
3. T. G. Shaw, *Wine, the Vine and the Cellar*, 1863, p. 284.
4. M.-A. Puvis, *De la culture de la vigne et de la fabrication du vin*, 1848, pp. 234–39.
5. René Pijassou, *Le Médoc*, Tallandier, 1980, p. 570.
6. Puvis, *De la culture de la vigne*, pp. 225ff.
7. Edmund Penning-Rowsell, *The Wines of Bordeaux*, 5th ed., Viking Penguin, 1985, p. 38.
8. Pamela Vandyke Price, *Enjoying Wine*, Heinemann, 1982.
9. Anthony Hanson, *Burgundy*, Faber & Faber, 1982, p. 100.
10. Charles Tovey, *Wine Revelations*, c. 1881, pp. 67–71.
11. Fiona Beeston, *Mes hommes du vin*, Plon, 1989, p. 134.
12. *Decanter*, September 1987, p. 42.
13. *Wine & Spirit*, August 1984, p. 24.
14. Hanson, *Burgundy*, p. 217.
15. *Decanter*, February 1984, p. 68.
16. *The Vine*, no. 12, January 1986, p. 32.
17. Jancis Robinson, *The Great Wine Book*, Sidgwick & Jackson, 1982, p. 93.
18. This is the only form of chaptalization that is permitted in California.

8. THE CHAMPAGNE GAME

1. H. Warner Allen, *A History of Wine*, Faber & Faber, 1961, p. 214.
2. See Malcolm Bell, "Romantic Wines of Madeira," *Georgia Historical Quarterly*, December 1954.
3. Kermit Lynch, *Adventures on the Wine Route: A Wine Buyer's Tour of France*, Farrar Straus & Giroux, 1988, pp. 12–13.
4. *The Wine Spectator*, November 30, 1986, p. 4.
5. Anthony Hanson, *Burgundy*, Faber & Faber, 1982, p. 120.
6. Auguste Petit-Lafitte, *La Vigne dans le Bordelais*, 1868, p. 189.
7. Anthony Hogg (ed.), *WineMine*, Peter Dominc Ltd, 1970, pp. 132–37.
8. Burton Anderson, *Vino*, Little, Brown & Co., 1980, p. 377.
9. Jancis Robinson, *The Great Wine Book*, Sidgwick & Jackson, 1982, p. 128.
10. Patrick Forbes, *Champagne*, Victor Gollancz, 1967, p. 378.

11. Robin Young, *The Really Useful Wine Guide*, Sidgwick & Jackson, 1987, pp. 90, 162.
12. In 1986 Miguel Champalimaud wrote to *Decanter* to say: "The reason why traditional port shippers are now offering single *quintas* is that they knew that in less than ten years the classic vintage port will be a single-*quinta* vintage port." (*Decanter*, August 1986, p. 9.) It does not appear likely that this prophecy will be fulfilled, at least not within the time scale Champalimaud has set for it. In another letter to *Decanter* two years later, he condemned British-owned port shippers for establishing a poor image for single-*quinta* by selling inferior wines under that label. (*Decanter*, February 1988, p. 12.)
13. T. G. Shaw, *Wine, the Vine and the Cellar*, 1863, p. 171.
14. In California, a wine labeled, for example, Carneros Chardonnay is permitted by law to contain 15 percent of grapes from outside the Carneros region and 25 percent of wine made from a variety other than Chardonnay.
15. Sheldon Wasserman and Pauline Wasserman, *Italy's Noble Red Wines*, Blandford Press, 1985, pp. 145, 152.
16. Nicolas Belfrage, *Life Beyond Lambrusco*, Sidgwick & Jackson, 1985, pp. 255–56.
17. Wasserman and Wasserman, *Italy's Noble Red Wines*, pp. 171–72.

9. THE LAW IS A ASS

1. Pliny the Elder, *Natural History*, A.D. 77, Book 14, Chapter 25.
2. *Wine & Spirit*, February 1985, p. 48. In California, some time ago, Gallo tried adding oak chips to their wines, and found that, although it gave an impression of age and complexity to their "ports" and "sherries," it did not do much for their table wines. (James Conaway, *Napa*, Houghton Mifflin, 1990, p. 122.)
3. Nicholas Faith, *Cognac*, Hamish Hamilton, 1986, p. 118.
4. *Wine & Spirit*, August 1986, Sherry and Spanish Brandy Supplement, p. 5.
5. Anon., "Wine and the Wine Trade," *The Edinburgh Review*, 1867, pp. 179–204.
6. James Suckling, *Vintage Port: The Wine Spectator's Ultimate Guide for Consumers, Collectors and Investors*, Wine Spectator Press, 1990, pp. 147–49.
7. Professor L. Grandeau of Nancy, quoted in *The Brewers' Guardian*, 1876, pp. 309, 336, 373.
8. "A popular writer"—I know not who—quoted in James L. Denman, *Wine and Its Adulterations*, 1867.
9. *The Pall Mall Gazette*, 1882, quoted in Faith, *Cognac*, p. 73.
10. *Wine & Spirit*, October 1984, p. 25.
11. G. Cosimo Villfranchi, *Oenologia Toscana*, 1773, quoted in A. Marescalchi and G. Dalmasso, *Storia della Vite e del Vino in Italia*, 1931–37, vol. 3, pp. 563–64.
12. *The Times*, April 21, 1986.
13. *The Observer*, August 11, 1985, p. 9.

14. *Wine*, January 1986, p. 6.
15. *Wine & Spirit*, April 1986, p. 45.
16. Fritz Hallgarten, *Wine Scandal*, Weidenfeld & Nicolson, 1986, pp. 68–69.
17. *The Sunday Times*, October 20 and November 3, 1974.
18. Nicolas Belfrage, *Life Beyond Lambrusco*, Sidgwick & Jackson, 1985, p. 227.
19. M. A. Amerine and E. B. Roessler, *Wines: Their Sensory Evaluation*, 2nd ed., W. H. Freeman, 1983, p. 73.
20. Pierre Bert, *In Vino Veritas*, Albin Michel, 1975, p. 65.
21. The most important exception to this rule is the Clos de Vougeot.
22. Noël Cossart, *Madeira*, Christie's Wine Publications, 1984, pp. 111–12.
23. Belfrage, *Life Beyond Lambrusco*, pp. 48–49.
24. *Wine & Spirit*, April 1987, pp. 49–51.
25. Belfrage, *Life Beyond Lambrusco*, p. 188.
26. *Wine*, June 1988, p. 13.
27. It is hoped that the absurdity of top-class *vini da tavola* will be ended by the 1992 Goria Law, which provides for the possibility of creating new denominations which are no larger than a single property. But this will take time.

10. VARIETAL WORSHIP

1. *The Wine Spectator*, March 15, 1989, pp. 21–25, March 31, 1989, p. 7, and April 15, 1989, p. 7.
2. A. d'Armailhacq, *De la culture des vignes, de la vinification et les vins dans le Médoc*, 1855; Jules Guyot, *Etude des vignobles de France*, 1868, vol. 1, pp. 455–56.
3. A. Jullien, *Topographie de tous les vignobles connus*, 1816, p. 107.
4. M. J. Lavalle, *Histoire et statistique de la vigne et des grands vins de la Côte d'Or*, 1855, pp. 164–65.
5. A burgundy is allowed to carry a varietal name on the label only if it is no more than half the height of the name of the *appellation*. The Institut National des Appellations d'Origine is considering banning varietal names altogether.
6. *The Wine Spectator*, January 31, 1990, p. 58.
7. *Wine and Spirit*, March 1986, p. 44.
8. *Decanter*, February 1991, p. 32.
9. Hugh Johnson, *Modern Encyclopedia of Wine*, Simon & Schuster, 1983, p. 51.
10. Nicolas Belfrage, *Life Beyond Lambrusco*, Sidgwick & Jackson, 1985, pp. 13–14.
11. Wilhelm Franck, *Traité sur les vins du Médoc*, 2nd ed., 1845, pp. 32–33.
12. Guyot, *Etude des vignobles de France*, pp. 455–56.
13. Vines had in fact been imported from Bordeaux to the east coast of America in colonial times. William Penn took vines from Bordeaux with him on his first trip to Pennsylvania in 1682. These may not have

included Cabernet Sauvignon, but it is likely to have been among the vines imported in 1805 by Peter Legaux of the Pennsylvania Vine Company from Châteaux Margaux, Lafite, and Haut-Brion. There is no evidence that these ever produced any wine, however. (Thomas Pinney, A History of Wine in America from the Beginnings to Prohibition, University of California Press, 1989, pp. 33, 113.)

14. He was killed in 1878 trying to stop a runaway horse. Charles L. Sullivan, Like Modern Edens: Winegrowing in the Santa Clara Valley and Santa Cruz Mountains 1798–1981, California History Center, 1982, pp. 24–26, 60.

15. Pinney, A History of Wine, pp. 346–48; Leon D. Adams, The Wines of America, 3d ed., McGraw-Hill, 1985, pp. 349–50.

16. Sullivan, Like Modern Edens, pp. 54–55, 58, 99.

17. Adams, The Wines of America, pp. 305–8, 318–19. The house Parrott built at Miravalle was later featured in the television drama Falcon Crest.

18. The New York Times, September 16, 1981.

19. The Wine Advocate, no. 45, June 1986, p. 2.

20. Miguel A. Torres, The Distinctive Wines of Catalonia, Hymsa, 1986, pp. 50–51, 66–68.

21. Wine & Spirit, December 1985, p. 57.

22. See Edward Hyams, Dionysus: A Social History of the Wine Vine, 1965, reprinted by Sidgwick & Jackson in 1987, pp. 122, 138–41.

23. Stan Hock, "Clonal selections: obstacles and opportunities with Pinot Noir," Practical Winery and Vineyard, May/June, 1989.

11. OLD WINE IN NEW BOTTLES

1. J. L. W. Thudichum and August Dupré, A Treatise on the Origin, Nature and Varieties of Vine, 1872, p. 548.

2. Emile Peynaud, Knowing and Making Wine, 2nd ed., Wiley, 1984, pp. 109–10.

3. M. J. Lavalle, Histoire et statistique de la vigne et des grands vins de la Côte d'Or, 1855, p. 30.

4. Anthony Hanson, Burgundy, Faber & Faber, 1982, p. 245.

5. Claude Arnoux, Dissertation sur la situation de Bourgogne, 1728.

6. Noël Cossart, Madeira, Christie's Wine Publications, 1984, pp. 102–3.

7. Peynaud, Knowing and Making Wine, p. 252; Jean Ribéreau-Gayon et al., Sciences et techniques du vin, vol. 3, Dunod, 1976, p. 705.

8. Decanter, December 1984, p. 36.

9. Pascal Ribéreau-Gayon, "Wine Flavor," in G. Charalmbous (ed.), The Flavor of Foods and Beverages, Academic Press, 1978, pp. 355–79.

10. Kermit Lynch, Adventures on the Wine Route: A Wine Buyer's Tour of France, Farrar Straus & Giroux, 1988, p. 203.

11. Something similar happened to Rioja in the 1970s. The foundation of many new bodegas and increased investment in old ones brought a corresponding increase in the proportion of new barrels that were used. This was just at the time that overseas importers started to interest themselves in Rioja as an alternative to red Bordeaux. They, and their

customers, acquired the image of Rioja as a very oaky wine—and have been disappointed ever since.

12. *The Wine Spectator*, October 15, 1988, p. 48.
13. Burton Anderson, *Vino*, Little, Brown & Co., 1980, pp. 168, 375.
14. Cossart, *Madeira*, p. 115.
15. Peynaud, *Knowing and Making Wine*, p. 191.
16. *The Wine Advocate*, no. 48, December 1986, p. 13; Robert Parker, *The Wines of the Rhône Valley and Provence*, Simon & Schuster, 1987, pp. 264, 280.
17. Anthony Hanson, *Burgundy*, p. 188.
18. Cossart, *Madeira*, p. 109.
19. René Pijassou, *Le Médoc*, Tallandier, 1980, pp. 783–84.
20. *The Guardian*, June 1, 1991.
21. Charles Metcalfe and Kathryn McWhirter, *The Wines of Spain and Portugal*, Price Stern, 1990, p. 79; *The Guardian*, February 10, 1990.
22. Theodore Zeldin, *France 1848–1945*, vol. 2, Oxford University Press, 1973, p. 760.
23. *Le Canard enchaîné*, October 14, 1987, p. 4.

12. KEEPING UP WITH THE JAYERS

1. Christopher Fielden, *Is This the Wine You Ordered, Sir?*, Christopher Helm, 1989, pp. 126–27; *Wine*, March 1989, p. 25.
2. Julian Jeffs, *The Wines of Europe*, Faber & Faber, 1971, p. 418; *Sherry*, 3rd ed., Faber & Faber, 1982, p. 226.
3. Noël Cossart, *Madeira*, Christie's Wine Publications, 1984, p. 70.
4. Ibid., p. 124.
5. Maurice Healy, *Stay Me with Flagons*, Michael Joseph, 1940, p. 246.
6. *Wine & Spirit*, December 1986, p. 63.
7. Cosimo Ridolfi, *Orali lezioni*, 1862, vol. 2, p. 299, quoted in Lamberto Paronetto, *Chianti*, Estampa, 1970, pp. 190–92.
8. *The Brewer's Guardian*, 1890, p. 340.
9. I am indebted for this story to Faber & Faber's wine editor Julian Jeffs.
10. *The Wall Street Journal*, March 14, 1986.
11. Henri Enjalbert, "Comment naissent les grands crus," *Annales*, 1953, pp. 457–63.
12. Although Forbes, who died in 1991, liked collecting old wines, his connoisseurship was questionable. On one occasion a wine broker, discovering that Forbes was born in 1919, sent him a message offering to sell him a case of 1919 La Tâche. A message came back thanking the broker for the offer, but explaining that Mr. Forbes already had several 1919 Bordeaux. (*Wine & Spirit*, September 1989, p. 102.)
13. *The Wine Spectator*, December 15, 1988, pp. 22–29.
14. Edmund Penning-Rowsell, *The Wines of Bordeaux*, 5th ed., Viking Penguin, 1985, p. 428.
15. *The Wine Spectator*, May 31, 1989, p. 7.
16. Penning-Rowsell, *The Wines of Bordeaux*, p. 428.
17. *The Wine Spectator*, December 15, 1988, p. 15.

18. Leonard S. Bernstein, *The Unofficial Guide to Wine Snobbery*, Elm Tree Books, 1984, p. 107.
19. Stephen Chadwick and Hugh Dudley, "Can Malt Be Discriminated from Blended Whisky?", *The British Medical Journal*, December 1983, pp. 24–31.
20. Marc Elliott, brand manager for Glenfarclas, quoted in *Wine & Spirit*, November 1985, p. 37.
21. Patrick Forbes, *Champagne*, Victor Gollancz, 1967, p. 157.
22. *Decanter*, July 1986, p. 47; *Wine & Spirit*, March 1987, p. 49.
23. Penning-Rowsell, *The Wines of Bordeaux*, pp. 363–64.
24. *Wine & Spirit*, June 1987, p. 55.
25. Penning-Rowsell, *The Wines of Bordeaux*, p. 270.
26. A. D. Francis, *The Wine Trade*, A. & C. Black, 1972, p. 235.
27. *The Wine Spectator*, July 15, 1989, p. 8.
28. The *Los Angeles Times*, February 8, 1990.
29. Ibid., November 14, 1991.
30. Quoted in James Conaway, *Napa*, Houghton Mifflin, 1990, pp. 248–49.
31. Charles L. Sullivan, *Like Modern Edens: Winegrowing in Santa Clara Valley and Santa Cruz Mountains 1798–1981*, California History Center, 1982, pp. 54–55.
32. Leon D. Adams, *The Wines of America*, 3rd ed., McGraw-Hill, 1985, pp. 18–21, 223–29; Vincent P. Carosso, *The California Wine Industry: A Study of the Formative Years 1830–95*, 1951, pp. 100–1, 183–85.
33. Henry Lachman, a San Francisco wine merchant, speaking in 1915, quoted in Thomas Pinney, *A History of Wine in America from the Beginnings to Prohibition*, University of California Press, 1988, p. 360.
34. Adams, *The Wines of America*, pp. 10–11.
35. Ibid., p. 330.
36. *The Wine Spectator*, June 15, 1991, p. 25.
37. *The New York Times*, February 13, 1991; *The Wine Spectator*, January 31, 1992, p. 12.
38. It was this tasting which convinced vine growers in Oregon that Pinot Noir was the right variety to plant. The tasting which put Oregon Pinot Noir on the map was a tasting of seven red burgundies and ten Oregon Pinot Noirs from the 1983 vintage, held at the International Wine Center in New York in 1985. This has been described in Chapter 5.
39. Penning-Rowsell, *The Wines of Bordeaux*, p. 167.
40. This view was expressed by Bruno Prats, the enlightened proprietor of Château Cos d'Estournel, in *Decanter*, August 1983, p. 24. I have been unable to substantiate it.
41. A. d'Armailhacq, *De la culture des vignes, la vinification et les vins dans le Médoc*, 1855, quoted in Penning-Rowsell, *The Wines of Bordeaux*, pp. 232–33.
42. *Decanter*, December 1984, p. 32.
43. Robin Young, *The Really Useful Wine Guide*, Sidgwick & Jackson, 1987, p. 44.
44. Christopher Fielden in *Decanter*, October 1984, p. 19.

45. *Wine and Spirit* Champagne Supplement, September 1991, p. 28.
46. Charles Tovey, *Wine Revelations*, c. 1881, pp. 32–39.
47. Edward Hyams, *Dionysus: A Social History of the Wine Vine*, 1965, reissued by Sidgwick & Jackson in 1987, p. 90.
48. It also excludes most California Cabernet Sauvignons. With the exception of Beaulieu Vineyards Georges de Latour Private Reserve, first produced in 1936, these simply have not been made for long enough to establish a track record. The first famous vintage was 1974, a hot year producing big wines; the first vintage in which elegant wines were generally produced was 1979. As a rule, the best California wines from these vintages have preserved their fruit rather than improved in the manner of fine red Bordeaux.
49. *Decanter*, September 1985, p. 4.
50. Ibid., December 1983, p. 9.
51. *The Wine Spectator*, September 15, 1989, p. 44.
52. *Wine & Spirit*, February 1990, p. 65.
53. Ibid., October 1986, p. 50.
54. Quoted in Simon Loftus, *Anatomy of the Wine Trade: Abe's Sardines and Other Stories*, Sidgwick & Jackson, 1985, p. 77.

13. THE FALERNIAN SYNDROME

1. Arthur Young, *Travels in France 1787–89*, 1792, p. 383.
2. *Wine & Spirit*, January 1987, pp. 47–50.
3. *The Wine Spectator*, December 31, 1990, p. 76.
4. *Wine & Spirit*, January 1987, pp. 47–50.
5. Stephen Brook, *Liquid Gold: Dessert Wines of the World*, Beech Tree Books, 1987, p. 99.
6. The 1983 Raymond-Lafon was excellent in its youth, but unfortunately —as has been described in Chapter 6—it was not filtered sufficiently and therefore re-fermented in bottle.
7. The "b" word is used, for example, by Clive Coates in *The Vine*, no. 10, November 1985, p. 2.
8. The failure of a similar gambling act explains why many of the Sauternes from the 1983 vintage—the year which marked the beginning of the region's recovery—have not turned out quite as good as they were cracked up to be. In 1982 most of the Sauternes growers had waited for noble rot to arrive, only to encounter rain. As a consequence, 1982 Sauternes tend to be rather dilute. In 1983, for fear of a repeat of their bad experience of the previous year, many growers picked their grapes too early, thus missing out on the noble rot that arrived only at the end of October. Notoriously, the first-growth Château Suduiraut, having produced a surprisingly good 1982, made a wine that was inferior to it in 1983.
9. Quoted in George Ordish, *Vineyards in England and Wales*, Faber & Faber, 1977, p. 64.
10. David Peppercorn, *Bordeaux*, Faber & Faber, 1982, p. 41.
11. Camille Rodier, *Le Vin de Bourgogne*, 1921, pp. 15–17.
12. George Ordish, *The Great Wine Blight*, 2nd ed., Sidgwick & Jackson, 1987, p. 196.

13. Anthony Hanson, *Burgundy*, Faber & Faber, 1982, p. 95.
14. Quoted in C. Ladrey, *La Bourgogne: revue oenologique et viticole*, 1861, p. 97.
15. Nicholas Faith, "Phylloxera—What Really Happened in the Médoc," in Patrick Matthews (ed.), *Christie's Wine Companion*, 1981, p. 114.
16. Michael Broadbent, *The Great Vintage Wine Book*, Knopf, 1980, p. 43.
17. René Pijassou, *Le Médoc*, Tallandier, 1980, pp. 777–78, 782, 829–30.
18. Hugh R. Rudd, *Hocks and Moselles*, Constable, 1935, pp. 10–11.
19. *L'Appellation d'Origine contrôlee*, 1985, pp. 78–79.
20. Julian Jeffs, *Sherry*, 3rd ed., Faber & Faber, 1982, p. 154.
21. The smuggling of cuttings of virus-infected vines from France into California is not without its dangers, however. It has been suggested that the mutant strain of phylloxera which is currently devastating Napa and Sonoma counties might have been introduced with one of these cuttings.
22. John Livingstone-Learmonth, *The Wines of the Rhône*, 2nd ed., Faber & Faber, 1983, p. 21.
23. *Decanter*, October 1984, p. 60.
24. Sir Edward Barry, *Observations Historical, Critical and Medical on the Wines of the Ancients, and the Analogy Between Them and Modern Wines*, 1775, pp. 437–39.
25. Pliny the Elder, *Natural History*, A.D. 77, Book 14, Chapter 8.
26. Wilhelm Franck, *Traité sur les vins du Médoc*, 1824, p. 121.
27. *Decanter*, December 1983, p. 18.
28. *Wine & Spirit*, October 1989, p. 71.
29. Livingstone-Learmonth, *The Wines of the Rhône*, pp. 81–82.
30. *The Wine Spectator*, March 15, 1990, p. 17.
31. Burton Anderson, *Vino*, Little, Brown & Co., 1980, p. 374.

14. WHAT'S YOUR POISON?

1. *The Guardian*, May 10, 1989. Ridley later resigned following the publication of comments about the Germans that he had made to the son of a former colleague, who also happened to be a journalist.
2. René Pijassou, *Le Médoc*, Tallandier, 1980, p. 830.
3. *Wine & Spirit*, December 1988, p. 22.
4. Columella, *De Agricultura*, c. A.D. 60, Book 12, paragraphs 16, 19.
5. *The Wine Spectator*, September 30, 1990, p. 58.
6. The threshold is 10 parts per million. Even organic wines generally have to carry sulphite warning labels, because they contain more naturally produced sulphites than this.
7. *What's Brewing*, November 1987, p. 9.
8. It is thought that very few of the people who are sensitive to sulphur react to less than 12 milligrams of sulphur dioxide. It is also thought that they react to the sulphites they inhale rather than to the sulphites they ingest. They do not react to all of even the relatively small portion of the total sulphur content that is "free" (that floats above the wine rather than being bound into it) but only to the portion of the free sulphur

dioxide that remains in molecular form (as SO_2), rather than to the portion which ionizes and floats above the wine as separate sodium or potassium ions. It is perfectly possible that a wine containing more than the proposed OGWA limit of 100 parts per million of sulphur dioxide will contain less than 12 milligrams of molecular un-ionized SO_2 in the portion of the wine (say half a bottle) that the sulphur-sensitive person might drink. (*Wine & Spirit*, March 1992, p. 29.)

9. *The Wine Spectator*, September 30, 1990, p. 63.
10. Ibid., September 15, 1991, p. 7; *Wine & Spirit*, September 1991, p. 9.
11. *The Wine Spectator*, April 30, 1987, September 30, 1987, November 15, 1987, and April 15, 1988. Orthene 50 was never sold in the United States.
12. J. F. Roques in *Outlook on Agriculture*, 1976, pp. 30–34, quoted in George Ordish, *Vineyards in England and Wales*, Faber & Faber, 1977, pp. 117–19.
13. Molière, *Le Bourgeois Gentilhomme*, 1670, Act 2, Scene 4, l. 179.
14. Fritz Hallgarten, *German Wines*, Publivin, 1976, p. 98.
15. Emile Peynaud, *Knowing and Making Wine*, 2nd ed., Wiley, 1984, p. 307.
16. *The Wine Advocate*, no. 46, August 1986, p. 26.
17. Kermit Lynch, *Adventures on the Wine Route: A Wine Buyer's Tour of France*, Farrar Straus & Giroux, 1988, pp. 140–42.
18. *The Wine Advocate*, no. 48, December 1986, p. 18.
19. Robert Parker, *Burgundy*, Simon & Schuster, 1990, p. 90.
20. Ibid., p. 315.
21. At Château de Beaucastel in Châteauneuf-du-Pape the skins of un-crushed grapes are heated to 176°F, but this is not pasteurization, as is sometimes alleged, because only the skins of the grapes are heated, not the pulp inside. Nevertheless, the process of heating cannot but affect the taste of the end product. The wine is not filtered before bottling.
22. Nicolas Belfrage, *Life Beyond Lambrusco*, Sidgwick & Jackson, 1985, pp. 35–36.
23. Anthony Hanson, *Burgundy*, Faber & Faber, 1982, p. 117.
24. *Decanter*, October 1982, p. 44.
25. John Locke, *Observations upon the Growth and Culture of Vines and Olives*, 1766, pp. 21–22.

CONCLUSION

1. J. C. Boudreau (ed.), *Food Taste Chemistry*, American Chemical Society, 1979, p. 24.
2. Pascal Ribéreau-Gayon, "Wine Flavor," in G. Charalambous (ed.), *The Flavor of Foods and Beverages*, Academic Press, 1978, pp. 355–79.
3. *Wine & Spirit*, September 1985, p. 70.
4. *Decanter*, May 1983, p. 11.
5. P. Morton Shand, *Bacchus, or Wine Today and Tomorrow*, 1927, pp. 47–48. This book was published during Prohibition, when most of the wine drunk in speakeasies, if it was not sweet and fortified, was likely to be sparkling.

6. Tom Stevenson, *Champagne*, Sotheby's Publications, 1986, p. 48.
7. Jean Ribéreau-Gayon et al., *Sciences et Techniques du Vin*, vol. 3, Dunod, 1976, pp. 475–82.
8. There were those who disagreed, it must be said. The wine merchant J. J. Lasseure, writing in 1843, ridiculed the idea that sparkling red burgundies were "too strong"; he claimed that even using grapes from top *grands crus* such as Richebourg and Le Chambertin, even in the ripest vintages, it was difficult to produce sparkling wines with *enough* body for English or Russian tastes. Admittedly, he was prejudiced, having been the person who introduced champagnization into Burgundy in 1822. See Camille Rodier, *Le Vin de Bourgogne*, Louis Damidot, 1921, pp. 67–69.
9. Not surprisingly, there has been considerable litigation over the respective rights of the American and Czech companies to the Budweiser brand name. The American beer Budweiser was given that name in 1876 in homage to the beers that were produced in Budweis (now called Ceske Budejovice) in Czechoslovakia, but the Czech brewery that currently produces Budweiser was not opened until 1895. As things stand, in the United States only the American beer may be sold as Budweiser; in much of Europe the Czech beer has the rights to the name; in Britain both are permitted. Anheuser-Busch has been trying to solve the dispute once and for all by buying the Czech brewery.
10. *What's Brewing*, August 1991, p. 13.
11. *The New York Times*, May 12, 1982.
12. Noble rot and gray rot are actually the same fungus: the difference is that noble rot affects ripe grapes, and gray rot affects grapes before they are ripe.
13. *The Independent*, May 4, 1991.
14. Edward Ott, *A Tread of Grapes*, n.d., pp. 38–39.
15. *Commentary*, February 1984.
16. Thomas Pinney, *A History of Wine in America from the Beginnings to Prohibition*, University of California Press, 1989, p. 151.
17. Matt Kramer, *Making Sense of Burgundy*, William Morrow, 1990, p. 208.
18. *The Wine Spectator*, April 30, 1990, p. 14.
19. Ibid., April 30, 1989, p. 7.
20. Nicholas Faith, *The Story of Champagne*, Facts on File, 1989, p. 21.
21. *The New York Times*, June 23, 1985.

Index

Aaron, Michael, 48, 55, 229
Accad, Guy, 197–98, 218
acephate, 266–67
acidity, 35, 70, 83, 89, 97, 100,
  102, 130, 184–85, 187, 195,
  273, 277, 285, 286; adding of,
  108–9, 261; of red burgundies,
  107–9
Adams, Leon D., 21, 216, 297
Adanti, Fratelli, 84, 129
Adelsheim, 64, 289
adulteration, 131–44; with artificial
  flavors, 134; bottling locale and,
  139–40; bringing to light of,
  141–44; with caramel, 134–35;
  with colorings, 135–37, 277;
  with dangerous chemicals, 10–
  11, 34, 94, 101–2, 139, 142,
  145, 148; detecting of, 141–46;
  with liquid sugar, 85, 110, 131,
  139, 143, 149; with oaky flavor-
  ings, 132–33; with seasonings,
  132; with water, 198–200, 261;
  with wood infusions, 133–34.
  See also blending; chaptalization;
  fortified wines
advertisements, 23, 50, 52–53, 54,
  68–69
aging, 184–200, 219–20; acidity
  and, 184–85; artificial methods
  of, 202–4, 205; bottle, 188, 189,
  193–94, 243, 275, 276; carbonic
  maceration and, 195–97; "closed
  period" and, 194–95; desire for
  exclusivity and, 205–7; development of wines intended for,
  204–5; fermentation temperature
  and, 185–86; and preference for
  old wine, 204. See also cask aging
Aglianico, 129–30, 164

alcohol content, 28, 82, 85, 87,
  89, 91, 92, 113. See also chaptalization
allergic reactions, 28–29
Alsace, 139–40, 175
aluminum, 261–62
Anderson, Burton, 193, 255
Angerville, Marquis d', 140–41
Anheuser-Busch, 286, 287
"antifreeze" scandal, 10–11, 34,
  94, 139, 142, 145, 148
Antinori, 177, 282
AP (Amtliche Prüfung) numbers,
  139
appellation contrôlée rules, 114,
  115, 120, 138–41, 143–44,
  146–51, 154, 161, 221, 223–24,
  235, 291
appellations, in California, 151–
  152, 158, 291–96
armagnac, 202
aroma, 19, 145–46, 243, 282,
  283–84, 288
asbestos filters, 272
Asti Spumante, 276
Au Bon Climat, 40, 65, 292
auctions, 205–6, 230
Auslesen, 80, 83, 89–91, 184,
  185
Ausone, Château, 53
Austin Nichols, 292
Australia, Australian wines, 18,
  83, 103, 109, 161, 261, 270,
  288, 294; blind tastings won by,
  68, 69–70; medal system in, 66,
  67, 69–70; spacing of vines in,
  180–81; yeasts in, 270–71. See
  also specific producers
Austria, Austrian wines, 10–11,
  94, 139, 142, 145, 148
Averys, 53, 147

Babycham, 209
Bachelet-Ramonet, 238
bacteria, 109, 146, 195, 259, 262,
　275
Bailey, Jenny, 101
Bailey, Lucy, 49–50
Bairrada, 119, 152, 153, 164, 193
Bandol, 174
Barolo, 129–30, 154–55, 185
Barton, Ronald, 117–18, 126, 128
Beaucastel, Château de, 243, 268
Beaufort, Jacques, 263–64
Beaujolais, 28, 115, 196, 197;
　Nouveau, 196–97, 274, 291
Beaumes de Venise, 85
Beauséjour-Bécot, Château, 225
Becker, J. B., Weingut, 91
beer, 39, 47, 48, 77, 119, 203,
　261–62, 284, 286–87, 297
Beerenauslesen, 80, 82, 83, 91–
　92, 96, 184
Belfrage, Nicolas, 51, 164–65, 276
Benedict (vineyard), 176
bentonite, 261–62
Berger, Dan, 63
Bernabei, Franco, 126–27, 130
Bernardi, Cesari, 203
Bernardins, Domaine des, 85
Bernkastel, 35, 221, 242
Bernstein, Leonard S., 207
Berry, Liz, 51, 72
Berry, Mike, 72
Bert, Pierre, 143, 144, 148
Bespaloff, Alex, 44
Bianchi, Fabrizio, 130
Bigi, 129
Billiot, Henri, 122
Bisquit Dubouché, 202
bitterness, innate dislike of, 37–38
Bize-Leroy, Lalou, 106–7, 114
"blackmail," 236–38
Blanchon, Roger, 151
Blandys, 152
Blass, Wolf, 66
blending, 112–30, 137, 140, 216,
　237–38, 270; character of indi-
　vidual vintages lost by, 118–20;
　by cooperatives, 141; of different
　vintages, 119–20; of grapes or

wines from different regions,
　66–67, 129–30; as hedge against
　weather, 116–17; of higher-
　yielding varieties, 128–29; house
　styles and, 118–21; of white
　grapes into red wine, 126–27; of
　wines meant to be drunk young,
　126–28. *See also* fortified
　wines
Blosser, Bill, 64
blue fining, 262
Blue Nun, 88, 253
blush wines, 78–79
boisé, 133–34
Bollinger, 72, 120, 123, 208,
　232–33
Bonny Doon, 83–84
Bordeaux, 55–59, 61, 71, 90, 97,
　98, 107, 110, 120, 123, 126,
　132, 141, 149, 154, 172, 188,
　194, 244, 246, 250, 252, 253,
　257, 267; "blackmail" and, 236–
　237, 238; blending of, 112, 116–
　120, 126, 127–28; blind tastings
　of, 68, 69, 70, 162, 163, 181;
　cascade system in, 146–48, 239;
　chaptalization of, 100, 101; *châ-
　teau* bottling in, 140; classifica-
　tion of *châteaux* in, 221–24;
　climate of, 174, 175; crop yields
　in, 101, 146–47, 148, 199, 234,
　239, 241–42, 247–49; Cruse
　scandal and, 143–44, 228; de-
　velopment of wines intended for
　aging in, 204–5; grape varieties
　in, 116–18, 126, 128, 159, 160,
　164, 166, 171, 182; harvests in,
　100–101, 104–5; investment in,
　227–31; in 19th century, 184–
　185; price of, 212–14, 227–29,
　231, 236–39, 247–48; quality of
　site, 173–74; soil of, 173–74,
　178–79, 199, 222; two-century
　old, 205–7; vat elimination in,
　238–40, 241; vine age in, 181–
　182; vinification methods in,
　171–72
Bordeaux mixture, 244, 245, 257,
　259

Borie, Jean-Eugène, 239
Bossard, Guy, 268
botrycine, 82
botrytis cinerea. See noble rot
bottle aging, 188, 189, 193–94,
    243, 275, 276
"bottle sickness," 203
bottling, 139–41, 187–88, 204,
    259
Bouchard Père et Fils, 99, 108, 256
Boudot, Gérard, 171
Boudreau, James, 281
bouquet. *See* aroma
Bourges, 173
Bourgogne Blanc, 147, 162
Bouron, Paul, 277
brandy, 86, 133–34; wines fortified
    with, 112, 113, 188–89
Braquessac, M. de, 247
Breuer, Bernhard, 90, 91, 96
Breuer, Georg, Weingut, 90
Brisson, Gérard, 196
Broadbent, Michael, 91, 228, 247
Brook, Stephen, 84, 92
Brunello di Montalcino, 40, 156
Brunier, Daniel, 274
Bual, 152, 194
Bureau of Alcohol, Tobacco and
    Firearms (BATF), 23, 24, 133,
    152, 159, 160, 162, 260, 293,
    294–95
Burgundy, burgundies, 28, 40, 45,
    57, 110, 123, 129, 132, 136,
    138, 154, 172, 199, 239, 244,
    246, 261, 267, 270, 290, 291;
    Americans' emulation of, 217–
    218, 287, 289–90; "ancient
    method" in, 188; "blackmail"
    and, 237–38; blind tastings of,
    68, 70, 181, 218–19; branded
    table wine from, 115; chaptaliza-
    tion of, 96–103, 108, 256; clas-
    sification of vineyards in, 221;
    climate of, 78, 115, 174–76;
    confusing nomenclature system
    of, 149–51, 220–22; crop yields
    in, 240, 241, 243, 246, 248;
    estate bottling of, 140–41; "ex-
    cess production," 147; fertilizer

use in, 246–48; grape varieties
    in, 115–16, 117, 125, 159,
    160–61, 164, 166, 172–73, 182,
    250, 285; harvests in, 104,
    105–6; multiple ownership of
    vineyards in, 220–21, 223, 224–
    225, 240; price of, 220, 227,
    236, 238; soil of, 178, 179–80;
    type of oak used in, 169
Burgundy, red wines of, 35, 54,
    63, 64, 70, 72, 78, 188, 218–
    219, 220, 288; acidity of, 107–9;
    blending of, 115–16, 127, 128,
    224–25; chaptalization of, 97,
    98–100, 102, 108; decline in
    quality of, 250–51; extracting
    more color for, 197–198; fortifi-
    cation of, 112, 113–115; pas-
    teurization of, 277; sparkling
    grand cru, 285–86
Burgundy, white wines of, 71, 89,
    102–3, 115, 121, 122, 160–61,
    192, 194, 243; California wines
    compared to, 162, 169, 170,
    287–88; defects in, 287–88
Burnap, Ken, 242, 254, 271

Cabernet Franc, 116–17, 118,
    160, 167, 171, 173
Cabernet Sauvignon, 41, 66, 104,
    116–18, 126, 128, 154, 156,
    158, 159, 160, 162–68, 171,
    172, 174, 175, 185, 241, 251;
    California, 63, 68–69, 71, 159,
    162–63, 167–68, 175–76, 194,
    255, 293; soil and, 177–80; su-
    perior clones of, 182; vine age
    and, 181–82
Cabernet-Shiraz Black Label, 66
Cafaro, Joe, 104
calcium phytate, 262
California, California wines, 15,
    17–18, 20, 24, 31, 35, 39, 40,
    41, 44, 48, 52, 59, 82, 83–84,
    123, 174, 199, 242, 282; appel-
    lation system in, 151–52, 158,
    291–96; blind tastings of French
    wines vs., 68–69, 70, 162, 163,
    169–70, 181; Cabernet Sauvi-

California, California wines
(*continued*)
  gnon, 63, 68–69, 71, 159, 162–
  163, 167–68, 175–76, 194, 255,
  293; chaptalization of, 103, 104;
  Chardonnay, 30–31, 40, 65,
  66–68, 71, 159–60, 162–63,
  167–71, 175, 192, 193, 249,
  287–89; climate of, 175–76,
  180; competitions between Australian wines and, 69–70;
  French names appropriated by,
  215–17; geographic associations
  lacked by, 291–95; grape varieties in, 159–60, 162–64, 166–68,
  175–76; high price and image
  of, 214–15, 220; misleading
  names of, 159–62; oaky flavor
  of, 132–33, 168, 169–70, 192;
  organic, 259–60, 264; Pinot
  Noir, 41, 72, 123, 175–76, 249,
  254, 255; rootstock in, 245; soil
  in, 179–80; spacing of vines in,
  180–81; sparkling, 210, 216–17,
  285, 286; uneconomic to produce, 254–55; vinification methods in, 168–69, 170–71, 270–
  271, 287, 289; White Zinfandel,
  31–32, 78–79, 88. *See also specific producers*
California, University of, at Davis,
  31, 163, 170, 182, 249
Callaway, 193
Campbell, Pat, 217
Canandaigua Wine Company, 79
Cantenac-Brown, Château, 221–22
Cantenac-Prieuré, Château, 223
caramel, 134–35
carbonic maceration, 195–97
Carignan, 172, 196
Carmenère, 166
Carneros, 163, 175, 177, 249,
  254–55, 286
Carré family, 273
cartãos de beneficio, 144–45
cascade system, 146–48, 239
casein, 261
cask aging, 67, 118, 132–33, 154–
  155, 189–95, 204; bottle aging

vs., 188, 189, 193–94; heating
  to achieve appearance of, 202–3;
  in Limousin oak, 168, 169–70;
  long, 171–72, 185, 187, 188,
  193; in new vs. old oak, 190–
  191, 192
Castello di Neive, 164
Catawba, 15–16, 32, 113, 217
Cauhapué, Domaine, 268
Caves Aliança, 132
Caves de la Madeleine, 68, 70,
  169–70
cellar yeasts, 270, 271
Centre Viticole de la Champagne,
  225
centrifuge, 92
Chaban-Delmas, Jacques, 143–
  144
Chablis, 18, 141, 162, 193, 243
Chalone, 55, 60, 169, 180, 249
Chambertin, 138, 183, 219
Champagne, champagnes, 62, 94–
  95, 103, 138, 172, 208–12,
  272, 284, 285, 286; blending of,
  120–23, 125–26, 128, 141; climate of, 78; comparative tastings
  of, 71–73; crop yields in, 148,
  251; *cuvée de prestige*, 210–12,
  232–33; fermentation of, 92, 94,
  121, 188; fraudulent labeling of,
  225–26; grape varieties in, 161,
  285; pink, 136–37; price of, 72–
  73, 122, 125, 208, 210–12,
  225, 227, 232, 233; sparkling,
  introduction of, 187–88, 284,
  296; uneconomic to produce,
  232–33; vintage dates of, 120.
  See also specific producers
"champagne method," 35, 209–10,
  216
Champalimaud, Miguel, 124,
  135–36
chaptalization, 35, 96–111, 112,
  131–32, 146, 157, 200; addi-
  tional acidity and, 108–9; alternatives to, 109–11; detection of,
  146; grape harvests and, 100–
  107, 109; price and, 102, 111;
  wine laws and, 98–99, 101, 108

Chardonnay, 32, 73, 102, 154, 155, 159–68, 172, 174–77, 179–83, 217, 249; Australian, 133, 270; California, 30–31, 40, 65, 66–68, 71, 159–60, 162–63, 167–71, 175, 192, 193, 249; 287–89; in champagne, 120, 121–22, 126; oak aromas of, 193; residual sugar in, 30–31, 67

Charles II, King of England, 112, 284

Charta, 88, 89

Chassagne-Montrachet, 140, 149, 238

Chasse-Spleen, Château, 119

Château & Estate, 229, 237

Châteauneuf-du-Pape, 112, 154, 171, 188, 195, 197, 243, 249

Chave, Gérard, 65, 107, 195, 268

Cheilly, 150

chemical sprays, 263–64, 266–70, 277

Chenin Blanc, 160

Chereau family, 273

Chevalier, Domaine de, 98, 186, 268

Chianti, 126–27, 130, 140, 156, 165, 187, 282

cholesterol, 22, 23

Christie's, 205–6, 228

Chroman, Nathan, 52

Churchill, 274

Ciravegna, Giovanni, 142

citric acid, 108–9, 262

Clair, Bruno, Domaine, 191

Clancy, Terrence, 193

Clape, Auguste, 268

Classic Wines (Boston), 60, 61

Clendenen, Jim, 175–76, 292

Clerico, Domenico, 269

climate, 77, 168, 174–77, 178, 180

clonal selection, 165–66, 182–83, 246, 248–50

Clos de l'Arbalestrier, 268

Clos de Vougeot, 220, 221, 290

Clos de Vougeot, Château de, 168

Clos du Bois, 287

Clos du Vieux Plateau Certan, 212

"closed period," 194–95

close planting, 180–81

coal tar dyes, 136

Coates, Clive, 9, 58, 63, 106

Coca-Cola, 33–34, 87

Coche(-Dury), J.-F., Domaine, 273

cochineal, 137

Cockburn, 123–24

Cognac, cognac, 93–94, 133–34, 138, 169, 202, 208, 246

colas, 33–34, 35, 87

cold fermentation, 282–83

cold maceration, 197–98, 218

Coldstream Hills, 288

collecting, 58, 59–61, 205–6, 230–31

Colli di Catone, 128–29, 156, 282

color, extracting of, 197–98

colorings, 135–37, 277

Columella, 259

Comtes de Champagne, 211–12

Condrieu, 127, 172

Congress, U.S., 22, 34, 161–62

Connecticut, 21

Consorte, Mario, 154

coolers, 21, 34–35

cooperatives, 141

Coppola, Francis Ford, 168

corkage charges, 43

corked wines, 44–45, 60

corking of bottles, 187

Cornas, 151

Corney & Barrow, 238

coronary heart disease, 22, 23

Cos d'Estournel, Château, 220

Cossart, Noël, 152, 189, 194, 198, 202

Cossart, Sidney, 152

Cossart-Gordon, 194

Coteaux d'Aix-en-Provence, 177

Côte de Beaune, 244

Côte de Beaune-Villages, 150

Côte d'Or, 238, 243, 247

Côte Rôtie, 60, 127, 151, 172, 194, 253–54, 295–96

Côtes de Provence, 188

Côtes du Rhône, 197
Coulée de Serrant, 269, 278
Crawford, Charles M., 33
Crema, La, 123
Croix, La, 239
Croizet-Bages, Château, 60
crop yields, 101, 144, 146–49,
    155, 233–34, 239, 240–51; cas-
    cade system and, 146–48, 239;
    clonal selection and, 246, 248–
    250; fertilizers and, 246–48,
    249; health of vine stock and,
    244–46; irrigation and, 199–200,
    254; quality and, 241–43; wine
    laws and, 144, 146–49, 155,
    243. See also harvesting
Cru de Coudoulet, 268
Cruse scandal, 143–44, 228
cryo-extraction, 83–84, 109–10,
    235
Cuvelier, Didier, 222

Dão, 119, 132, 145, 152–53, 242
Dauvissat, Jean-Claude, 141
Dauvissat, René, 141
Dauzac, 223
Davies, Jack, 217
Day, Douglas, 169
Decanter, 50–51, 53, 58, 106–7,
    283
Deinhard, 51, 56, 88, 93
Delaunay, 51
Delbeck, Pascal, 53
Delicato, 79
Delmas, Jean, 73
Delon, Michel, 105
Delorme, André, 51
De Luca, John, 265
denominazione regulations, 126,
    154–56
Dezize, 150
diethylene glycol, 10–11, 34, 94,
    139, 142, 145, 148
Doisy-Daëne, Château, 92
Dominus, 293
Domitian, 180
Dom Perignon, 211–12
Doudet-Naudin, 57
Douro, 100, 124, 144, 153, 205

Draper, Paul, 164, 204, 290–91
drinking age, 38, 265
Drouhin, Bernard, 198
Drouhin, Domaine, 162, 219
Drouhin, Robert, 162, 183,
    218–19
Drouhin-Laroze, Domaine, 198
"dry" label, on sweet wines, 32
Dry Sack, 32
Duboeuf, Georges, 197
Dubois-Challon, Heylett, 53
Dubourdieu, Pierre, 92
Ducru-Beaucaillou, Château, 118,
    213, 239
Dupré, August, 90
Dupuy, Michel, 275
Durante, Nelson, 40
Duvault-Blochet, M., 105

Echézeaux, 224
Eddy, Rusty, 264
1855 classification, 222–23
Eiswein, 83–84
Ek, Fred, 60, 61, 231
El Aliso Vineyard, 167
elderberry juice, 135–36
electrolysis, 203
Elk Cove, 217
El Vino (London), 208
estate bottling, 140–41, 237
European Community, 67, 92, 93,
    94, 110, 129, 133, 157–58, 199,
    209, 257, 258, 261
eutypiose, 246
Evesham Wood, 218
excimer lasers, 259
exclusivity, 205–19; of champagne,
    208–12, 225–26; price and,
    205–7, 208, 210–15, 219, 232,
    251; seeming to be in short sup-
    ply and, 226–27; use of French
    names and, 215–17
Eyrie Vineyards, 64, 183, 218–19

Faith, Nicholas, 202, 247, 296
Falernian, 252
fan-leaf virus, 242, 245–46, 250
Federacão dos Vinicultores do
    Dão, 153

fermentation, 28–29, 40, 77, 82, 85, 86, 92, 94, 102, 121, 126, 128, 146, 168–71, 188, 197, 243, 250, 269, 288, 289–90; carbonic maceration and, 195–197; of German wines, 82, 87, 90–91, 92, 156–57; malolactic, 28–29, 89, 102, 109, 157, 169, 196–97, 262; of organic wines, 259–60, 270; temperature of, 176, 185, 198, 282–283. *See also* chaptalization; yeasts

Fernandes, José de Sousa Rosado, 154

fertilizers, 178, 244, 246–48, 249, 258, 268, 269, 281

Fetal Alcohol Syndrome, 24

Fetzer Vineyards, 264

Fèvre, William, 243

Fieuzal, Château de, 275

Figeac, Château, 227

Filhot, Château, 295

filtration, 92, 195, 196, 233, 262, 272–75

Finigan, Robert, 56, 57

Finkenauer, Carl, Weingut, 91

Florentin, Emile, 151

Florey, Charles, 25

Flurbereinigung, 252–53

Fonsalette, Château de, 225

Fonseca (port producer), 63

Fonseca, J. M. da, 153–54

Fontodi, 127, 130

food, wine with, 39, 40–41, 73

Food and Drug Administration (FDA), 260, 265, 267

Forbes, Malcolm, 205–6

Forbes, Patrick, 94

Forman, Rick, 67

Forstmeister Geltz Zilliken, 57, 90–91

fortified wines, 33, 34, 97, 112–115, 188–89

Francis, Alan, 214

Franck, Wilhelm, 166

Franco, Antonio, 153–54

Frascati, 128–29, 144, 155, 156, 282

Fraud Squad, 98–99, 143–44, 200, 258

French Colombard, 160

"French Paradox," 23

Frey Vineyards, 259

Friuli, 101

fuchsine, 136

Fulda, Bishop of, 81

fusel oils, 133–34

Gaglioppo, 129–30, 164

Gainey, 176

Gaja, Angelo, 177

Galestro, 282

Gallagher, Rolland, 19

Gallo, Ernest, 53–54

Gallo, Ernest & Julio Winery, 17–18, 33, 34, 162, 226, 264, 282

Gamay, 115–16, 140, 172–73, 196, 247

Gardine, Château de la, 171

Gardinier, Xavier, 266

Garganega, 155–56

gas chromatography, 145–46, 165

Gault Millau "Wine Olympics," 70, 176, 218

Gentaz, Marius, 191

geographic associations, 291–96, 297

Gérin, Alfred, 253

German Viticultural Association, 149

Germany, German wines, 11, 56, 57, 229, 259, 262, 266, 287; confusing nomenclature system of, 220, 221, 222; crop yields in, 242, 243–44, 248; dry, 47, 88–89, 243; historic status of, 219–20; price of, 220, 248; red, 156–58; sulfur in, 184; sweetness of, 80–83, 85–93, 96; uneconomic to produce, 252–53; vine age and, 181–82; wine laws in, 131, 138, 139, 142–43, 148–51, 156–58, 199, 200. *See also specific wines and producers*

Gevrey-Chambertin, 149

Gibbs-Smith, Lavinia, 256–57

Gibert, André, 149
Gigon, Michel, 173
Girardin, Armand, Domaine, 190–91
Giscard d'Estaing, Valery, 143–44
glasses, 43, 283, 284
Gleave, David, 51
Glenfarclas, 208
Glenlivet, 149–50
Glynn, Patrick, 290
Goheen, Austin, 182
Gorden Valley, 152
Goudal, 140
Gouges, Henri, 140–41
governo process, 130
Graciano, 164, 172, 251
Graff, Dick, 169, 180
Graham, Randall, 83–84
Graham & Co., 124–25
grapes, 77, 78, 174–81; climate and, 77, 168, 174–77, 178, 180; clonal selection and, 165–66, 182–83, 246, 248–50; close planting of, 180–81; cut off in midsummer, 240, 241; drying after picking, 84–85; extracting color from, 197–98; gas chromatography and, 145–46, 165; harvesting of (See harvesting); health of vine stock and, 244–246; increase in size of, 250; irrigation and, 199–200, 254; organically grown (See organic wines); rootstock and, 245; soil and (See soil); vine age and, 184; yields of (See crop yields)
Gratien, Alfred, 123
Grave, Domaine La, 270
Graves, 149
gray rot, 80, 156–57, 233
Graziano, Gregory, 123
Great Britain, 20, 23, 39, 56, 69, 87–88, 112, 136, 138, 205, 209, 213–14, 219, 220, 251, 252, 256, 261, 262; wine investment in, 228, 229–30; wine retailers in, 48, 49, 55; wine writers in, 49–51, 55, 56, 58
Grechetto, 129, 164

Greece, Greek wines, 84, 85, 226–27
Grenache, 164, 172, 249–50
Griñon, Marqués de, 199
Grivot, Jean, Domaine, 221
grocery stores, wine sold in, 20, 21
Guermonprez, Philippe, 217
Guibert, Aimé, 177, 179
Guigal, Marcel, 60, 127, 191, 254, 295–96
gum arabic, 262

Haag, Fritz, 83
Hallcrest Vineyards, 259
Hallgarten, Fritz, 87, 272
Halliday, James, 288
Hamilton, Thomas, 16
Hancock, John, 113
hangovers, 28–29
Hanson, Anthony, 51, 98–99, 105–6, 114–15, 188, 198, 277
Hanzell, 168
Haraszthy, "Count" Agoston, 167
harvesting, 100–107, 176, 185, 235; late, 105–7, 109; selective picking in, 233–35, 236
Harveys, 134, 220
Haut-Bages-Averous, Château, 105
Haut-Bailly, Château, 213
Haut-Brion, Château, 73, 149, 213–14, 235
Haute Serre, Château, 101
Hawley, John, 287
Haynes, Hanson & Clark, 51
headaches, 133, 262
Heitz, Joe, 168, 215, 292, 293–94
Heitz Wine Cellar, 59–60
Henderson, Alexander, 89
Henry, Scott, 240–41
Herbemont, Nicholas, 292
herbicides, 268. See also chemical sprays
herbs, 132
Hermitage, 107, 112, 127–28, 151, 172, 194, 195, 253
Hess, John and Karen, 33
Hessen, Langraf von, 57
Hetterich, Paul, 79

Heublein, 168
Heyl zu Herrnsheim, Weingut
    Freiherr, 267, 269
Heyman Brothers, 103
Heymann-Lowenstein, 91
histamine, 28–29, 262
histidine, 28
Hoggart, Simon, 30
Holbach, Brigitte, 143
hot-bottling, 276
house styles, 118–21
Huet, Gaston, 269
hundred-point system, 55–56
Hyams, Edward, 227, 242–43
hygiene, 289–90

Inglenook, 168, 293
insecticides, 266–67. *See also*
    chemical sprays
insects, 244, 266–68
Institut National des Appellations
    d'Origine, 147, 148
International Wine Center (New
    York), 64, 72
investment in wines, 227–31
irradiation, 203
irrigation, 199–200, 254
Italy, Italian wines, 39, 88, 193–
    194; blending of, 126–30; chap-
    talization of, 103, 146;
    concentration methods in, 110–
    11; grape varieties in, 163–65;
    hot-bottling of, 276; methanol
    scandal and, 34, 101–2, 142;
    passiti, 84–85; wine laws in,
    126, 131–32, 154–56. *See also*
    specific wines and producers
Ivaldi, Domenico, 84, 85

Jadot, Louis, Maison, 102, 192–93
James I, King of England, 187
Jamieson, Ian, 51
Jayer, Henri, 218, 242, 292
Jefferson, Thomas, 15, 16, 81,
    206, 207
Jeffs, Julian, 32, 201, 249
Jensen, Josh, 180
Jermann, Silvio, 156
Jobard, François, 273

Johnson, Hugh, 51, 56, 164, 227
Joly, Nicolas, 278
Jones, Brice, 123, 292
Josephshöf, 57
jug wines, 31

Kabinett, 252
Kacher, Robert, 190–91
Kaiser, Bruce, 230
Kendall-Jackson, 31, 66–67, 287
Kesseler, August, 157
Kesselstatt, von, 57
Kessler, George, 208–9
Klein, Pierre, 215
Klenkhart, Erwin, 142
Kobler, Hans, 285
Koehler-Ruprecht, 91
Korbel, 216, 217
Krug, 73, 125
Krug, Remi, 121

labels, 260–63; fraudulent, 48–49,
    53, 225–26; warning, 22, 23–24
Labrusca, 20
Lafarge, Michel and Frédéric, 103
Lafite, Château, 69, 73, 105, 140,
    205–6, 207, 213, 219, 220, 227
Lafon, Domaine des Comtes, 273
Lail, Robin, 293
Lambert (champagne), 71
Lambrusco, 88, 276
Lamothe, 97–98
Lamouroux, Château, 179
Lancers, 154
Landiras, Château de, 270
Lanson, 94, 120
Lardière, Jacques, 102, 192–93
Larrivet-Haut-Brion, 149
Latour, Château, 51, 70, 97–98,
    100, 105, 140, 185, 186, 199,
    203, 204, 219, 241–42, 247–48,
    257
Latour, Louis, 275, 276, 277
Laube, James, 58, 63
La Vigneronne (London), 51, 72
Lazy Creek Vineyards, 285
lead, 265
lead oxide, 85
Leboeuf, M., 211

Le Cirque (New York), 43
Leclerc, Philippe, 63
Lee, Terry, 271
lees, 170–71, 272–73, 287
Leeward Winery, 23
Lefranc, Charles, 167
Léglise, Max, 108
Leighton, Terry, 22–23
Le Montrachet (New York), 45
Leonnet, Alain, 48–49
Léoville–Las Cases, Château, 105,
    118, 213, 270
Léoville-Poyferré, Château, 222,
    270
Le Pavillon (New York), 45
Lequin-Roussot, 161
Leroy, Domaine, 269
Lett, David, 64, 183, 219
Levett, William, 203
Lichine, Alexis, 223
Liebfraumilch, 88, 141, 242, 253
Lillet, 132
limestone, 179–80
Lindgren, Henry Clay, 61
Lingenfelder, Rainer, 157
liquor stores, 19–20, 21. See also
    wine merchants and retailers
Listel, 258
Livingstone-Learmonth, John,
    250, 253
Locke, John, 277
Loeb, Otto, 86, 92
Loire Valley, 35, 287
London Food Commission,
    265–66
Longoria, Rick, 176
Longworth, Nicholas, 15–16, 32,
    33, 35, 217
Loosen, Ernst, 90, 149, 242, 252
Lopez de Heredia, 194
Loubat, Mme. Edmond, 212
Lur-Saluces, Comte Alexandre de,
    234–35
Lutèce (New York), 43, 207
Lynch, Kermit, 113, 191, 274
Lynch-Bages, Château, 105

Maccioni, Sirio, 43
McCloskey, Leo, 203, 290–91

McCrea, Fred, 168
maceration, 137; cold, 197–98,
    218
McRitchie, Bob, 64
Madeira, madeiras, 112–13, 152,
    188–89, 194, 198–99, 201–2
Mahoney, Francis, 249
Malbec, 118, 166, 167, 171, 195
malic acid, 102, 109, 185, 285
Malmsey (Malvasia), 128, 152,
    164, 251, 282
malolactic fermentation, 28–29,
    89, 102, 109, 157, 169, 196–
    197, 262
Malvasia, 128, 152, 164, 251, 282
Malvasia di Candia, 155
Malvasia di Lazio, 155
Mansell, Sir Robert, 187
Mansson, Per-Henrik, 54
manure, 246–48, 268
Maranges, Les, 150
Margaux (appellation), 179, 223
Margaux, Château, 167, 179
Marne et Champagne, 225
Marsanne, 127
Martin, René-Claude, 144
Martini, Louis, 80
Martin-Jarry, 144
Marvel, Tom, 17
Mas de Daumas Gassac, 177, 178,
    179, 269
Masi, 198
massal selection, 248, 250
Masson, Paul, 242
Matrot, Thierry, 192
Maudiére, Edmond, 62
Médoc, 105, 116, 140, 146, 166,
    179, 212, 222, 224, 234, 241,
    249
Melbourne Show, 66
Méo-Camuzet, Domaine, 292
mercaptans, 266
Merlot, 105, 116, 118, 119, 126,
    128, 162, 166, 167, 171, 177,
    185, 236, 241
Mesnil, Le, 211–12
Metcalfe, Charles, 56
methanol, 34, 101–2, 142
Metternich, Prince, 81

Meursault, 68, 122, 192, 199, 273
Michael, Peter, 67
Middle Ages, 78, 81, 132, 135, 172–73, 204
mildew, 245, 247, 257
Millardet, Pierre, 257
Minervois, 196
Miravalle, 167–68
Mission Haut-Brion, Château La, 70
Mitchelton Winery, 66
Moët et Chandon, 62, 209, 211, 227
Monbazillac, 235
Mondavi, Michael, 68–69, 175, 179, 226
Mondavi, Robert, 214, 215
Mondavi, Robert, Winery, 24, 41, 68–69, 175, 226, 227, 264
Monsanto, 130
Montelena, Château, 68, 163, 169–70, 269
Montepulciano, 130, 164, 255
Montepulciano d'Abruzzo, 193
Montesquiou d'Artagnan, Maréchal de, 284
Monticello (estate), 15
Monticello Cellars, 169
Montille, Hubert de, 97, 113
Montlouis, 35
Montpellier, 277
Montrachet, Le, 168, 245
Mont Redon, Château de, 171
Morey-Saint-Denis, 227
Morgon, 196
Morrell, Peter, 55
Mosel, 35, 83, 85–89, 92, 98, 129, 149, 174–75, 177, 220, 245, 252–53
Moser, Lenz, 269
Moss Wood, 273
Motto, Vic, 255
Moueix, Christian, 293
Moueix estate, 269
Mount Eden, 67, 168, 242, 249
Mourvèdre, 174, 249
Mouton-Baronne-Philippe, Château, 222

Mouton-Cadet, 224
Mouton-Rothschild, Château, 68, 105, 185, 206, 213, 214, 215, 227
Mugneret-Gibourg, Domaine, 65
Mugnier, Frédéric, 291
Müller-Thurgau, 93, 155, 242, 253
Mumm, 122, 210
Murrieta, Don Luciano de, 172
Murrieta, Marqués de, 194
Musar, Château, 269
Muscadet, 49–50, 144, 272–73
Muscat (*Moscato*), 84, 85
must, 78, 82, 86–87, 91, 263; concentrated, 110–11, 146; sugar added to (*See* chaptalization)
must heating, 197, 198
Musto, David F., 25–26
Myrat, Château, 235, 236

Nadrasky, Otto, Sr., 10–11
Nahe State Domain, 179
Nalys, Domaine de, 197
Napa Valley, 151–52, 159, 162–163, 164, 174, 175, 245, 293–95
Napa Valley Wine Auction, 214–15
Napoleon III, Emperor of France, 276
Navarro, 35
Nebbiolo, 129, 164
New Almaden Vineyard, 167
Newton, Andrew, 198–99
New York State, New York wines, 20–21, 24, 217, 230
New Zealand, 83, 209, 251
Niebaum, Gustav, 168
Nightingale, Alice and Myron, 82
Night Train, 54
nitrates, 258
Nixon, Richard M., 216–17
noble rot, 80–83, 233–36, 287–288
Noblet, André, 106
Noblet, Bernard, 106
Novellucci, Ulisse, 202

nuclear magnetic resonance spectrometer, 146, 203–4
Nuits-Saint-Georges, 239

oak casks. See cask aging
oak chips, 132
Oakmore, 132–33
oenin, 203, 290
Offley, 124
oidium, 166, 172, 245, 257
Oiron, 173
Opus One, 214, 215, 293
Orange County Wine Fair, 67
Ordish, George, 245
Oregon, Oregon wines, 56, 182,
  217–19, 245, 249; Pinot Noir,
  41, 64–65, 72, 183, 217–20,
  240–41, 289–90. See also specific producers
Oregon State University, 182
Organic Grapes into Wine Alliance (OGWA), 260
Organic Wine Company, 256
organic wines, 256–78, 281–82;
  anti-alcohol lobby and, 264–65;
  chemical sprays and, 263–64,
  266–67, 269, 270, 277; fermentation of, 259–60, 270; filtration
  and, 272–75; good producers of,
  268–69; misinformation about,
  256–57; natural vs. cultured
  yeasts in, 259–60, 270–72; pasteurization and, 275–77; sulfur
  and sulfite levels and, 257–64,
  270
Orthene 50, 266–67
Orvieto, 129
Ott family, 267–68
Owades, Joseph, 286–87
oxidation, 67, 193, 194, 203, 204,
  259, 263
oxygenation, 189, 190, 263, 276

Pacific Wine Company, 220
Paillard, Bruno, 73
Palmer, Château, 222, 223
Panther Creek, 108, 289–90
Parker, Robert, 55–57, 60–61, 63,
  170, 197, 230, 273, 274–75

Parrott, Tiburcio, 168
Passe-Tout-Grains, 115
passiti, 84–85
Pasteur, Louis, 189, 276
pasteurization, 275–77
Pato, Luis, 153, 164
Pauillac, 146–47, 224, 239
Pellier, Pierre, 167
Penfolds, 65–66
Penning-Rowsell, Edmund, 9, 68,
  98, 212
Pepe, Emidio, 119, 193–94
Peppercorn, David, 51, 244
Peppercorn & Sutcliffe, 51
Pepsi-Cola, 33, 34
Perignon, Dom, legend of, 296
Pernin, André, 107
Perrier, Laurent, 94
pesticides, 258, 266–67. See also
  chemical sprays
Peter Dominic, 71
Peterson, Joel, 164
Petite Syrah, 18
Petit-Lafitte, Auguste, 117
Petit Verdot, 118, 184–85
Pétrus, Château, 59, 205, 212,
  236, 241, 293
Peuillets, Domaine des, 196
Peynaud, Emile, 185–86, 190,
  191, 195, 272
Peyraud, Lucien, 174
Phélan-Ségur, Château, 266
Philip the Bold, Duke of Bur-
  gundy, 172–73
Phillips, Alan, 169
phylloxera louse, 137–38, 163–64,
  166, 172, 174, 201, 202, 243,
  245, 247
Pichon-Lalande, Château, 118–19,
  213, 224
Pieropan, Leonildo, 155–56, 269
Piesporter, 151, 221
pigeage, 290
Pin, Le, 212
Pinot Blanc, 127, 160–61
Pinot Droit, 108
Pinot Gris, 127, 160–61, 166
Pinot Meunier, 73, 128
Pinot Noir, 41, 73, 78, 84, 98,

104, 107–8, 115–16, 117, 129, 140, 154, 160, 172–76, 217, 244, 250, 286, 289; California, 41, 72, 123, 175–76, 249, 254, 255; in champagne, 120, 121, 122, 126; clonal selection of, 249; crop yields and, 240–41, 246, 247, 249; extracting color from, 197–98; German, 156–57; Oregon, 41, 64–65, 72, 183, 217–20, 240–41, 289–90; soil and, 179–80

Piper-Heidsieck, 71, 123

piquettes, 136

Pisani, Edgard, 105

pitch, 132, 204, 259

plafond limite de classement (PLC), 147, 148, 239

Plant, Moira, 24–25

Pleasant Valley Wine Company, 217

Pliny, 132, 252

Pojer, Mario, 155

Pojer e Sandri, 156

Polignac, Alain de, 94

pomace, recyling of, 197, 198

Pombal, Marques de, 153

Pomerol, 105, 116, 177, 241

Pommard, 140

Pommery, 210

Pontac, Arnaud de, 213

Pontac, François-Auguste de, 213–14

Pontac, Max de, 235, 236

Pope Valley, 152

"pop" wines, 34

port, 63, 85, 86, 100, 112–13, 138, 153, 205, 252, 274; adulteration of, 134–36; blending of, 123–25; sites classified for production of, 144–45; tawny, 134–135, 145, 189; vintage, 153, 189

Portugal, Portuguese wines, 132, 164, 165, 201–2; wine laws in, 144–45, 152–54. *See also specific wines, regions, and producers*

potassium ferrocyanide, 261, 262

Potel, Gérard, 99–100, 114, 275

Pouilly-Fuissé, 48

Pouilly-Fumé, 251

Pousse d'Or, Domaine de la, 99–100, 114, 220, 275

pregnant women, 22, 24–25, 46, 265

preservatives, 97, 259, 260

press trips, 49–50, 52

Prial, Frank, 27, 42, 69, 170

price, 102, 111, 178; "blackmail" and, 236–38; exclusivity and, 205–7, 208, 210–15, 219, 232, 251; of good vs. bad vintages, 236–38; investment potential and, 227–31; popularity and, 251–52; quality and, 72–73, 210–11, 212, 222–23, 232, 239, 251; restaurant markups and, 41–43; of wines uneconomic to produce, 232–35, 252–55

Price, Pamela Vandyke, 98

Prieuré-Lichine, Château, 223

Primitivo, 163–64

Priorato, 242

Prittie, Terence, 86, 92

procymidone, 267

Prohibition, 16–17, 19, 21, 25, 33, 297

Proposition 65, 264, 265

Prüm, J. J., 91

Pulcini, Antonio, 156

Puligny-Montrachet, 48

QbAs (*Qualitätsweine bestimmter Anbaugebiete*), 253

Quantas Wine Cup, 69–70

quercetin, 23

Questa, La, 167

Quinta do Noval, 124

Rabot, Noël, 171

Rahoul, Château, 270

Raimat, 199–200

raisin wines, 136

Rákóczi, Prince, 81

Ramonet-Prudhon, 238

Rand, Margaret, 9

Raney, Russ, 218

Rasmussen, Kent, 163, 254–55

Rausan-Ségla, Château, 179, 213
Rauzan-Gassies, Château, 213
Ravenscroft, 187
Ravenswood, 164
Ray, Cyril, 28
Ray, Martin, 168, 169
Rayas, Château, 154, 225, 243,
     249
Raymond-Lafon, Château, 82, 236
RC (Récoltant-Coopérateur), 141
recioto, 84
Redding, Cyrus, 89
red wine: consumption of white
     wine vs., 27–31, 37–41; flavor
     components of, 203–4. See also
     specific wines
reefers, 113–14
refrigeration, 30, 31, 289
Reguengos de Monsaraz, 153–54
Remoissenet, Roland, 53, 147
Renaud, Serge, 23
rendement annuel, 147, 239
rendement de base, 147
resin, 132, 191, 204, 259
restaurants, 38, 39–46, 47, 203,
     273; consumption of red vs.
     white wine in, 40–41; decline of
     wine sales in, 45–46; ignorance
     of wine service in, 43–45;
     markup on wines in, 41–43
retsina, 132
Reynaud, Jacques, 154, 177,
     224–25
Reynaud, Louis, 154
Rheingau, 83, 88, 89, 90, 149,
     185, 243
Rheinhessen, 149, 253
Rheinpfalz, 149
Rhenish in the Must, 86–87
Rhine Valley, 92, 98, 174–75, 220
Rhodes, Bell and Barney, 59
Rhône Valley, 56, 60, 65, 127,
     151, 172, 197, 237–38, 253–54,
     295–96
Ribera del Duero, 166
Ribéreau-Gayon, Jean, 190
Ribéreau-Gayon, Pascal, 190
Ricasoli, Baron, 126
Rice, David, 65

Richter, Dirk, 87
Ridge Vineyards, 162, 164, 203–4,
     290–91
Ridley, Nicholas, 256
Riesling, 89, 93, 129, 149, 160,
     167, 174–75, 177, 242, 248,
     252, 253
Rieussec, Château, 236
Rioja, 100, 119, 132, 166, 171–
     172, 194, 196, 197, 201, 251–
     252, 257
Riunite Lambrusco, 34, 35
Rixford, Emmett H., 167
RM (Récoltant-Manipulant), 141
Roberts, Jim, 272
Robinson, Jancis, 25
Rocheret, Bertin de, 284
Rodenstock, Hardy, 206, 207
Roederer, Louis, 94, 123, 285
Romanée-Conti, Domaine de la,
     44, 105–7, 114, 183, 220, 221,
     244
Romans, 84, 85, 202, 204, 206,
     227, 252, 265
rootstock, 245
Roque, La, 174
rosé, 251
Rostaing, René, 127
Rothschild, Baron Philippe de,
     213, 214, 215
Rothschild, Elie de, 213
Roulot, Guy, 68
Round Hill, 42
Roussanne, 127
Rousseau, Armand, Domaine, 244
Rudd, Hugh, 248
"rule of 1 percent," 108
Rutherford & Miles, 152

Saar, 150
Sagrantino d'Arquata, 84
Sagrantino di Montefalco, 84
Saint-Apollinaire, Domaine, 258
Saint-Emilion, 105, 116, 225, 241
Saint-Evremond, Marquis de, 284
St. James's Club (London), 219
St. Jean, Château de, 30–31
St. Johannishof, Weingut, 90
Saint-Joseph, 151

Saint-Julien, 118, 224
Saint Pierre-Sevaistre, Château, 257
Saintsbury, 171, 286
Sampigny, 150
Samuel Adams Boston Lager, 287
Sancerre, 173, 251
Sanders, Jean, 213
Sandri, Fiorentino, 155
Sanford, Richard, 175–76
Sangiovese, 126, 163, 164
Santa Barbara County, 175
Santa Cruz Mountain Vineyard, 242, 271
Santa Maria Valley, 175, 179
Sassicaia, 66, 156, 158
Saumur, 173
Sauternes, 80–84, 87, 92, 103, 109–10, 132, 184, 233–36, 287
Sauzet, Etienne, Domaine, 171
Scharzberg, 150
Schiettekat, Mark, 212
Schlossböckelheimer Kupfergrube, 179
Schloss Johannisberg, 81
Schloss Rheinhartshausen, 56
Schloss Vollrads, 88
Schmidt, 287
Schoonmaker, Frank, 17, 44
Schramsberg, 216–17
Schumacher, John, 259
Scuppernong, 15, 33
Seagram, 229
seasonings, 132
Sebastiani, Don, 159–60
second labels, 239
Seitz, 87
Selle, Château de, 267–68
Semillon, 80
Senard, Philippe, 218
Sénéjac, Château, 101
Sercial, 152
serving temperature, 29–30
Shand, Morton, 284–85, 286
Shanken, Marvin, 52–54, 58
Shaper, Gerald, 22
Shaw, Thomas George, 97
sherry, 32, 138, 201
Siben, Wolfgang, 87

Sichel, Allan, 89, 90
Sichel, Peter M. F., 88, 231
Siegrist, Thomas, 157
Silvaner, 253
Silverado Vineyard, 163
Simi, 171
Simon, Abdullah, 17, 18, 45–46, 228–29, 237
Simon, Joanna, 44–45
Sinskey, 104
Sionneu, Lucien, 214
Siran, Château, 223
skins, 28, 40, 78, 80, 104, 127, 137, 185, 188, 190, 197, 198, 250, 288
Smith, George, 149–50
Smith, Marcia, 293
"smoked wines," 202
Soave, 84, 144, 155–56, 165
soda pop, 33–34, 35, 87, 136
soil, 146, 173–74, 177–81, 194, 199, 222, 246, 268
Sokol Blosser Winery, 64, 72
Sokolin, William, 206, 230
soleras, 201–2, 220
Soltner, André, 43, 207
sommeliers, 43
Sonoma County, 174, 245
Sonoma-Cutrer, 171, 292
sorbic acid, 109
Soter, Tony, 264
Soulé, Henri, 45
Soverain, Château, 39
Spain, Spanish wines, 119, 164, 165, 172, 199–200. See also specific wines and producers
Spanna, 129–30
sparkling wines, 32, 34, 35–36, 94–95, 208–9, 284–86; California, 210, 216–17, 285, 286. See also Champagne, champagnes
Spätburgunder, 156, 157
Spätlese, 89, 143, 253
spices, 132
Spottswoode, 264, 269
Spurrier, Steven, 68, 163
Stag's Leap (appellation), 152
Stag's Leap Wine Cellars, 63, 68, 163, 214–15

stainless-steel tanks, 168, 169, 185, 186, 282
states, liquor controlled by, 19–21
Steele, Jed, 31
Steinberger, 220, 272
Steiner, Rudolf, 278
Stevenson, Tom, 285
Stony Hill, 168
Strong, Rodney, 40
Stuart, Jack, 163
Suckling, James, 48, 54, 207
Suduiraut, Château, 234
sugar, 107, 128, 199; addition of, 85–86, 92, 93–95, 131, 139 (See also chaptalization); grape ripeness and, 100, 102, 103, 107, 109; liquid, 85, 110, 131, 139, 143, 199; residual, 30–31, 67, 85, 91, 94, 96
sulfites, 259–61, 262, 270
sulfur, 82, 87, 92, 97, 184, 187, 197, 245, 257–58, 259, 262–64
Sumisclex, 267
Sumitomo, 267
sur lattes scandal, 225
Süssreserve, 86–88, 89, 90, 92–93, 131
Sutcliffe, Serena, 10, 51, 106–7
Sutter Home, 31, 32, 78, 79
sweet wines, 37–38, 80–95, 96, 131, 291; Americans' preference for, 30–34, 38
synthetic wines, 290–91
Syrah, 191, 249, 250

Tachis, Giacomo, 282
Tafelwein, 157–58
Taittinger, 94, 211
Talinda Oaks Ranch, 176
tannins, 29, 37, 41, 69, 97, 104, 126, 127, 128, 130, 133, 134, 169, 171, 184, 185, 187–90, 194, 197–98, 203, 250, 263
tartaric acid, 108, 109, 273, 276, 285
tartrazine, 136
tastings, 48, 53, 62–73, 97; actuality vs. potential of wines in, 65–68; by committee, 63–65;

personal preferences and, 62–63; promotional uses of, 68–69
tasting tests, 138, 139, 147–48, 153
Taylor (port producer), 124
Taylor, Jean Sharley, 52
Taylor-Gill, Simon, 51
Taylor Wine Company, 20
temperance movements, 21–26, 46, 297. See also Prohibition
Tempier, Domaine, 174, 269
Tempranillo, 164, 166, 172
Terme, Marquis du, 206
Terres Blanches, 269
Terry (brandy producer), 134
Terry, Anthony, 143
Thienpoint family, 212
Thorncroft Vineyard, 209
Thudichum, Johann, 90
Thunderbird, 34, 54
Tiefenbrunner, Herbert, 116
Tignanello, 156
Tinta Negra Mole, 152
Tokay, 81
Tolar, Joseph, 286
Torres, Miguel, 70, 176–77
Touriga Nacional, 153, 164
Tovey, Charles, 99, 225
transportation problems, 113–14
Trebbiano, 126, 128–29, 155, 255
Trefethen, 289
Tremblay, Gérard, 141
Tremblay, Suzanne, 141
Trévallon, Domaine de, 269
Trinchero, Bob, 31, 32, 78, 79
Trockenbeerenauslesen, 80, 82, 83, 91–92, 96
Tschida, Siegfried, 142
tyramine, 28–29, 262
Tyrell, Werner, 143
Tyrrell, Bruce, 271
Tyrrell, Murray, 271, 282

Ugni Blanc, 128
Usseglio-Tomasset, Luciano, 193

Valencia, 119
Valentini, Edoardo, 255
Vallana, Antonio, 129

Valpolicella, 84, 165, 198
Van Asperen, Ernie, 42
varietals, 31–32, 159–83; and matching of region to ideal grape variety, 173–81; predominance of technique over grape variety in, 168–72. *See also specific grape varieties*
Varoilles, Domaine des, 51
vat elimination, 238–40, 241
Vaucelles, Comte Henri de, 295
Vauthier, Alain, 53
vermouth, 132
Victoria, Duque de la, 172
Vieux Château Certan, 116, 173, 212, 241
Vieux Lazaret, Domaine du, 171
Vieux Télégraphe, Domaine du, 195, 274
Vignes, Jean-Louis, 167
Vigoroux, Georges, 101
Villaine, Aubert de, 269
Villars, Bernadette, 119
vin de Fimes, 137
Vin des Liqueurs, 86–87
vin de table, 146, 147, 157–58
Vinding-Dyers, Peter, 270, 271
Vinival, 119
vino da tavola, 157–58
Vino Nobile di Montepulciano, 156
Vin Santo, 156
vintage dates, faked, 201–2
Viognier, 127
Voepel, Manfred, 88
Voerzio, Roberto, 155
Voillot, Joseph, 246
Volnay, 188
Vosne-Romanée, 65, 129, 224
Vouvray, 35

Wädenswil clone, 183
Wallace, Steven, 55
Ward, Dick, 158, 286
warning labels, 22, 23–24
Washington, George, 113
Wasserman, Sheldon and Pauline, 130
water, adding of, 198–200, 261

Jimmy Watson Trophy, 66, 67
Waugh, Harry, 250
Webb, Brad, 168
Wehlener Sonnenhur, 129
Weinstuben, 16
Wente Brothers, 39
Wetmore, Charles, 167, 216
Weymarn, Peter von, 267
whiskey, 133–34, 138, 149–50, 207–8
white wine, 35, 102, 186, 273, 282–83; consumption of red wine vs., 27–31, 37–41. *See also specific wines*
White Zinfandel, 31–32, 78–79, 88
William III, King of England, 188
Williams, Burt, 292
Williams Selyes, 292
Wilson Daniels, 114
Wine, 9, 50, 51, 58, 56
Wine Advocate, The, 55–57
Wine & Spirit, 56, 142
wine importers, 51, 77, 113–14
wine laws, 131–58, 199–200; and bringing to light of adulterations, 141–46; chaptalization and, 98–99, 101, 108; crop yields and, 144, 146–49, 155, 243; improvement and innovation hindered by, 155–58; misleading names and, 138–45, 149–52, 159–62; on planting of grape varieties, 154, 159–60, 172–73, 174, 180; practices of majority imposed by, 131–32; status quo protected by, 154–55. *See also appellation contrôlée rules*
wine merchants and retailers, 48–49, 51, 55, 237–38
Wine Society, The, 9, 53
Wine Spectator, The, 18–19, 21, 22, 25, 40, 44, 45, 52–61, 64, 65, 72, 114, 207, 228
wine writers, 47–61; advertising and, 50, 52–53, 54; American, 51–61; British, 49–51, 55, 56, 58; collecting and, 58, 59–61;

wine writers (*continued*)
  descriptive language of, 56; financial interests of, in wine
  businesses, 51, 52; perks received by, 49–52; subjectivity of,
  47
Winiarski, Warren, 163, 215
Wooden Valley, 152
wood infusions, 133–34
Woolley, Robert, 214–15
World Health Organization, 260,
  261
Wright, Ken, 108, 289–90

Yamhill Valley Vineyards, 64,
  65
Yapp, Robin, 65

yeasts, 77, 82, 87, 90, 91, 92,
  108, 118, 146, 170–71, 186,
  273, 275, 285, 289; natural vs.
  cultured, 259–60, 270–72, 287;
  starter, 272
yields. *See* crop yields
Young, Arthur, 233
Young, Robin, 124–25, 223
Yquem, Château d', 17, 81, 82,
  233–35, 236

Zellerbach, James D., 168
Zilliken, Hans-Joachim, 90
Zinfandel, 18, 31, 78, 79, 163–
  164, 167, 194; White, 31–32,
  78–79, 88